Insects and Human Life

Insects and Human Life

Brian Morris

Oxford • New York

English edition
First published in 2004 by
Berg
Editorial offices:
1st Floor, Angel Court, 81 St Clements Street, Oxford, OX4 1AW, UK
175 Fifth Avenue, New York, NY 10010, USA

Berg is the imprint of Oxford International Publishers Ltd.

Library of Congress Cataloguing-in-Publication Data
Morris, Brian, 1936–
    Insects and human life/Brian Morris. — English ed.
        p. cm.
    Includes bibliographical references.
    ISBN 1-85973-847-8 (cloth)
        1. Beneficial insects—Malawi. 2.   Insect pests—Malawi.
    3.   Beneficial insects—Ecology—Malawi. 4.   Insects—
    Ecology—Malawi. I.   Title.
        SF517.3.M67 2004
        595.716'3'096897—dc22   2004006120

British Library Cataloguing-in-Publication Data
A catalogue record for this book is available from the British Library.

ISBN   1 85973 847 8 (cloth)
             1 84520 075 6 (paper)

Typeset by Avocet Typeset, Chilton, Aylesbury, Bucks
Printed in the United Kingdom by Biddles Ltd, King's Lynn

www.bergpublishers.com

To my lifelong friends, Anne and John Killick

Contents

List of Tables   ix

List of Figures   xi

Preface   xiii

Introduction   1

1. Folk Classifications of Insects   13

2. Insects as Food   49

3. Bees and Bee-keeping   93

4. Insects and Agriculture   109

5. Household Pests and Locust Swarms   145

6. Insects and Disease   161

7. Cultural Entomology   181

Appendix: Insect Life of Malawi   217

Bibliography   291

References   293

Index   311

List of Tables

Table 1.1	Navajo Classification of Insects	22
Table 1.2	Number of Folk Generics per Insect Order	23
Table 1.3	Relationships of Generics to Taxa in the Main Insect Orders	40
Table 2.1	Nutritive Values of Four Edible Caterpillars per 100 gm Dry Weight	88
Table 2.2	Caterpillar Collections in Kasungu National Park, 1994–2000	90
Table 4.1	Armyworm Infestations in Malwi, 1994–5	113
Table 4.2	Crops Attacked by Various Genera of Termites in Southern Malawi	117
Table 4.3	Incidence of Termite Damage by Crop	118
Table 4.4	Numbers of Farmers in the Lower Shire Valley Identifying Particular Cotton Pests as Important to them	126
Table 5.1	Numbers of People Considering Specific Insects their most Troublesome Household Pests (of a Total of 70 Interviewees from Villages around Kapalasa Farm)	150
Table 6.1	Morbidity and Mortality from Various Causes, Mulanje Mission Hospital, 1998: Children under Five	162
Table 6.2	Morbidity and Mortality from Various Causes, Mulanje Mission Hospital, 1998: Adults	163
Table 7.1	Types of Insect Mentioned in Malawian Proverbs and Riddles	209

List of Figures

Fig. 1   Peter Mofor, drying termites, Kapalasa,
           December 2000.   61
Fig. 2   Meria White with nest of *Ntchiu* (*Anaphe panda*,
           the processionary caterpillar), Kapalasa.   78
Fig. 3   Mary Malata cooking *Ntchiu* caterpillars
           (*Anaphe panda*), Kapalasa.   79
Fig. 4   *Bunaea alcinoe*, caterpillars, Kapalasa.   81
Fig. 5   Market vendor, Zomba, selling insecticides.   143
Fig. 6   Number 2. *Blatoidea, Periplaneta americana*,
           Cockroach, Mphemvu, Makwawa, 3 July 2001.   219
Fig. 7   Number 7. *Mantidae, Polyspilota aeruginosa*,
           Barred Mantis, Chiswambiya, Kapalasa,
           14 March 2001.   222
Fig. 8   Number 10. *Pamphagidae, Lobosceliana brevicomis*,
           Toad Grasshopper, Tsokonombwe, Kapalasa,
           20 January 2001.   224
Fig. 9   Number 17. *Acrididae, Gastrimargus africanus*,
           Yellow-Winged Grasshopper, Chidyamamina,
           Makoka, 23 May 2001.   228
Fig. 10   Number 18. *Acrididae, Acrida sulphuripennis*, Sulphur
           Acrida, Chigomphanthiko, Kapalasa, 30 May 2001.   229
Fig. 11   Number 19. *Acrididae, Catantops spissus*, Blue-
           Winged Grasshopper, Nakagunda, Kapalasa,
           12 May 2001.   230
Fig. 12   Number 26. *Acrididae, Ornithacris magnifica*,
           Common Locust, Mphangala, Makwawa,
           14 March 2001.   232
Fig. 13   Number 26. *Acrididae, Ornithacris* (*orientalis*) *cyanea*,
           Oriental Locust, Chiwala, Kapalasa, 12 February
           2001.   233
Fig. 14   Number 27. *Acrididae, Acanthacris ruficornis*, Tree
           Locust, Chiwala/Dzombe, Kapalasa, 14 March 2001.   234
Fig. 15   Number 30. *Tettigoniidae, Homorocoryphus vicinus*,
           Common (Green) Katydid, Bwanoni, Kapalasa, 24 May
           2001.   235

Fig. 16   Number 56. *Dynastidae, Oryctes boas*, Rhinoceros
          Beetle, Chipembere, Blantyre, 3 October 2000.   245
Fig. 17   Number 59. *Cetoniidae, Amaurodes passerinii*
          (*Mecynorrhina passerinii*), Nsopa Beetle, Kapalasa,
          30 November 2000.   247
Fig. 18   Number 59. *Cetoniidae, Ranzania petersiana*
          (*Taurhina splendens*), Green Flower Beetle, Kapalasa,
          3 February 2001.   247
Fig. 19   Number 62. *Buprestidae, Sternocera (variabilis)*
          orissa, Jewel Beetle, Nkumbutera, Makwawa,
          26 January 2001.   249
Fig. 20   Number 63. *Elateridae, Tetralopus terotundifrons*,
          Black Click Beetle, Chindenga, Zoa, 11 February
          2001.   249
Fig. 21   Number 72. *Cerambycidae, Ceroplesis orientalis*,
          Redbanded Longhorn Beetle, Ligombera, Kapalasa,
          6 January 2001.   253
Fig. 22   Number 76. *Cerambycidae, Mecosaspis plutina*,
          Blue Longhorn Beetle, Mwase, Kapalasa, 9 November
          2000.   254
Fig. 23   Number 106. *Thaumetopoeidae, Anaphe panda*,
          Processionary Moth, *Ntchiu*, Collective Cocoon on
          Bridelia micrantha, Kapalasa, 2 February 2001.   268
Fig. 24   Number 107. *Psychidae, Eumetia cervina* (*Clania*
          moddermanni), Bagworm Moth, Ntemankhuni,
          Kapalasa, 12 May 2001.   269
Fig. 25   Number 130. *Xylocopidae, Xylocopa mossambica*
          (*caffra*), Pied Carpenter Bee, Bemberezi, Kapalasa,
          11 November 2000.   281
Fig. 26   Number 130. *Xylocopidae, Xylocopa flavorufa*,
          Rufous Carpenter Bee, Bemberezi, Kapalasa,
          2 October 2000.   281
Fig. 27   Number 130. *Xylocopidae, Xylocopa nigrita*, Large
          Carpenter Bee, Bemberezi, Kapalasa, 6 May
          2001.   281

Preface

I have always experienced an intense joy in the natural world, particularly in regard to what the Taoists described as the 'ten thousand things' – the myriad of life-forms that inhabit the earth – for me insects, plants, fungi, frogs, birds and mammals having an especial interest. The first book I ever owned was called *Look and Find Out Birds* (by W. P. Westell), and the first article I ever published was entitled 'Denizen of the Evergreen Forest' (in *African Wildlife* 1962), describing the habits and life history of a rather rare pouched rat *Beamys hindei*. I have thus never considered myself a 'real' anthropologist – nowadays they all seem to be obsessed with language, metaphor and hermeneutics. I belong, rather, to a tribe of scholars who became extinct in the nineteenth century; they described themselves as 'naturalists', as students of natural history. My intellectual tendencies and aspirations thus tend to be fundamentally empirical, realist and historical. That's why my favourite authors are all orientated towards history and biology – Darwin, Kropotkin, Dubos, Mayr, Jonas and Bookchin.

This, my latest book, is about insects, or rather, about the relationship between humans and insects in Malawi. It reflects an interest that goes back a long way, as I was an avid reader of the essays of Jean-Henri Fabre in my youth, and I made notes and sketches on insects in Malawi when I lived at Zoa and Limbuli during the years 1958–1965. I actually discovered then an insect new to science – *Hemimerus morrisii*, which, believe it or not, is a parasitic, flightless earwig that lives in the nest of the pouched rat. As it has no relevance at all to the lives of Malawians, this insect is not mentioned in this book. One of my earliest published articles in anthropology was in fact an analysis of Navajo ethnoentomology (1979), which explored the relationship between the Navajo classification of insects and their symbolism.

This present study is specifically based on ethnoentomological research undertaken in 2000–2001, which was sponsored by a grant from the Leverhulme Trust. For this support I am grateful.

As research is always a collective enterprise, I would very much like to thank the following people for supporting and encouraging in various ways my research studies in Malawi.

Firstly, I should like to thank those who gave me institutional support; and I was happy again to be affiliated to the Centre of Social Research, University of Malawi, Zomba. I should therefore particularly like to express my thanks to Eston Sambo, the university research co-ordinator, and Wycliffe Chilowa, the director of the centre, for their warm and continuing support of my research endeavours.

Secondly, basing myself at Kapalasa farm near Namadzi, I should like to express my thanks to the late Sven Grüner and his family for their support and hospitality, and all the people of Kamalo village for tolerating my intrusions, and for offering me friendship, instruction and insights into their cultural life, especially with regard to insects. In this respect I should also like to thank Feston Damson, Christina Kasiya, Jackson Kasinja, Mary Malata, Biswick Mataya, James Matanika, Peter and Teresa Mofor, Joyce Molombo, James Stima, Meria White and Andreya Zakaliya.

Thirdly, I should like to thank people at several research institutions, all of whom welcomed me as a visiting scholar, and helped me in my research. At the National Archives in Zomba, I much appreciate the help given to me by Stanley Gondwe and Elliam Kamanga in tracking down old reports and documents relating to insects. At Bvumbwe Agricultural Research Station I much valued the support of director Noel Nsanjama, the entomologists Godfrey Chig'oma and Tony Maulana, and especially help given to me by Julius Kambalame in the identifications of my insect collections.

At Mimosa Tea Research Station, Mulanje, I much valued the enlightening discussion I had with James Biscoe and Pritam Rattan on coffee and tea insect pests respectively, on which both men are recognized authorities.

At Makoka Agricultural Research Station I appreciated the help from the always welcoming Tobias Mtwanga and the librarian Iwalani Chinkhata and the invaluable advice given to me by Julian Mchowa and George Phiri, who provided me with introductions to cotton pests and the maize stalk borer respectively.

At the Forestry Research Institute in Zomba, the director Dennis Kayambazinthu was warmly supportive of my project and I appreciated the help of the assistant librarian Tiyesi Chirwa and the generous advice given to me on insects as a food resource in Malawi by Gerald Meke and Lawrence Chikaonda.

Fourthly, I would like to express my thanks to many people throughout Malawi, some of whom I have known for over twenty years, who have offered me friendship and given me helpful advice and instruction on insects – whether as food, medicine or pests – as well as wider aspects of

Malawian culture. In this regard I would like to thank: Samuel Banda (Nsanje), Moses Allan (Neno), Alexander Boatman (Thyolo), Wyson Bowa (Mlangeni), Salimu Chinyangala (Domasi), Christopher Gongolo (Balaka), Biton Gulumba (Zoa), Booker Kauta (Neno), Mai Late Malemia (Domasi), Chiwanda Uka Lyoka (Mzuzu), Simon Mbewa (Chiradzulu), Helen Mgomo (Domasi), Henry Moyo (Nchalo), Daulos Mauambeta (Limbe), Joyce Nkhonjera (Chitimba), Benjamin Phiri (Nkhamenya), Boston Soko (Ekwendeni), Arnold Wasi (Neno) and Samson Waiti (Namadzi).

Fifthly, I would also like to thank the following for giving me constructive advice, intellectual support and help relating to the insect identification: Alex Banda, Mike Bingham, Birgitt Bossen, Chieko Ando, Robin Broadhead, Stephen Carr, Roy Ellen, Susan Greenwood, Peter Hayes, Mike Froude, Irmgaard Hoeschle-Zeldan, Tim Ingold, Robert Kruszynski, Paul Latham, Ray Murphy, the late Sally Singh, Arthur Stevens, Angela Travis, and James Woodburn.

Sixthly, I am grateful to many friends in Malawi for offering me warm hospitality and continual support, and would especially like to thank Shay Busman, Father Claude Boucher, Neville and Rosemarie Bevis, Les and Janet Doran, Cornell and Sandy Dudley, Carl Bruessow and Gillian Knox, John and Anne Killick, Janet Lowore, Janet and Douglas Mwenitete, Martin Ott, Hassam and Martha Patel, Dilys and Paul Taylor, Brian and June Walker, Pat Royle, John and Fumiyo Wilson, and Pat and Mike Whitbread. Cornell Dudley and John Wilson, both experienced entomologists and wildlife conservationists, were particularly helpful in giving me guidance on insect identification. But there is one person to whom I owe especial thanks, and that is John Kajalwiche, who acted as my guide, mentor and friend throughout the year I spent at Kapalasa.

Finally, I should like to thank my family and colleagues at Goldsmiths College for their continuing support, and Emma Svanberg and my daughter Ketta, who helped me to type up the manuscript.

Introduction

Others have reproached me with my style ... they fear lest a page that is read without fatigue should not always be the expression of the truth. Were I to take their word for it, we are profound only on condition of being obscure.

Jean-Henri Fabre, Souvenirs Ethnomologiques

This book explores the role of insects in the social and cultural life of the matrilineal people of Malawi. It forms a part of an ongoing project in which I have attempted to describe the complex and multifaceted ways in which Malawian people relate to the natural world, my earlier studies having focused specifically on medicinal plants, fungi and mammals.

Insects, of course, are the most abundant terrestrial life-form, yet anthropologists on the whole have been little interested in insect life, although in recent decades, with the emergence of enthnobiology and cultural entomology as sub-disciplines, a growing interest has developed in insect-human interactions. Thus scholars have been studying not only the practical uses of insects as food or medicine, but the role that insects have played in the cultural life of human societies – with regard to literature, mythology, music, art, religion, folklore and recreation (Bodenheimer 1951; Clausen 1954; Hogue 1987; Van Huis 1996). This study aims to contribute to this growing literature, but it is integrative and not specific in its focus, and combines anthropology with a historical perspective.

Humans have often tended to see themselves as the ultimate form of life on earth, as either the 'apogee of evolution' or as created in the 'image' of god, and thus having 'dominion' or 'stewardship' over the planet. But as (some) humans seem bent on self-destruction, and as insects, are, it appears, several times more resistant to radiation than humans, humans can hardly claim to be the dominant species (H. E. Evans 1970: 18). Indeed, one could well argue that it is the insects that are the truly dominant life-form, for their numbers on earth are quite staggering, and the total number of known (described) insect species in the world is thought to be around one million. It is, however, estimated that

1

there may be at least nine million species of insects in the world, mostly unknown and undescribed. When one compares these numbers with the known number of species of animals and higher plants, this relative abundance of insect species becomes dramatically evident.

Number of Species

	Worldwide	Malawi
Mammals	4,327	195
Birds	9,672	630
Reptiles	6,550	124
Fish	22,000	338
Flowering Plants	262,000	3,600

One family of beetles, the *Curculionidae* (weevils) has around 60,000 species, more than the total number of mammals, birds, reptiles and fish put together, and it is estimated that around 80 per cent of all living animals are insects. Cornell Dudley has thus recently calculated that there are probably well over two hundred thousand species of insects to be found in Malawi, many of which are still undescribed, although only around four thousand species have been collected (Hammond 1992; Dudley 1996). I must therefore emphasize that the many species of insects that are described in this book, and that are known and used by Malawian people, constitute only a tiny fraction of the thousands of species that are to be found in Malawi.

But not only is there a wealth of insect species: the actual number of individual insects can be quite staggering. I watched at intervals a column of red driver ants, *Linthumbu* (*Dorylus* sp.) moving near my house at Kapalasa. The column, four or five abreast, was marching for the greater part of the day, and the colony must have numbered millions. On another occasion, in mid-November at the onset of the rains, I had an equally enlightening experience. Early one morning I suddenly noticed thousands of small termites, *Chiswe* (*Fulleritermes* sp.) emerging from cracks in the veranda of my house, and within minutes the whole of the veranda was swarming with termites, both workers and alates. They must have numbered many thousands. Half an hour later, the veranda was swarming with thousands of small red driver ants, which appeared suddenly, emerging from the same holes and cracks in the veranda. Although the worker ants were smaller than the termites, they attacked the termites furiously. Within half an hour, hardly a termite was to be seen, and thousands of swarming ants had taken over the veranda. In another twenty minutes or so, no ants were to be seen – they mysteriously disappeared. All this took place within about two hours. The numbers of insects, in fact, is so vast, that it can hardly be imaged, let alone estimated.

Although largely terrestrial – few insects are found in the sea – insects have invaded almost every habitat on earth, from the most arid deserts to the most luxurious tropical forest, from marshy swamps to the tops of the highest mountains, and are even found in the depths of the Antarctic. From an evolutionary or ecological perspective, the insects are probably the 'most successful of animals on earth' (Waldbauer 1996: 11–24), and they were around long before the dinosaurs and flowering plants, having evolved some four hundred million years ago. Insects belong to that great group of invertebrate animals known as *Arthropoda* (those with jointed legs), and as a class they are characterized – as adults – by having a body with three distinct segments – head, thorax and abdomen, a pair of antennae (feelers) and six legs. Their success as a life-form can be attributed to their ability to live in diverse habitats – they have an external skeleton of hardened cuticle and have an extremely tenacious hold on life; a high reproductive capacity; and a remarkable proclivity to consume all kinds of food; and to their being the only invertebrates that have wings – though not all insects are winged. And it is worth noting that although Europeans often express an extreme aversion towards insects, probably less than 2 per cent of the insects in the world make life difficult for humans – by damaging our crops, transmitting diseases or destroying our material possessions. Indeed, the vast majority of insects are neither a blessing (useful) nor a curse (harmful) to humans, but are simply there in the environment, indispensable links in the web of life that sustains all living things, including humans.

The focus of my study will be on insects, but I am less concerned with insects *per se*, than with exploring human–insect interactions in Malawi, although I have to admit I find insects – particularly ants and termites – an especially fascinating group of organisms. I can well understand why scholars like Morton Wheeler and Edward Wilson have spent a lifetime studying ants! (For useful general studies of insects see Imms 1947; Newman 1965; H. E. Evans 1970; and Waldbauer 1996.)

This study is focused on the matrilineal peoples of Malawi, and specifically on the people living in rural areas who constitute the majority of the population. In earlier studies I have discussed at length the socio-economic life of Malawian people, their kinship organization, agriculture, hunting traditions, life-cycle rituals and religion, and the salience of the main ethnic communities – Nyanja/Chewa, Lomwe, Yao and Tumbuka. To these earlier writings (Morris 1998, 2000) the reader is referred. And as with those earlier texts, the theoretical perspective that informs this study may well be described as one of the empirical/dialectical naturalism or historical/emergent materialism, although I tend to employ the term evolutionary holism myself (Dewey 1929; Bookchin 1990; Bunge 1996; Foster 2000; Morris 2001b).

In recent years the academy has been besieged by the rhetoric of so-called postmodernists who, following in the footsteps of Nietzsche, Dilthey, Husserl, Heidegger and the later Wittgenstein, have had a rather baneful influence on the social sciences, including anthropology. The postmodernists (Baudrillard, Lyotard, Derrida, Rorty, Butler *et al.*) have tended, in oracular fashion, to advance the following rather questionable tenets.

Firstly, they have propounded an idealist and subjectivist metaphysic that denies the reality of the material world. In Mary Douglas's memorable phrase they suggest that 'all reality is social reality' (1975: 5). The natural world thus becomes a social construct and facts (events, happenings, natural objects) and concepts (ideas, intentional objects) are seemingly conflated. Anti-realism has thus now become the vogue in anthropology, and things in nature are now seen as having 'no independent existence apart from how they are defined by culture', as David Schneider long ago put it (1976: 204). That nature – defined as that which is not humanly created – pre-exists humans is taken for granted, of course, by all ordinary people, including Malawians. Indeed, the social constructivist thesis not only conflicts with common sense, but with everything we know about the material world prior to the emergence of humans (Margulis and Sagan 1986; Bunge 1999: 48).

Secondly, the postmodernists (and interpretative anthropologists) have tended to disparage, or even to repudiate entirely, empirical social science. There has thus been a growing obsession with symbolism, ritual, narratives, myth, metaphor and language more generally, and anthropology has been reduced to semiotics, or hermeneutics or even autobiography. Social life, indeed the world, has been seen as a 'text', to be interpreted, rather than as something real to be described and explained. Viewing social life simply as text, or a collection of 'discourses', is an 'idealist extravagance' that undervalues the natural world and bypasses economic and political realities (Bunge 1996: 343–6).

Thirdly, as there is no immediate relationship between consciousness (or language) and the world – an idea that has been part of the common currency of the social sciences ever since Marx – postmodernists now take this premise to extremes and posit no relationships between language and the world, and thus espouse an absolute epistemological (and moral) relativism. Truth is thus either repudiated entirely (Tyler) or seen simply as an 'effect' of local cultural discourses (Rorty, Geertz, Flax) or is seen as something that will be 'disclosed' to or 'revealed' by elite scholars through poetic evocation (Heidegger) – truth and meaning being conflated in the process. Thus we are told that there are no objective truths, and that the natural world (and social facts) even if they exist, can never be known. Such relativism, of course, has a long history, and has been critiqued by many scholars (Gellner 1973: 50–77; Devitt 1984; Bunge 1996: 338-42; Searle 1999; Bricmont 2001).

Finally, there has been a growing tendency among postmodern academics – again following Heidegger – to express themselves in the most obscure and impenetrable jargon, under the misguided impression that obscurity connotes profundity, and that a scholastic, neo-baroque prose style is the hallmark of radical politics. Much of this Heideggerian style of writing is mystifying, and this too has provoked much recent criticism (Harris 1999: 153-60; Sokal and Bricmont 1999).

In this present study, in opposition to the nihilistic ethos of postmodernism, I continue to affirm the indispensability of a realist (materialist) ontology – an acknowledgement that the natural world *exists* independently of human sense experience and cognition – and the crucial importance of upholding such conceptions as truth as correspondence, human agency and empirical social science. In my article *In Defence of Realism and Truth* (1997) I have offered my own critical reflection of the anthropological followers of Heidegger, and suggested that an anthropology worthy of the name will embrace what Adam Kuper (1994) has described as the 'cosmopolitan project' – linking with other social sciences (as well as with humanities) to contribute towards a comparative study of human life. Thus an understanding of human social life will entail both interpretation/hermeneutics (humanism) and also explanations in terms of causal mechanisms (naturalism). Implicitly, this is the theoretical perspective that informs the present study. Equally, I have tried to write in a style that is readable, lucid and accessible to a wide range of people – not just to academics, but also to lay persons who may be interested in insect–human interactions, especially Malawians. I thus try to write, as the pioneer entomologist S. H. Skaife put it, in 'plain everyday language' (1955: preface), even though the subject–matter itself may be complex.

This book is essentially an ethnographic study, and is primarily based on a year's anthropological fieldwork, undertaken in the years 2000–2001, although I have lived and worked in Malawi for more than a decade. But it differs from other ethnographic texts in a number of ways.

The first is that most of the empirical data on which this text is based are essentially derived from *my own* fieldwork experiences in Malawi, that is, from my own active participation in social activities relating to insects (such as collecting bugs or termites), and from conversations in

Chewa/Nyanja I have had with numerous Malawians – mostly informally and in an outdoor setting – and from my own observations of Malawian social life. During the year I discussed insects with practically everyone I met in Malawi, and even drinking in a local bar I invariably turned the conversation around to a discussion of insects, to the amusement (normally) of my companions, who were somewhat incredulous that a European should be familiar with such insects as *mafulufute* and *nyenje*. Unlike, it seems, most anthropologists, I never employed a team of undergraduates, or what are described in Malawi as research 'enumerators', to go out into villages with tape-recorders, interview schedules and questionnaires to gather empirical data on my behalf. In fact, given the welter of data now being published on 'research methods', I have to admit that I never utilized any questionnaire or formal research schedule. I simply participated in those social activities relevant to my purposes, or chatted (*cheza*) with local people, making inquiries about insects – their recognition, habits, uses and cultural significance. All the data I gathered were jotted down on bits of paper carried in my pocket, and then written up in a journal – data that would make sense to nobody but myself. I thus have no typed field notes, no interview schedules that I could bequeath to prosperity or deposit in some library; just personal journals – eighteen in all – that are full of notes, maps, sketches of insects and newspaper cuttings, and that form the basis of this ethnography.

Secondly, although I was based at Kapalasa farm near Namadzi, and spent most of my time engaged in research studies on the farm and in Kamalo village, and I had close and intimate relations with all my neighbours, this study is not rooted in a particular community, as is the custom with many ethnographic texts. In fact – of necessity – I travelled widely in Malawi during the year, covering over 16,000 km on my Yamaha DT125 motorcycle. Had I sat under a mango tree in Kamalo village, armed with a tape-recorder, discussing the esoteric details of some rituals with the local chief (whom I knew well) or some well-known spirit medium – which appears to be some anthropologists' conception of fieldwork – my understanding of human–insect interactions in Malawi would have been severely limited. Thus I travelled widely: to the northern lakeshore (Chitimba), to observe and learn about *nkhungu*, the lakefly; to Nchalo to study firsthand the insect pests of sugarcane; to the Chimaliro forest and the Kasungu National Park to research edible caterpillars; to Mulanje and Thyolo mountain to observe, discuss and record the insect pests of tea and coffee; to Zoa in order to learn what it means to gather honey and to learn something about local beekeeping; to the Dedza highlands to join young boys in collecting grasshoppers; to Neno to join in the collection of the *nkhunguni* shield bug and the search out the *mphalabungu* caterpillars, and to Bangula in the Lower Shire valley to study cotton pests firsthand. I would have learnt precious little about insect interactions had I spent all my days in Kamalo village. The focus of this study is, therefore, neither on a particular locality, nor on a specific ethnic community, but rather on Malawi as a whole, as both a geographical and social unit, the subject of my study being the matrilineal people of Malawi (who share a common cultural heritage) and their relationship to insects. I use Nyanja/Chewa terms in the text not because I see them as 'representative' of the Malawian people – as one critic has suggested, completely misunderstanding my work on mammals – but because this has long been the national language, and is the language I personally used in my conversations with Malawians. Most of my research in the Shire highlands at both Makwawa and Kapalasa has in fact been mainly with Yao and Lomwe speakers, and almost all my close Malawian friends are also Yao or Lomwe.

Thirdly, as I am particularly concerned not only to describe and interpret Malawi social life and culture, as it relates to insects, but also to explicate it in a social-historical context, I have incorporated into the study not only data derived from my own fieldwork and experiences but also historical and ethnographical data from a wider range of sources. This book thus includes data from newspaper reports, economic surveys, unpublished articles, early ethnographic studies and archive material. I have thus delved into the records of early missionaries such as Rev. Robert Laws and Father Louis Denis, as well as into the early colonial reports of the governmental entomologists. In the text I thus pay tribute to, rather than disparage, the pioneering work of William Lamborn, Colin Smee, Jessie Williamson and Charles Sweeney. I am certainly not the first person to study human–insect interactions in Malawi. I have also incorporated into the text comparative material where this seems to be of interest and relevant. Indeed, the book has a deliberate cross-cultural focus, and is not only concerned with Malawi but with human–insect interactions throughout the world, and each chapter incorporates comparative data from a wide range of cultures. The notion that ethnography should 'break' with the 'trope' of history and social structure and be simply a kind of autobiography (Marcus 1995) seems to me to be both limiting and unnecessary, a redundant form of 'textualism'. I have, therefore, given my realist aspirations, declined to make this study into a postmodernist text, into a kind of rather self-indulgent account of fieldwork where we learn more about the anthropologists than about the people that they are supposed to be studying. This book is certainly not a record of my own 'self-exploration', a 'visionary' quest into a supposedly unknown and exotic culture; it is rather a modest account of human–insect interactions in Malawi and elsewhere. Thus I have not made this study into a record of my own fieldwork experiences, nor have I enlivened the text with personal vignettes and anecdotes about my friends and informants. What shoes my friend Mary Malata was wearing when we were collecting termites together seems to me hardly relevant to the purposes of my ethnography, though it might have given my account a more colourful, 'authentic' ring, and indicated that I might have literary pretensions. Heaven forbid! The realist texts of Malinowski, Firth and Monica Wilson (for example) are, it seems to me, much more enlightening about their subject-matter and make much more exciting and interesting reading that most of the so-called 'new' ethnographies, which are invariably wrapped up in Heideggerian jargon. And Heidegger, as Paul Edwards remarked, was, along with the likes of Wittgenstein, a 'pompous purveyor of platitudes' (Honderich 1995: 22; cf. Bunge 1996: 295). No doubt some equally pompous academic will declaim that I have not undertaken 'real' fieldwork and that this book is not a 'real' ethnography; but I trust that readers will understand why at intervals I left Kamalo village , and took off on my motorcycle to study human–insect interactions in other parts of Malawi, and why I am reluctant to indulge in autobiography. I trust, too, that they will be able to recognize the empirical data derived from my own fieldwork experiences, and those that I have obtained from other sources – whether from books, newspaper articles, reports or archival material – for data of the latter type are always clearly indicated in the text (and not in the more fashionable footnotes).

In the past decade there has been a growing tendency among scholars to set up not simply a contrast, but a radical and rather gnostic dualism between the worldviews of hunter–gatherers (and tribal people more generally) and that of 'Western' people. On the one hand Western thought/culture is equated quite simplistically with the ultra-rationalism of Cartesian philosophy; with a mechanistic paradigm that sees the world as lifeless and mechanical; with a dualistic ontology that posits a radical dichotomy between humans and nature; with the Baconian (Capitalist) ethic of a 'domination' over nature, such that land and all living things are seen as simply resources to be exploited; and with subject–predicate logic, so that organisms (including humans) are seen as self-existent entities – isolated, lifeless, passive, rigidly demarcated, wholly unconnected with other living beings. Western people's relationship with nature and especially with animals, we are told, is impersonal, detached, anthropocentric and disparaging, and their culture generally one of domination and oppression. It is even suggested that 'Western' people have no sensuous understanding of nature, and are quite unable to experience – see, smell, hear, feel – the myriad life-forms (birds, insects, frogs, spiders, fungi, trees) that always and everywhere (even in cities) form an essential component of their life world.

Tribal people, on the other hand, especially hunter-gatherers, see the world, we are informed, as 'living and sacred'. The whole of nature is thought by tribal people to be 'animated' or 'enspirited' (the two notions are invariably and misleadingly conflated), and so all living things are seen as interconnected in a 'spiritual unity' or in a complex 'web of life'. Nature, for tribal people, is composed, it is suggested, not of impersonal inert 'objects' (as with Europeans) but of 'persons' with subjective agency. Their relationship to nature, especially towards animals, is therefore interpreted as one of trust and caring; it involves participation and reciprocal exchange, and implies a relational, and not an objective, epistemology (Abram 1996; Hartmann 1999; Ingold 2000; Peterson 2001; Milton 2002).

Although all people have much to learn from studying the social life and culture of tribal peoples. thus enriching our own understanding of the world, as Kropotkin (1902) long ago taught us, setting up a gnostic dualism between tribal people (interpreted as sensuous religious mystics) and Western people (Europeans) (seen as mechanistic materialists alienated from nature) is crude and simplistic. Such monolithic portrayals of both tribal and Western worldviews are misleading and simplistic, and verge on caricature. For no human culture is homogeneous, and, as I have tried to show in my earlier studies, people's relationship to nature, and specifically animals, is, in all societies, always one that is complex, diverse and multifaceted, and even contradictory, embracing many different perspectives on the world – empirical, pragmatic, practical, aesthetic, realist and sacramental (1998: 168–9). Thus Malawi people's interactions with insects, and the accompanying attitudes, are complex: they do not view insects in homogeneous fashion, and they neither see insects as 'persons' nor as 'enspirited' – certainly not as 'voices of the infinite' (Lauck 1998), nor as simply 'inert objects' to be utilized as a 'resource'. What I am thus trying to explore in this study is the diverse ways in which human–insect interactions are expressed in Malawi, and each chapter is focused on a particular form of interaction.

In Chapter 1 I outline the folk classifications of insects in Malawi – the basic insect natural history of Malawian people, with regard to the hundred or so insects that are given a phenomenal recognition that has varying degrees of cultural salience. This recognition of generic kinds implies a form of empirical naturalism that acknowledges that all things are causally interconnected – what Whitehead (1929: 196) described as the 'mode of causal efficacy' – for an awareness that all things are interconnected is fundamentally a feature of our common-sense understanding of the world, and ought not to be conflated with 'totemic' thought or so-called 'spiritual ecology'.

As an appendix I give, as background material, a descriptive outline of the common insects of Malawi. Under each species I give a short description of the insects, their common names, and notes on their distribution and ecology, and I draw heavily on the seminal studies of African insect life by two pioneering entomologists, Sydney Skaife (1979) and Charles Sweeney (1970).

In Chapter 2 I focus on those insects that are utilized as food in Malawi, and give details regarding the collecting strategies employed by Malawians, and their cooking procedures. I emphasize throughout that insects are an important source of protein and fat, the principal edible insects being termites, lakefly, crickets, bugs, grasshoppers and caterpillars.

Chapter 3 is on bees and beekeeping, for both opportunistic honey-hunting and traditional beekeeping have been widely practised in Malawi for many centuries. I outline the three types of bee from which honey is obtained and discuss the introduction of modern beekeeping methods to Malawi with the formation of beekeeping clubs by development agencies.

Chapter 4 is focused on the relationship between insects and agriculture, and discusses the many insects that are perceived as pests with regard to the main agricultural crops in Malawi – whether subsistence crops such as maize, beans, cassava and sweet potato, cash crops such as cotton and vegetables, or estate crops such as tea, sugar, tobacco and coffee. The principal pests are termites, elegant grasshoppers, various bugs, and crucially, the larvae of many moths and beetles. I conclude this chapter with a discussion of insects and pesticides.

In the following Chapter 5 I discuss those insect pests associated with domestic households, which are invariably considered to be troublesome by local people – ants, cockroaches, termites, bed bugs, maize weevils and the itch mite, as well as the forest pests. In regard to the latter, those of most economic importance are the various aphids that have in recent years attacked pine plantations and cedar forests throughout Malawi, inflicting considerable damage. I conclude this chapter with a historical account of the many locust swarms that have, at intervals, scourged the Malawian countrywide.

In Chapter 6 I discuss the complex relationship between insects and disease, and focus specifically on the two insects that have historically had such a vital impact on the social life of the Malawian people – the mosquito and the tsetse fly, which are, of course, the principal vectors of malaria and sleeping sickness respectively. I discuss in some detail the impact of these two diseases on the well-being of the Malawian people.

The final Chapter 7 examines the inter-cultural significance of insects in Malawi. After an introductory section examining cultural entomology in a comparative perspective, the chapter discusses the role of insects in medicine, in oral literature and in folklore and religion in Malawi.

–1–

Folk Classification of Insects

Ethnobiological Classifications

'To classify is human', and many forms of classification are ubiquitous in all human societies. Indeed, practical classifying has been described as the 'stuff of cultural anthropology – how people classify their everyday worlds, including everything from colour to kinship' (Bowker and Star 1999: 59). But classification is not some detached, intellectual activity – which is how some anthropologists appear to define it (and then repudiate it!) – for, like all forms of knowledge, it is derived from our engagement with the natural world, from practical action, not passive contemplation, as scholars like Dewey (1929) and Roy (1940) taught us long ago. Classifying is therefore inherently both a practical activity and a social process.

Over the past two decades there have been a wealth of studies on ethnobiological classifications. Much of this material has, inevitably given their salience, focused on the larger vertebrates and the flowering plants, to the general neglect of fungi and insects. In a path-breaking work on the principles of categorization of plants and animals Brent Berlin (1992), for example, makes no mention of fungi, and only very briefly discusses insects. But what is of interest is that in listing the major 'morphotypes' of arthropods, Berlin refers to the principal insect orders and families, and not to biological genera and species, which are the levels of classification that are given prominence in his discussions of mammals and flowering plants (1992: 266–7). Equally interestingly, there is hardly any mention of African people in the whole text.

Ethnobiological classification is all about recognition and relating to the world: it constitutes one of the ways in which people organize their knowledge about plants, animals and fungi. It is focused on 'natural kinds' (in a holistic sense) – the basic kinds of living beings that make up the diversity of nature. To set up a dichotomy between 'things' (supposedly reflecting a Western logic) and 'events' (supposedly the preoccupation of tribal people), as do some anthropologists (cf. Bird-David 1999) is quite misleading, and an example of the exoticism that besets anthropology. Not only do events presuppose the existence of concrete 'things' (*onta*), living or otherwise, but to speak about the relationships and activities of organisms, such as insects or elephants, also presupposes their recognition as living entities. Moreover, to focus on the classification of natural kinds – organisms – as the fundamental units of life, with the properties of reproduction, growth, metabolism, autonomous agency and self-maintenance, and with natures specific to their own kind (Goodwin 1994), does not in the least entail, as Ingold (2000) seems to misleadingly infer, that a natural kind is therefore a distinct entity with no relationship to the surrounding world at all. Equally obfuscating therefore is the setting up of a dichotomy between 'natural kinds' – things – and relationships, as if these are antithetical perspectives. There are no relations without relata, and no relata without relations. As the social ecologist Murray Bookchin put it, in critiquing the spiritual mechanism of Capra and Bateson, who, as with Ingold and Nurit-Bird, seem to deny the world its very physicality: 'The temptation to abandon the study of THINGS – living or not – for a study of relationships between them is as one-sided and reductionist as the temptation to abandon relationships for the things they interrelate.' Such reductionism involves debasing concrete organisms into abstract relations and subjectivism. An organic way of thinking, which Bookchin advocates – and which people in Malawi also share, does not imply the repudiation of the reality of concrete things (Bookchin 1990: 156–7; Bunge 1996, 1999: 246).

It has long been recognized that organisms, as species-beings, reflect what Mayr describes as 'real discontinuities in organic nature' (1988: 331), which delimit the natural entities that are described by ethnobiologists as folk 'generics'. Thus nobody perceives the world as 'formless matter' which is then, as cultural idealists would have it, (Leach 1964; Douglas 1990), culturally constructed in a unique and specific way by a particular 'culture'. For species-beings or generics have a reality in nature, and are not merely arbitrary mental (or cultural) constructs; they are, as Mayr put it, 'the products of evolution not of the human mind'. They thus form the 'basic' units, not only of biology, but of the folk-biological classifications of ordinary people throughout the world (Mayr 1988; Gould 1980: 170–7; Atran 1990). Ingold also repudiates the distinction, emphasized by Scott Atran (1990: 56), between living beings and inanimate objects, suggesting that this is not universally recognized, as the Ojibway view stones (some stones, in specific contexts!!) as 'persons' (2000: 95–7). Reacting against his own earlier writings, which expressed a very dualistic metaphysic (cf. Morris 1989), Ingold now *conflates* our common perceptions of the world and specific cultural conceptions of that same world. We no more perceive stones as animate (as having inherent properties and capacities such as self-replication, metabolism, growth, and self-maintenance) or as 'persons' than we directly perceive a shrine, or a wink, or somebody melancholy, or an insect as a food resource. A relational epistemology, which Dewey advocated more than half a century ago, does not entail conflating events (facts) (and an insect generic is a pattern of events) with ideas (concepts) about events.

The history of taxonomy, wrote Mayr (1982: 149), starts with Aristotle, and Aristotle is often depicted as an advocate of a subject–predicate logic that tends to conceive of an existent thing as requiring 'nothing but itself in order to exist' – and thus to deny the crucial importance of relationships (Whitehead 1929: 64). But Aristotle was fundamentally a naturalist whose years in the eastern Aegean (347–335 BC) were largely devoted to natural history studies. Although he expressed a natural teleology and conceived the natural world as essentially eternal, with each 'species' being essentially fixed and unchanging with an inherent nature (*physis*) or form (*eidos*), his approach to animal life was essentially empirical. In his well-known study '*Historia animalium*' (1965–70)Aristotle was not particularly concerned with providing an exhaustive classification of animals, or working through some deductive logic, but largely with recording the ecology, activities, and dispositions, as well as the morphology of animals. In fact, in *De partibus animalium* Aristotle (1937) specifically repudiates dichotomous division as a classifying principle, and goes to some length to indicate the limitations of the method of 'twofold division' (642b). Whitehead rightly suggests that Aristotle was not an Aristotelian (1929: 66), and Mayr (1982: 153) argues that the level of natural history went steadily downhill after Aristotle. Aristotle thus never conceived of animals simply in morphological terms, as self-existent isolated entities (does anyone?), but has essentially an ecological or relational perspective, emphasizing the relationships of various kinds (*genos*) of animals to the world. He noted and described the diverse feeding habits of the various forms (*eidos*) of animals; the fact that they have agency and provide themselves with specific habitations (488a); their varying dispositions towards humans; that cranes, ants, wasps and bees are, like humans, essentially social animals; that the morphologies of birds or animals clearly have functional correlates, in that birds of prey have talons and hooked beaks (592b).

The main life-forms (*genos*) of animals recognized by Aristotle were the following; quadrupeds, birds, fish, serpents (the presence of blood being a key distinguishing feature of these groups), various forms of marine animals (about which Aristotle seems to have been very knowledgeable) and insects. With respect to insects (*entoma*), which he described as those creatures that have insections on their bodies, get their food on land, and do not have blood or take in air (487a), Aristotle noted the following:

> That some insects have membraneous wings, those of the cockchafer and the dung and blister beetles being sheathed; that four-winged insects like wasps have a sting at their rear, while two-winged ones have a sting in front, e.g. fly, horse fly, gadfly, gnat (490a); that among some kinds of insects, such as the ant and glowworm, both winged and wingless forms are found (523b); that the insect body consists of three parts, and that its hardness 'ensures their safety' (532a); that insects can perceive objects that have a smell from a long distance (534b); that bees will not settle on anything that is putrid, but those feeding on thyme make the best honey with regard to sweetness and consistency (554a); that males are generally smaller than females in insects, and to copulate the male mounts the larger female (550b); that ichneumon wasps kill venom spiders as food for their larvae and make mud nests (552b).

Aristotle clearly had a very detailed knowledge of the ecology and habits of many species of insects, particularly the edible kinds such as the cicadas (556a), and mentions around forty different genera of insects. Nevertheless, although he recognized that most insects produce animals of the same kind as themselves, he also thought some insects are produced spontaneously, out of dew, wood or putrefying mud and dung (550b).

Aristotle was first and foremost a naturalist who expressed an organic way of thinking – as Bookchin (1990) emphasized – and he thus recommended that we should study animals without any aversion 'knowing that in all of them there is something natural and beautiful' *(De partibus animalium* 645a). Clearly Aristotle did not share that disdain for nature that David Abram (1996: 94) sees as intrinsic to European civilization. For Aristotle, however, the natural order was eternal and unchanging, and everything in nature has its purpose, there being an essential unity between the form *(eidos)* of an organism and its purpose or function *(telos)*. He was thus not an evolutionary thinker, though Mayr has suggested that Aristotle's principle of *eidos*, which was quite distinct from that of Plato, is akin to the modern conception of a 'genetic programme' (1988: 56–7).

It is worth noting that Aristotle placed little emphasis on the conception of nature *(physis)* as a totality, over and above the natures of particular things. As one writer put it: Aristotle's nature is '*not* transcendent but immanent as the species or soul of individuals' (Preus 1975: 184). And in classifying these various species-beings or natural kinds Aristotle focused not only on their morphology, but on how their natures were nourished, moved and reproduced. Through its activities and its relationships with the manifold aspects of nature, the adult form of the animal was realized, its nature (*physis*) becoming 'actual' (French 1994: 43–6, for further studies of Aristotle's biology see Gotthelf and Lennox 1987; Atran 1990; Lennox 2001).

Ethnobiologists have postulated that folk-biological classifications typically relate to five taxonomic levels; yet those that seem to have particular salience for Aristotle, and for many ethnobiologists, are the taxonomic ranks, life-form and generics. These roughly correspond to Aristotle's concepts of kind (*genos*) and form (*eidos*).

Although people throughout the world (and Malawians are no exception) clearly recognize distinctions between animals and plants, this is rarely given significance in folk terminology. Many people thus have no terms for the 'animal' and 'plant' kingdoms. It has been suggested that both these concepts are relatively recent phenomena in the development of taxonomic nomenclature (Berlin 1972; Morris 1980). But throughout the world people have higher-order categories, generally referred to as 'life-forms', that embrace a diverse number of folk generics. Their number is usually small, and includes such taxa as 'bird', 'fish', 'tree', 'herb' and 'quadruped'. The Ndumba of Papua New Guinea, for example, have an animal taxonomy that includes four life-forms – *fai* (marsupials and monotremes), *kaapa'raara* (reptiles, eels, centipedes and worms), *Kuri* (bats and birds) and *tovendi* (insects and arachnids). These include most of the folk generics (Hays 1983: 602). Unlike folk generics, which as 'natural kinds' are seen by biologists – as species – as the real units of nature, the life-form categories are to some extent culturally determined, and, as a general rule, do not correspond closely to scientific taxonomy. There has indeed been much debate among ethnobiologists regarding the character of life-form taxa and whether or not they can be perceived as natural categories, as distinct from being purely utilitarian or practical taxa (Hunn 1982; Randall and Hunn 1984; Berlin 1992: 161–71). Equally important is the fact that many generics are unaffiliated to the main life-form categories (Ellen 1993: 99–102). Among the Tzeltal of Southern Mexico, for example, whose plant classification embraces four life-form categories, *te'* (tree), *wamal* (shrubs), *ak* (grass) and *ak'* (vine), around 21 per cent of folk plant generics are unaffiliated to any life-form category (Berlin 1992: 172).

Although folk generics do not exactly match the biologist's concepts of genera and species, many studies have indicated that there is a fairly close correspondence between folk generics and biological classifications. In Brent Berlin and his associates' pioneering study of Tzeltal plant taxonomy, which recorded 471 plant generics, 61 per cent corresponded to two or more species of the same genera (Berlin, Breedlove and Raven 1974). Similarly, Eugene Hunn (1975) found that 75 per cent of Tzeltal animal generics corresponded to biological species, with a further 11 per cent corresponding to two or more species of the same genus. Thus there is little evidence to suggest that folk generics are purely mental or cultural constructs. Most generics are monotypic, but some generics, particularly those relating to cultivated plants, may be polytypic, and divided into two or more specific (binomial) categories. The number of polytypic generics seem to be between 10 and 20 per cent in most folk-botanical taxonomies (Berlin 1992: 129; D'Andrade 1995: 96).

Folk generics as natural kinds (organisms) tended to be perceived as a *gestalt*, as a configurational, dynamic unity, rather than as an entity with a discrete list of properties – though people everywhere described generics with reference to certain key attributes. Such attributes, as Aristotle recognized, refer not simply to an animal's morphological characteristics, but also to its inherent powers, capacities and essential activities. Not only hunter-gatherers like the Nayaka, but people everywhere, are interested in what animals do (events!), and not simply in what they look like. Hunn has made a useful distinction between the referential meanings of animal and plant generics, which are specific, and their various cultural meanings. He suggests that once the referential meaning has been established 'a whole world of other cultural meanings is accessible to the student of that system of traditional ecological knowledge' (1993: 20). This relates again to the distinction between morphological (or general-purpose) and functional (or special-purpose) classifications. Functional classifications are defined in terms of the use or function of a particular plant or animal – terms such as weed, timber, rubber, relish, herb are functional categories – and many ethnobiologists, particularly Brent Berlin, have tended to see them as extra-taxonomic, since they are not natural kinds, but rather refer to the way certain objects/generics are used. The problem is that removing functional terms from general folk classifications not only results in lexical gaps, but also ignores the fact that in many languages both the life-forms and intermediate categories have a mixture of morphological and functional features – as I have attempted to demonstrate in my earlier studies (1996: 32–47, 1998: 133–52; D'Andrade 1995: 103). Equally important is the fact that the 'general-purpose' classifications based predominantly on morphological criteria, to the exclusion of functional or cultural factors, tends to be more evident as societies become increasingly complex, and, as Ellen puts it, 'less semantically attached to the natural world' (1993: 110; cf. Abram 1996).

Many symbolic and postmodern anthropologists seem to hold very disparaging opinions of ethnobiology, engrossed as they are in delineating the 'symbolic logic' of some particular ethnic group, or discussing in labyrinthine detail some ritual performance or their own fieldwork experiences. Yet ethnobiologists have provided us with a wealth of information and ideas on how non-Western peoples themselves categorize and utilize the diversity of living kinds. Offering an interdisciplinary perspective, they have thus made an important contribution to our understanding of people's everyday knowledge of the biological world (Brown 1984; Berlin 1992; Medin and Atran 1999).

Folk Classifications of Insects: a Comparative Perspective

Folk classifications are far less comprehensive than the taxonomic systems of professional biologists, and, as Fikret Berkes writes, the gap between the two classificatory systems increases as the cultural and practical significance of the animal or plant decreases. Thus trees and the larger mammals are often clearly recognized, and there is an almost one-to-one correspondence between folk and scientific nomenclature with regard to the more conspicuous plants and mammals (Morris 1996, 1998: 156–64). However, among most communities only a small fraction of the insects and other invertebrates in an ecosystem may be recognized (Berkes 1999: 42). In fact insects are rarely recognized as a life-form category, but are usually incorporated with other invertebrates into a category that has a residual status. Often insects seem to be unaffiliated to any life-form category (Berlin 1992: 165–6). Among the Itzaj Maya of Guatemala, insects along with other small invertebrates form a 'residual' life-form category *Mejen B'a'al Che* ('small forest animals') that Atran suggests does not have a conceptually distinctive role in their 'economy of nature' (1999: 124). In an early study of the ethnozoology of the Tewa Indians of New Mexico, Henderson and Harrington explicitly note that these people have no word for 'insect', though they recorded the names of several kinds of insects. Around twenty local names are mentioned, and they seem to be correlates of the main orders of insects (1914: 58–60, cf. Posey 1983).

For comparative purposes we may briefly outline the classification of insects among four societies for which we have fairly detailed studies – the San, Tzeltal, Nuaulu and Navajo.

The Central Kalahari San categorize insects as *goowaha* – 'useless things', and found it highly amusing that the anthropologist should even be interested in such life-forms. Even so, these hunter-gatherers utilize eighteen kinds of insects as food, and also use insects as medicine, arrow poison and decoration – so they are hardly useless. Around 70 species of insects are known to the allied !Kung San (Yellen and Lee 1976: 37), while Nonaka (1996) records around 104 folk generics among the Central Kalahari San. Many of these folk generics cover several insect species, which often belong to several distinct families. For example: *ciecebe* seems to cover most of the adult forms of *Lepidoptera*; *kama* many species of beetles, which though focused on dung beetles, also covers beetles from several other families, and seems to be polytypic; while *fkeme* is a general term for the larger grasshoppers. Although inhabiting a rather arid, inhospitable terrain, the San hunter–gatherers of the Central Kalahari thus have a fairly detailed folk taxonomy of insects.

In his pioneering study of Tzeltal folk zoology Eugene Hunn (1977) recorded in detail their folk classification of insects, which in general outline is similar to that of the San hunter–gatherers, although the Tzeltal Maya have a very different mode of subsistence. It is of interest that although both the dragonflies (*Odonata*) and butterflies/moths (*Lepidoptera*) are composed of hundreds of species under several families, they are each categorized by the Tzeltal under a single taxon – *Tultus* and *Pehpen* respectively. The various species are then described by attributes relating to size and colour – 'small', 'large', 'red', 'streaked', 'black'. In contrast the grasshoppers (*Orthoptera*) have a fairly detailed classification, which Hunn suggests: 'may be explained in terms of the cultural significance of these insects,' many of which are considered edible or cause damage to crops (1977: 281–8). The folk generics of the Tzeltal seem roughly to correspond to biological families, only a few being identified at the species level, while the 'covert complexes' that Hunn delineates relate mainly to insect orders. Around 95 generics were recorded.

The Nuaulu, swidden cultivators of South Central Seram, have been extensively studied over many years by Roy Ellen (1978, 1993). From his analysis of their animal categories it would appear that, unlike many other communities, the Nuaulu have few clearly defined life-form categories, apart from *Peni* (loosely, large game), *Mnaha* (rats and mice), *Manue* (birds/bats) and *Ikae* (fish and marine animals). This means that intermediate or generic levels of classification are of primary importance, and that many of these 'basic categories' are polytypic, consisting of 2–17 terminal (specific) categories. Ellen recorded some 49 folk generics – the 'basic categories' – relating to insects that together comprised around 113 terminal taxa (Ellen 1993: 100–1). Thus the generic category *Kauke* (grasshoppers, crickets, mantids) embraces 14 terminal categories; while Rikune (bugs) covers around 9 terminal categories (mostly of the families *Coreidae* and *Pentatomidae*), with the cicadas (three generics) and such bugs as the common stainer (*Makarota pina*) and the cicadas (three generics) being considered distinctive. Taking into account these discriminations, the number of insect categories (generics) of the Nuaulu seems comparable to that of both the San and Tzeltal.

The ethnoentomology of the Navajo (Diné) of New Mexico has been described in great detail by Wyman and Bailey (1964), who noted that these people seem to be ideal subjects for anyone interested in folk classification, for they love to categorize and are ready and willing to argue about hair-splitting taxonomic distinctions. They also never fail to give a name to any specimen shown to them, even if it means inventing a new variety. The number of terminal taxa recorded by these ethnobiologists may therefore be somewhat misleading, and should be treated with some scepticism. Table 1.1 gives a summary of the Navajo classification of insects:

Although there are some Navajo generic terms that cover biological species from more than one insect order – the taxon *asa nayehe* 'pot carrier', for example, embraces both blister beetles (*Meloidae*) and robber flies (*Asilidae*) – it is evident that there is a fairly close correspondence between biological nomenclature and Navajo taxonomy (see my re-analysis of Navajo folk taxonomy and symbolism, Morris 1979). There is some disagreement among writers regarding the taxonomic status of insects among the Navajo; Perchonok and Werner (1969: 231) regard the insects as forming a distinct class *Ch'osh*, whereas Wyman and Bailey (1964) indicate that insects may fall under any of the more general categories, such as water, flying or moving animals. But the term *Cos* seems to cover small crawling insects or worms, and *wo* is a general term for ants, and such insects as sand crickets, cicadas, and bed bugs. Navajo names are descriptive on the whole, particularly in relation to terminal (specific) categories, but, unlike plants, insects are frequently named after their habits and behaviour, especially in relation to movement, which is a pervasive theme in their taxonomic ordering. Thus *na'azq'zi*, 'the stinger' refers to the mutillid wasp; *k'ini'si*, 'urine squirter,' to darkling beetles; and *ca'nilma'si*, 'dung roller,' to dung beetles; while *nahacagi*, 'that which hops here and there,' is focused specifically on the grasshoppers and locusts, but is also applied to leaf hoppers and some beetles. Navajo generic names refer essentially to insect orders and families, rather than to biological species and genera; thus the order *Hymenoptera*, of which 188 species were collected and examined, are categorized by the Navajo into essentially only seven generics – *de'acahi* (pinching ant), *na'ilc'ai* (listening ant), *loci* (red ant), *lazini* (black ant) – all forms of *wo* – *na'azqzi* (mutillid wasp), *cisna* (bee) and *ja'dneis'di* (leg dragger – wasp). Similarly, in a detailed re-analysis of the Navajo classification of the order *Coleoptera* (beetles) I noted that some 197 species of beetles belonging

Table 1.1 Navajo Classification of Insects

Order	Common Name	Species	Navajo Taxa	(Literally)	Number
Thysanura	Bristetails	4	Le'esoli	Soil blower	2
Odonata	Dragonflies	11	Tani'l'ai	Spread on water	9
Blattaria	Cockroaches	1	Celca	Rock beaver	
Orthoptera	Grasshopper cricket		Nahak'izi	Which move in crevices	9
			Nahacagi	It hops here and there	19
Isoptera	Termites	1	Ciny'ani	Wood-eater	
Hemiptera	Winged bugs	31	Wonescidi	(Cicada)	7
			Na'da bicos	Cornbug	
	Bugs	66	Yo deelci'hi	Red horned insect	
			Talka Dilyohi	Water surface runner	
Anoplura	Lice	1	Ya	Louse	
Neuroptera	Lacewings	19	Tani (l'ani Anlt'ani	Ripener	
Trichoptera	Caddis flies	1	Icai	Moth	
			C'i'I	Gnat	
Lepidoptera	Butterflies	92	Icai	Moth	32
	Moths		Ka'logi	Butterfly	12
Diptera	Flies	105	Ce'edqi	Fly	17
			C'i'I	Gnat	
			Dezi	Horse fly	6
Siphonaptera	Fleas	1	Le'cai biya	Dog's flea	
Coleoptera	Beetles	201	Yon'zi	Hard insect	
			K'ini'si	Urine squirter	21
			Je'iya'h	Ear traveller	4
			Nada bicos	Corn bug	
			Nlcago	Rain beetle	5
			Le'soli	Soil blower	
			Celca	Rock beaver	6
			Yo Bicos	Water bug	
Hymenoptera	Ants, wasps, bees	188	Cisn'a	Bee	10
			Wo'lazini	Black ant	14
			Woloci	Red ant	8
			Na'azqzi	Stinger	
			Ja'dneis'di	Leg dragger	4

to 24 biological families were categorized by the Navajo into only 23 folk generics. Although there was some overlap, essentially a clear correspondence between folk generics and biological families was evident (Morris 1979: 122–3). It is probable that the detailed classification of both beetles and bugs with regard to folk generics is related to their importance as agricultural pests. Equally noteworthy is the fact that the cicada (*wo 'nescidi*) is the only insect used as food by the Navajo – at least, this is what Wyman and Bailey report. They recorded 105 folk generics, of which 42 were differentiated into species (terminal categories), although many of the generics were not insects, but spiders, scorpions, millipedes, centipedes and earthworms. Their researches therefore seem to indicate around 64 generic names of insects, although some of the terminal taxa may have generic status, while others may be simply the idiosyncratic invention of individual Navajo informants.

Table 1.2 summarizes the distribution of the folk generics of the four societies according to insect orders.

Table 1.2 Number of Folk Generics per Insect Order

Order		San	Tzeltal	Nuaulu	Navajo
Odonata	Dragonflies	—	2	1	1
Blattodea	Cockroaches	3	2	1	—
Isoptera	Termites	7	—	1	1
Mantodera	Mantids	1	1	2	1
Phasmatodea	Stick insects	2	1	2	—
Dermaptera	Earwigs	—	1	1	—
Orthoptera	Grasshoppers	11	10	2	4
Phthiraptera	Lice	1	2	2	3
Hemiptera	Bugs	7	7	6	15
Neuroptera	Lacewings	1	1	—	1
Coleoptera	Beetles	26	16	12	23
Siphonaptera	Fleas	—	1	3	1
Diptera	Flies	8	8	5	4
Lepidoptera	Butterflies and moths, adult	1	2	1	3
	larvae	16	10	1	—
Hymenoptera	Wasps	7	10	3	2
	Bees	3	11	1	1
	Ants	10	10	5	4
Total		104	95	49	64

(*Source*: After Wyman and Bailey 1964; Hunn 1977: 254–308; Ellen 1993: 260–7; Nonaka 1996: 43–6.)

In a seminal paper relating modes of subsistence to folk-biological taxonomies, Cecil Brown (1985) suggested, and attempted to demonstrate, that significant differences exist between the ethnobiological classifications of hunter–gatherers and those of small-scale agriculturists. With regard to both botanical and zoological taxa, agricultural people generally have a much larger inventory of labelled biological generics than do hunter–gatherers, and tend to use binomial names much more commonly. Thus small-scale agriculturists have between 400 and 800 zoological generics, compared with 250–400 among hunter–gatherers. There are clearly problems regarding the lack of data comparability in such an analysis, as Brown acknowledged; but these findings are nonetheless suggestive, especially as I had earlier been struck by the relative lack of interest in folk classifications expressed by one hunter–gathering community, the Hill Pandaram, as compared with the peoples of Malawi (Morris 1976). Several factors are suggested by Brown to explain why subsistence agriculturists tend to have larger inventories of folk generics and more binomial categories – that agriculturists usually inhabit regions of the world that are biologically richer than those of hunter–gatherers, who have tended to be pushed into more marginal areas – like the Kalahari desert; that subsistence cultivation creates a local environment that tends to increase biological diversity; that, given problems of food shortages, subsistence cultivators will often utilize wild plant and animal resources more intensively than do hunter–gatherers; and finally, given that higher populations tend to increase health risks from infectious diseases, that subsistence cultivators are inclined to exploit more those organisms in the environment, especially plants, that have medicinal value (Brown 1985: 48–50). I have noted the fact that Evans-Pritchard (1937) mentions walking along a path for about two hundred yards and collecting about a hundred plants to treat diseases and lesions – more, it seems, than the entire !Kung and Hill Pandaram pharmacopoeia (Morris 1996: 24–5).

It is of interest, then, that there is little difference in the total number of insect generics of the Central Kalahari San, compared with those of the three agricultural communities described above.

Nyanja Classification of Insects

Folk classifications of animals in Malawi essentially refer, as in other societies, to two basic levels, that of life-form categories, and that of folk generics – which refer to natural kinds. Such natural kinds do not, of course, exist apart from a specific social situation and a local ecological context, as Ellen affirms (1993: 71). Whether or not a natural kind, as the basic form of a living being, can be equated with the biological concept of 'species' has long been debated, although evidence suggests, as noted above, that there is a close correspondence between folk generics and biological species (Dupré 1981; Posey 1983; Mayr 1988: 335–58; Ellen 1993: 67–71; Goodwin 1994: 163).

I have discussed in some detail elsewhere life-form categories relating to plants and animals among the Nyanja (*Chewa*) and related peoples of Malawi (Morris 1996: 33–6, 1998: 140–2). With regard to animals – which are to be distinguished from woody plants (*mitengo*), grass (*maudzu*), fungi (*bowa*) and ancestral spirits (*mizimu*) – there are essentially five main life-form categories. These are: *nyama* (a polysemic term meaning both meat and any form of edible quadruped), *nsomba* (fish and edible freshwater crustaceans), *mbalame* (birds), *njoka* (snakes and intestinal worms), and *chirombo* (useless and harmful organisms). The key life-form categories *nyama* and *chirombo* are prototypically functional categories, with respectively positive (meat) and negative (as harmful) connotations. Together they are used by Malawians quite flexibly, and, according to context, may have taxonomic relevance. Needless to say, in Nyanja (*Chewa*) thought, humans (*anthu*) form a separate and unique category.

Chirombo may refer to any hostile wild animal – and a kudu or bushbuck, which are typically *Nyama*, maybe referred to as *chirombo* if they invade gardens and damage cultivated crops. The leopard and hyena are archetypal *chirombo*. Essentially, however, *chirombo* means any useless or harmful living thing, and it includes most invertebrates. Like *nyama*, the term also has important ritual and symbolic connotations, being associated not only with wild animals of the bush, but also with malevolent spirits and with masked dancers (who impersonate the spirit of the dead in the form of wild animals) at certain ceremonials (Morris 2000: 143–50). *Chirombo*, however, is an important functional rather than a residual taxonomic category, and although it includes most invertebrates and such animals as lizards and frogs, it does not correspond to the category of 'creeping things' of the Authorized Version of Genesis, nor to Brown's (1979) conception of 'Wug' for small animals that are not incorporated into the categories of fish, bird or snake. The archetypal *chirombo*, as has just been noted, are large mammals, the lion, leopard and hyena, and the term can be extended to cover the crocodile (*ng'ona*) and monitor lizard (*ng'anzi*).

The smaller forms of animals that are considered useless or harmful are described as *kachirombo* (*ka*, diminutive; plural, *tizirombo*), and this term thus comes to cover a wide variety of small animals – insects, millipedes, centipedes, scorpions, spiders and crustaceans. Insects may thus be glossed as *kachirombo* – although edible insects like the cicada (*nyenje*), winged termite (*ngumbi*) and locust (*dzombe*), while important as relish, are not usually described as *nyama*, nor are they usually thought of as *chirombo* – but rather as *cholengwa basi*. They are simply 'created things,' or existents. Thus generic taxa of insects in Malawi may be thought of as essentially unaffiliated, to be described as *kachirombo* (*kalombo*) according to a specific context or set of circumstances. The term *chirombo* may also be used as a term of abuse, to describe a person considered useless or worthless. But *nyama* and *chirombo* (Yao, *chikoko*) seem to be concepts that resonate throughout much of eastern and southern Africa. The Rangi of Tanzania, for example, seem to have four major life-form categories relating to animals – *Ndee* (birds and bats), *Vanyama* (mammals, but exlcuding humans), *samaki* (fish) and *makoki* ('creeping things'). The anthropologist here suggested that the *makoki* life-form category includes snakes (*njoka*), lizards, snails, and slugs, as well as most arthropods, including insects (Kesby 1979: 42–4).

Given its rich biodiversity there are many, many thousands of insect species to be found in Malawi, and only a tiny fraction of these have salience for local people. Three factors seem to be important in giving one of these organisms its cultural salience – its perceptual salience, or relative size and visibility; its ecological salience in terms of its distribution and abundance; and its cultural significance, the role that the insect may play in folk tales, as a ritual symbol, or as food or medicine (Hunn 1999). It is, however, never simply a dichotomy as to whether insects have perceptual or intellectual salience 'simply because they are there' in the world (Brown 1995: 52) – many common and conspicuous insects in Malawi are not recognized by local people – or whether they have utilitarian or functional significance – for insects impinge on human life in diverse ways, causing bodily pain through their stings or blistering fluid, or may impair people's livelihoods – as agricultural or domestic pests or as vectors of disease.

As with the Tzeltal and Kayapo (Hunn 1977; Posey 1983), people of Malawi tend to express a 'covert' classification of insects, which suggests a broad correspondence between folk generics and the main orders of insects. We may therefore outline the main generic taxa of insects in Malawi with reference to the biological orders as follows.

Tombolombo   Order: Odonata   Dragonflies
This taxon covers all the many species of dragonflies and damsel flies, which belong to several different biological families. These include the following species:

Anax imperator
Ictinogomphus ferox
Rhyothemis semihyalina

Brachythemis leucosticta
Philonomon luminans
Palpopleura lucia
Elattoneura glauca

The robber fly *Alcimus rubiginosus* (order: *Diptera*) is also frequently described under this taxon, given its similar predatory habits – resting on a perch prior to swooping after its prey. The lacewing *Palpares cataractae* (order: *Neuroptera*) is also identified as *Tombolombo*. This taxon therefore covers insects from three different orders – though archetypally it refers to the larger dragonflies. People may distinguish various forms of dragonfly by reference to their colour, but these distinctions have little cultural significance. They are not utilized as food or as medicine.

Mphemvu   Order: *Blattodea*   *Cockroaches*
All the three common species of cockroach:

Periplaneta americana
Blatella germanica
Blatta orientalis

fall under this taxon, as well as many common woodland species such as *Euthyrrapha pacifica* and *Gyna* spp. Local people see the cockroach as quite distinct from both the grasshoppers and the mantids.

Chiswe is a generic term for all termites, local people distinguishing between essentially four specific kinds: the mainly subterranean termites *chiswe cha micholo* ('of the hole'), which have little or no mound; *nthusi*, the harvester termite; *chiswe chapachulu* (of the termite mound) which embraces the larger termites of the genus *Macrotermes* that build large conspicuous termite mounds; and *chiswe cha chikula* (of the mound that can be overturned), focused on the genus *Cubitermes*. The winged termites are distinguished: the *Macrotermes* sp. are *ngumbi/inswa*; the winged alates of *Odontotermes* sp. are *mbereswa*; and the winged termites of those species that are not considered edible are described as *gontham'kutu* ('deafen the ears'). It is said that eating these termites will make a person deaf. A distinction is also made within the mound termites (*Macrotermes*) between the alates (*ngumbi*) that fly in the afternoon (*chamadzulo*), and those that fly at night (*chausiku*, or *kauni*).

The taxon *kalanzi* covers the workers of all those termites – of several genera – that enter the house or settlement and cause damage to timber or crops. People also distinguish the soldier termites of *Macrotermes*: *agang'a* or *mgagadula*.

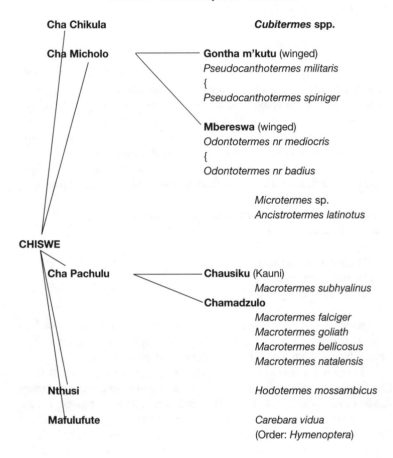

Chiswe   Order: *Isoptera*   Termites

Cha Chikula

Cha Micholo

Cubitermes spp.

Gontha m'kutu (winged)
Pseudocanthotermes militaris
{
Pseudocanthotermes spiniger

Mbereswa (winged)
Odontotermes nr mediocris
{
Odontotermes nr badius

Microtermes sp.
Ancistrotermes latinotus

CHISWE

Cha Pachulu

Chausiku (Kauni)
Macrotermes subhyalinus
Chamadzulo
Macrotermes falciger
Macrotermes goliath
Macrotermes bellicosus
Macrotermes natalensis

Nthusi

Hodotermes mossambicus

Mafulufute

Carebara vidua
(Order: *Hymenoptera*)

Importantly, the thief ant *Carebara vidua* (order: *Hymenoptera*) is considered as belonging to the taxon *chiswe*. This is understandable, as the worker ants are minute and reddish-yellow, and it lives as a parasite in termite nests.

Chiswambiya   Order: Mantodea   Mantids
All species of mantids are included under this taxon: those specifically identified and common are the following:

Polyspilota aeruginosa
Tenodera sp.

Pseudocreobota wahlbergi
Rhomboderella scututa
Popa spurca
Damuria thunbergi
Epitenodera capitata
Otomantia rendalli

The common name means to 'break pot' (*ku-swa*, to break, *mbiya*, water pot). *Chiswamphika* is a synonym (*mphika*, cooking pot). The mantis is shown much respect. If anyone touches or kills the mantis it is believed that he or she will, thereafter, be continually dropping or breaking pots. The alternative names *chilandamphuno* or *mdulamphuno* (to seize, or cut, the nose), refer to its habit of holding its front legs, which it uses to capture its prey – largely other insects high in a clasping position. The taxon *chiswambiya* also covers the stick insects (order: *Phasmatodea*).

Katambala   Order: Dermaptera   Earwigs
This taxon covers the earwigs, specifically the common earwig *Forficula senegalensis*.

Chitete Order: *Orthoptera* Grasshoppers and Crickets

Family: *Pamphagidae*

Tsokonombwe   *Losbosceliana brevicomis*
Lobosceliana loboscelis
Lobosceliana haploscelis

Wang'ono *Chrotogonus hemipterus*

Family: *Pyrgomorphidae*

M'Nunkhadala   *Zonocerus elegans*
Taphronata cincta
Dictyophorus griseus

CHITETE

Wankulu *Phymateus viridipes*

Family: *Tettigoniidae*

Bwanoni   *Homorocoryphus vicinus*
Tylopsis rubrescens
Pseudorhynchus pungens
Bvimbvi   *Enyaliopsis petersi*

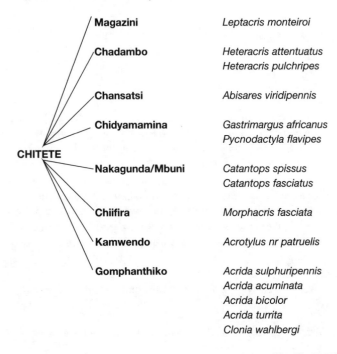

Magazini	*Leptacris monteiroi*
Chadambo	*Heteracris attentuatus* *Heteracris pulchripes*
Chansatsi	*Abisares viridipennis*
Chidyamamina	*Gastrimargus africanus* *Pycnodactyla flavipes*
Nakagunda/Mbuni	*Catantops spissus* *Catantops fasciatus*
Chiifira	*Morphacris fasciata*
Kamwendo	*Acrotylus nr patruelis*
Gomphanthiko	*Acrida sulphuripennis* *Acrida acuminata* *Acrida bicolor* *Acrida turrita* *Clonia wahlbergi*

CHITETE

(Family: *Tettigoniidae*)

Other species

Euproacris cylindicollis
Maura bolivari
Cardeniopsis pauperatus
Tmetonata abrupta
Microcentrum rhombifolium

Family: *Acrididae*

Dzombe/Chiwala

Acanthoxia gladiator
Afroxyrrhepes acuticerus
Afroxyrrhepes procera
Homoxyrrhepes punctipennis
Cyrtacanthacris tatarica
Cyrtacanthacris aeruginosa
Ornithacris magnifica
Ornithacris cyanea
Acanthacris ruficornis
Nomadacris septemfasciata

Family: *Tettigoniidae*

Cymatomera denticollis

Family: *Gryllidae*

Nkhululu — Brachytrypes membranaceus

Kalijosolo — Gryllus bimaculatus
Gryllus campestris

'CRICKET'

Family: *Gryllotalpidae*

Bololo — Gryllotalpa africanus

Family: *Stenopelmatidae*

Chiboli — Henicus sp.

Although the taxon *chitete* is often used as a generic or intermediate category to cover grasshoppers generally, essentially it refers to the smaller grasshoppers, especially those considered edible. The larger grasshoppers and locusts are described as *chiwala* (*ku-wala*, to shine, on account of their colourful hind wings) or *dzombe*. Many species belonging to the order that have salience have their own generics, while crickets tend not to be identified as *chitete*. The four species of crickets also have their own generic terms. Grasshoppers that are not considered edible, such as *chansatsi* (*Abisares viridipennis*) may also be described as *gontham'kutu* ('to deafen ears'). Given its carnivorous habits, *Clonia wahlbergi* is sometimes described as *fisi* ('witch').

Nsabwe   Order: Phthiraptera   Lice
This is the common human louse *Pediculus humanus.*

Order: Hemiptera   Bugs
The order *Hemiptera* (true bugs) consists of 12 folk generics, the majority of which have a functional status, either as edible insects (green shield bug and cicada) or as crop pests. Aphids that are a serious pest on plants, such as the cotton aphid (*Aphis gossyphi*) are described as 'plant lice' (*nsabwe za zomera*).

Family: *Pentatomidae*

Nkhunguni

Nezara robusta
Nezara viridula
Antestiopsis lineaticollis

Nsesenya

Sphaerocollis ocellatus

Family: *Coreidae*

Nandoli

Anoplocnemis curvipes
Anoplocnemis montandoni

Family: *Pyrrhocoridae*

Cham'matowo

Dysdercus intermedius
Dysdercus fasciatus
Dysdercus nigrofasciatus

Family: *Reduviidae*

'BUGS' —— Molosi

Platymeris

Family: *Belastomatidae*

Nyamalaza

Lethocerus niloticum

Family: *Nepidae*

Mwinimadzi

Laccotrephes ater

Family: *Cimicidae*

Nsikidzi

Cimex hemipterus

Family: *Cicadae*

Nyenje

Loba leopardina
Platypleura brevis
Platypleura polydorus

Family: *Jassidae*

Majasidi

Empoasca fascialis

Family: *Coccidae*

Kodikodi

Phenacoccus manihotus

Family: *Aphididae*

Nsabwe za Zomera

Aphis spp.

As with the bugs, there is no taxon that embraces all the beetles, although people recognize their similarities in that most are strong fliers and have hard sheathing on their forewings. The beetles comprise sixteen distinct generics, many of which are familiar to most Malawians, although only one beetle, the jewel beetle (*nkhumbutera*) is eaten. *Chikodzera* (Yao, *namtundira*) ('that which urinates') covers not only the ground beetle *Tefflus cypholoba*, but also the armoured ground cricket *Enyaliopsis petersi*, more commonly known as *bvimbvi*, which also exudes fluid that may blister the skin or irritate the eyes. Many of the generic terms express the ecology or habits of the beetles – *chitutamanyi*, 'to carry dung', the dung beetles; *nankafumbwe* 'that which eats into grain' – the maize weevils; *kafadala*, the snouted beetles that have a habit of feigning death (*ku-fa*, to die).

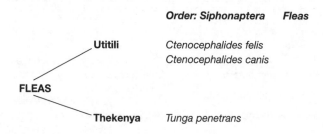

Order: Siphonaptera   Fleas

Utitili	*Ctenocephalides felis*
	Ctenocephalides canis
FLEAS	
Thekenya	*Tunga penetrans*

The fleas are covered by two generics. The status of the human flea (*Pulex irritans*) in Malawi is uncertain.

Order: Diptera   Flies

The taxon *Ntchenche*, which prototypically refers to the common house fly *Musca domestica*, is often used as a generic concept to cover flies more generally, especially those associated with human settlements. Only the lake fly *Chaobora edulis* is considered edible. Nine taxa of flies were recorded during my research.

Order: *Coleoptera* Beetles

	Family: *Carabidae*
Chikodzera	*Tefflus cypholoba*
	Tefflus carinatus
	Family: *Dytiscidae*
Chisambi sambi	*Cibister vulneratus*
	Family: *Dynastidae*
Chipembere	*Oryctes boas*
Matono	*Heteronychus licas*
Mbozi zoyera	(larvae)
	Family: *Scarabaeidae*
Chitutamanyi	*Garreta azeurus*
	Catharsius satyrus
	Anachalus procerus
	Heliocopris hamadryas
	Family: *Cetoniidae*
Nkangala	*Goliath albosignatus*

'BEETLES'

	Family: *Buprestidae*
Nkhumbutera	*Sternocera orissa*
	Psilotera amaurotica
	Family: *Elateroidea*
Chindenga	*Tetralopus terotundifrons*
	Family: *Lampyridae*
Chiphaniphani	*Luciola caffra*
	Family: *Tenebrionidae*
Kafadala	*Dichtha inflata*
	Family: *Curculionidae*
	Brachycerus nr labrusca
Nankafumbwe	**(several families)**
	Tribolium confusum
	Rhizopertha dominica
	Prostephanus truncatus
	Sitophilus zeamays
	Cycas puncticollis
Dzodzwe/Ligombera	**Family: *Meloidae***
	Mylabris dicincta
	Family: *Cerambycidae*
	Ceroplesis orientalis
Chipokodzi	*Monochamus leuconotus*
Mwase	*Mecosaspis plutina*
	Family: *Galerucidae*
Mkupe	*Ootheca mutabilis*
	Family: *Chrysomelidae*
	Prosimidia conifera
	Family: *Passalidae*
Nyangi	*Didymus sansibaricus*

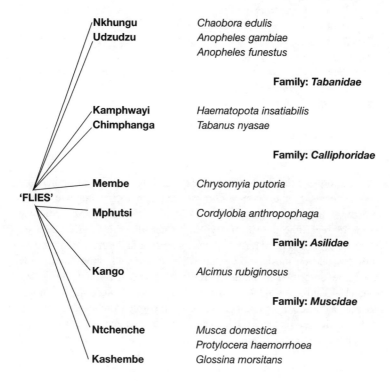

Family: *Culicidae*

Nkhungu — Chaobora edulis
Udzudzu — Anopheles gambiae / Anopheles funestus

Family: *Tabanidae*

Kamphwayi — Haematopota insatiabilis
Chimphanga — Tabanus nyasae

Family: *Calliphoridae*

Membe — Chrysomyia putoria

Mphutsi — Cordylobia anthropophaga

Family: *Asilidae*

Kango — Alcimus rubiginosus

Family: *Muscidae*

Ntchenche — Musca domestica / Protylocera haemorrhoea
Kashembe — Glossina morsitans

'FLIES'

Order: *Lepidoptera Butterflies and Moths*

Gulugufe is a general taxon that covers all adult forms of the order *Lepidoptera*. All butterflies and moths encountered during my research – and there are over 500 species of butterflies alone in Malawi – were denoted by this term, although moths may be described specifically as *chifukufuku*. At Kapalasa I recorded the following common species, which were all identified as *gulugufe*.

Bematistes aganice
Acraea eponina
Acraea encedon
Melanitis leda
Mycalesis ena
Neptis alta
Eurytela dryope
Hypolimnas misippus

Precis octava
Papilio ophidicephalus
Papilio nireus
Papilio dardanus
Eurema hecabe
Mylothis chloris
Hippotion celerio
Enmonodia capensis
Bunaea alcinoe
Erebus macrops
Anaphe panda

Unlike other cultures, Malawians express little interest in delineating specific forms of the taxon *Gulugufe*, although they recognize that it embraces many distinct morphotypes. But in contrast they have a complex taxonomy regarding the various types of caterpillars, many of which are eaten. *Mbozi* is a general term that covers larvae of all kinds, but is specifically focused on the larvae of butterflies, moths and some beetles. Fly larvae are described as *mphutsi*. I recorded and identified during my research 19 generics relating to the taxon *mbozi* (caterpillars). This is probably a conservative number, for I have records, from various sources, of about thirty edible caterpillars, each with its own generic name.

Although some of the generic terms listed above denote morphological attributes – *fiira* (red), *minga-minga* (with spines) – the majority express ecological relationships – *zamdothe* (of the soil), for 'cutworms'; *mtemankhuni* (to cut firewood) for the bagworm. Many of the generics refer to the tree on which the caterpillar generally feeds, for example *mabwabwa* – of the *Cussonia arborea* tree (*mbwabwa*). It is of interest that the majority of the generics refer to caterpillars that are either edible or infringe on human well-being in some way, with stinging hairs (*chiyabwe* – which covers caterpillars from several families with irritant hairs, from *yabwa*, 'to itch'), or are troublesome agricultural pests, either of maize or cotton. *Mbozi* is therefore a general taxonomic category, while the generics highlight only those species that have cultural salience for local people. Out of many hundreds of different caterpillars (*mbozi*) that they may encounter in their environment, specifically in the woodlands and cultivations, only a limited number of species are specifically recognized and named. Most caterpillars are disregarded as useless and not worth bothering about – *mbozi chabe* – 'only caterpillars'. As Silow writes regarding the Mbunda of Zambia: 'People are seldom or never acquainted with caterpillars that are not traditionally known and named. The fact that one larvae [sic] does not have any name is regarded as a proof that it is without interest for man' (1976: 202).

		Family: *Noctuidae*
	Mbozi ya Chifilika	*Helicoverpa armigera*
	Ntchembere Zandondo	*Spodoptera exempta*
	Mphalabungu	*Spodoptera* sp.
	Mbozi ya Minga-Minga	*Earias biplaga*
		Earias insulana
	Mbozi Yofiira	*Diparopsis castanea*
	Kapuchi	*Busseola fusca*
		Sesamia calamistis
		Chilo partellus
		(**Family:** *Pyralidae*)
	Mbozi zamdothe	*Euxoa segetis*
		Euxoa ypsilon
		Family: *Gelechiidae*
MBOZI	Mbozi ya Pinki	*Pectinophora gossypiella*
		Family: *Thaumetopoeidae*
	Ntchiu	*Anaphe panda*
		Family: *Psychidae*
	Ntemankhuni	*Eumetia cervina*
		Family: *Limacodidae*
	Chiyabwe	*Latoia vivida*
		Family: *Sphingidae*
	Chilumphabere	*Acherontia atropus*
	Nthowa	*Nephele comma*
		Family: *Saturniidae*
	Mabwabwa	*Bunaea alcinoe*
	Maphombo	*Nudaurelia wahlbergi*
	Chilungulungu	*Gonimbrasia zambesina*
		Gonimbrasia belina
		Gonimbrasia rectilineata
	Mapala	*Imbrasia ertli*
	Matondo	*Pseudobunaea pallens*
		Athletes gigas
		Athletes semialba
	Kawidzi	*Cirina forda*

He noted for example that the large and colourful caterpillar of the death's head hawk moth *Acherontia atropos* (family: *Sphingidae*) is not known or named by the Mbunda – though it is recognized and eaten elsewhere. But it is worth noting that Malawians who collect edible caterpillars have detailed empirical knowledge of the life-cycle, ecology and habits of the various caterpillars signified by specific generics.

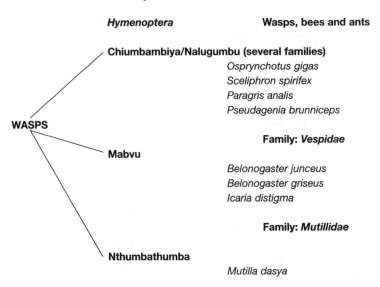

| | **Hymenoptera** | **Wasps, bees and ants** |

Chiumbambiya/Nalugumbu (several families)
Osprynchotus gigas
Sceliphron spirifex
Paragris analis
Pseudagenia brunniceps

WASPS

Family: *Vespidae*

Mabvu

Belonogaster junceus
Belonogaster griseus
Icaria distigma

Family: *Mutillidae*

Nthumbathumba

Mutilla dasya

Wasps are essentially classified under three taxa: those colourful species associated with, or parasitic on, the wasps that build mud nests in houses (*Chiumbambiya*, 'to make pot'); the social wasps, who can often inflict powerful stings (*Mabvu*); and the velvet ants, which can also inflict painful stings if the female is accidentally trodden upon. There are numerous species of wasp to be found in Malawi, belonging to several families, but only those that impinge on human life in some way seem to have cultural recognition.

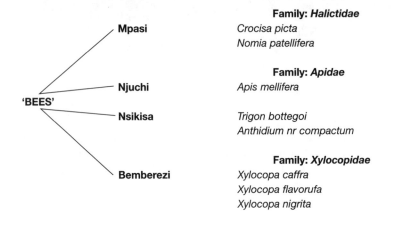

Family: *Halictidae*

Mpasi
Crocisa picta
Nomia patellifera

Family: *Apidae*

Njuchi
Apis mellifera

'BEES'

Nsikisa
Trigon bottegoi
Anthidium nr compactum

Family: *Xylocopidae*

Bemberezi
Xylocopa caffra
Xylocopa flavorufa
Xylocopa nigrita

Four taxa of bees are recognized and familiar to most Malawians, and three of these produce honey that is gathered eclectically and eaten. The carpenter bees (*bemberezi*) are well known, as they often make their nests in the beams or rafters of houses.

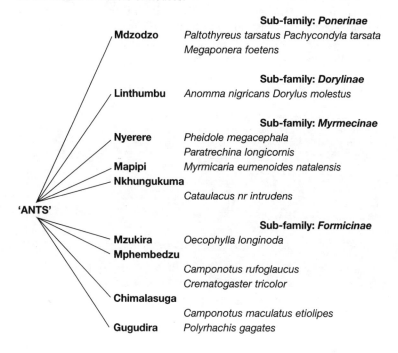

Sub-family: *Ponerinae*
Mdzodzo — *Paltothyreus tarsatus Pachycondyla tarsata Megaponera foetens*

Sub-family: *Dorylinae*
Linthumbu — *Anomma nigricans Dorylus molestus*

Sub-family: *Myrmecinae*
Nyerere — *Pheidole megacephala Paratrechina longicornis*
Mapipi — *Myrmicaria eumenoides natalensis*
Nkhungukuma — *Cataulacus nr intrudens*

'ANTS'

Sub-family: *Formicinae*
Mzukira — *Oecophylla longinoda*
Mphembedzu — *Camponotus rufoglaucus Crematogaster tricolor*
Chimalasuga — *Camponotus maculatus etiolipes*
Gugudira — *Polyrhachis gagates*

Ants are ubiquitous in Malawi, and nine generics are clearly recognized, although they are never eaten, and have few other uses. Thus Malawians are neither purely detached intellectuals, nor do they think entirely through the stomach, as Malinowski famously suggested: their relationship with the world is one of engagement, complex and multi-faceted – intellectual, aesthetic, ecological, sacramental and functional (Malinowski 1974: 44; Morris 1984; Berlin 1992: 285–8; Brown 1995).

A total of 103 insect generics have been recorded from Malawi, a figure comparable to that of both the San hunter–gatherers and the Tzeltal Maya. As with these other communities, the majority of taxa relate to four groups of organisms – grasshoppers and crickets (*Orthoptera*), beetles (*Coleoptera*), caterpillars of moths/butterflies (*Lepidoptera*) and wasps, bees and ants (*Hymenoptera*) – which for all three communities together constitute roughly 70 per cent of the total number of generics. The two other important groups are the termites (*Isoptera*), an important source of food, and bugs (*Hemiptera*), many of which are well-known agricultural pests. Also significant is the fact that some generics can be identified with biological orders (which may of course consist of numerous species), while other generics relate to genera and species, particularly if the insects have pragmatic significance. The contrast between the taxonomy of adult butterflies/moths and their larvae is significant in this respect.

Table 1.3 gives details of the main orders of insects, and the relationship of the generics to biological taxa.

Table 1.3 Relationships of Generics to Taxa in the Main Insect Orders

Primary Orders or 'Covert' Categories of Insects	Number of Folk Generics	Number of Biological Species Identified	Number of Edible Generics	Level of Identification		
				Order	Family	Species Genera
Odonata						
Dragonflies	1	9	–	1		
Blattodea						
Cockroaches	1	5	–	1		
Isoptera						
Termites	5	14	3		2	3
Mantodea						
Mantids	1	9	1	1		
Dermaptera						
Earwigs	1	1	–	1		
Orthoptera						
Grasshoppers	13	44	8		4	9
Crickets	4	5	4			4
Phthiraptera						
Lice	1	1	–	1		
Hemiptera						
Bugs	12	19	4		2	10
Coleoptera						
Beetles	16	28	1		6	10
Siphonaptera						
Fleas	2	3	–	2		2
Diptera						
Flies	9	11	1		1	8
Lepidoptera						
Butterflies/moths						
Adults	2	19	–			
Larvae	19	27	10			19
Hymenoptera						
Wasps	3	8	–		3	
Bees	4	8	3		4	
Ants		9	12	–		9
Total	**103**	**223**	**35**	**7**	**22**	**74**

Reflections on Folk Classifications

Living in a largely oral culture it has to be recognized that Malawians have no standardized terminology when it comes to insects, and the names given to insects vary widely. Not only are there ethnic and regional variations throughout the country – these are detailed in the appendix – but there are numerous cases of interchangeable synonyms, even with regard to a single individual. Thus both *mafulufute* and *nyamu* may be used to signify the thief ant *Carebara vidua*; either *pherupheru* or *gulugufe* may be employed to refer to adult butterflies and moths; *gonondo* and *kafadala* both signify snouted beetles. Moreover, there is often wide variation, both local and personal, in the pronunciation and structure of generic terms. The common cricket, for example, may be referred to as *chijosolo*, *kalijosolo*, *kajosolo* or *nakajosolo*. The taxon for the larger grasshoppers and locusts *dzombe* likewise has many synonyms; *nazombe*, *sombe*, *nyadzombe*, *khwiya*, as well as *chiwala*, which alludes to the brightly coloured hindwings. As ecological relationships are often emphasized, a specific association of an insect with a particular plant, such as the castor oil shrub *nsatsi* (*Ricinus communis*), will link together under the same term insects of diverse orders – in this instance the grasshopper *Abisares viridipennis* and the edible caterpillar *Nudaurelia wahlbergi*. The term itself may be variable – *masatsi*, *nakasatsi*, *kam'satsi*, *chansatsi*. Given the nature of Bantu languages, and the desire of many Malawians to be helpful and practical, local people will often coin their own names for insects. A small grasshopper with reddish wings will be described as *chafiira* (fiira, red), an insect that is common in low-lying marshy areas *chadambo* (of the '*dambo*'); a bug that emits an unpleasant smell, such as *Nezara spp. chinunkha* (*ku-nunkha*, to smell); the snouted beetle will be called *chifadira* – although most people use the generic *Kafadala* (*ku-fa*, to die). These may be valid names, but are highly idiosyncratic. Those I have listed in the previous section are the ones more widely recognized in the Shire Highlands, the outcome of discussions I have had in the field with numerous people. It is however common for people to use the singular term very rarely when discussing insects: thus Yao-speakers rarely use *lupeu* and/or *litendeu* for the cockroach and social wasp respectively, but always use *mbeu* and *matendeu*. Likewise Nyanja-speakers described the social wasps as *mabvu* and very rarely use the singular (*dabvu*, *babvu*). (In what follows, where the terms used for a species among Yao-specific speakers and speakers of Nyanja (chewa) differ, the former will sometimes be found differentiated by a bracketed upper-case letter Y following the name, and the latter by a bracketed upper-case letter C.)

In the classification of plants in Malawi, many intermediate, functional categories are recognized, relating to potency medicines, relish, latex or ecological niches or relations (Morris 1996: 40–5). But with insects few intermediate taxa seem to be evident, and the many generics are unaffiliated to any life-form category – apart from the general class of small useless organisms (*kachirombo*). Many of the generics, however, are widely used as general rubrics to cover several insects within a particular domain, or 'covert' class. Thus *chitete* is used as a general category to cover all grasshoppers of the three main families (*Pyrgomorphidae, Acridae* and *Tettigoniidae*), although I never heard the taxon used to describe the four species of crickets. Similarly, *ntchenche* covers many of the more conspicuous flies (of which there are several hundred species in Malawi, belonging to more than twenty different families); while *nyerere* is often utilized as a general category for ants. As with the classification of plants, certain species are seen as prototypes or exemplars of a particular generic. Thus the common *katydid* or cone grasshopper *Homorocoryphus vicinus* is widely known as *bwanoni* (syn. *noni*), and is familiar to all Malawians, as it is an important insect food, rich in proteins and fat. This is the true *bwanoni* (*weni-weni*, 'truly'), recognized by most Malawians by its pointed head and long slender antennae. But other similar grasshoppers may also be described as *Bwanoni*, such as *Tylopsis rubrescens* and *Pseudorhynchus pungens*, and less knowledgeable individuals may even describe *Acrida* spp. as *bwanoni* because of their similar size and appearance, even though they are quite distinctive, with characteristic short, blade-like antennae. The latter genus is more widely known as *chigomphanthiko* ('to peck at the porridge stick'). The importance and psychological reality of prototypes has been stressed in cognitive studies (D'Andrade 1995: 115–21), but they are also evident and salient in everyday folk classifications of insects. For insect generics tend to have a core reference – *njuchi* is the honey bee *Apis mellifera* – that is then extended to less familiar but similar species – such, in this instance, as the leaf-cutting bees (*Megachile* spp.).

Equally common is the use of the term *nzache* (neighbour, relative) to describe the relationship of an unknown insect to a more familiar generic. Thus the unusual, but rather uncommon, grasshopper *Cymatomera denticollis* may be described as *nzache wa bwanoni*. When classifying insects – and Malawians are usually ready and eager to name, describe and differentiate the various forms of insects – people tend to use the terms *gulu* and *mtundu*, which may roughly be translated as kind, sort, tribe or assembly. As with the Nuaulu, Malawians clearly seem to operate with a concept of 'natural kinds' (cf. Ellen 1993: 68), although this in no way precludes a fervent interest also in the insect's activities, habits, ecology, and relationships – particularly in regard to what they eat. As with the mammals, *amadya*, 'it eats' is commonly invoked when people describe insects. Equally importantly, when discussing insects people clearly recognize the existence of morphotypes within a generic, and often allude to the name that it is given in another region or language. Thus someone will describe the *tombolombo* (dragonfly) as a creature (*kachilombo*) that flies and lives near water, and is given the Lomwe name *mweteteri*. They will suggest that it often feeds on winged termites, capturing them on the wing, and drinks with its tail (dragonflies deposit their eggs in this manner), as well as noting that there are many different forms. In discussing such morphotypes they invariably refer to colour – *agrilini* (green), *amangamanga* (spotted), *ofiira* (red), or *akuda* (dark, black). But such distinctions have little real cultural significance.

As with plants, people's knowledge of insects, in regard to both nomenclature and usage, is extremely variable. Many Malawians living in urban areas have very little knowledge of insects, and some people found it incredible, or highly amusing, that I should even know the names of such insects as *mafulufute* or *chiswambiya*. To ascertain the extent of and variations in people's folk knowledge of insects I conducted interviews with fourteen people I knew well – indeed, some of them, such as Salimu Chinyangala and Helen Mgomo, I have known for over twenty years. I questioned them on 64 common insects that I had collected and preserved, belonging to the following groups:

	Number
Dragonflies	1
Cockroaches	1
Mantids	1
Grasshoppers and crickets	18
Lacewings	1
Bugs	7
Beetles	16
Flies	3
Butterflies and moths	2
Wasps/bees	7
Ants	7
TOTAL	64

The people were of varied background: four were women, two were local herbalists (*sing'anga*), the ages varied from 25 to 65 years, and although all were living in the southern region they came from diverse ethnic backgrounds – Nyanja/Chewa, Yao, Lomwe, Ngoni. They were all essentially subsistence cultivators, though some had supplementary occupations, and they all spoke little or no English. What I learned from these intensive interviews with selected friends was what I had intuitively understood from wider contexts and observations. The results may be briefly summarized as follows:

- There are many insects that are clearly recognized and named by everyone, and whose habits and ecology are well known. These include:

Periplaneta americana	Mphemvu
{	
Cockroach	
Philonomon luminans	Tombolombo
{	
Orange dragonfly	
Homorocoryphus vicinus	Bwanoni
{	
Common Katydid	
Losbosceliana Naploscelis	Tsokonombwe
{	
Toad grasshopper	
Enyaliopsis petersi	Bvimbvi
{	{
Armoured grasshopper	Namtundira
Zonocerus elegans	M'Nunkhadala
{	
Elegant grasshopper	
Brachytrypes membranaceus	Nkhululu
{	
Giant cricket	
Gastrimargus africanus	Chidyamamina
{	{
Yellow winged grasshopper	Gulumamina
Platypleura brevis	Nyenje
{	
Cicada	
Brachycerus nr Labrusca	Kafadala
{	{
Snouted beetle	Gonondo
Eumetia cervina	Ntemankhuni
{	{
Common bagworm	Lipepedwa

Xylocopa nigrita	Bemberezi
{	
Carpenter bee	
Carebara vidua	Mafulufute
{	
Thief ant	
Anomma nigricans	Linthumbu
{	
Red driver ant	

- There are also many insects that are clearly familiar to people, but for which the names that are given tend to be variable, as a result of either ethnic or regional variations or personal proclivities. Knowledge of the habits of these insects also tends to be variable – and sometimes quite limited. Examples are:
  - *Polyspilota aeruginosa*, the barred mantis, which has been described under several names – *chiswambiya, chikasachiwiga* (Y), *chiswamphika, chilandamkphuno, gogofuno, chiswambali*;
  - *Belonogaster junceus*, the social wasp, which was similarly described by several names – *mabvu, matendeu, mphang'ombe, mabvunkhomo*; and
  - *Mutilla dasya*, the mutillid wasp, variously described as *mwayi, chisulu* and *nthumbatumba*.
- It is also evident that many insects, although common and widespread and fairly conspicuous, are not recognized or named by Malawians – who generally know little or nothing about their ecology and habits. These include, in particular, many beetles. For example:

Goliathus albosignatus
{
Goliath beetle
Anomalus heraldicus
{
Grey beetle
Taurhina splendens
{
Flower beetle
Catemerus rugosus
{
Moss beetle
Lycus constrictus
{
Orange net-winged beetle

It is evident that cultural factors influence – but do not determine – our perceptions of insects: and that these arthropods are not named simply because they exist in the life-world.

- Finally there are many insects that are known and have a recognized name – and even usages – but that are unfamiliar to many people – either because of local distribution, or because they have little relevance to the people concerned. These include insects such as the blister beetle, *dzodzwe* (*Mylabris dicincta*), the giant water bug, *Lethocerus niloticus* – which is often aligned to the jewel beetle, *nkhumbutera*; the green long-horned grasshopper, *chigomphamthiko* (*Clonia wahlbergi*), and the ichneumon wasp, *namlondola* (*Osprynchotus gigas*). Most people I interviewed recognized and named around 75 per cent of the insects shown to them.

While there are gender variations in the ethnobotanical knowledge of plants and fungi, as I have shown elsewhere (Morris 1987b, 1996), there seems little difference between men and women in the recognition and knowledge of insects.

What is of interest, however, is that there appears to be little or no relationship between the folk classification of insects, and their edibility status, certainly not in terms of the concept of 'anomaly'. In spite of the criticisms I made long ago of the theory of classificatory 'anomalies', put forward by Leach (1964) and Douglas (1966), which postulated that those animals that are considered impure and inedible are those that transgress a 'symbolic order' or classificatory schema (Morris 1976, 1987a: 203–10), this theory is still bandied about as if it were a valid hypothesis (Douglas 1999; Bowie 2000: 50–2). But none of the insects considered by Malawians to be inedible and described as bad (*woipa*) are classificatory 'anomalies', at least not in terms of their folk classifications, although they may be seen as impairing people's social well-being. As with the Hebrew classification of 'unclean' birds – all of which are either scavengers or birds of prey, and were not anomalous according to their symbolic schema – most of the insects not eaten in Malawi are explicable in terms of material considerations. They are either predators, such as *chigomphamthiko* (*Clonia wahlbergi*) and the mantids (*Polyspilota aeruginosa*), which are not considered to have a good taste; or they are considered harmful and 'poisonous' (an English word commonly used by Malawians), such as *mtemankhuni* (*Eumetia cervina*), *bvimbvi* (*Enyaliopsis petersi*), *dzodzwe* (*Mylabris dicincta*) and *namtundira* (*Tefflus cypholoba*); or they are associated with faeces and human waste, such as *chidyamamina* (*Gastrimargus africanus*), *chitutamanyi* (*Garreta azeurus* and associates) and *mphemvu* (*Periplaneta americana*). Certain insects, if eaten, are said to cause deafness, and so are described as *gontham'kutu* ('deafen the ear'). As was noted earlier, these include some winged termites, as well as the crested grasshopper *chansatsi* (*Abisares viridipennis*). Cultural factors are clearly important in interpreting dietary rules; but social practices rarely if ever simply follow or replicate some cultural logic, or symbolic and classificatory schema (Holy 1986: 9; Morris 2000: 42–3).

The importance of the classifications, as Darrell Posey (1983) long ago suggested, is that they serve as a guide to culturally significant domains, and point to the crucial social and cultural practices of a community. The remainder of this study will be devoted to exploring the importance of insects in the social and cultural life of the matrilineal people of Malawi.

−2−

Insects as Food

Prologue

Throughout the world, and across the centuries, insects have formed an important part of the human diet. As Vincent Holt put it in his well-known little book *Why Not Eat Insects?*, which was aimed to counter the deep-rooted prejudices of Europeans towards insects: 'From almost every part of the inhabited globe instances and examples can be brought of the eating of insects, both in ancient and modern times' (1885: 32).

From the historical record it seems that humans, like their closest primate relatives, have been essentially eclectic omnivores, eating leafy matter, roots, fruits and nuts, and a variety of animals, including insects. With regard to the common primates of Southern Africa – the chacma baboon, the vervet monkey and the blue monkey – they are omnivorous, but feed primarily on fruit and leaves. The chacma baboons feed mostly on above-ground items, as the gathering of roots and bulbs can be time-consuming, and may, occasionally, collectively hunt small mammals – but the latter represent only about 1 per cent of their diet. Insects, however, are important, forming a more complete and concentrated form of protein than plant material, and wherever baboons have been feeding one usually finds almost every stone turned over as they hunt for insects and other arthropods. Vervet monkeys are also primarily vegetarians, but they too eat insects, grasshoppers and termites having been recognized from their stomach contents. The same is true of the blue (or samango) monkey, which, although essentially frugivorous, commonly eats insects, especially caterpillars (Skinner and Smithers 1990: 157–64). Studies elsewhere have confirmed that insects, of various species, form an important part of the diet of many primates, although monkeys may reject those insects with cryptic or warning coloration, such as the two species of *Nunkhadala* – *Zonocerus elegans* and *Phymateus viridipes*, which both exude a distasteful frothy liquid (Mackenzie 1930).

Although chacma baboons may prefer animal matter, including insects, to other kinds of food, it has been concluded that no larger primate could satisfy its energy requirements solely on an insect diet. But when readily available – and insects are often found in local abundance – then insects constitute an important source of energy and protein for primates. The consumption of insects, usually gathered singly, is an individual activity. Hamilton concludes that the overconsumption of meat and sugar by contemporary human populations may, in part, be based on the 'dietary predilections' of our primate ancestors (1987: 122–6).

It seems more than likely that the gathering of insects, particularly caterpillars, winged termites and grasshoppers, formed an important part of the diet of early human populations. General accounts of human evolution, however, though devoting much discussion to the respective roles of hunting, gathering and scavenging, have tended to ignore insects (cf. Diamond 1991; Foley 1987; Jones *et al.* 1992; Ingold 1994). Indeed, as Bodenheimer remarked in his pioneering study of 'Insects as Human Food' (1951), it is quite astonishing that the 'real and basic importance' of insects as food for early humans and contemporary human societies has largely been ignored by scholars (1951: 7). For the salience of insects, spiders and other invertebrates in the diets of many cultures throughout the world has frequently been overlooked, even though there are many scattered references to insect-eating in the early writings and accounts of travellers, naturalists and anthropologists. Many of these data were collated and presented by Bodenheimer in his classic study. Bodenheimer not only discussed the importance of edible insects in classical antiquity – focusing on the locust, cicada, and the larvae of the cossus beetle (*Cerambyx cerdo*) – but detailed the many hundreds of species used as food among the Australian Aborigines, as well as in Africa, Asia and the Americas. It has been estimated that the reported total amounts to around five hundred species in more than 260 genera and 70 families of insects. But this is a rather conservative estimate, for the actual number of insects eaten in the world is far greater, and probably runs into many thousands. And the volume of the insects eaten as a percentage of the total animal proteins that are consumed within a community is also much greater than might at first be realized (DeFoliart 1989: 22).

In recent decades, with the emergence of 'cultural entomology' as a sub-discipline, there has been a wealth of studies on the role that insects play in the diet of peoples throughout the world. Much of this research on insects as a food resource has been summarized in recent papers and in the journal *Food Insects Newsletter* (1988–) pioneered by Gene DeFoliart (DeFoliart 1989: 22–6; 1999: 23–40; Van Huis 1996: 6–8).

It is beyond the scope of the present study to review this extensive literature here, but it may be useful to discuss two relevant topics: the use of insects as food among hunter–gatherers (who tend to be ignored in recent surveys), and the Western aversion to insects, which is an undoubted factor in explaining why insects tend to be overlooked by anthropologists, and by food and agricultural scientists.

Jared Diamond tells us that the 'hunter–gatherer lifestyle is often characterized by anthropologists as "Nasty, brutish, and short"' (1991: 164). Actually, it was the philosopher Thomas Hobbes who said this, and anthropologists have, over many decades, devoted themselves to repudiating the Hobbesian portrait of humans as unitary, isolated, competitive and egocentric individuals (Howell and Willis 1989). But in comparing hunter–gatherers with farming communities Diamond suggests that hunter–gatherers are: 'healthy, suffer from little disease, enjoy a very diverse diet, and do not experience the periodic famines that befall farmers'. He emphasizes that early hunter–gatherers enjoyed a varied diet, with adequate amounts of protein, vitamins and minerals, and indeed describes agriculture as bad for the health (1991: 167–9). Yet although critiquing the mystique of 'man the hunter' in the 'rise' of the 'third' chimpanzee (humans), Diamond makes no mention at all of insects. Surprisingly, this is also partly true of Richard Lee's excellent socio-economic study of the !Kung San, for Lee suggests that 'Insects do not play an important role in the diet' of these foragers, even though 70 species of insects were known to the San. He notes the importance of wild honey, a species of antlion, three click beetles and six caterpillars – yet these seem to be considered infrequent 'delicacies' rather than as part of the staple diet (R. B. Lee 1979: 101). Lee also notes the crucial role that beetles play in the production of arrow poison for hunting – the larvae of three species of beetles of the family *Chrysomelidae* being involved (*Polyclada flexuosa* and *Diamphidia* spp.), together with their parasites, the larvae of *Lebistina* spp. (family *Carabidae*) (1979: 102; cf. Marshall 1976: 147–8; Skaife 1979: 130–1; Nonaka 1996: 36–7).

Other studies of Kalahari hunter–gatherers seem to confirm Lee's observations that, although insects are important in their diet as delicacies and though they are highly esteemed, they do not form a substantial part of their diet. In his study of the G/wi of the central Kalahari Silberbauer noted that they robbed bees' nests for honey only infrequently, and that the insects consumed were mainly winged termites and caterpillars – both occurring sporadically and highly localized (1981: 216–17).

In his important paper on the ethnoentomology of the Central Kalahari San Kenichi Nonaka (1996) suggested that earlier studies of the San tended to be rather biased, in that insects were thought to be useless or marginal to San subsistence. But he too seems to confirm the earlier portraits of Lee and Silberbauer, suggesting that the limited contribution of insects to the diet as a resource is due to the purely seasonal concentrations of the insects (collected mainly during the rains), their year-to-year fluctuations, and the fact that they have a low cost–benefit ratio, i.e. that they supply only a low caloric intake in relation to the energy expended in collecting them (1996: 40). Yet he notes eighteen kinds of insects, and three kinds of honey as being utilized as food by the San – focusing particularly on harvester termites (*Hodotermes mossambicus*), grasshoppers (*Cyrtacanthacris tatarica*), edible catterpillars, ants (*Camponotus* spp.) and the jewel beetle (*Sternocera orissa*), as well as wild honey.

Among the Mbuti of the Ituri forest in the Congo, Colin Turnbull records a similar situation. Although honey-collecting is of vital importance, both symbolically and structurally, as well as from the nutritional point of view, the gathering of insects for food seems to be rather sporadic, and insects are mainly considered as 'delicacies'. Only termites and certain ant species are mentioned by Turnbull, and their gathering is equally practised by men and women (1965: 166). This dearth of information on edible insects may not reflect the true situation, for evidence suggests that the hunter–gatherer people of the Congo forests also collect many species of caterpillar, the larvae of palm weevils (*Rhynchophorus phoenicis*) and longicorn beetles (Family: *Cerambycidae*), as well as termites (Bodenheimer 1951: 195–8, Bahuchet 1999: 91). Indeed Mitsuo Ichikawa (1987) noted that the important insect food species among the Mbuti included the larvae of beetles, termites, edible caterpillars and honey from sixteen species of bees. But again the insects seemed to be only a small part of their intake of animal food – which focused especially around the hunting of the duiker.

Among the Australian Aborigines ethnographic studies indicate that insects formed an important part of their diet. Besides the importance of honey-gathering – from several species of bees – they focused around the following insect species: honeypot ants (*Melophorus* spp.), the well-known witchetty grubs (the larvae of the wood moth *Xyleutes leucomochla,* family: *Cossidae*), grubs of longicorn beetles (*Cerambycidae*), *bugong* moths (*Agrotis infusa*), the sugary secretions (manna) of scale insects (*Psyllidae*) that were found on eucalyptus trees, and certain cicadas (Bodenheimer 1951: 70–134; Cherry 1993a). Many of these insects had totemic associations and were gathered by the women, who engaged in more specialized foraging than the men. What is of interest compared with the African context – both among foragers and subsistence cultivators – is that termites and leaf-eating caterpillars were only rarely collected by the Australian Aborigines (Bodenheimer 1951: 13). Neither is mentioned in a recent text (Menzel and D'Alvisio 1998: 18–29).

One can but conclude that, although insects are important as a food resource among hunter–gatherers, it is among subsistence agriculturists that the collection of relish sources – whether mice, fungi or insects – reaches its most complex elaboration – although one cannot fail to acknowledge the intense passion that most hunter–gatherers have for honey.

The main purpose of Vincent Holt's classic text *Why Not Eat Insects* (1885) was to counter Western prejudices against the eating of insects. He emphasized that insects are eaten throughout the world and quotes from Leviticus a text that suggests 'these ye may eat' of the locust, the cricket and the grasshopper, and their kind (11: 22). He continually points out that most of the insects that are considered edible are 'vegetable feeders, clean, palatable, wholesome and decidedly more particular in their feeding than ourselves' (Preface). Why eat scavengers such as the lobster and pig, he asks, and neglect those 'wholesome foods', the insects. The general abhorrence of insects, Holt suggests, is a 'foolish prejudice', and of comparatively recent origin. John the Baptist lived in the desert exclusively upon locusts and wild honey (Matthew 3: 4). Aristotle records how much the Greeks enjoyed the cicada, while both Herodotus and Pliny the Elder describe such delicacies as the locust and the larvae of the longicorn beetle (Cossus – probably *Cerambyx cerdo*). He notes that in the past insects were often utilized by Europeans as medicine. Holt thus concludes by stressing the need to overcome our prejudices and to encourage people – particularly the working classes – to eat insects, especially those that damage crops: 'Thus you would not only save all the produce of the little garden, but also pleasantly vary your monotonous meal with wholesome and savoury dishes' (1885: 93). The text, of course, is now somewhat dated, and rather patronizing towards the 'labouring classes'; but Holt makes an important plea for us to overcome our negative prejudices towards insects. Interestingly, the book has recently been re-issued by the British Museum (Natural History).

In a similar fashion Bodenheimer argues that the aversion to insect food that is so conspicuous in Western civilization is based on 'custom and prejudice', for there is no evidence at all that humans have an instinctive dislike of insects as food. On the contrary, throughout human history insects of many kinds have been eaten by human communities, not simply as a 'famine' food but as an intrinsic part of their diet. His book documents insect consumption throughout the world, over many centuries, and in varied social contexts. He emphasizes too the nutritional value of insects, which are among the 'richest' of foods, high in calories, protein, fat and minerals (Bodenheimer 1951: 7–37).

Bodenheimer also indicates that the aversion against the eating of insects among Europeans is of comparatively recent origin. He documents the history of entomophagy from classical antiquity, noting that early scholars such as Aristotle and the elder Pliny detailed the importance of insects as food and expressed favourable attitudes towards them. Enlightenment scholars too – Réaumur, Kant, Cuvier, Linnaeus – wrote of the importance of insects as food, especially edible locusts and the larvae of the palm weevil (*Rhynchophopus palmarum*). That 'inimitable observer' of insect life (as Darwin called him) Jean-Henri Fabre also tried to counter the widespread bias against insects. He experimented with locusts, frying them in butter and salt, as the Arabs prescribed. All his family were induced to partake of this 'queer dish'. Fabre concluded that it was 'far superior' to the cicada extolled by Aristotle (1917: 245–8).

But besides Fabre other entomologists have expressed an interest in insects as food, and have tested the edibility of certain insect species – cicadas, locusts, white grubs – and attempted to counter the Western bias against insects. Bodenheimer outlines the work of such scholars as C. V. Riley (1876), L. O. Howard (1915) and J. Bequaert (1921) (1951: 57–63; cf. DeFoliart 1999: 40–2). Over half a century ago Bodenheimer thus concluded that perhaps in due time Europeans may overcome our 'repugnance at eating insects and accept them as part of our diet' (1951: 146).

It is possible that this aversion to insects is related to what Norbert Elias described as the 'civilizing process'. For, in his history of European manners, though not specifically mentioning insects, Elias described a process, stemming from the aristocratic court, whereby the standards of 'good behaviour' implied the growing social control of bodily functions and instinctual life (Elias 1994: 68–105). Touching anything greasy with the fingers was therefore held to be 'impolite', and eating in a particular way with a knife and fork was seen as good 'etiquette' and extolled. Insects would thus come to be associated with 'uncivilized' behaviour, and the eating of insects to be deemed 'primitive'. As Vane-Wright writes: 'the very fact that eating insects belongs to the hunter–gatherer stage of human evolution may be a major factor in their rejection by western people: we may unconsciously reject entomphagy as primitive' (1991: 2).

But the eating of insects is not particularly confined to hunter–gatherers; it reaches its most unique elaboration in more complex societies, particularly those of sub-Saharan Africa and Asia. For example, 80 species of insects have been reported as food from Thailand, and the trade in grasshoppers averages about $6 million per year (DeFoliart 1999: 32–3). The interesting question, however, is why insects have not been domesticated as food, given that they are so important as food throughout Africa, Asia and South America. Bees have been domesticated for their honey, and silk moths for the silk produced by their larvae, but no insects have been cultivated in a systematic way as a food resource.

DeFoliart has suggested that insects may not have been competitive as food items because 'the agriculture that initially spread to Europe originated mainly in the Fertile Crescent of the Middle East'. It was here that sheep, goats and cattle were first domesticated, and such basic crops as wheat, barley and various legumes first originated. But compared with Africa and Asia, in the Middle Eastern economy insects were of minor importance. Only the locust, grasshoppers, crickets and the 'manna' of the Bible (Exodus 16: 13–35) – the white excretion of a scale insect on the tamarisk tree (Bodenheimer 1951: 217–23) – were there utilized as food. Thus, no insects were ever domesticated specifically as food (DeFoliart 1999: 43).

In recent decades there has been a resurgence of interest in edible insects throughout the world. This has to some degree been a response to the adverse effects of global capitalism, which has resulted in a reduction of biodiversity, the dominance, through multinational corporations like McDonalds, of Western cuisine, and the deterioration of living standards for subsistence farmers and rural people throughout the world. Structural adjustment programmes, pushed through by capitalist agencies like the World Bank and the IMF have had a devastating effect on rural people in the 'Third World', leading to what is euphemistically called 'food insecurity' – the fact that around 20 per cent of the world's population are chronically undernourished or starving. In these circumstances the Western bias against the eating of insects, and the dominance of Western consumption patterns generally, only aggravates what is already a very serious problem. Many scholars have thus envisaged the need to enhance the nutritional contribution of edible insects to the rural diet by whatever means possible. This may entail: countering the Western bias against insects as food, and emphasizing the crucial role that insects play in the provision of calories and protein for many rural people; establishing wider communication and awareness among scientists and development personnel regarding the human use of insects as food – as well as in providing animal feed; and the development of the controlled mass production of and trade in indigenous insects as food resources (DeFoliart 1989: 30–3, 1999: 44–5; Illgner and Nell 2000: 337–8).

Edible Insects of Malawi

Writing half a century ago, Bodenheimer remarked that: 'Africa is perhaps today the continent where insects still play the most important role in the native diet' (1951: 22).

This is certainly true of Malawi, and, long before the emergence of cultural entomology, the pioneer ethnobiologist Jessie Williamson was writing graphically of the edible insects that were recorded during the Nyasaland Survey 1938–1940 (Williamson 1941, 1992). Williamson was quite a remarkable woman. Dr William Berry, who was a member of the survey team, described her as a 'small, slight, dark haired, very sunburnt woman in her early thirties' who was known as Jabe, and he writes warmly of her enthusiasm, energy, modesty, and compassion for local women (W. T. C. Berry 1984: 43). To local women however, Williamson was known as *Mwadyachiani* – 'What do you eat?' – for this was the question she invariably asked when in the villages conducting her food survey. Williamson recorded more than twenty species of insects commonly eaten as food in the Dowa and Nkhotakota districts, and offered notes on their methods of cooking, palatability and nutritional value. Such data were later incorporated into the various editions of the *Malawi Cookbook*, which always included a section on the common insects eaten – the 'traditional delicacies'. About a dozen species were described and illustrated, and notes were given on cooking procedures. What these books particularly emphasized was that insects had long been recognized as a valuable source of food in Malawi, and were a very good and cheap source of protein (Shaxson, Dixon and Walker 1974: 21–3; CCAM 1992: 139–43). It is surprising, then, that Chimwaza's thesis on food and nutrition in Malawi (1982) has scant discussion of insects, and makes no mention at all of Jessie Williamson's pioneering studies.

Leaving aside the importance of honey, edible insects in sub-Saharan Africa focus essentially around five orders or groups of insects – termites, grasshoppers/locusts/crickets, bugs, beetles and caterpillars. The total number of edible insects in Africa probably amounts to several hundred species – or even more; but the common species recorded in the literature number 113. These belong to the following families:

Isoptera	Termites	7
Orthoptera	Locusts, grasshoppers, crickets	27
Hemiptera	Bugs	11
Coleoptera	Beetles	9
Diptera	Lakefly	1
Lepidoptera	Edible caterpillars	54
Hymenoptera	Ants/bees	4
Total		113

(After Bodenheimer 1951: 137–98; Van Huis 1996: 7; Illgner and Nel 2000: 341–5.)

There have been many detailed studies of edible insects in sub-Saharan Africa, and all such studies indicate that the consumption of insects is widespread throughout the continent. In any particular locality between 35 and 70 species of insects may be commonly eaten, and edible caterpillars and winged termites seem to be the usual favourites. The number of edible insect species recorded for different countries is as follows:

	Species	Families
Congo	65	22
Zambia	60	15
South Africa	35	16
Zimbabwe	40	14

(DeFoliart 1999: 23–31)

Such insects are not simply famine foods, nor infrequent 'delicacies' (as they seem to be among many hunter–gatherers), but are an intrinsic part of the diet. In the Congo, Gome, Hault and Cullin (1961) estimated that insects furnished 10 per cent of the animal proteins produced annually, compared with 30 per cent for game animals, 10 per cent for domestic livestock, 48 per cent for fishing, and 2 per cent for poultry. In some districts insects furnished around 37 per cent of the animal proteins consumed. In many parts of Africa termites and edible caterpillars are preferred as relish to meat and chicken. What is equally important is that termites and caterpillars are collected during the early part of the rainy season – which is typically the 'hunger' season for many African people. As insects are high in energy value, protein and many vitamins and minerals, they are a crucial food source. During the season, and if in abundant supply, insects are widely marketed in urban areas – caterpillars and termites especially, which often attain a higher market price than imported meat (Quin 1959; Nkouka 1987; Holden 1991; DeFoliart 1999: 23–31).

We may discuss the edible insects of Malawi under broad headings, which roughly correspond to categories recognized by local people.

Termites (Isoptera)

The winged termite is the relish *par excellence* in Malawi, and, it appears, throughout sub-Saharan Africa. As a food source it is greatly esteemed, and most people – but not all – consider it superior as a relish to chicken or meat. Bodenheimer long ago described termites as an 'African manna', and described the collection of winged termites among peoples throughout Africa, together with their cooking procedures and nutritional value.

His general conclusion was that although termites are highly favoured as a delicacy everywhere, they also, especially during the early part of the rainy season, form a crucial part, as relish, of people's regular diet. Normally people eat the winged reproductives, but also, on occasions, the soldier termites and queens. Among the important species he mentions are: *Acanthotermes spiniger, Macrotermes goliath, Odontotermes* sp. and *Bellicositermes* sp. (Bodenheimer 1951: 144–60). Recent studies have confirmed the crucial role that termites play in the diet of African people, particularly those associated with the genus *Macrotermes* (McGregor 1995; DeFoliart 1999: 30).

Although there are probably around a hundred species of termites in Malawi, the edible species of termites focus around the family *Termitidae*, and I found little evidence of local people eating the small mound termites *chiswe cha chikula* (*Cubitermes* spp.) or the harvester termites *nthusi* (*Hodotermes mossambicus*), although both these species are common throughout Malawi, at least in suitable localities. The generic term for termites is *chiswe*, and Malawians make a general distinction between those termites associated with termite mounds (*chulu*) (*Macrotermes* spp.*)* and the smaller termites, which often do not construct conspicuous mounds (*Odontermes* spp.*, Microtermes* spp.*, Pseudocanthotermes* spp.). The latter, generally described as Chiswe Cha Micholo (termite of the hole) are not a favoured food, although the alates of the larger species *mbereswa* (*Odontotermes* spp.) are often collected by young children, and eaten raw. They gather them up as they emerge from the holes on their nuptial flight – often in their thousands. They normally take to the wing around midday during the rains.

Termites of the genus *Macrotermes* are common throughout Malawi, and are especially characteristic of *Brachystegia* woodland, although also common along the Lakeshore and in the Lower Shire Valley. Several species have been recorded, including *Macrotermes goliath, Macrotermes bellicosus* and *Macrotermes natalensis*. Some of the mounds are enormous: those of *M. bellicosus* are perpendicular, and reach the height of a mango tree, some 4–5 metres, while those of *Macrotermes falciger* may be 20 metres in diameter, and form forested islands in cultivated land. This latter species was common in the Namadzi area, and is the termite with which I am most familiar.

My first encounter with termites, and one of the most memorable experiences of my life, happened on a December evening at Zoa in 1958. I was reading a book one evening when I suddenly became aware of a great commotion taking place on the verandah (*khonde*) of the house. I went outside and confronted an amazing sight. The whole verandah was filled with thousands of winged termites, which had evidently been attracted by the light, some flying around, some crawling on the ground, and amongst them was the watchman Justin of Khuguwe village, frantically trying to collect them – with the aid of a bucket and a hessian bag. This is one method of collecting the winged termites, collectively known as *inswa* (C) or *ngumbi* (Y). Local people speak of two kinds of *ngumbi* (the winged *Macrotermes* spp.): *ngumbi chausiku* (termites of the night) or *kauni* (*Macrotermes subhyalinus*), and the *ngumbi chamasana* (of midday), although the nuptial flight of *Macrotermes falciger* tends to be in the late afternoon, around 5 p.m.

To capture the night form kauni men collect several bundles of dry thatching grass, *kamphi* (*Hyparrhenia filipendula*) and make them into a bundle (*chisakata*). They also dig a hole at the base of the termite mound, where they suspect nuptial activity is taking place. Around midnight when the winged forms (*ngumbi*) begin to emerge collectively the men light the grass bundles to form a torch, and this is held over the pit. The winged termites are attracted to the light, and falling to the ground as they seek to mate, they are swept (*-sesa*) by both men and women (and helping young children) into the pit. They are then collected and taken away in a bucket or bag.

To collect the termites of the day (*ngumbi chamasana*), which are described as much larger and darker (*-kuda*) than those of the night – which are reddish-brown (*-fiira*) – is a much more complicated affair. An active termite mound is sought, and when one is discovered in the wood-land (*thengo*) any person has a right to claim it as his or her own and may mark it with a stick or stone. But not until he or she has built a bamboo frame (*litala*) over it does he or she have exclusive rights to the termites – although such rights are only usufruct for that season, and cease if the *litala* is not maintained (Rangeley 1948). Individuals, usually men but sometimes young women, often have long-term rights over particular termite mounds, negotiated through the village headman or estate owners. The alates of *Macrotermes sp.* begin emerging from December onwards, and are evident throughout the rains. Once a potential mound has been identified, with nuptial activity suspected, the vegetation is cleared from one side of the mound and it is scraped level (*kupalapala*) with a hoe to form a broad smooth pathway (*kanjira*), down which the emerging termites will fall. At the lower end of the 'scrape' a pit is dug, and in it is placed a tin or bucket – in the past it was an earthenware pot (*monjo*). Over the site is then placed a framework of branches or split bamboo (*litala*), and around its base aromatic grass (*mpobvu*) and asparagus stems *tsitsilamanda* – 'root of the graveyard' (*Asparagus africanus*) – are placed. Such medicine is said to induce the winged termites to emerge. After water has been sprinkled on the mound the top of the framework is completely covered with either more grass or leaves. Other people are said to use *chamba* (*Cannabis sativa*), another aromatic herb, as medicine. The smoke of the herb is gently blown (*-fukiza*) into the galleries (*mcholo*) of the termite mound. The medicines are said to have a good smell that encourages the alates to emerge. Water may or may not be placed in the tin or pot.

With the emergence of the winged termites late in the afternoon, great excitement may be generated, and several family members may gather to help in the collection of the termites. Much effort has to be expended in closing down all the other openings on the termite mound from which the alates may be emerging – and there may be many – so as to ensure that the alates only emerge from the holes beneath the *litala* framework. When they do emerge, the winged termites arise in their thousands, and the soldier termites (*mgagadula*) come to the surface to offer protection, along with many workers. Almost every creature in Africa enjoys eating termites – at least those who are not herbivores, especially humans – and those termites that manage to escape beyond the *litala* and fly into the air are eagerly pounced upon by scores of birds that surround the termite mound during collecting activities. As the winged termites emerge – a process described graphically as 'papapa' – birds gather them up. Among those species recorded by John Wilson as feeding on emerging termites in Zomba township were the following: pygmy kingfisher, white-eared barbet, lesser honey-guide, black-eyed bulbul, Heuglin's robin, collared sunbird, olive sunbird, spectacled weaver and yellow-eyed canary. Around forty species of birds were recorded. Those termites that fall to the ground, shedding their wings in the process, are immediately seized upon by other invertebrates, including a parasitic fly.

As termites emerge in their thousands, the tin or pot may quickly be filled, and so the insects have to be continually scooped out and placed in a bag – usually, these days, an old fertilizer bag (*thumba*). Although termite collectors may cover their hands with bits of plastic, this may be a very painful exercise, as soldier termites bury their mandibles into the skin, and can draw blood. Collecting termites is thus a rather exciting and hectic activity, particularly as termite mounds are rich in clay, and so, if it is raining, one slips and slides all over the place. It is important to note, however, that in any particular locality, many termite mounds appear to be dormant, and contain no insects. In a transect of 900 metres on Kapalasa farm ten termite mounds were recorded, each some 20 metres in diameter and covered with trees or bamboo; yet only two of these termite mounds produced nuptial flights, and thus the collection of winged termites, during the year I was there.

Figure 1 Peter Mofor, drying termites, Kapalasa, December 2000.

After collection the termites are boiled in a pot of water, the women stir-ring (*-phatikiza*) the termites continually with a porridge stick (*mthiko*), and removing by hand any leaves or debris. The next morning the termites are put in the sun to dry (*-yanika*), usually being spread over a rocky outcrop (Figure 1). When they are dried, the women winnow (*-peta*) the termites to remove the wings and any further debris. The termites are then in a suitable condition for cooking, or storing for future use, or, if there is a surplus, selling in the local market. The termites – the gathering may include many soldiers amongst the winged alates – are cooked in the same manner as grasshoppers and crickets: heated in a pan over the fire with a little water and salt, the salt dissolving in the water (*-sungunuka*) and penetrating the body of the insect. As the winged termites contain a lot of fat or oil (*mafuta*), which is why they are so esteemed, no cooking oil is usually used in their preparation. The termites are usually eaten as a side dish or relish (*ndiwo*) with maize porridge. This method of capturing and cooking winged termites has a long history, and was noted by earlier scholars (Johnston 1897: 371; Williamson 1992: 271).

During the dry season, if relish is particularly short, women and young children will collect soldier termites. A piece of dry grass or straw is lowered into openings in the termite hill, and quickly extracted when the soldier termite seizes the grass stem in its powerful mandibles. They may be eaten raw, or cooked later. These termites are rich in protein (cf. Ellert 1984: 114).

Termites are eaten throughout Malawi, and when I travelled by motor-cycle from Nsanje to Chitimba in February 2001 I noticed termite traps (*litala*) on almost every stretch of the road, and termites were being sold on the roadside by young men and women – holding baskets or buckets of termites aloft. Termites were also to be found in the local markets. At that time the termites were selling at 5 or 10 mk per small plate. One of my close friends who made a speciality of collecting termites suggested to me that during the season he obtained around 1,400 mk from selling termites locally – which was a useful income when the wage for a watch-man or agricultural labourer was only 1,000 mk (£10) per month. Williamson estimated that during the rains men usually consumed around 30–60 gms of termites per day (30–40 termites), with women and chil-dren eating lesser amounts (Berry and Petty 1992: 107).

The nutritional value of termites has long been affirmed. A hundred grams of fried termites have a value of 561 calories, which makes them one of the richest of foods, and contain some 40 per cent fat and 36 per cent protein, as well as being rich in such minerals as phosphates and potash. The high fat content of *kauni* (*Macrotermes subhyalinus*) was reflected in their high energy value, 613 kcal/100 gm; they also have 38 per cent protein, and contain such minerals as phosphorus, magnesium and iron. Thus, besides being a well-liked delicacy and relish, termites have a very high nutritional value (Bodenheimer 1951; 29–30; DeFoliart 1975; 161–2, 1989: 26; Nkouka 1987).

Equally important is that pregnant women often eat the soil of termite mounds, particularly old mounds. They suggested to me that this is not because it is medicine, or that they are sick, but rather because of its rich smell (*-nunkira bwino*), and that it is this that they desire ardently (*-lakalaka*).

There is one species of *chiswe* that it is appropriate to discuss here, although it is not strictly speaking a termite, but an ant. This is *mafulu-fute*, the thief ant (*Carebara vidua*, subfamily *Myrmecinae*). The worker ants are tiny, reddish-yellow, and around 1–2 mm long, and can inflict an irritating itch. The thief ants are found only in association with termite mounds or nests, and they are essentially predators living within the colony and carrying off the eggs and young of the termites as food. Given their size and colour, and the fact that they are associated with termite mounds/nests, it is not surprising that they are described as *chiswe* by local people.

The winged ants emerge from the termite mounds or from holes in the ground at the beginning of the rains, usually at the end of November. Like the *mbereswa*, they emerge around midday or in the early afternoon, usually after a shower of rain. The female ants are large, a shiny black and around 25 mm long (and thus enormous in comparison with the worker ants); the males are smaller with a black head and thorax, a large ochre-yellow abdomen, and some 17 mm long. The flying ants are described as *mafulufute* or *nyamu* (*nyama*, meat), and are highly esteemed as a relish, especially the female, which has lots of fat. The CCAM cookbook notes that the *mafulufute* 'consist of females which are big, black, very oily and tasty. The males are small, brown and not so tasty' (1992: 141). The flying ants come out of their holes singly and at intervals, and patience is required in collecting them – as I discovered from my own experience. Hence the proverb that runs:

Mafulufute akamatuluka
Usamawatsinire ku dzenje

which roughly translated means:

When the flying ant comes out
Do not squeeze them at the hole.

It signifies: have patience, let them completely emerge before collecting them. Before roasting, or cooking in salted water, the brown wings are removed. Locally people correctly refer to the male winged ant as *mphongo*. The large females of *Carebara* seem to be highly prized as a delicacy not only in Malawi, but throughout sub-Saharan Africa, and are eaten raw, roasted or cooked (Bodenheimer 1951: 193; Gelfand 1971: 168).

Locusts (Orthoptera)

Locusts and grasshoppers have been eaten by humans since time immemorial, and they are one of the few insects clearly recognized as food in the Mosaic dietary rules. They are mentioned fifty-six times in the Bible, and appear in seventeen different books – which indicates their importance as food (or pest) in Biblical times. They appear more often than any other insect, and around nine different generic names are described in the scriptures (Cansdale 1970: 238–9). They are specifically distinguished from all 'winged creeping things' – which are deemed abominations – by the fact that they 'have legs above their feet, to leap withal upon the earth' (Leviticus 11: 20–3). The generic names probably refer to various grasshoppers, locusts and crickets – all of which were considered edible.

Grasshoppers and locusts, however, were not only eaten by the ancient Hebrews but are a favoured food throughout the Middle East and North Africa. They are considered a great delicacy, and in the Islamic tradition they are lawful food – provided they are taken alive and ritually killed by Muslims – as the prophet himself used to eat them (Bodenheimer 1951: 43). Among Greek historians, such as Diodorus of Sicily (2nd century BC) we even find references to a people called Acridophagi – the locust-eaters (Gr *Acris*, grasshopper) (1951: 41).

Throughout Africa locusts and grasshoppers are a major source of food, and, in the past a swarm of locusts was often considered a mixed blessing, destructive of crops, but 'manna' for others. Bequaert records that in South Africa the *Nganga* (medicine man) often attempted in his ritual incantations to bring locusts, rather than rain (1921: 193). It has been suggested that governmental control of the migratory locust in Zimbabwe, although curbing serious locust outbreaks, has also deprived people of an important source of food (DeFoliart 1999: 31).

In Malawi, a distinction is made between the larger grasshoppers and locusts (*chiwala/ dzombe*) and the smaller, less conspicuous grasshoppers, which are described as *chitete*. *Chiwala* is never used as a general term for insects, as suggested by Sherry and Ridgeway (1984: 21), but is essentially applied to the large, winged, colourful grasshoppers. All the larger grasshoppers – the term locust is usually reserved for those species that have a swarming phase (Latin *Locusta*, grasshopper) – are considered edible in Malawi and eagerly sought. The term *dzombe*, and its correlates, includes the following nine species, all short-horned grasshoppers (family: *Acrididae*):

Bush Grasshopper	*Afroxyrrhepes acuticerus*
	Afroxyrrhepes procera
	Homoxyrrhepes punctipennis
Yellow Locust	*Cyrtacanthacris tatarica*
	Cyrtacanthacris aeruginosa
Common Locust	*Ornithacris magnifica*
	Ornithacris cyanea
Tree Locust	*Acanthacris ruficornis*
Red Locust	*Nomadacris septemfasciata*

Although local people describe all the larger grasshoppers by the term *dzombe*, and see them as flying insects (*kachirombo kamauluka*), they do recognize that there are many different kinds, some with red (*-fiira*), others with yellow (*-achikasu*) wings.

The *dzombe* grasshoppers are collected in two ways. The first involves mainly women or young children going out very early in the morning, usually armed with a stick or branches, to beat down the grasshoppers in the gardens or grasslands. Anyone who has tried to capture the larger grasshoppers around midday – many of them can fly twenty metres or more in a single flight – will realize why collecting is done around daybreak, when the grasshoppers are still numbed by the cold of the night. The second method of obtaining the larger grasshoppers is by hunting (*ku-saka*) with bow and arrow (*nakasaka*). This is usually undertaken by young men. The arrows consist of a long bango reed (to 1.5 m in length) armed with a three-pointed prong made from the spokes of a bicycle wheel. The youths approach the grasshoppers quite closely, and impale the insects to the ground with remarkable accuracy (see the photograph in my book *The Power of Animals* 1988: xii). The youths will often, when they have collected a sufficient amount, roast the grasshoppers over a fire themselves, and consume the insects as a snack.

The usual method of cooking is quite simple: the women take off (*-sadzula*) the wings and the lower part of the hind legs (the tibia is usually armed with sharp spines); they are then put in a cooking pot or frying pan (*silepani*) with salt and a little water, and heated over the fire until the water has evaporated. If available, women will often put in cooking oil to make the insects taste good (*-koma*). They can be eaten at this stage, either as a snack or a meal, or be cooked later with tomato, onions or groundnut flour (*nsinjiro*) as a relish dish (*ndiwo*). If the grasshoppers are in abundance, after cooking they may be spread on the rocks to dry (*-yanika*), and then sold in a local market. One Lomwe woman informed me that female grasshoppers containing eggs are particularly well-liked, and that, if kept dry and salted, the insects may be stored for more than a year, and a portion taken (*-tapa*) as and when needed. When cooked the *dzombe* grasshoppers tend to be a reddish colour and have a good taste. The grasshoppers tend not to be killed when captured, but have their legs and wings removed and are placed in the cooking pot while still alive. Although found throughout the year, the larger grasshoppers are particularly plentiful at the end of the rains, or in the early dry season (March–July). At Kapalasa farm the bush grasshopper *Afroxyrrhepes acuticerus* was particularly abundant in abandoned cultivations during May and June.

Locusts and grasshoppers are not only considered a tasty relish by local people – Hovington (1971: 99) considered the taste a 'little rancid' – but are extremely nourishing, with a high protein, fat and vitamin content. As dry matter the red locust (*Nomadacris septemfasciata*) has 63 per cent protein, and 14 per cent fat, as well as traces of essential minerals (Bodenheimer 1951: 32; DeFoliart 1975: 162). David Livingstone is said to have compared the taste of locusts to that of caviare (DeFoliart 1975: 164).

The large coffee locust *Phymateus viridipes*, which is allied to the elegant grasshopper (family *Pyrogomorphidae*) and common throughout

Malawi – especially in montane grassland, is not usually described as *dzombe*, nor is it considered edible. When provoked it exudes a poisonous frothy secretion.

Grasshoppers (Orthoptera)

Chitete is a generic term used in Malawi to cover all the smaller grasshoppers, most of which are considered edible. There are well over a hundred small grasshoppers in Malawi (Whellan 1975), the majority belonging to the family *Acrididae*, and most of these are probably utilized as food. I joined a group of three young boys collecting grasshoppers near Dedza. Their mode of foraging was quite simple. It was a cool overcast afternoon, and they walked through the grassy meadow, each with a stick, waving it from side to side across the sward. As soon as the movement of a grasshopper was detected it was pounced upon, and sharply hit with the stick. This was quite a skilled operation, and compared with these three boys I was a rather incompetent collector of grasshoppers. Dead or alive, the insects were then placed in a small tin – to be roasted later. What is of interest is that this small collection yielded around ten different species of small grasshoppers, mostly around 30–40 mm in length.

The common species of *chitete* include the following:

Acrididae

Chilwa Grasshopper	*Leptacris monteiroi*
Green-striped Grasshopper	*Heteracris attentuatus*
	Heteracris pulchripes
Sulphur Acrida	*Acrida sulphuripennis*
	Acrida acuminata
	Acrida bicolor
	Acrida turrita
	Morphacris fasciata
	Tmetanota abrupta
	Cardeniopsis pauperatus
Blue-winged Grasshopper	*Catantops spissus*
Scarlet-winged Grasshopper	*Acrotylus nr patruelis*
Yellow-spotted Grasshopper	*Euproacris cylindicollis*

Tettigonidae

Common Katydid	*Homorocoryphus vicinus*
	Tylopsis rubrescens
	Pseudorhynchus pungens

Pyrgomorphidae

Elegant Grasshopper	*Zonocerus elegans*

All these species are considered edible, and mostly collected by women, or by young herdboys while out tending cattle. I particularly observed boys collecting grasshoppers at Mulanje, Mangoche, Ntcheu and Dedza, usually in small groups. Women suggested to me that if they are out hoeing in the gardens, and lots of *chitete* (small grasshoppers) seem to be around, they encourage the young children to capture them by hand, with the help of a stick. They are prepared and cooked in similar fashion to the larger grasshoppers (*dzombe*) with a little salt and water, or roasted on a stick.

But there are two grasshoppers (*chitete*) that have particular salience for local people. The first is *bwanoni* (*Homorocoryphus vicinus*), a small green (or pale brown) grasshopper with a pointed head, which is very well liked, as it contains lots of fat (*mafuta*). One man told me that *bwanoni* excelled all other grasshoppers in its fat content, and was liked very much by all people (*Ndaposa ziwala zonse ndi mafuta achilengedwa ndipo anthu ambiri amandikonda*). This grasshopper often swarms, and comes to the light at night. Some years ago, I was informed, swarms of *bwanoni* came to the street lights in Blantyre, and hundreds of people came out with bags and buckets to collect the insects. This brought traffic to a standstill in the city centre, and riot police were called out, with tear gas, to disperse the crowds – so well liked is the *bwanoni*. Such an occurrence has been recorded elsewhere, for this, or the allied species *Homorocoryphus nitidula*, appears to be eaten throughout Africa, and is usually described as a 'cone-headed grasshopper' (Bodenheimer 1951: 140; DeFoliart 1989: 25; Van Huis 1996: 8). Two other very similar small grasshoppers (HB 25–40 mm), both green with pointed heads and long antennae – *Tylopsis rubrescens* and *Pseudorhynchus pungens* – are also eaten, and often described as *bwanoni*, but Malawians are clearly able to distinguish the prototypical *bwanoni*. Its body fat is so well liked that people suggest they are seduced (*-kopa*) by it. In the past *Homorocoryphus vicinus* was often noted as a serious agricultural pest. Some people confuse *bwanoni* with the similar green bush grasshoppers *Acrida* spp. – the illustration in the CCAM cookbook (1992: 142) is of an *Acrida* sp., not *bwanoni* – but Malawians do not equate them, for *Homorocoryphus vicinus* has long antennae and carries fat in the body. *Acrida* spp. in contrast have short blade-like antennae, and are usually described as *chigomphanthiko*.

The other grasshopper that has salience is the *nunkhadala* (*Zonocerus elegans*). A sluggish, very brightly coloured grasshopper, it exudes a yellowish, smelly fluid (hence its name) and is also a serious agricultural pest on a wide variety of crops. It is very common, particularly in the Lower Shire, where it is known as *mbobo*. People are ambiguous as to its edibility. Some consider it distasteful, and will not touch it as food, given its obnoxious smell (*-nunkha*); others consider it edible. Williamson recorded that it was not liked by men because of its foul smell, but that it was 'eaten occasionally by women and in considerable quantities (twelve at a time) by children having been roasted on a stick' (1992: 270). The wings and legs are removed before eating. Others suggest that it is edible provided it is boiled in water initially and the water is discarded, before it is cooked like other grasshoppers.

But not all grasshoppers are eaten as food, and several species in particular are singled out as inedible, although all at times may be described as *chitete*. The toad grasshopper *tsokonombwe* (*Lobosceliana* spp.) is well known to all Malawians, its call being a harbinger of the coming rains. A fat, wingless (in the female) medium-sized grasshopper (HB 70 mm), greyish brown with chocolate patches on the thorax, *tsokonombwe* has important cultural relevance, but it is rarely eaten. Williamson records that they were eaten only by children, who roast them in ashes in the early part of the rains (1992: 270). One Lomwe woman suggested to me that the Angoni people eat them – but not the Lomwe themselves.

Another slow-moving, plump and wingless grasshopper, *Maura bolivari*, which is very common in the Shire Highlands, is also never eaten. Nor is the dull-coloured crested grasshopper, *chansasi* (*Abisares viridipennis*), which is, as its name suggests, associated with the castor oil shrub. The common yellow-winged grasshopper *chidyamamina* (*Gastrimargus africanus*) is also not eaten, for it is reputed to eat human mucus – hence its common name. It has however been recorded as edible in the Sahel (Van Huis 1996: 7). Finally two members of the family *Tettigoniidae* are also not eaten – *gomphanthiko* (*Clonia wahlbergi*), a large green carnivorous grasshopper with long springy legs, and *mvimbvi* (*Enyaliopsis petersii*), the armoured ground cricket – although strictly speaking it is not a cricket. The latter has a thorax armed with short spines, and exudes a whitish rubbery liquid than can blister the skin. People view it as a harmful species, and it is not eaten.

Crickets (Orthoptera)

There are numerous species of cricket to be found in Malawi, mainly of the family *Gryllidae*; but three species have particular relevance as a food source. The giant cricket *nkhululu* (*Brachytrypes membranaceus*) is very well known, is widely distributed, and seems especially adapted to abandoned cultivations, gardens, and cleared areas in woodland. A rather plump, dark chestnut insect (HB 47 mm) it lives in burrows in the ground – to a depth of 20 cm, the males calling at their entrances in the early evening during the rains. It feeds on the roots of plants, and can at times cause serious damage to crops. It is usually obtained by being dug from its burrow, and women hoeing in coffee gardens or in similar situations will often dig up around fifty crickets during the morning. Loveridge records that in the Mulanje district young boys will often capture the cricket by means of a black army ant *mdzodzo* (*Megaponera foetens*) tied to a piece of cotton, which is lowered into the burrow – the cricket making a hasty retreat to the surface, to be captured by the boy (1954: 283). I often observed this when I worked on Limbuli estate. Williamson records that they are killed by crushing the head between the fingers; the wings are then torn off, and they are roasted in ashes or on a piece of earthenware (1992: 270). The crickets are cooked in similar fashion to the locusts; the wing cases are removed, and the crickets heated over the fire in a pan with salt and a little water. As they contain a large amount of fat they are well liked as a relish. Williamson recorded that people consumed 30–60 gm of giant cricket daily during the season (5–10 insects) – mainly March–April in the Lakeshore (Berry and Petty 1992: 107). This species seems to be eaten throughout Africa (Gelfand 1971: 171; Van Huis 1996: 7).

People have rather mixed feelings about the common crickets *kalijosolo* (*Gryllus* spp.), some species of which are particularly associated with entering houses and damaging clothes. *Gryllus bimaculatus* and several associated species are particularly common, but they are rarely eaten, and never mentioned in the early literature.

The king or black cricket *chiboli* (*Henicus* sp.) is a well known wingless cricket that is also said to have a lot of fat, and is dug out from its burrow towards the end of the rainy season. It is a shiny brown, almost black insect – rather smaller than the giant cricket (HB 32 mm).

Finally, Malawians think highly of the small and rather unique species, the mole cricket *bololo* (*Gryllotalpa africanus*). Of the family *Gryllotalpidae*, it is a cosmopolitan species, and is found in low-lying or marshy (*dambo*) areas throughout Malawi. It is slender, furry, and a rich reddish brown, with the front-legs adapted to digging – hence its common name. Like the other crickets, it is dug up by means of a hoe. The CCAM cookbook suggests that they should be caught by putting a wet stick into their holes and 'pulling it out quickly, as soon as the insect bites' (1992: 142). They are cooked in a similar fashion to the locusts and grasshoppers.

Bugs (Hemiptera)

Only three species of bugs are commonly eaten in Malawi, and apart from the cicada bugs are very rarely mentioned in the literature on the insect foods of sub-Saharan Africa. Bugs seem to be more often eaten in Asia, and the giant water bug (*Lethocerus indicus* – the allied species *L. niloticum* is plentiful in the Lower Shire – is commonly sold in food shops in Canton – along with cockroaches (*Periplaneta americana*) and water beetles (*Cybister* sp.) (Bodenheimer 1951: 276–7). None of these species are eaten in Malawi. Bugs in Malawi have salience not as food but as serious agricultural pests – aphids, jassids, mealy bugs, scale insects, cotton stainers and mosquito bugs – on cassava, cotton and a wide variety of food plants.

The cicada was often mentioned in the literature of antiquity, and considered a great delicacy among the Greeks (Aristotle 1965–1970: 556b). They were particularly made famous by the great French naturalist Jean-Henri Fabre – he never described himself as an entomologist – who recorded in detail their very complex life-cycle. For cicadas are among the longest-lived insects, often spending up to a decade underground as larvae, feeding on the roots of trees. The adults, in contrast, only live a few weeks, and during that time males make an incessant 'song' that fills the *Brachystegia* woodland – or in the Mediterranean region the olive groves. Fabre noted that the cicada was a great 'ventriloquist' and that it was commonly used as medicine among the Greeks – as it was believed to have diuretic properties. He concluded: 'Four years of hard labour underground, and a month of feasting in the sun; such is the life of the cicada' (1911: 11–59).

In Malawi the cicada (*nyenje*) is highly esteemed as food. The generic term includes several species of cicada, of the commoner genera *Ioba, Platypleura* and *Pycna*. In Yao a distinction is made between the larger cicadas, such as *Ioba leopardina* (*nyesele*) and the smaller species *Platyspleura brevis*, which is described as *lilangwe*. All species of cicada seem to be considered edible. They are collected by the use of latex. A long stem of *bango* reed (*Phragmites mauritianus*) or *nsenjere* grass (*Pennisetum purpureum*) is cut, some 3–4 metres long, and on the tip of the reed is smeared some plant latex (*ulimbo*) usually that taken from the freshly-cut inner bark of the *kachere* tree (*Ficus natalensis*). As with the use of latex in trapping birds, several other plants may be utilized to obtain the latex. Significantly in trapping birds a winged termite may be used as bait (for a discussion of the plants used as *ulimbo*, and the preparation of the latex see Morris and Patel 1994).

The collection of the cicada is an apparently simple procedure. People wander through the woodland, listening for the song of the cicadas, usually in the early morning. On detecting the whereabouts of the cicada on the branch of a tree, the reed is slowly and carefully directed to the cicada, the latex adhering to its wings. The procedure is simplicity itself. Yet for the unskilled it is by no means easy, for it needs very sharp eyes and hearing to detect the exact location of the cicada on the tree – for they are well camouflaged, and, as Fabre suggested, they seem to be ventriloquists. After gathering a suitable quantity, they are either roasted as a snack with the wings removed, or cooked in salted water as a side dish. Williamson noted that cicadas were much liked and eaten in urban areas during the rains (1992: 271). I was informed that they were often sold in Balaka market. As with other bugs, cicadas are often drawn to light at night, and at Liwonde I learned that the main form of collection was by means of fire at night – in some woodland at the end of the dry season (October–December). Gerald Meke records that when he was a boy in the Mangochi district cicadas were 'hunted' at night using fire torches (Meke *et al*. 2000: 7). Many suggest that the cicada is a kind (*gulu*) of *chiwala* (grasshopper), but its taste is superior, and comparable to that of the winged termite.

The green shield bug *nkhunguni* (*Nezara robusta*) is not mentioned in the early report of the nutrition survey (1938–1940), but *Pentatomid* bugs seem to be eaten widely in Southern Africa (Bodenheimer 1951: 190–1). *Nkhunguni* – a name shared with the common bed bug, although the pronunciation is slightly different – is a common bug in the Mwanza, Neno and Thyolo districts, and is associated with *Brachystegia* woodland and blue gum plantations. It is alternatively called the green stink bug, for it has a powerful smell, and is often described as *chinunkha* – 'that which smells'. In the Thyolo district the bug is collected from *Eucalyptus* trees at daybreak, when there is still a chill in the air, and the bugs are dormant. The bole of the tree is hit (-*gunda*) or beaten very abruptly with a log or heavy implement. This has the effect of shaking the tree suddenly, and the insects fall to the ground, to be gathered up by the women. In the Neno district collection of the bug is more organized. It is done by means of a collecting bag, called *apolo*. This consists of a long bamboo pole, some 4–5 metres long, which carried aloft a plastic funnel in the form of a bag, at the base of which is a collecting pouch. The collection is done by thrusting the *apolo* vertically upwards into the leaves of the trees, where the *nkhunguni* bug feeds, causing the bugs to fall into the pouch. When the pouch is full, the insects are transferred into a woven bamboo basket, which has a lid. The shield bug is usually found at around 1,200 m in *Brachystegia* woodland, often in shady kloofs that are cool, the collectors suggesting that it likes a cool (-*ozizira*) environment. It is particularly associated with such trees as *msuku* (*Uapaca kirkiana*), *nchumbe* (*Brachystegia spiciformis*), *kasokolowe* (*Uapaca nitida*) and *tsamba* (*Brachystegia floribunda*). Care is always taken not to kill the bugs, and they are kept alive in the bamboo basket when being carried back to the village. The bug contains a bitter juice that causes brown stains on the fingers and is painful if it enters the eyes. It is described as oil (*mafuta*), and as bitter (*-wawa*). To prepare the bug for eating it is therefore washed several times in tepid water. It thus ejects its bitter juices and loses its powerful smell (*fungo*). It is never put in boiling water, as this kills the bug immediately, and it thus retains its 'poison' or toxicity. It then has a dark patch on its underside and a bitter taste. After washing the bug loses its green coloration, and becomes a pale golden yellow. It is then cooked with a little water and salt. In the Neno hills I was given some to taste along with *chimbamba* beans (*Phaseolus vulgaris*) and maize porridge. It may be eaten as a snack or as a side dish, and, if there is a surplus, may be sold in local markets. The water used to wash the bugs is said to be used as a pesticide, to counter damage done by termites to crops or houses (Meke *et al.* 2000: 3). Collection of the shield bugs is usually from June to September.

Other stink bugs, often with a local distribution, may be eaten. Williamson records the bug *nsesenya* (*Sphaerocoris ocellatus*), which was collected at the end of the rains (April to June) in the Nkhotakota district. It is a small green insect, with red and black markings, HB 12 mm, and seems to be especially associated with abandoned cultivations and such shrubs as the tree cassava, *mpira* (*Manihot glaziovii*). Owing to widespread deforestation some edible insects are becoming rare, and when I asked one woman about *nsesenya* she replied that she had seen it long ago, but that now she is a grandmother, and has forgotten about it (*Panopo ine munthu wankulu ndiye ndakaiwala*).

The final bug that may form part of the local diet, although it seems to be eaten only infrequently, is the bow-legged bug, *nandoli* (*Anoplocnemis curvipes*). A dark greyish-brown stink bug (family *Coreidae*), it is a common wayside insect, and many note its edibility. But I have no records of people actually eating it as a relish.

Beetles (Coleoptera)

Beetles are ubiquitous in Malawi, and found in every type of habitat. The total number of species in the country is unknown; it probably amounts to several thousand species. But few species seem to be recognized as food. A number of edible beetles have been recorded from sub-Saharan Africa, and among the more important are the following: the larvae of three beetles – the palm weevil, *Rhynchophorus phoeniceus*, the giant click beetle, *Tetralobus flabellicornis*, and the rhinoceros beetle, *Oryctes boas*; and the adult beetle *Sternocera orissa* (Bodenheimer 1951: 142–3, 186; DeFoliart 1999: 25). In Malawi only this last species seems to be widely recognized as an edible beetle. I showed the large grubs of the rhinoceros beetle, which feed on horse manure, to some young men in the

Blantyre district; they not only failed to recognize the larvae, but indicated extreme disgust at the thought of eating it. The jewel beetle, *nkhumbutera* (*Sternocera orissa*) is however different, and this attractive, metallic beetle is widely recognized and commonly eaten, both the adult and its rather large white eggs (5 mm). As Sweeney writes: 'The females are sometimes kept in little pens by children who eat the eggs when they are laid' (1970: 47). It is described as an insect that flies high and fast, and feeds on the leaves of *mombo* trees (*Brachystegia longifolia*) and it is cooked in salted water in the same way as locusts (*dzombe*). It is usually collected in January and February. One person described it to me as 'meat' (*nyama*). Among the central Kalahari San this beetle is considered a great delicacy, and they liken the taste of a female containing eggs to that of roasted eland meat (Nonaka 1996: 33).

It is significant that neither of the Malawi 'cookbooks' mention edible beetles (Shaxson *et al.* 1974: 21–3; CCAM 1992: 139–43); but the *Nyasaland Survey 1938–40* mentions two beetles, the jewel beetle (*nkhumbu* (C)), which is roasted and eaten by children, and the cockchafer *chikumbu* (Family: *Melolonthidae*). This latter species is dug for by women and children, and roasted, or cooked with oil as a side dish (CCAM 1992: 272). Meke records the *chikumbu* as a large black beetle that feeds on the leaves of *Brachystegia spp.* and is collected as a relish or snack at the beginning of the rainy season (Meke *et al.* 2000: 4).

The grubs of two species feeding on *chiwale* palms (*Raphia farinifera*) – *sakanjale* and *namungorongoro* – have been recorded from the Mulanje district, but their specific identification is uncertain.

Lake-fly (Diptera)

One day in September many years ago I was travelling on my motorcycle from Chitimba to Rumphi. It was a beautiful clear day, with not a cloud to be seen. However, as I was climbing the Chiweta escarpment I saw across the lake what appeared to be a large dark cloud. It struck me as rather odd. I got off my motorcycle near the top of the escarpment and stopped a local man who was transporting firewood on a rather ramshackle bicycle. I asked him about the cloud. 'It's not a cloud (*mtambo*)', he said; 'it is *nkhungu* – relish (*ndiwo*).' That was my first encounter with the lake fly of Lake Malawi.

All earlier travellers to Malawi had written about the famous *nkhungu*, or lake fly. In his account of his Zambesi expedition the famous missionary-explorer David Livingstone had written:

> ... clouds, as of smoke rising from miles of burning grass, were observed bending in a south easterly direction, and we thought the unseen land on the

opposite side was closing in, and that we were near the end of the lake. But next morning we sailed through one of the clouds ... and discovered that it was neither smoke nor haze, but countless millions of minute midges called '*kungo*' (a cloud or fog). They filled the air to an immense height, and swarmed upon the water, too light to sink in it. Eyes and mouth had to be kept closed while passing though this living cloud.

And Livingstone continues:

Thousands lay in the boat when she emerged from the cloud of midges. The people gather these minute insects by night and boil them into thick cakes, to be used as relish – millions of midges in a cake. The *kungo* cake, an inch thick ... was offered to us; it was very dark in colour, and tasted not unlike caviare or salted locusts (Livingstone 1865: 261–2).

Around the turn of the nineteenth century, another missionary wrote of the Nkhungu fly: 'This is a small fly which comes in great clouds resembling columns of smoke. The natives make them into cakes and eat them and declare that they are really good. They make a buzzing noise like a swarm of bees and are caught in a basket by a quick movement of the hand' (Mills 1911: 262).

More recently Archie Carr devoted a whole chapter of his travel book *Ulendo* to the *nkhungu* fly, describing it in terms of a 'dense blue-black smoke', of swirling 'grey mists', and with 'spouts' that consist of billions of flies rising vertically from the lake. Describing the *nkhungu* clouds as something that fills the traveller with awe and wonder, Carr concludes 'I know nothing in Africa that more wholly astounds the mind than the *kungu* clouds ... There is nothing anywhere that so overpoweringly seems to show the mindless drive of life as these vast up-pourings of protoplasm show it' (1965: 62–64).

The *nkhungu* fly of Lake Malawi is a tiny black fly, *Chaoborus edulis* (Family: *Chaoboridae*) that is allied to the mosquitoes. It forms dense swarms over the lake, such swarms having a distinctive structure, with a narrow vertical column. These swarms are undoubtedly associated with the fly's mating behaviour. The adult phase is relatively short-lived, and most of the life-cycle is spent as aquatic larvae that feeds on zooplankton. As the larvae, in turn, are eaten by various fish species, particularly usipa (*Engraulicypris sardella*), the *Chaoborus* fly thus forms an essential component of the lake's ecology. The larvae during the day feed at depths of 200 m, migrating to the surface of the lake at night. Observations made by Irvine from Senga Bay indicated that lake-fly swarms at the southern end of the lake were sporadic and seasonal, usually occurring during the rains (November–February). The swarms were usually accompanied by northerly winds. The life-cycle may be linked to lunar periodicity, swarms occurring at the dark moon (Irvine 1995). Sweeney notes that the lake-fly sometimes occurs in such numbers that the sky is darkened, and people out fishing who are trapped in such a cloud of billions of tiny flies are liable to suffocate to death (1970: 69). Whellan records seeing the swarms at a distance of forty miles (60 km) [BRS/A23]. But Washington Banda, who came from Nkhata Bay, suggested that the Nkhungu flies appear around July, August and September, at a time when the lake is 'fruitless' … so he wrote, 'people find *nkhungu* as manna' (S. W. Banda 1967: 70). My own observations suggest that the *nkhungu* lake-fly swarms throughout the rains from October to March; but what is important from the perspective of local people is that there is an on-shore wind. Around Mangoche I found few people that knew about *nkhungu* fly – this may be due to its sheltered location, or to the fact that the majority of the population there are Muslims. As with the eating of the *nchenzi* (cane rat), there is some dispute among Muslims as to whether or not the lake-fly is a prohibited relish.

Local people do not associate the lake-fly with mosquitoes (*udzudzu*), and are puzzled as to the origins of the swarms. One person at Nkhotakota told me that people believed that the *nkhungu* came from a large fish that lived in the lake, while Washington Banda suggests that people at Nkhata Bay feel that the lake-fly come from the clouds. He suggests that they usually appear after a cloudy morning, and that the flies dance in their large swarms until they are carried ashore by the wind – and are often to be found 2–3 km inland (S. W. Banda 1967: 70). Although harmless, the flies may become troublesome when they enter houses, as they are moist and sticky. Their appearance is often seen as heralding bad weather.

When a swarm of lake-fly has been blown ashore and comes to cover the bushes along the lakeshore, or on the nearby hillside, the women go out with their baskets (*dengu*) and in a sweeping motion beat the bushes. Women talk about beating the leaves (*kugunda masamba*), allowing the insects to enter the basket. The women then separate out the leaves and woody debris, put in a little water, and then squeeze or press (*-finya*) the tiny, black, sticky flies into a cake or ball (*mpira*). These are then placed in the sun to dry or wrapped in banana leaves and placed in hot ashes (*-ocha pa moto*). When dried – as either a black cake or powder – they are ready for eating, and are usually cooked with tomatoes or onions as relish (*ndiwo*) to be eaten with maize porridge (*nsima*). Other people suggest cooking the lake-fly with termites, using only salt. The lake-fly cakes, if kept dry, can be kept for long periods – like tea, one person said to me. The CCAM cookbook suggests that, since they are rich in protein, calcium and iron, they make an extremely nourishing dish (1992: 141), and that this is a relish that is well liked by Malawians. One woman cooked some especially for me, and I found the lake-fly tasty – but a little oily and fishy. In contrast, Archie Carr found it 'had a taste of dry chocolate and badly kept anchovy paste' (1965: 77). The lake-fly is also used as medicine, and evidence suggests that it has a very high iron content.

It is of interest that although the lake-fly (*Chaoborus* sp.) is an important source of protein in Uganda, it is absent from Lake Tanganyika (DeFoliart 1995: 1; Eccles 1985).

Caterpillars (Lepidoptera)

Along with the winged termites, edible caterpillars are the commonest and most esteemed of the edible insects – and seem to be eaten throughout sub-Saharan Africa. Tessman at the beginning of last century recorded that the Pangwe of the Cameroon consumed more than twenty different kinds of edible caterpillar, and recognized each by its specific name and knew its particular host tree (Vide Bodenheimer 1951: 188). More recently Carl Silow (1976) has recorded thirty-one edible caterpillars from mid-Western Zambia (among the Mbunda), and in a detailed survey of the edible caterpillars of sub-Saharan Africa Malaisse and Lognay (2000) recorded fifty-six species that had nutritional value, belonging to several families, although more than half the edible species belong to the family of the emperor moths, *Saturniidae (Attacidae)*.

Little detailed research has been undertaken on the edible caterpillars of Malawi, although the White Father, Louis Denis, in his *Chewa Dictionary*, recorded the names of around twenty-five edible caterpillars. In a more recent survey Gerald Meke (1995b) noted fourteen edible caterpillars from the Chimaliro forest reserve, north of Kasungu (although his preliminary study is without scientific determinations), in what he describes as a declining food resource (cf. Abbot 1998, appendix, for a similar listing).

In many areas of Malawi, particularly where *Brachystegia* woodland is still to be found, edible caterpillars form an important source of food, as well as of petty cash through their sale in local markets. About ten species of caterpillar are fairly common and widely recognized, though vernacular names vary according to locality. We might discuss each of these in turn

Mphalabungu Family: Noctuidae. Belonging to the family *Noctuidae*, *mphalabungu* is common throughout Malawi and is particularly associated with grasslands, whether in marshy (*dambo*) areas in the Shire Highlands – I found it common at Kapalasa – or in montane grassland at the higher altitudes – in the Kirk range, on Dedza and Zomba mountains, or in the Chimaliro forest. It is a gregarious caterpillar, some 30 mm long, smooth, and pale green, with orange-yellow head and legs. It is particularly associated with *utheka* grass (*Hyparrhenia* spp.), and people suggest that it first lays its eggs on the *ndema* or *nthupa* shrub (*Dolichos kilimandscharicus*) and then, some days after hatching, the larvae move to the grasses. In Neno the caterpillars come second only to the *nkhunguni* bug (*Nezara robusta*) in importance as an insect food resource, both for subsistence and for income generation. The caterpillars are collected by women and children from the grassland usually in the early morning – for the caterpillars are rarely in evidence after midday. The season for collection is usually at the end of the rains, from February to April – when the maize ripens. People clearly distinguish this species from the allied and similar caterpillars, the stalk borer and army worm, that infest maize. After collection the caterpillars are washed and boiled in salted water for a few minutes, and then they are put in the sun to dry. They are rarely squeezed, and are usually eaten fresh on the same day. But they are often dried for future use, mixed with *mfutso* leaves. For relish they are boiled with dried leaves, especially dried cowpea leaves, *mfutso wa chitambe* (*Vigna unguiculata*) for ten minutes, before adding tomatoes and salt (CCAM 1992: 141). Meke notes that some people eat them dry as a snack, and that in Neno, with the expansion of population and the opening up of gardens, there has been a marked reduction in the number of these caterpillars (Meke *et al.* 2000: 4). It was suggested to me that *mphalabungu* has a different and 'sweeter' (*-koma*) taste than the caterpillars of the processionary moth (*Anaphe panda*), because it eats grass rather than leaves. There is a children's song relating to this caterpillar, which runs:

Mphalabungu zachepa, zizizaza mkapoto
Hmm walira, walira, walira, magileti (×2)

When the caterpillar is scarce, the pot is wild;
[she] cries, cries, cries, Margaret,

alluding to the fact that the child is unhappy if they fail to find the *mphalabungu* caterpillar. Among the Mbunda of Zambia this species is known as *lixanjungu* (Silow 1976: 50–4).

Sven Grüner reported to me that when, some twenty years ago, there was a serious outbreak of armyworm (*Spodoptera exempta*) in the

Namadzi area, the caterpillars were eagerly gathered by local women as food.

Ntchiu Family: Thaumetopoeidae (Notodontidae). The caterpillar of the African silk moth or processionary moth (*Anaphe panda*) is common

Figure 2 Meria White with nest of *Ntchiu* (*Anaphe panda*, the processionary caterpillar), Kapalasa.

throughout Malawi, and is particularly associated with the *nsopa* tree (*Bridelia micrantha*). The caterpillars are gregarious, and are often seen moving in long processions, head to tail, with more than a hundred caterpillars in a line. The caterpillars are dark grey, almost black, and covered in fine, dirty white long hairs, with reddish-brown head and legs. They are

Figure 3 Mary Malata, cooking *Ntchiu* caterpillars (*Anaphe panda*), Kapalasa.

around 35 mm long. At pupation the caterpillars come together to construct a collective cocoon, robust, oval-shaped, and pale yellowish-brown in colour (Figure 2). Not until they have formed the cocoon, when they have lost much of their hair, are the caterpillars usually collected as food. This usually takes place at the end of the rainy season, around April. Meke notes that while in Zomba and Kasungu districts people wait until the collective cocoon has been constructed before collecting the caterpillars, in Neno they collect the third and fourth instars as they feed (Meke *et al.* 2000: 4).

After collection or removal from the cocoon the caterpillars are first roasted (*-ocha*) or burnt (*-waula*) to remove the hairs, which are slightly irritant. The common Lomwe name, *awauleni*, relates to this initial singeing of the hairs. After being dried in the sun, and then winnowed to remove the remaining hairs, the caterpillars are slowly fried (*-kazinga*) in a frying pan, together with a little salt (Figure 3). The caterpillar is then eaten as relish, or, if fully dried and salted, may be kept for future use. As *Anaphe panda* is particularly associated with the *Bridelia* tree, it often shares its name: *maleweza* (C), *masopa* (Nyanja). Its local name in Neno, *ntchiu*, refers to the tree *Dombeya rotundifolia* (*torrida*) on which it also feeds.

Another species of *Anaphe* sp., *kamonde* is associated with the *msolo* tree (*Pseudolachnostylis maprouneifolia*). In Zambia Silow described a similar species, *liungu luanda* ('the caterpillar that spins a web') – so called after its habits of spinning a cocoon – *Anaphe infracta*, which is associated also with the *msolo* tree. As in Malawi, it is greatly esteemed as food, as well as being utilized as medicine (1976: 114–24). As the processionary caterpillar has a high fat content, 35 per cent, it is well-liked, as well as being rich in protein (45 per cent). Its calorific value is 543 kcal, which is higher than both meat (237 kcal) and kidney beans (336 kcal) (Latham 1999: 138).

Chilumphabere Family: Sphingidae. The caterpillar of the death's head hawk moth (*Acherontia atropos*) is well known in Malawi, because it is large and colourful, usually green or yellow, with a curved horn at the end of its body, and it feeds on the sweet potato plant *mbatata* (*Ipomoea batatas*), as does the allied species, the convolvulus hawk moth (*Herse convolvuli*), which can be a serious pest on potato. In Zambia the large and gaudily coloured caterpillar of *Acherontia atropos* is not usually eaten (Silow 1976: 202); but sketches and photographs of this shown to Malawians were all identified as either *chilumphabere* or *nthowa*. Denis gives them the alternative names *kambuma* and *mbinimini*. Pinhey described these caterpillars as 'delicacies to the African palate' (1962: 7), for they are widely eaten in Malawi and elsewhere. In Zambia, the Mbunda name refers to them as *liungu kandolo* ('caterpillar of the sweet potato plant'), and by the Mbunda they are considered a delicacy, though only found in small numbers (Silow 1976: 11–14).

The caterpillar of the allied hawk moth *nthowa* (*Nephele comma*) is also commonly eaten in Malawi. It is very variable in colour, but has a characteristic horn (*nyanga*) or tail (*chira*) at the end of its body, and is particularly associated with the *thombozi* tree (*Diplorhynchus condylo-carpon*), which shares the Tumbuka name *mtowa*. In Zambia the Mbunda name for this caterpillar, *chikilakila*, refers to the conspicuous tail (*-kila*) (Silow 1976: 1–2). In Malawi it is often gregarious, and is collected in the early part of the rains, October–December.

Mabwabwa   Family: Saturniidae.   This is probably the commonest and most widespread edible caterpillar, the larva of the common emperor, *Bunaea alcinoe* (Figure 4). Its local name is derived from its association with the *mbwabwa* tree, *Cussonia arborea*, although it is to be found on a wide variety of trees: *Bauhinia, Croton, Ekebergia, Maesa* and *Terminalia*. At Bvumbwe I found it on a *chisomanga* tree (*Liquidambar styracifolia*), being eagerly collected by local women. The caterpillars are extremely colourful; the head and body is black, with black spines on the first two segments, and six rows of ivory-white spines on the remaining

Figure 4 *Bunaea alcinoe*, caterpillars, Kapalasa.

segments, and with orange spiracles along the sides. It is large, around 65 mm long. It is of interest that it is not listed by Meke *et al.* (1995) from the Chimaliro forest, although I recorded it with Hassam Patel in the Mzuzu botanical gardens. It is usually collected by women, who use long bamboo poles to knock down the caterpillars, or shake the tree vigorously to unsettle them. To prepare the caterpillars for eating several distinct steps are undertaken, as was graphically described to me by one person: the caterpillars are first squeezed (*-finya*) from the head downwards to remove the guts; then the caterpillars are washed (*-tsuka*) several times to clean them; then they are cooked (*-phika*) in a little water; then they are put in the sun (*-yanika*) to dry; finally they are fried (*-kazinga*) in a little oil. They are not usually fried with tomatoes, although salt is usually added to make them into a relish, to be eaten with maize porridge (*nsima*). Jessie Williamson noted that: 'Native potashes may be used in the cooking. Much liked. Eaten occasionally in the hill village in the rains' (1992: 271).

I noted them being collected mainly between January and April. The preparation and cooking of the caterpillars, noted above, is common to all the *Saturniid* caterpillars – and this particular family is specifically associated with *Brachystegia* woodland. Around 70 species of emperor moths have been recorded from Malawi, and the caterpillars of most of these are probably deemed edible by local people – although further research studies are needed. As with other caterpillars, if they are found in abundance, they will be sun-dried and stored (*-sunga*) for later use. People always speak of the propensity that *mabwabwa* caterpillars have for completely stripping the leaves off the branches of the *Cussonia* trees. It is very well liked (*-koma kwambiri*) and thought to be superior to both *mphalabungu* and *ntchiu*. As one woman described *mabwabwa* to me: '*Chili nambala wani, eeh ndithu!*' 'It is 'number one', yes!' Indeed! In Zambia this species, under the taxon *lixaxa* (Mbunda) is equally well-liked, and considered to have a 'nice taste'. It is not systematically gathered, but only collected in passing (Silow 1976: 70–3). The *mabwabwa* caterpillar is rich in protein (65 per cent) and fat (10 per cent) and high in calories – 443 kcal (Latham 1999: 138).

Maphombo.   The caterpillar of this emperor moth (*Nudaurelia (imbrasia) wahlbergi*) is similar to the *mabwabwa*, with a black body, but has red spines and white spiracles along the sides of the body. It is also 65 mm long. In Tumbuka it is usually called *viphombo*, and is particularly associated by local people with the *msuku* tree (*Vapaca kirkiana*). But it is also found on mango trees, and is usually collected towards the end of the rains, March–June.

Chilumgulungu. Caterpillars described under this name essentially relate to three species of *Gonimbrasia* that are very similar.

Gonimbrasia zambesina is probably commoner and more widespread. Its head and body is black, with the body mottled with blue, yellow and red speckling, and with dark red to black spines. It has been noted on mango, oleander and *msumwa* (*Diospyros mespiliformis*) trees.

Gonimbrasia rectilineata has a similar mottled body, but has a pale red head and short red spines. It seems to be particularly associated with shrubby plants, *nduma* (*Eriosema ellipticum*) and *mphilipwiju* (*Mucuna stans*), and to be collected mainly during the rains, February–March.

The third species is the well-known '*mopane* worm' (a misnomer), the caterpillar of the anomalous emperor (*Gonimbrasia belina*). The head and body of this caterpillar are black, the body densely speckled with yellow, white and bluish-grey, and with short black spines. Although recorded from Kasungu National Park (Munthali and Mughogho 1992: 145) it is very much associated with the *mopane* or *tsanya* tree (*Colophospermum mopane*), which is not found in Kasungu, but is essentially a tree characteristic of hot low-lying areas, such as the Shire Valley. All three *Gonimbrasia* caterpillars are however very similar, quite large, circa 80–100 mm, and are harvested in the early rains November– December, although I noted *Gonimbrasia belina* at Liwonde in April.

The '*mopane* worm' is common and widespread throughout Southern Africa, and is the subject of a very extensive literature. In South Africa Dreyer and Wehmeyer (1982) record that the *Gonimbrasia belina* caterpillar is widely sought after as a relish, and to a substantial degree supplements the predominantly cereal diet – of maize. It also forms an important item of trade, and it is estimated that more than 1,600 metric tons of dried caterpillars are annually traded through co-operative markets. The '*mopane* worms' (*masonja*) among the Pedi are preferred to meat (Quin 1959: 114). In Botswana women will travel long distances into the bush to harvest the caterpillars, which are then cooked and sun-dried to be sold in the city markets. For the women 'these caterpillars mean business' and constitute an important 'cash crop' during the rainy season (Menzel and D'Alvisio 1998: 127–9).

Mopane worms are such a sought-after delicacy in southern Africa that they form the basis of a huge cash industry, and, in good seasons, a person harvesting the caterpillars can earn in a few weeks a substantial income – almost equivalent to a year's income as a farm labourer. Such systematic caterpillar collecting for the urban market as has developed in recent years may be having serious ecological consequences, particularly as more than 90 per cent of Botswana's *mopane* caterpillar production is exported to South Africa annually (Illgner and Nel 2000; 340–9). The '*mopane* worm' (Mbunda , *muyaya*,) is equally popular in Zambia, and is the most well known of all the spiny caterpillars. It is collected by men, women and children, for both subsistence and trade (Silow 1976: 64–70). Given its cultural importance, it is of interest that the '*mopane* worm' is depicted on the Botswana 5 pula coin (Green 2001).

Because of their spines the *Gonimbrasia* caterpillars, as with *mabwabwa*, may often be described as *malasalasa* (-*lasa*, to cut, wound).

Mapala. The caterpillars of the diverse emperor (*Imbrasia ertli*) seem to be evident at all altitudes from the Lower Shire to the Nyika plateau, and are widely eaten as a relish. The caterpillars have a reddish brown head and a black body, covered with long, fine white hairs, which are loosely attached. The head and body are around 70 mm long. It feeds on a variety of trees associated with *Brachystegia* woodland – *chitimbe* (*Piliostigma thonningii*), *mtondo* (*Julbernardia paniculata*), *mpapa* (*Brachystegia spiciformis*) and *mombo* (*Brachystegia longifolia*). Ray Murphy suggested to me that it was probably the commonest of the *Saturniid* moths in Malawi. The caterpillars are collected at the end of the rains, May–July, usually by cutting the branches of the trees, or even cutting down the trees themselves – which is often the case with other edible caterpillars. Because of their long white hairs the caterpillars are often described as *makoloaimvi* (*makulaimvi*), the 'grey hair of the ancestors' (*makolo*, ancestors, *imvi*, grey hair). As with other caterpillars, the body is squeezed to remove the gut, and then washed and fried to remove the hair, and finally cooked in salted water. When sun-dried it may be stored for future use, usually in dried *msuku* (*Uapaca*) leaves. In Zambia this caterpillar (*Mbunda, lipanda*) seems to be harvested three times a year (Silow 1976: 101–3).

Matondo. The speckled emperor moth *Gynanisa maia* has been noted as the *matondo* that is harvested in Kasungu National Park (Munthali and Mughogho 1992: 145). But Ray Murphy informs me that this moth has not been recorded from Malawi, and tends to be restricted to the dry, low veld of Zimbabwe and South Africa. *Matondo* seems to cover a variety of emperor moths whose caterpillars are large, green and without conspicuous spines, and which are specifically associated with the *mthondo* tree (*Julbernardia paniculata*). Three species seem to be particularly identified: *Pseudobunaea pallens*, *Athletes gigas* and *Gynanisa carcassoni*. The caterpillars are collected in the early rains, October–December.

Kawidza. The caterpillars of the pallid emperor (*Cirina forda*) are widely used as a food resource, and tend to be gregarious. They are yellowish, with long white hairs, and black segmented bands. Head and body around 60 mm long. They are particularly associated with the *mkalati* or *kawidzi* tree (*Burkea africana*), from which their name is derived, but they tend to feed on a variety of trees, *Ekebergia, Carissa, Rhus* and *Euclea*. They are harvested during the rains, January–February, and Williamson suggested they were much liked as a side dish (1992: 271). In Zambia this caterpillar (Mbunda, *kakomba*) is noted as feeding not only on *Burkea* trees, but also on the ordeal tree *mwabvi* (*Erythrophleum africanum*), and it is considered to be bitter, and even to cause sickness – diarrhoea, vomiting, dizzy spells. Thus the caterpillars are always squeezed thoroughly and boiled before eating (Silow 1976: 88–93). It is widely eaten in the Congo, and in Nigeria it is the most widely marketed edible insect, and sells for about twice the price of beef (Latham 1999: 136; DeFoliart 1999: 25).

I have outlined above some of the main species of edible caterpillars recognized by Malawian people. Although the generic term for caterpillars is *mbozi* (which seems to cover the larvae of both caterpillars (*Lepidoptera*) and some beetles (*Coleoptera*)), only a select number of caterpillars are known and named, and considered edible. I have records, from various sources, of about thirty edible caterpillars, although their scientific determinations are still uncertain. As for the edible caterpillars, people have extensive knowledge with respect to their morphology, ecology and habits. Of key importance to local people in the recognition of caterpillars are their colour and size and the presence of spines or hairs. The three primary colours, red (*-fiira*), black (*-kuda*) and white (*-yera*), are mainly used in the descriptions of larvae, and the 'finger' is utilized to indicate size. It is of interest that the edible caterpillars are mainly species that are relatively large in size (as with the larvae of the *Saturniid* moths) and are gregarious. Small and solitary caterpillars, or those with irritant hairs (recognized collectively as *chiyabwe*) are not eaten. The colour of the head is also a diagnostic feature; but people never mention the colour of the spiracles.

People are also familiar with the ecology and feeding habits of the caterpillars, and frequently the name of the caterpillar is derived from its principal host tree. Thus *mabwabwa*, the larva of the common emperor moth, relates to the well-known tree *mbwabwa* (*Cussonia arborea*) (Tumbuka, *chipombora*). But generally caterpillars are not host-specific, and people will name the various trees with which they are associated. However, they often suggest that the moths lay their eggs on a specific host, and that later the caterpillars move and disperse to other trees in the surrounding woodland. Thus *matondo* is specifically associated with the *mthondo* tree (*Julbernardia paniculata*), but when mature they move to and feed on other trees, where they are collected at the beginning of the rains in November and December. People also recognize that the caterpillars pass through several distinct stages before becoming mature, and they are generally collected in their final stages prior to pupation – which usually takes place in the ground. Silow recorded that in Zambia rural people had several theories about the reproduction of caterpillars, including the views that caterpillars come with the rain, or that they lay eggs and bring forth their own young. People in Malawi, even older, non-literate people, seem to be fully conversant with the life-cycle of the moth. When in Tsamba forest near Neno I picked up the wing of an emperor moth that had recently been eaten by some bird. My companion Arnold Wasi immediately related to me the life-history of the moth (*nkhani agulugufe*) – from the egg (*dzira*), through the birth of the caterpillar (*kabadwa kambozi*), to its maturity (*pang'ono pang'ono yakhula*) – 'little by little it matures' – to the making of its cocoon (*panga chikwa*). The stages are seen as involving transformations (*-sanduka*). For Arnold the caterpillar was edible; the adult moth was not.

As with the gathering of mushrooms, the collection of caterpillars is mainly associated with the rainy season, from November to March, although processionary caterpillars and the *mapala* are collected mainly in the early part of the dry season. Although several species of moth may have more than one brood during the year, people associate the caterpillars with specific seasons. And importantly, caterpillars are especially gathered at the beginning of the rainy season, which for subsistence cultivators in Malawi is the 'hungry season', when relish is often scarce. Thus caterpillars provide a valuable source of protein at a difficult time.

The gathering of caterpillars is undertaken by men, women and children, but, as with the gathering of mushrooms (Morris 1987b), it seems to fall principally within women's economic sphere, and they are the primary collectors. In their eclectic gathering in the woodland, or when out collecting firewood – and in rural areas this is an important and time-consuming occupation – women are always on the lookout for caterpillars during the season. The whereabouts of the caterpillars, which often feed high in the crowns of trees, are detected by their droppings on the ground. These are blackish, pellet-like, and some 10–12 mm long. Women will collect the caterpillars by any means possible; hand-picking from the leaves, cutting the branches of the tree, or even cutting down the whole tree. In the Chimaliro forest, which is a part of the Viphya mountains and a protected area, women, I was told, often go to the forest at night to cut down the trees in which caterpillars have been found – thus evading the forest guards. Although recognizing that caterpillars are an important food source for local people, the Department of Forestry has always looked with disfavour on this wanton cutting-down of trees, seeing its role as protecting the forest as a timber resource, as well as its importance in protecting fragile watersheds. For the women, of course, the enterprise is not purely destructive, for not only does the felling give easy access to the caterpillars, but the felled tree may be an important source of future firewood. Sometimes branches holding immature caterpillars may be cut and brought back to the village, where they are allowed to mature before being collected as food.

There is evidence to suggest, as with termites, that the person who first finds a tree in the woodland with caterpillars may lay claim to this resource by marking the tree, putting grass around its base. If the signs of proprietorship are not respected, then disputes may arise, which are taken to be heard by the local chief (*mfumu*). In the case of *mphalabungu*, the children lay claim by making a loop, tying a knot in the grass (Berry and Petty 1992: 91).

There is wide variation in the degree to which caterpillars are considered edible, and cultural and individual factors determine whether or not caterpillars are regarded as edible. Many people I met in Malawi, particularly those living in urban areas or who were devout Christians, refuse to eat caterpillars, and view them with disdain. But in rural areas they are highly regarded, and next to termites, caterpillars are considered the most tasty insect relish. Four species are particularly well-liked: *matondo*, *mapala*, *mabwabwa* and *chilungulungu*. There seem to be wide variations among different ethnic groups in Africa with regard to the utilization of edible caterpillars as food, and Meke notes that many edible caterpillars are not eaten by people in the Liwonde district, although common there (Silow 1976: 206–7; Meke *et al.* 1995: 11).

It is important to realize that the availability of caterpillars is extremely erratic, and within specific localities there are wide variations from year to year in their abundance. In some years caterpillars may be extremely plentiful, and women may be engaged for many days, or even weeks, in collecting the larvae: in other years hardly a caterpillar is to be found. This is true of other edible insects. This variability may relate, not only to predation or climatic factors, but to the burning cycles of *Brachystegia* woodland, for there is evidence to suggest that the early burning of the woodland is conducive to higher caterpillar yields (Munthali and Mughogho 1992: 149).

In the past controlled early burning, particularly through local chiefs, may have been encouraged precisely because late bush-fires tend to destroy the caterpillars (Holden 1991).

We have discussed above the preparation and cooking of the various caterpillars. A common pattern tends to prevail. The gut contents are first squeezed out, and the caterpillars are then washed, and put in a pot with salted water and boiled until dry. Sometimes potashes (*chidulo*) may be added. For future use – and when in abundance caterpillars are often stored or sold in local markets – the caterpillars are put out on rocks for a day to dry. Caterpillars may also by roasted in an earthenware pot or frying pan. Caterpillars are rarely eaten raw, and are either eaten as a snack in a crispy, dry condition, or eaten as a relish with maize porridge, when powdered groundnuts may be added. When stored they are often mixed with dried leaves (*mfutso*) and stored in a gourd cup (*chikho*) or in leaves (*chikwatu*). People recognize that the taste of caterpillars varies with the tree on which the caterpillar feeds, and, as some trees have toxic qualities, such caterpillars are usually boiled thoroughly before eating.

All scholars have emphasized in recent years that edible caterpillars are an important food resource for local people, given that they have a very high protein value. The nutritive value of four edible caterpillars is indicated in Table 2.1.

Table 2.1 Nutritive Values of Four Edible Caterpillars per 100 gm Dry Weight

	Protein (gm)	Fat (gm)	Carbohydrate (gm)	Calories (kcal)
Mabwabwa (*Bunaea alcinoe*)	65.7	10.0	19.3	443
Kawidzi (*Cirina forda*)	51.9	13.0	29.4	447
Mapala (*Imbrasia ertli*)	48.6	11.1	16.9	—
Ntchiu (*Anaphe panda*)	45.6	35.0	9.2	543

Source: After Latham 1999: 138.

As a protein source, caterpillars are of especial importance to the poorest people in rural areas, who cannot afford meat, fish or beans (Meke *et al*. 1995: 10).

In recent years with an expanding human population and extensive deforestation – which has resulted in a loss of *Brachystegia* woodland, particularly in the southern parts of Malawi – caterpillars are becoming increasingly scarce as a food resource. I asked a man on one of the Mulanje tea estates why few caterpillars were eaten by local Lomwe people, and his answer was quite adamant: so much of the land was now under tea estates or village cultivations (mainly maize) that there was little woodland left – and thus no habitat for the caterpillars. Extensive agriculture and high population growth has indeed been the main cause of the rapid decline of Malawi's rich biodiversity. In 1990, both to provide direct economic benefits to the rural communities around Kasungu National Park, and to counter the negative attitudes that local people have towards wildlife protection in Malawi (see Morris 1998: 95–6, 2001), the Department of National Parks and Wildlife initiated a pioneering scheme to encourage wild-life based enterprises within the park – specifically beekeeping and the collection of edible caterpillars. In a seminal paper, significantly titled 'Economic incentives for Conservation', Munthali and Maghogho (1992) describe and assess the viability of the scheme. With regard to caterpillar utilization, two species of caterpillar are involved: *chilungulungu* (*Gonimbrasa belina*) and *matondo* (*Gynanisa maia*). What these scholars emphasized is that in a rural situation where the basic wage was less than 3MK a day, and a kilogram of dried caterpillars sold for 29MK in Kasungu Market, a considerable income could be derived from the sale of caterpillars. Indeed, they go so far as to suggest that caterpillar utilization is superior to agriculture as a source of rural income, and that the gross margin on caterpillar collection was 418MK per ha, as against 174MK per ha for maize cultivation (Munthali and Mughogho 1992: 150–1). They argue that agriculture is 'unsustainable due to low productivity and insufficient income accruing from it' (1992: 144), and they extol caterpillar utilization (and beekeeping) as important in diversifying rural people's economic base. Although promoting cater-pillar collection in National Parks and protected areas is salutary, both as a means of encouraging positive attitudes towards wildlife conservation and in providing economic benefits for local people, three important facts have to be kept in mind in assessing this pioneering scheme.

Firstly, subsistence agriculture in Malawi is not geared to income generation but to subsistence – survival – and many rural households do not even produce enough maize to sustain the household through the year. As Munthali and Mughogho themselves note: 50 per cent of smallholder farmers in the study area run out of food stocks by November each year (1992: 152).

Secondly, caterpillars are entirely non-existent outside the park, owing to the absence of large tracts of *Brachystegia* woodland – and so the conservation area is able to provide caterpillars – whether as a protein source or as income – for only a very limited number of people.

And finally, the erratic occurrence of caterpillars in the park hardly makes caterpillar collecting a viable alternative to subsistence agricul- ture, or even a provider of a regular supplementary income. Mkanda and

Munthali note that while caterpillars occurred in abundance in 1990, in the following two years people were unable to harvest caterpillars (1994: 41). In recent years the data in Table 2.2 below on caterpillar collections in Kasungu National Park are relevant.

Table 2.2 Caterpillar Collections in Kasungu National Park, 1994–2000

Year	Number of collecting days		Caterpillars fresh weight (kg)
1994	8		2,557
1995		No collection	
1996		No collection	
1997	2		No data
1998	3		1,024
1999	12		4,979
2000		No collection	

Source: WRU 50/12/1.

Although the stated aim of the caterpillar collecting is to help communities neighbouring the park – around twelve villages – to generate income and to improve food security, it can be seen from the above data that caterpillar utilization is a very unpredictable enterprise, and is hardly a viable alternative to agriculture as a form of livelihood. In addition many wildlife officers expressed concern at the number of trees felled in the process of collecting caterpillars. One wrote in a report: 'It was really distressing to see the hundreds of mature *Julbernardia paniculata* [trees] down on the ground ... all were mature with a height of at least 5 metres. The estimated damage by local people was about 9 trees per hectare'. Another wildlife officer concluded that the 'wanton felling of trees in the park in the name of *matondo* collection is shameful, disheartening and mind-boggling', and called for clear guidelines and a proper monitoring of caterpillar collecting within the park.

But these records confirm the enthusiasm that women exhibit in collecting the edible caterpillars when they are available, and suggest that the average harvest of an individual woman was around 11 kg dry weight, enabling them to generate about 80MK as income (WRU 50/12/1). In a situation where there is a severe protein shortage among rural people, and the daily wage is only around 3MK per day (1993) the caterpillar collections make a significant contribution to food security. Thus, as Munthali and Mughogho came to conclude, the advantages of caterpillar utilization (along with beekeeping) are: 'Strong incentives for the rural people to adopt wildlife management as an adjunct to conventional subsistence agriculture, and therefore, provide conservation of natural ecosystems and wildlife habitats in the face of growing human population and demand for land' (1992: 152).

–3–

Bees and Bee-keeping

Opportunistic Honey-Hunting among Hunter–Gatherers

Throughout history the gathering of honey by humans has been an important source of food, and 'opportunistic honey hunting' by humans goes back to prehistoric times. This involves simply raiding a bees' nest when found, and harvesting the honeycombs from it. Mesolithic rock art, particularly from Europe and Africa, illustrates the various techniques utilized in honey-gathering, with the use of rope ladders and lianas, as well as portraying bees swarms and collecting baskets. It has been suggested that many of the allegedly 'entopic' figures depicted, such as the concentric circles, may well in fact represent the combs on the underside of rock overhangs (Bodenheimer 1951: 14–15; Crane 1999: 49–51). Humans seem to have an innate liking for sweetness, and this no doubt derives from the importance of fruits and honey among early human communities. Baboons and chimpanzees certainly have a taste for honey, and are especially prone to raid the nests of stingless bees (*Meliponinae*).

Honey-hunting is common and widespread among contemporary hunter–gatherers. As there are no honey-bees (*Apis* spp.) native to Australia, Australian Aborigines harvest the honey – as well as collecting the brood and wax – of small stingless bees (*Trigona* spp.). To locate the 'honeybag' of the bees the hunter–gatherers would examine trees likely to hold nesting colonies, watching for the movement of the bees, or putting their ears close to the trunk of the tree to listen to the sound of the bees through the wood, or they would attach a piece of fluff or a petal to a foraging bee by means of sticky resin, and then follow the bee to its nest. Men, women and children all engage in honey-gathering. The nests are usually to be found in hollow trees, rock crevices or termite mounds. Most of the honey gathered was consumed on the spot. The honey comb was consumed whole, the inedible wax being spat out. Nests of the *Trigona carbonaria* bee yielded about 2 kg of honey (Bodenheimer 1951: 115–25; Cherry 1993a: 10; Crane 1999: 88–90).

Among African hunter–gatherers opportunistic honey-hunting both for the honey-bee (*Apis* sp.) and the stingless bee (*Trigona* sp.) plays an

important, even if sporadic, role in their lives. Honey is almost universally highly valued as food, even though its collection may be unsystematic and quite destructive. James Woodburn thus records that, among the
Hadza of Tanzania, when a nest of wild bees is found and raided for its
honey 'No portion of the comb is left to encourage the bees to stay.
Moreover, little effort is made to leave the nest suitable for reoccupation'
(1968: 53). To illustrate the importance of honey-gathering among
African foragers we can briefly outline studies of two communities, the
Central Kalahari San and the Mbuti of the Ituri forest, Zaire.

The San of the Central Kalahari collect honey from three types of bees.
The first is the honey of *Anthophorid* bees, which resemble small, hairy
carpenter bees. They make nests in the ground, in deep tunnels. The
honey is so thin that it is eaten only as a snack by children. The second
type is the honey from the leafcutter bee (*Megachile* spp.), which is
sporadically collected when cutting firewood, as the bee nests in hollow
stems. The honey is very sweet, and is also given mainly to children. But
the most important is the honey of the honey-bee (*Apis* sp.), which nests
in tree hollows. The San generally come across the bee colonies when out
foraging, although they may search for the bees by following the tracks
of the honey badger, or the flights of bee-eaters. Honey is considered a
'superb delicacy', even if it is only sporadically gathered. Silberbauer
remarks that among the G/wi 'beelore' is remarkably extensive, considering that they rob the nests only infrequently, and that the 'notorious
aggressiveness' of the African honey-bee hardly allows close observation
(Silberbauer 1981: 76, Nonaka 1996: 35).

Interestingly, R. B. Lee's detailed study of the !Kung San (1979) has
little mention of honey-gathering among these people, whose diet seems
to focus around meat and *mongongo* nuts, while Marshall notes that,
though they 'delight in honey', they seldom find it (1976: 129).

In contrast, honey-gathering among the Mbuti of the Ituri forest is of
vital importance in their socio-economic life, especially during the honey
season, which lasts around two months (May–July), when the net-hunting
bands split up into smaller groups. They recognize many different kinds
of honey, and collect honey from more than ten species of bees, although
the bulk of the honey gathered is that of the African honey-bee (*Apis
mellifera adansonii*), which nests in hollow branches up to 30 metres high
in the forest trees. Other honey gathered is that of stingless bees, which
nest low down in trees, or in the ground. While honey from the *Apis* bee
is always collected by men and youths who can climb the high trees,
women often collect the honey of the stingless bees, which belong to
several genera (including the species *Meliponula bocandei, Trigona
braunsi* and *Dactylurina staudingeri*). The Mbuti suggest that the honey

from the stingless bees can be toxic and cause diarrhoea, or aching joints. Honey is their favourite food, and Turnbull writes that: 'There is a craving for honey during the season that never seems to be satisfied. No amount of alternative foods, even meat, can reduce this passion for honey' (1965: 170).

In a seminal paper on the ecological and sociological aspects of honey-collecting among the Mbuti, Mitsuo Ichikawa notes that during the months of May to July it is their main subsistence activity. The Mbuti, like other forest hunter–gatherers, are skilful tree climbers, and collect honey usually in the early morning. Within a few hours a person may find 2–3 hives. When the bee colony is opened, they blow in smoke through a tube, and do not seem unduly worried by the bees, in spite of the 'aggressive' reputation of African honey-bees. During a twelve-day period at one camp, Ichikawa recorded that they collected honey from the hives of forty-five honey-bees and four stingless bees. This amounted to 229 kg of honey, and as the camp consisted of twenty-three persons, it was estimated that 0.83 kg of honey was consumed by each person per day. Thus during the honey season honey was not only deemed to be their favourite food, but constituted around 70 per cent of their diet – and 80 per cent of their calorific intake. Equally importantly, honey is widely shared in the camp, and thus, as Ichikawa writes, it functions as a 'lubricant' of social relationships. Opportunistic honey-hunting is thus not only important to the Mbuti from a nutritional point of view, but also structurally (Turnbull 1965; 168, Ichikawa 1981: 59–65).

Although the Mbuti have, historically, a close 'symbiotic' relationship with neighbouring agriculturalists, they seem to trade very little honey – unlike the Hadza and the forest hunter–gatherers of South Asia (see my study of the Hill Pandaram of South India, *Forest Traders*, for details of honey-gathering and trade among these foragers 1982: 84–7).

Opportunistic bee-hunting is, of course, widespread throughout Africa, and by no means confined to hunter–gatherers. Over the past two millennia it has been, perhaps, the main means of acquiring honey among subsistence cultivators. Indeed, given the fact that much of sub-Saharan Africa is covered with either tropical forest or open savannah woodland, a *Brachystegia*-type woodland familiarly known as *miombo* woodland (cf. Morris 1970; Malaisse 1978), the African sub-continent has been described as 'good bee country' (Crane 1999: 49). In Malawi, and elsewhere in Africa, the unsystematic collection of honey, from both the honey-bee and the stingless bee, has been a common practice for many centuries. Whenever bees established nests in grain silos at Zoa half a century ago, it was never difficult to find local men willing and able to remove the colony of bees – and collect their honey in the process. But opportunistic honey-gathering, whether from rock crevices or hollow trees, is sporadic and limited. It simply involves the finding of the nest – and in the past, the behaviour of a small bird, appropriately named the honey-guide (*Indicator indicator*), may have been significant in this (see Laws 1934: 240; Foran 1958: 124–8; Hooper 1989) – the use of an axe, hoe or panga to open up the nest cavity, and the smoking of the bees. The collection of honey is often described as simply a 'raid' on the hive. As with the Hadza, this could often be a destructive exercise – and, as Alex Banda (1991) suggests, quite dangerous (one of my close Hill Pandaram friends, Kuttan, though an expert climber, lost his life after falling from a tree while collecting honey from the large Asian bee *Apis dorsata*).

Traditional Bee-keeping

As the African honey-bee, unlike its Asian counterpart, is a cavity-nesting bee, bee keeping using fixed hives developed in Africa from a very early period. Indeed, so-called 'traditional' bee-keeping was evident in Egypt from around 2400 BC. Bees and honey are mentioned several times in the Bible, and though the phrase may be simply metaphorical Canaan is described as 'a land flowing with milk and honey' (Exodus 3:17). Both wax and honey were important as items of trade, and wax had invaluable uses for writing tablets, for candles, and for embalming (Cansdale 1970: 245). Several factors may have been conducive to the development of bee-keeping – an abundance of bee forage but a lack of suitable nesting sites, a growing human population that practised agriculture and had an increasing need for honey and wax, and the availability of pots and baskets to make suitable hives (Crane 1999: 161). Thus the earliest records that we have of African peoples south of the Sahara, including those in Malawi, suggest that bee-keeping was widely practised. It involved the making of artificial beehives of various kinds and placing these high in trees in a suitable woodland locality. Among the more common types were cylindrical bark-hives made from the outer bark of *Brachystegia* trees, log hives, woven or basket hives made of split bamboo or various plant materials, and clay pots. The making of these hives often indicated superb craftsmanship. There was, however, less ingenuity in bee-management in Africa, Crane suggests, than in other more temperate parts of the world (1999: 258).

In Malawi, as throughout much of south-central Africa where *Brachystegia* woodland is predominant, log and bark hives seem to have been in common use during the pre-colonial era. The cylindrical bark hives, made from the outer bark of *mombo* (*Brachystegia Boehmii*) meas-ured around 150 cm long and 40 cm in diameter. The log hives were usually made of the wood of the *mlombwa* (*Pterocarpus angolensis*) or *mtondo* (*Cordyla africana*) trees. But considerable skills were utilized by local people in their bee-keeping, although the African honey-bee (*Apis mellifera*) is notorious for its swarming habits. For not only is there the normal reproductive swarm, in which around half the worker bees swarm and with the old queen bee search out a new nesting site – such swarms can be very spectacular, but the whole colony may at times abscond, leaving a particular site in search of new foraging areas for food, or because unduly disturbed. It is estimated that more than 90 per cent of the absconding bee colonies in Malawi are due to the lack of food resources at a particular site (A. S. Banda *et al.* 1991: 46). Local bee-keepers therefore use various aromatic herbs, such as *mpungabwe* (*Ocimum canum*) to induce the bees to colonize the hives, as well as smearing the interior of the hives with wax or propolis – the resin collected by bees from various trees. Yet, to be successful, local bee-keepers had to know which were the best sites in which to place the hives, both in relation to microclimatic conditions and suitable forage, how best to make the artificial hives attractive to bees, and how to counter the maraudings of ants and the honey badger.

Contemporary bee-keepers, like earlier colonial administrators, tend to emphasize the destructive nature of traditional bee-keeping – the making of a log or bark hive involved the destruction of a mature tree, and the harvesting of the honey often entailed the liberal use of smoke and fire, which resulted in the colony's either being killed or absconding, or even in the burning of the woodland itself. In ecological terms traditional bee-keeping is therefore deemed to be both expensive and outdated. But the economic importance of honey in pre-colonial Africa, including Malawi, cannot be doubted – as a food resource, in the making of alcoholic drinks, and in the use of both honey and wax as items of trade, as well as its having a cultural significance (on early bee-keeping in Africa see Bodenheimer 1951: 165–85; Crane 1999: 258–69).

Although bee-keeping was always important as an economic activity in Malawi, over the last fifty years or so the craft has largely disappeared. This has been due mainly to an increasing human population – which has doubled since I first came to Malawi in 1958, and now stands at over 10 million; and this growth has largely been at the expense of the *Brachystegia* woodland. The opening up of areas for subsistence agriculture, as well as the development of estates devoted to such cash crops as tea, coffee and tobacco, has inevitably led to a reduction in areas of woodland for bee forage. In addition, around 20 per cent of Malawi's land area is protected, either as forest reserves or as wildlife protection areas. Honey-hunting and traditional bee-keeping – like hunting – have therefore become marginal activities among Malawian people, even though the demand for honey among the urban population is high. This has led in recent years to a sustained effort, on the part of the Malawi government and various development agencies, to encourage modern methods of bee-keeping.

Bees and Beeswax

In Malawi the honey from three types of bees is widely recognized, even though the honey of the stingless bee is infrequently gathered, and then only by means of opportunistic honey-hunting.

The first of these is the small mining bee *mpasi* (family *Halictidae*), which lives in small colonies, usually in the ground, and often in a bank. Several species may be involved – but the group has been little studied in Malawi, although over seventy species have been described from Africa. The honey of the *mpasi* is well liked. Little is known of this family of bees, and there appears to be no record in the literature of people gathering its honey (cf. Crane 1999), and I am reliant on Sweeney regarding its identification (1970: 217).

The second is the so-called *mopane* bee, *nsikisa* (*Trigona bottegoi*), tiny stingless bees that construct their nests in crevices in walls or rocks, in hollow trees, or in termite mounds. There is usually a slender tube at the entrance of the nest. Again, several species of the sub-family *Meliponidae* are probably involved. Both the honey and the brood of these bees are eaten by Malawians; the honey is very sweet, well liked, and usually described as *tongole*. The honey of stingless bees is eaten throughout Africa, and in many other parts of the world (Crane 1999: 15–16). But neither species of the stingless bees is well known to many Malawians, as opposed to being simply recognized. The honey of these bees often has toxic qualities, and may cause illness; but as with the edible caterpillars, the toxins may derive from the trees on which the bees feed, rather than from the honey itself (Crane 1999: 61).

It is the third species of social bee that is familiar to Malawians, the African honey-bee *njuchi* (*Apis mellifera*) – which is ubiquitous throughout the country. The Malawi honey-bee belongs to the sub-species *Apis mellifera scutellata*, which is the common savannah bee of east and southern Africa, and like many members of the genus (but not all), it nests in cavities and has multiple comb nests. On Nyika plateau, above 1,500 m, the mountain bee of east Africa, *Apis mellifera monticola*, is found. It is larger and darker than the common honey-bee.

The African honey-bee has a reputation for aggressiveness, and for its readiness to defend its colonies, often fiercely attacking people without any provocation. When exploring a dry river-bed in Mwabvi game reserve, looking for bushpig and hyrax, accompanied by a Malawian game guard, I was viciously attacked by the bees, and stung about ten times. I was quite unaware of their nest, and spent the night sweating, intensely itching and experiencing a kind of out-of body feeling ... which lasted about six hours. Several deaths of young children stung by a swarm of bees have been recorded from Malawi, and the newspapers regularly report bees attacking mourners at a funeral – which usually take place in a wooded graveyard (*manda*) – so that the ceremony has had to be abandoned. One report described how the bees had 'launched' their attack from a hive in a nearby tree, and many people 'ran for their lives including the flower carrying women'. The bees, it noted, landed on the coffin, putting an end to the whole of the proceedings (*Daily Times* 28 August, 1998).

Yet I have seen Malawians taking honey from nests in hollow trees or houses, wearing no protective clothing and seemingly untroubled by the bees, as well as bee-keeping handbooks that carry photographs of young African boys opening, and helping themselves to the honey from, top-bar hives, dressed in ordinary clothes and without any protection at all (Clauss 1982). Not understanding and puzzled by this seeming contradiction, I asked an experienced bee-keeper at Zoa Biton Gulumba, to explain to me the real nature of African bees. His response was quite simple. Bees are not usually angry or hostile; they are normally gentle creatures, and only become aggressive when under stress. If he receives reports, he told me, that his bees are attacking women working in the gardens that are close to his hives he simply ascertains what is troubling the bees. Are they being attacked by ants (*nyerere*), or being unduly disturbed, or is the hive short of food or water? He then, he suggested to me, did what he could to rectify the situation. Moreover, he stressed to me that the smoking of bees was not to subdue them, or in any way injure them, but rather to make them docile, and any kind of material that produces acrid smoke, such as paraffin, only serves to make the bees angry (*-kwiya, -bvuta*), and thus more likely to attack the intruder. He always used dried cow dung, and swore by it. In east Africa the dried powder from the puffball fungus (*Lycoperdon* sp.) is used to 'stupefy' the bees (Bodenheimer 1951: 175). The smoking of bees must therefore be done gently and with care, and with materials that have an appropriate aroma. Apparently, the bees suspect bushfire, and so will fill themselves with honey. They then become slow and docile and less likely to sting (Clauss 1982: 31). Killing bees also makes other members of the hive agitated and angry, and liable to attack anything that moves.

In his encyclopaedic study on *British Central Africa* the early adminis-trator Harry Johnston recorded that honey-bees were found throughout Malawi in all forested areas, and made delicious honey and excellent wax. He noted two things: one was the importance of wax as an article of export; the other was that local bees were 'very ill-tempered', that he had been attacked by a swarm of bees while travelling in the upper Shire valley, and that bees were a great nuisance in the houses in Zomba, then the capital of the protectorate (1897: 374). We may briefly discuss both these issues.

Throughout the colonial period exports of beeswax from Malawi (then Nyasaland) were an important item of trade. In 1891 the first beeswax was exported from the country, and in 1895, 2.5 tons (valued at £174) was exported. Along with *Strophanthus*, beeswax reached an export peak in 1906, with an export of 58 tons (£6,000) of beeswax. Although beeswax continued to be exported in later years, virtually without a break, its rela-tive importance declined, and along with such indigenous products as ivory and *Strophanthus*, as an export commodity beeswax gave way to such export crops as tobacco, tea and cotton (C. A. Baker 1962: 18). As beeswax had a relatively high market value throughout the colonial period, the government attempted to encourage the collection of wax by local people. Bee-keeping seemed to be fairly widespread, with cylindrical hives made from the bark of a tree, but the method of collecting the honey, one administrator remarked, tended to be rather extravagant, for often the majority of the bees in the hive were killed by the use of fire. The response to government requests was varied, but in 1933 beeswax exported from Nyasaland had the value of £1,348. In the ten-year period prior to the Second World War the value of beeswax exported annually varied from £455 to £1,492, averaging £940 (MNA/NN/1/3/1, M2/24/15). This indi-cates that traditional bee-keeping was commonly practised throughout the colonial period. It is worth noting that yields from traditional bee-keeping range from 7–10 kg of honey and about 1 kg of wax per hive, with a maximum of as much as 39 kg of honey (Peham 1996).

The other issue relating to bees that concerned the colonial adminis-tration was the continual invasion of bees into the houses and government offices in Zomba. Attacks from bees often hindered administrative work, and the public works department (PWD) was continually called in to clear buildings of what had become a troublesome pest – a 'very disagreeable nuisance', as one administrator put it. Local bee-keepers were engaged by the PWD to undertake the task of removing the bees, and, when all else failed, local medicine was used as an insecticide to kill the bees – the well-known herb *mlozi* (Y, *mkuta*), *Adenia gummifera*. As Williamson records, the roots of this plant, which contain cyanogenetic glycoside, are dug and burnt, fresh or dried, and the smoke is used to stupefy the bees (1975: 21, MNA/51/544/20).

The Introduction of Modern Bee-keeping

Although bee-keeping with frame hives had first been introduced by early missionaries at the end of the nineteenth century, throughout much of the colonial period the collecting of honey was either through traditional bee-keeping methods, or by sporadic and rather opportunistic 'raiding' of the hives in order to obtain the honey. Soon after independence the Malawi government, principally through the Ministry of Agriculture, began to implement various feasibility studies and surveys in order to ascertain the viability of bee-keeping and to encourage the development of bee-keeping projects. The aim was both to increase the production of honey and beeswax – for there was little honey available in the shops, and it was at a very high price by local standards, and also to provide a viable source of alternative income for rural people. Between 1968 and 1973 a bee-keeping survey was established in the northern region, at Mzimba, Karonga and Rumphi, by the Agricultural Planning Unit. Some fourteen bee-keepers were recorded, with around, 1978 hives, and they produced 2,630 kg of honey and 295 kg of wax (A. S. Banda *et al.* 1991: 3). In the following decade further small projects were established at Salima and in the vicinity of Nyika National Park. But the important breakthrough came in July 1989, with the establishment of the Malawi German Beekeeping Development Project, with its headquarters at Mzuzu, and with financial assistance from the German government through GTZ. Its overall aim was to develop modern bee-keeping throughout Malawi. Its main focus of attention, however, was on the 'border zone' adjacent to Nyika National Park, the largest conservation area in Malawi, covering an area of some 3,134 km^2. An important water catchment area, and holding viable populations of the larger mammals – particularly zebra, reedbuck, eland, roan, leopard and hyena, the park was enlarged in 1978 to include all the escarpment areas. This involved the resettlement of several local villages to other areas (S. A. Johnson 1995: 11). As access to the park was denied – areas that had formerly been used for subsistence hunting as well as for bee-keeping – much resentment was created between local people and the Department of National Parks and Wildlife. This enmity, it was realized, was not conducive to long-term wildlife conservation. With the introduction of community-based wildlife conservation in the 1980s, largely inspired by the late Richard Bell, who had been research officer at Kasungu National Park (see my article on wildlife conservation in Malawi, Morris 2001a), it was felt that it was important to allow local people to utilize resources within the conservation area on a controlled and sustainable basis. The most important resource, besides edible caterpillars, was of course honey – particularly as there was a long tradition of bee-keeping in the area. The bee-keeping project therefore had two principal objectives:

1. To induce a change of attitude among local people around the national park towards the conservation of natural resources – especially the wildlife, which was an important tourist attraction.
2. To develop bee-keeping as an alternative income-generating activity for rural people, who are principally subsistence agriculturalists. In addition, through the project it was hoped to make honey more readily available, and at an affordable price, for the average Malawian salary-earner (A. S. Banda *et al.* 1991: 6).

In order to achieve these objectives the project, over the seven years of its existence – it was phased out in 1996, attempted in a number of ways to develop bee-keeping as an economically viable activity among rural people – by helping to establish bee-keeping clubs, and giving training, advice and support to local bee-keepers; by training extension workers in bee-keeping; by encouraging local NGO's to support and take over bee-keeping projects, especially those relating to the marketing of honey and wax; and to introduce modern bee-keeping methods that were both affordable and sustainable. It also produced a 'Beekeeping Handbook', but this was never available to the general public, though some material found its way into a useful booklet 'Kuweta Njuchi' ('conserve the bee'), written in Nyanja by Francis Epulani, and produced by the Wildlife Society of Malawi, with the support of GTZ.

The project recognized and emphasized the fact that successful bee-keeping was only possible if certain crucial conditions were met. What was essentially needed was an area of woodland in which hives could be placed, and which held enough suitable vegetation – the 'bee pasture' – to enable bees to collect nectar (for honey), pollen (for bee bread) and propolis (resin for sealing the hives). Climatic conditions and access to water were also crucial. The project also emphasized the important benefits that local people could derive from bee-keeping – the honey, which is particularly nourishing and well-liked; a viable source of income from the sale of honey and wax; the ecological importance of bees as pollinators – essential in the generation of plants; the enjoyment that bee-keeping offered as an activity or pastime; and the fact the bee-keeping does not compete with other agricultural activities. But what was particularly important about the project was in the promotion of the top bar hive as the most viable form of hive for local bee-keepers – in contrast to both the traditional log or bark hives and the frame hives that had long been used by European bee-keepers. The top bar hive is in the form of a long box, measuring some 120 cm × 50 cm, with sloping sides and a narrow base, and a movable protective lid. The most common timber used for the hive is *malaina* (*Gmelina arborea*), which is rich in resin and resistant to termites. Entrances to the hive consist of ten small triangular holes 10 mm across at one end. The hive is hung from a tree 1–3 m from the ground by means of a wire.

In many of the project's reports the name of the American clergyman/ bee-keeper the Rev. L. L. Langstroth is often mentioned. For in 1851 Langstroth essentially perfected the first practical hive with movable frames – the frame hive, for he noticed that bees in building their combs respect a gap of 8–9 mm – what he described in his notebook as 'bee space'. The colony strictly follows this rule, to enable bees to move freely on adjacent comb surfaces. Yet although the frame hives are now the most sophisticated and, under certain conditions, the most productive of all hives, yielding high-quality honey, they are expensive and exacting to make, especially for an ordinary village carpenter. The project therefore decided to promote the top bar hive developed in Kenya in the 1970s. Here a project team discovered that if top bars, exactly 33 mm wide, were placed in a wooden hive with sides sloping at an angle of 67 degrees the bees left a 'bee space' both between the combs and the sloping walls. This made possible the making of a much simpler hive, with top bars instead of frames (A. S. Banda *et al.* 1991; Crane 1999: 422). The top bar hive (*mng'oma*) has the advantages that it is easily made by a local carpenter, has small entrance holes at the side that keep out natural enemies, especially 'robber' bees, and is easily opened and inspected, with a movable lid and removable top bars. It has a disadvantage in that combs easily break if not held in an upright position. Top bar hives may be placed on stands, but usually they are hung by wire in suitable localities – either in gardens where bee forage is plentiful or in the woodland.

Bee-keeping Clubs

An important aspect of the Malawi–German Beekeeping Development Project was the establishment of bee-keeping clubs in the 'border zone' areas neighbouring Nyika National Park and the Vwaza Game Reserve. As most of the extension workers from the Department of National Parks and Wildlife had no experience themselves with bee-keeping, the staff involved in the bee-keeping project had initially to be trained, at a series of workshops, in the theoretical and practical aspects of bee-keeping, and in the harvesting and processing of honey and beeswax. It seems that extension workers and the potential bee-keepers underwent this training at almost the same time. The bee-keepers were also offered support by the project in the formation and registration of bee-keeping clubs, and offered loans in order to purchase bee-keeping equipment – protective clothing being especially emphasized, although in the past men tended to collect honey clothed only in the briefest shorts! By 1997 some 104 bee-keeping clubs had been formed, with an overall membership of 872 bee-keepers – interested people were organized in groups of around ten – the majority (612) being men. However, some nineteen bee-keeping clubs consisted of women only. They utilized both top bar hives and the traditional log and bark hives. The top bar hives numbered 1,746, around 75 per cent of the hives containing bee colonies; while traditional hives numbered 852 hives, with 70 per cent holding bees. This only amounts to three hives per person.

In his important report on the bee-keeping clubs Alex Banda (1997) recorded that the average production of honey for the whole project area for the 1995/6 season was around 8 kg per colonized hive. But some individual clubs produce more honey, averaging 12–15 kg per hive, and some individual hives in the Phoka area yielded up to 40 kg per hive. He noted that youth involvement in bee-keeping was very minimal. Although the Department of National Parks and Wildlife was the main agency in initiating the bee-keeping project, both the forestry department and community development agencies have extension officers involved in promoting and supporting bee-keeping clubs. As it was decided that all project activities should eventually be taken over by a non-governmental organization, rather than being the concern of government, in 1992 the Beekeepers' Association of Malawi was formed. It had as its primary role the marketing of honey and wax collected by the various bee-keeping clubs. However, the Association soon ran into difficulties and became defunct; but over sixty bee-keeping clubs still continue to flourish in the Nyika/Vwaza area, supported by extension staff of the Department of National Parks and Wildlife. Most of the honey now available in the shops in Malawi comes from this area, and is produced by these bee-keeping clubs (A. S. Banda 2001). Even more encouragingly, largely stimulated by the German-funded project, bee-keeping using top bar hives has spread throughout Malawi, supported by development and conservation agencies such as World Vision and the Wildlife Society of Malawi. Many tobacco and tea estates now have bee-keeping projects, and in suitable locations gardens in Blantyre, Lilongwe and Zomba may hold a number of top bar hives. Even so, one person I know, a highly respected agricultural consultant, had to abandon the idea of keeping bees in his garden, as the bees continually attacked the gardener!

But one problem that is troubling bee-keepers is the high degree of vandalism that seems evident – either the wilful destruction of hives or the theft of honey. This vandalism severely limits the expected income of the bee-keepers. Vandalism may thus either be perpetrated professionally by other bee-keepers, who simply rob the hive – this takes place usually outside the national park – or committed within the park, this usually involving the destruction or burning of the hives by poachers (Berg and Critchlow 2001).

A similar but smaller project to encourage bee-keeping was established at Kasungu National Park. By allowing people to practise bee-keeping within the park, the aim was thus both to change people's attitudes towards the park – then extremely negative – so that they would come to support wildlife conservation; and to develop income-generating activities that might supplement agriculture among the subsistence cultivators living outside the park. Bee-keeping, it was felt, along with caterpillar collection (discussed in the last chapter) could help rural people to diversify their economic base. In a survey of public attitudes towards the conservation area, it was found that honey was the most coveted resource that people would like to derive from the park – followed by caterpillars, firewood and building materials – and that 90 per cent of people who responded to the questionnaire expressed the wish to be involved in the bee-keeping project (Mkanda and Munthali 1994).

The bee-keeping project in Kasungu National Park was initiated in 1990, and three years later it had six bee-keeping clubs that seemed to be flourishing, each club consisting of ten members. Most of the clubs had harvested once or twice, but extension workers felt that the club members were over-optimistic about potential financial returns – which were felt to be rather small. The six clubs had fifty hives, some 76 per cent (38) of which were occupied by bees. Honey was harvested in June and December and amounted to 199 kg, that is 5 kg per occupied hive, and 33 kg per bee-keeping club. The following year (1994) five new clubs were formed. Membership of the clubs seemed to consist only of men, none of whom could be classified as a resource-poor farmer. As the formation of the bee-keeping clubs was supported by a grant of 28,000MK from the World Wildlife Fund, and as the potential earnings of a member of a bee-keeping club were estimated at only 30MK per year – the project seems to have fallen far short of its goal (WRU/1/54/10).

Collecting Honey

In discussions I had with Biton Gulumba it is clear that one of the difficulties bee-keepers face in Malawi, whether they use bark or a log hive, or the top bar hive, is that bee populations are extremely unstable. Within any apiary, many of the hives at any one time do not hold a colony of bees – as the above records indicate. People like Biton therefore spend an inordinate amount of time and care encouraging bees to colonize particular hives – making sure that the entrance is downwind, and not troubled by adverse local climatic conditions; rubbing the hives with beeswax and propolis, or using aromatic herbs such as lemon grass (*Cymbopogon citratus*) or beer residues to encourage a bee swarm to take up residence in a hive; and selecting a site for the hive where there is adequate forage and a perennial water supply. All the hives at Zoa were thus placed by Biton close to riparian forest or near dams. He also took great care to ensure that no ants (*nyerere*) could gain access to the hives, cutting down branches and creepers near the hive, and smearing the wires that hold the top bar hives with a liberal amount of engine oil or grease, which the ants disliked intensely. If the red driver ants (*linthumbu*) reach the hive they can completely destroy the colony. Any disturbance to the hive at any time of year, bushfires, human interference, too much wind, the intrusion of ants (whether the small *nyerere* or the *linthumbu*), pests such as the waxmoth, and most important of all, a lack of food (bee fodder) will cause the bees to 'abscond' – completely leaving the hive. The highest incidence of absconding occurs in the dry season, which is the main swarming time. Biton regularly opened up his hives, to inspect them, and to make sure that the bees were content and not agitated. But out of eighty-four hives that he tended, only 76 per cent (64) produced honey, and his harvest for the year (2000) was seventy-one candles, nine wax tables and 82 litres of pure honey. As on the Nyika, vandalism and theft were an acute problem at Zoa. Interestingly, Biton always insisted that the top bar hive needed only five entrance holes.

The collection of honey (*ku fula uchi*) at Zoa took place around dusk – when the bees were settled. Biton already had a sense of which hives would contain honey, and always wore protective clothing. He had his equipment ready at hand, torch, plastic bucket, knife, dried cow dung wrapped in a piece of hessian, matches, a rope. He first climbed the tree, released the wire that holds the top bar hive (*mng'oma, syn. mzinga, muoma*) and gently lowered the hive to the ground using the rope, having already cut back the undergrowth beneath the tree. He then smoked the bees, gently blowing the smoke from the smouldering cow dung into the hive. Carefully lifting the lid, he inspected the colony to ascertain its condition and contents. Honey, he suggested to me, is usually ready for collection some 3–5 months after the bees first entered the hive. If there are 5–6 honeycombs available, Biton only takes 3–4 combs, and always left 1–2 combs for the bees: otherwise, he said, they would starve (*njala*).

He tries not to disturb the queen, or the bee brood towards the front of the hive. As there are some thirty top bars to a hive, the queen bee (*dzimwe, m'manthu*) is usually positioned towards the middle 9–12 bars. Biton took the greatest care not to harm any of the bees – for any bee that stings the clothing, or is crushed accidentally, not only reduces the bee colony, but agitates the other members of the colony, which can then become very aggressive. Often a person has to stop collecting honey, since the bees have become too aggressive. There is in Malawi, as elsewhere, an extensive vocabulary focused around bee-keeping; the honeycomb (*chisa*), honey (*uchi, madzi anjuchi*), the bee swarm (*nthenje*), the larvae (*ana anjuchi*), eggs (*madzira*), beeswax (*sera, phula*) and a bee sting (*-nyeteza*), while the bees' mating flight is described as *ku-kwatana* ('to mate'). Malawians, of course, are not only fond of honey, but also eat the bee brood, either raw or roasted, sometimes with pounded groundnuts. The nutritional value of honey hardly needs emphasizing: ripe honey contains less than 18 per cent water, about 79 per cent honey, and 3 per cent other substances, such as minerals, proteins and vitamins. Honey naturally crystallizes. It also has high energy value, 280–330 kcal/100g. Its medicinal properties are also well documented, and throughout history honey has played an important part in religious rituals and art (Crane 1999: 593–608).

Harvesting of the honey usually takes place during two main seasons, September–November, when *Brachystegia* spp. are in flower, and at the end of the rains, from March onwards, depending on the locality and the flowering of the woodland trees. But Biton wrote in his notebook that with regular feeding (of sugar solution) and under 'good and beautiful management' (as he expressed it in English) honey could be harvested four times a year. Although in most cases traditional hives yield less than 10 kg of honey per year, under good conditions a productive colony in a top bar hive may produce around 30 kg of honey in a year.

To conclude, we may note that while bees forage on a variety of plants – as can be seen in any garden – not every plant is a bee plant. In *Brachystegia* woodland the most important plants foraged by bees are the following:

Nyowe	*Syzygium cordatum*
Tsamba/Mombo	*Brachystegia* spp.
Kamponi	*Julbernardia globiflora*
Msolo	*Pseudolachnostylis maprouneifolia*
Muula	*Parinari curatellifolia*
Chitimba	*Piliostigma thonningii*
Msuku	*Uapaca kirkiana*

In spite of widespread deforestation honey-bees are still common in Malawi, and there seems plenty of scope for further developing bee-keeping as a viable rural occupation, for honey is an important and vital source of food, as well as providing a useful supplement to household income if marketed.

–4–

Insects and Agriculture

Agriculture in Malawi

An insect pest is often described as any insect that is in the wrong place – from a human point of view. It has been defined as those species that are injurious or a nuisance, and the control of which is felt necessary for social or economic well-being. Thus any insect that does economic damage to crops or domestic animals, or is harmful to human health, constitutes a pest (Clark 1970; Dempster 1975). The Nyanja concept *chirombo* encompasses this notion, and it implies a relationship of conflict or opposition between humans and insects.

There is a general recognized feeling that in Africa at the present moment humans 'are waging an undeclared war against insects in the competitive struggle for existence'; as Kumar puts it (1984: 4), and almost no crop in Africa is free from attacks by insects, at least to some degree. It is estimated worldwide that crop losses from insects amounts to around 14 per cent of the potential crop (1984: 8), and this figure may be higher in Africa. Given these losses to subsistence farmers in 1996 the Malawi government instituted a four-year project, supported by the British government through the Department for International Development (DFID), and costing some £1.7 million. The aim of the project was to improve the welfare of poor farmers in Malawi by reducing crop losses from insect pests, weeds and diseases, and to encourage the adoption of low-cost, sustainable pest-management strategies. The project focused on four important food crops grown by smallholder farmers in the Shire Highlands – maize, beans, pigeonpea and sweet potato – and advocated an integrated pest-management strategy involving biological, chemical and cultural forms of pest control (cf. Van Alebeek 1989). Although this was heralded as a new approach, the combination of various strategies of control in relation to insect pests – integrated pest management (IPM) – had been advocated by the government entomologist Colin Smee some 80 years ago.

But members of the project soon recognized that pest management alone could not solve the acute problems facing smallholder farmers in

Malawi, locked as they are within the capitalist system, with declining soil fertility, high costs of fertilizer and low prices for agricultural products (Orr *et al.* 2000).

Malawi is one of the poorest countries in Africa, with an estimated population of 11 million, and an annual population growth of 3.2 per cent. It has one of the highest population densities in Africa, 96 persons/sq. km, low urbanization (12 per cent), and a very low GNP per capita of US$210 (1992). Thus the average Malawian has an income of around half a dollar a day. As in the rest of the world, income inequalities are high, and a rich person in Malawi – whether a Malawian or an expatriate – may spend more on a Sunday lunch in Mount Soche Hotel in Blantyre than an agricultural worker will earn in a whole month – roughly the equivalent of US$14 (2001). Life expectancy at birth is 44 years, and more than one in five children in Malawi die before the age of five years – this mortality being mainly due to malaria and malnutrition.

Although agriculture only contributes around 35 per cent of the GDP, it employs almost 90 per cent of the workforce, and accounts for about 90 per cent of the foreign exchange earnings – largely from the export of such agricultural crops as tobacco, tea, coffee and sugar. These are produced mainly in the estate sector, which has expanded rapidly since the 1970s and now covers an estimated area of 1.2 million ha. Around 40 per cent of the cropped land on estates is under tobacco, which constitutes over 70 per cent of export earnings. The Malawian economy is therefore highly dependent on tobacco. The smallholder sector is mainly focused on subsistence food production, and within this sector – of around 3 million ha – over 80 per cent of the cultivated land is under maize. Thus smallholder agriculture is the primary means of livelihood for the majority of Malawians. But with a growing population there has, however, been an increasing pressure on land, with a reduction in soil fertility on cultivated land through continuous maize cropping, and expansion into marginal areas, with adverse environmental consequences – deforestation and a loss of biodiversity. Overall per capita food production – especially with regard to maize, cassava, sorghum and groundnuts – has decreased, along with the size of smallholdings. It is generally recognized that under subsistence agriculture holdings of less than 1 ha are not viable, and cannot provide the household with its basic food requirements. Around 50 per cent of rural households, however, now cultivate less than one hectare of land, and over 30 per cent of these households are described as 'female-headed', in the sense of having no attached male. Under these circumstances it is not surprising that around 60 per cent of Malawians in rural areas live below the poverty line – one based on the basic needs for food, clothing and shelter. As most households are unable to produce their basic food requirements, let alone a viable cash crop, most rural Malawians are thus forced to seek alternative sources of livelihood, or sell what little agricultural crops they have in order to obtain a cash income to buy such basic requirements as soap, paraffin and clothing (NRI 1996).

It is within this setting that the ravages of insect pests in Malawi have to be understood; and although insects make a crucial impact on rural livelihoods, most rural people in Malawi respond to their crop losses with either disregard or equanimity. In this chapter I shall focus on those insect pests that damage the main crops in Malawi, specifically in relation to three contexts: the main subsistence crops associated with the cultivations (*munda*) – maize, sorghum, beans, pigeonpea, cassava, groundnuts, sweet potato – although in Malawi there is no clear-cut division between subsistence and cash crops; those crops associated with smallholder agriculture that are specifically grown for the market – cotton, and such vegetables as tomato and cabbage, which are grown in low-lying or irrigated *dimba* gardens; and finally those commercial crops associated with the estates – tea, coffee, tobacco and sugar. Again, it is important to note that some crops – tea, tobacco, maize – are grown in both the smallholder and the estate sectors.

Insect Pests and Subsistence Crops

Maize, Chimanga (Zea Mays)

Maize is cultivated throughout Malawi, and from planting, usually at the onset of the rains, until harvest takes from four to five months. It forms the staple food of all Malawians, being cooked as a stiff porridge (*nsima*), as well as fed to children as a thin gruel (*phala*). Around 65 per cent (1,326,978 ha) of the total cultivated area of Malawi is under maize production. Sorghum and millet are also cultivated, but on a much smaller scale. Owing to over-cropping and subsequent loss of soil fertility, average yields of local maize varieties have fallen over the last decade, and are now less than 900 kg/ha (NRI 1996: 28).

Numerous insect pests attack maize (and the allied cereals), but there are wide variations in the insects involved and the degree of severity of the attack, and in relation to the stage in the plants' life-cycle at which they are attacked. The following are the six major insect pests associated with maize:

Armyworm, Ntchembere Zandondo (Spodoptera exempta) (Family: Noctuidae). This is one of the most serious pests of maize as well as of other cereal crops, as the caterpillars are particularly associated with two families, *Gramineae* and *Cyperaceae*. The adult moths are of migratory habits and disperse over long distances, sometimes hundreds of kilometres, immediately after emergence. Outbreaks of the caterpillars occur at sporadic intervals, and it has the habit of appearing suddenly in vast numbers, moving through the maize gardens like an 'army' – hence its name. In fact it appears to have two phases: a solitary phase when the larva is rather pale-coloured, and passive, feeding in a cryptic fashion; the other phase is gregarious and in this the larva is dark-coloured, green and velvety black, and very active. It is only under certain conditions that the active phase is produced; but when the caterpillars move into the maize they can be very destructive, completely destroying the crop. Outbreaks have been noted between November and May, but seem to occur mainly in two distinct periods – the early rains from December onwards, and March–April. Such outbreaks have been recorded throughout eastern and southern Africa: the pest has thus been the subject of numerous research papers. Outbreaks of the armyworm always occur without warning, and they appear not to be correlated with weather conditions, although Colin Smee attempted to ascertain some of the climatic and ecological factors that may have been involved (1943: 7–8).

Ever since the first outbreak was recorded in 1915, they have occurred regularly at intervals in Malawi. During the colonial period the armyworm was particularly widespread in the years 1929–30, 1936–7, 1939–40, 1942–3, 1955–6 and 1960–61. Outbreaks were particularly noted on the Phalombe plain, but they occurred at intervals throughout Malawi – Zomba, Mulanje, Lilongwe, Ntcheu, Chiradzulu, Nkhotakota and Kasungu. There were conflicting reports regarding whether or not the armyworms were eaten by local people – but one agricultural officer noted that 'if they were gathered culinary taste and not crop safeguard was the motive'. Sven Grüner informed me that armyworms were gathered as food during an outbreak near Namadzi many years ago. Local names recorded were *ntchembere za gwada* and *nyan'amile* (BRS/A16A).

Since independence, sporadic outbreaks of armyworm have continued to occur. In 1971 at the end of December there was a widespread outbreak in the Mulanje district, and in 1976–7 heavy outbreaks were reported throughout the southern and central regions, and over 100,000 ha of maize had to be replanted. In the 1981–2 season some 350,000 ha of maize crop were affected, and an estimated 940,000MK were spent on control measures. Six years later, in 1987–8 another outbreak occurred, affecting maize gardens throughout Malawi from Nsanje and Chikwawa in the south to Karonga in the north.

In the widespread outbreak of armyworm that occurred during the rainy season of 1994–5, the records of the geographical spread of the infestation and the crops affected were as given in Table 4.1.

Table 4.1 Armyworm Infestations in Malawi, 1994–5

	Nsanje	Phalombe	Rumphi	Machinga	Dedza	Total
Maize	7	2	3	3	4	19
Sorghum	4	2		1	4	11
Millet	4		3		4	11
Rice		1		3	3	7
Pasture	4	2	1	2	4	13
Totals	19	7	7	9	19	61

Source: BRS/ENTA 16D.

During my year in Malawi 2000–2001 only one outbreak of armyworm was noted: some 300 ha of maize and cassava were attacked in the Chitipa and Karonga districts, and the outbreak seems to have been quickly brought under control by chemical spraying (*Daily Times*, 22 December, 2000).

Armyworm has always proved difficult to control once it is in the gregarious phase. In the early days a tobacco extract or pyrethrum powder were among the insecticides used: later DDT, BHC, Sevin (Carbaryl), Sumithion and Fenitrothion were used as control measures.

If its favoured ecological and climatic conditions are met it seems difficult to prevent outbreaks of armyworm, and though such outbreaks are sporadic they can be widespread and devastating, causing, for the farmer, the loss of his or her entire maize crop – as well of other cereals (on the biology and ecology of the armyworm see Hattingh 1941; Smee 1943; Whellan 1956; E. S. Brown 1970; Luhanga 1988).

Maize Stalk Borer, Kapuchi *(Family:* Noctuidae*).*   The term *kapuchi* in Malawi essentially covers three similar small caterpillars that burrow into the stem of the maize, and thus cause the wilting of the leaves, and usually a complete failure of cob formation. The three species involved are the maize stalk borer (*Busseola fusca*), the spotted stalk borer (*Chilo partellus*) and the pink stalk borer (*Sesamia calamistis*). All three originally fed on wild grasses, and only became pests when cultivated cereals were introduced. In a study of the relative importance of crop pests in sub-Saharan Africa, Geddes estimated that the maize stalk borer ranked the No. 1 pest of maize, ahead of cutworms, beetle larvae, armyworms and termites (1990: 47). Bernard Smit likewise considered the larvae of

Busseola fusca to be the worst pest of maize throughout southern Africa, causing enormous crop losses. He estimated that about 10 per cent of the maize crop could be destroyed (1964: 212–13).

Although maize ranks high as a staple food crop, George Phiri (1995) noted that little research had been undertaken into the management of the stalk borers in Malawi, compared with the amount of research that had been devoted to tobacco, tea and cotton pests. Indeed, he wrote that the control of the stalk borer presented a rather unique problem, for not only did the insect display flexibility in its ecological adaptation, but for most of their life-cycle the larvae lived in protected habitats, within the leaf whorls and stem of the host plant. Moreover, chemical control through the use of Endosulfan and other insecticides recommended by the government was quite beyond the reach of subsistence farmers, who simply could not afford the cost. Phiri's own researches were on the relationship between the stalk borer and the parasitic wasp *Lotesia sesamiae* (Family: *Braconidae*), and explored the latter's role as a potential biological control agent. But what his pioneering study revealed was that *Chilo partellus* tended to be common at the lower altitudes, while *Busseola fusca* was found primarily above 1,200 m; that the majority of farmers (70 per cent) perceived the stalk borer to be *the* major pest problem in maize; that over 60 per cent of the fields examined had at least 13 per cent of the plants showing infestation by stalk borers; and, finally, that 75 per cent of the farmers did not use any control measures against the stalk borers. Among those who did attempt some pest manage-ment, only 2 per cent used chemical pesticides, while about 20 per cent used physical means (putting ash into the leaf whorls to suffocate the larvae), or natural pesticides (Phiri 1995: 38–51). The latter involved two well-known natural insecticides, the shrubs *mphanjobvu* (*Neorauthania mitis*) and Ombwe (*Tephrosia vogelii*) – both of which are also used as fish poison (Morris 1996: 379–86). In a survey of maize fields adjacent to Kapalasa farm I found a similar pattern, with around 20 per cent of the maize plants showing signs of stalk borer infestation and loss of crop, and people making little or no effort to control the pest. The development economist Stephen Carr (2001) suggested to me that perhaps 92 per cent of smallholder agri-culture in Malawi was now under a maize monocrop, and that 5–10 per cent of the crop each year was perhaps lost to the stalk borer. Compared with neighbouring countries this, he remarked, was 'no real problem'. Certainly local people do little to curb the infestation of *kapuchi* – although as Phiri stressed, subsistence farmers in Malawi hardly have the funds to buy fertil-izer, let alone insecticides. Research in Kenya, however, has indicated that the planting of Napier grass, *nsenjere* (*Pennisetum purpureum*) and sudan grass (*Sorghum sudanense*) around maize fields tends to attract the stalk borers away from the maize itself (Killick 2001).

But what clearly helps to keep the stalk borer under control is destroying the old maize stalks, either by burning or burying, at the end of the growing season. This is a common practice throughout Malawi.

Elegant Grasshopper, M'Nunkhadala *(*Zonocerus elegans*) (Family:* Pyrgomorphidae*).* This slow-moving, colourful grasshopper is common throughout Malawi, and familiar to all Malawians. Only about 5 per cent of adults have wings, and it emits juices that have an offensive smell – hence its common name. It is a very destructive pest throughout southern Africa, and in Malawi it feeds on a variety of plants. Besides maize it has been recorded on cassava, pigeonpea, rice, groundnuts, cowpea, sorghum and cotton. The incidence of the pest is mainly during the rainy season, between November and March. High populations of *m'nunkadala* can cause total crop loss. In the Lower Shire Valley it is described as 'public enemy number one' by all farmers, and along with termites it is one of the most serious pests on both maize and cotton – as well as being found on many other crops. Near Ngabu people will plant pigeonpea (*nandolo*) late in January, as they believe that by then the main emergence of the elegant grasshopper will have passed. The only control of the *mbobo*, as it is called in the Lower Shire, is by hand-picking or by beating the grasshoppers off the plants by means of a stick (Munthali *et al.* 1990: 94). In the Shire Highlands all surveys indicate that the elegant grasshopper is considered one of the most troublesome pests of maize gardens, whatever the type of inter-cropping, especially during the early vegetative stages. During the early part of the season it is also a serious pest of sorghum.

Cutworms, Mbozi Zamdothe *(*Agrotis segetis*) (Family:* Noctuidae*)*
Like the elegant grasshopper, cutworms – the smooth, greyish caterpillar of a small moth – feed not only on maize but on a wide variety of crops – cabbage, sorghum, beans and tomatoes. The caterpillar characteristically lives underground during the day, and comes to the soil surface at night to feed on the plants, often cutting the succulent stem of the plant. This usually results in its death. Throughout Southern Africa it is considered an important pest of maize, and can destroy the whole crop (Smit 1964: 214). In one survey in the Shire Highlands 7 per cent of the maize was found to have been attacked by cutworm (Munthali *et al.* 1992), and its presence is recognized by farmers throughout the Highlands.

Mbozi Zoyera *(White Grub), the larvae of the Black Maize Beetle* (*Heteronychus licas*). The larvae of many species of beetle, belonging to several families, can be serious pests of maize, especially during the early planting season. Mainly belonging to the family *Scarabaeidae*, they include such chafer beetles as *Schizonycha* spp, *Anomala* sp., *Orphnus* sp., and *Heteronychus licas*. At least thirty species of scarabeid beetles are thought to be involved in crop damage in Malawi, but their habits are little known to local people. The larvae of the beetle are generally known by the rubric *mbozi zoyera* – white grub or caterpillar. They are dirty white, C-shaped, with a pale brown head.

During the Soil Pests Project (1990–2) white grubs, together with termites and the elegant grasshopper, were found to be the most important pest during the sprouting and vegetative stages of the maize, and in a survey of 110 gardens, between 3 and 4 per cent of the gardens showed signs of being 'attacked' by white grub (Munthali *et al.* 1993: 81). In 1995–6 there was an exceptional outbreak of the black maize beetle in one locality surveyed in the Blantyre district, and in the *dambo* areas the farmers were forced to abandon the maize fields. The larva of the beetle feeds on the seeds, roots or the stem of the plant just below the soil surface, and can cause a total wilting of the plant. The beetle is locally known as *matono*, and one woman recalled that her parents described the white grubs as *kaufiti* ('little witch') – the name of the parasitic weed *Striga asiatica* (E. A. Banda and Morris 1986: 150). Of course, her parents would have been relating the insect devastations to the machinations of a local witch (*mfiti*). White grubs also cause serious damage to sorghum and millet. Apart from the usual banking of the maize and hand-killing, no control strategies appear to be employed by local people. Seed dressing with pesticides in order to control soil pests like the 'white grub' have been advocated by the Ministry of Agriculture for many decades, and up to the 1980s organochlorine pesticides (DDT, Aldrin, Dieldrin) were often used for this purpose. Less environmentally damaging insecticides are now recommended as seed dressing in order to reduce white grub damage – but of course, few subsistence farmers can afford these expensive chemicals (Ritchie and Mayaso 2000: 3/524).

In Zimbabwe the larva of the black maize beetle is a serious pest on sugarcane. As with maize, it feeds on the roots and underground shoots, resulting in the wilting and yellowing of the leaves. In the worst affected areas there may be 100 per cent loss of the sugarcane. Around 6 million Zimbabwe dollars are spent annually on chemical insecticides in an effort to control the pest (Clowes and Breakwell 1998: 213). According to Henry Moyo, the black maize beetle is not a serious pest on sugarcane in the Lower Shire Valley.

The larvae of other beetles can also be serious pests of maize, particularly those known as 'wireworms', which may cause considerable damage during the sprouting stage of the maize. The best known are the larvae of the dusky brown darkling beetle, *Gonocephalus simplex* (family: *Tenebrionidae*), but the term also includes the larvae of the click beetles (family: *Elateridae*). The larvae are smooth, tough-skinned, wiry and yellowish, and they feed on the roots and stems below the soil surface, and cause the wilting and death (*ku-fa*) of the young plants. Besides attacking maize, the 'wireworms' also cause minor damage to cotton, beans, pigeonpea and cowpea.

Termites, Chiswe *(Order:* Isoptera*).* Many surveys have shown that termites are among the most important pests of maize, and on average, during the early part of the rainy season, between 18 and 26 per cent of plants may be infested with termites. The cumulative effect of termite damage is indeed said to be very high, and not only maize but pigeonpea, groundnuts, beans, cowpea, sorghum and cotton, as well as the estate crops, tea, sugar and coffee, may also be attacked in varying degrees by termites. The soil pests project recorded at least 24 species of termites from nine genera damaging crops in Southern Malawi, and some of the essential data are summarized in Table 4.2.

Table 4.2 Crops Attacked by Various Genera of Termites in Southern Malawi

Termite genera	Pigeonpea	Beans	Cowpea	Groundnut	Cotton	Sorghum	Maize
Anustrotermes	X				X		
Hodotermes					X		X
Macrotermes	X			X	X	X	X
Microtermes	X				X	X	X
Odontotermes					X	X	X
Pseudocanthotermes		X	X	X			X
Trinervitermes					X	X	X
Synacanthotermes							X
Allodontermes							X
Totals	3	1	1	2	6	4	8

Source: after Munthali *et al.* 1992: 88.

It can be seen that, while termites also attack pigeonpea, cotton and sorghum, maize is the plant most often damaged by termites. This is confirmed by the termite damage recorded by the project on ten important crops – the survey was conducted with regard to 103 farmers from eight localities in the Southern region.

Crops such as pigeonpea and cotton were, like maize, much more seriously attacked during the early stages of growth, up to 26 per cent of maize plants being infested. Thus one can but conclude that termites are

Table 4.3 Incidence of Termite Damage by Crop

Crop	% of Plants Attacked at Harvesting Stage
Maize	13
Sorghum	9
Beans	0.6
Cowpea	11.3
Groundnuts	6.8
Pigeonpea	4.6
Cassava	9.5
Crownpea	–
Pumpkin	–
Cotton	2.5

Source: Munthali *et al*. 1992: 90.

a serious pest of maize, although local people tend to rank the white grub (*mbozi zoyera*) and the elegant grasshoppers (*m'Nunkhadala*) as more harmful pests than the termites. No control measures are used against termites, although when they become too problematic the queen termite may be dug out and destroyed – yet people are reluctant to do this, as the winged termites (*ngumbi*) are a favoured and important source of relish. There is a general feeling that farmers who burn all crop residues, rather than simply burying them (*kunojeka*) in the usual fashion, tend to have less problems with termites, and with other insect pests. It is also evident that monocropping with maize tends to increase termite attack. People are also aware that certain trees have toxic qualities and are thus repellent to termites: for example, the persian lilac tree *ndya* (*Melia azedarach*) and the milk bush *nkhadze* (*Euphorbia tiricalli*) (Morris 1996). Their use as an insecticide was described long ago by Jessie Williamson (1975); but although these trees may be planted near the homestead, I found little evidence that they were ever planted in the maize gardens as a control measure against termites. To some extent termites play a positive role in agriculture, in breaking down the dead wood and other unwanted debris. Equally important to note is that ants play a crucial role in controlling maize pests – particularly termites and white grubs; several genera of ants are involved, including *Camponotus*, *Acantholepsis*, *Tetramorium*, *Pheidole*, *Paltothyreus* and *Ocymyrmex* (Munthali *et al*. 1993: 126–9).

Beans and Peas

Among subsistence cultivators in Malawi, four pulses have particular importance, namely the kidney bean, *nyemba* (*Phaseolus vulgaris* and its many varieties); the pigeonpea, *nandolo* (*Cajanus cajan*); the groundnut, *ntedza* (*Arachis hypogaea*); and the cowpea (*Vigna unguiculata*) which has two distinct varieties, the cowpea proper (*khobwe*) and the crownpea (*nseula*), which has smaller pods and peas. The area under the three main pulses is as follows:

	Area in hectares
Nyemba, *Phaseolus vulgaris*	132,509
Nandolo, *Cajanus cajan*	70,598
Ntedza, *Arachis hypogaea*	61,059
(NRI 1996: 40)	

All four pulses seem prone to attack by termites in Malawi, especially the pigeonpea, one survey indicating that in its vegetative stage up to 33 per cent of the plants showed damage by termites. Pigeonpea, as Williamson noted long ago, seems particularly prone to various insect pests, and thus tends to be grown from seed each year (1975: 91). But all pulses are prone to attacks by a variety of insect pests – aphids, sap-sucking bugs, wireworms and other beetle larvae, and the African boll-worm (*Helicoverpa armigera*). This last species is also a serious pest of cotton and tobacco.

Four species are of particular importance as pests on legumes; the striped bean weevil (*Alcidodes leucogrammus*); the bean fly (*Ophiomyia spencerella*); the leaf beetle (*Ootheca mutabilis*); and the groundnut bug (*Hilda patruelis*). Although these insects do a considerable amount of damage to legumes, they are hardly known to local people, and have no recognized names. The leaf beetle was described to the IPM project as *tizilombo touluka* – which simply means 'useless flying organism'. We may described these four pests in turn.

*Striped Bean Weevil (*Alcidodes leucogrammus*) (Family:* Curculionidae*).* The larvae of this tiny yellow and black striped weevil (HB 8 mm), and of other members of the same genus, are serious pests on beans and peas, and up to 8 per cent of cowpeas have been recorded as being attacked by this insect. The larvae feed on and pupate in the stem just below the soil surface, and cause serious defoliation of the plant, or stunted growth. The intensity of the damage of this weevil on kidney beans (*nyemba*), can be quite severe in certain areas, and some gardens in the Blantyre district indicated that between 16 and 26 per cent of bean plants may be attacked, although infestation may be sporadic or local (Munthali *et al.* 1993: 96–7).

*Bean Fly (*Ophiomyia spencerella, Ophiomyia phaseoli*) (Family:* Agromyzidae*).* The bean fly is a minute, shiny black fly (HB 2 mm), the maggot of which is a 'leaf miner', burrowing into the leaf stem of beans and cowpeas and causing considerable damage through wilting (*kunyala*), often killing the plant. Anything up to 70 per cent of the plants may be attacked. Along with the striped bean weevil the fly can cause serious crop losses, and farmers in the Namwera district do not attempt to grow the first crop of beans (*nyemba*) owing to a combination of heavy rains and the prevalence of bean fly (Ritchie and Muyaso 2000: 1/47). The wilting of the beans is often ranked as the most important pest problem of beans, although farmers are unaware that this is caused by the bean fly maggot, and have no control measures. The bean fly mainly attacks beans and cowpea, rather than pigeonpea, and is generally consid- ered to be one of the most destructive pests on legumes in Africa, includ- ing Malawi. Infestations usually occur around eight weeks after planting, in the middle of the rains (February–March) (Mvula and Nyirenda 1995). The recommended use of an insecticide, such as Endosulfan as a seed dressing, is beyond the reach of most subsistence farmers.

Leaf Beetle, Mkupe *(*Ootheca mutabilis, Ootheca bennigseni*) (Family:* Chrysomelidae*).* This is a small colourful beetle with an orange thorax and a shiny blue elytra (HB 6 mm), which is more commonly associated with pumpkins, so that *Ootheca mutabilis* could well be described as the pumpkin beetle. The adults cause damage to cowpea and beans, feeding between veins on the leaves, and can cause considerable damage, particu- larly to seedlings. Along with the bean fly maggot – which causes wilting – it is considered one of the major pests of beans. It seems not to attack pigeonpea.

*Ground Bug (*Hilda patruelis*) (Family:* Tettigometridae*).* This is a well- known pest of groundnuts, although it also feeds on beans and cowpea. It is a sapsucking bug causing wilting, retarded growth, and eventually the death of the plant. On groundnuts – which generally seem to be free of pests – its damage can be sporadic, but in certain areas, such as the Lakeshore, it can be a serious pest.

In the Namadzi area, and throughout the Shire Highlands, pigeonpea is a very common legume, and is widely grown as a maize intercrop. Drought-resistant, it is an important source of relish during the early rains, and is also widely sold to augment income. The insect that is partic- ularly associated with the pigeonpea by local people is the blister beetle, particularly the red-spotted blister beetle (*Mylabris buqueti*), usually described as *dzodzwe*. This is a colourful, medium-sized black and red beetle (HB 34 mm) that feeds on the flowers of many shrubs, including pigeonpea. As there are many varieties of pigeonpea in Malawi, with indeterminable flowering periods, the blister beetle does not constitute a serious pest problem.

Several other insects feed on beans and peas, and can at certain times, and in some localities, become major pests. These include the green shield bug, *nkhunguni* (*Nezara viridula*), the bow-legged bug, *nandoli* (*Anoplocnemis curvipes*), and the small green weevil, *Systates perblandus*.

The main control measure in relation to pests on beans and peas is that local people may – but often don't – uproot the infested plants and burn them.

Cassava, Chinangwa *(*Manihot esculenta*).*   Cassava is a native of tropical America whose production is mainly concentrated in the northern region and along the lakeshore, and elsewhere it is grown as a security crop, as it is drought resistant. The area under cassava is estimated at 75,050 ha (1993), only half of that under maize. Many varieties of cassava are cultivated, differing in relation to the bitterness of the tubers. Both the leaves and the tubers are eaten, the latter being dried and processed as flour, from which *nsima* is made.

Cassava is attacked by a great diversity of insect pests, but significantly it seems resistant to the larger grasshoppers. However, the elegant grasshopper *m'nunkhadale* (*Zonocerus elegans*) is a common pest of cassava, and elsewhere in Africa crop losses of up to 60 per cent have been reported when young plants have been attacked by this grasshopper. Along with termites and aphids, it appears to be a troublesome pest, and is familiar to everyone. The white fly, *Bemisia tabaci*, is also important as a vector of the mosaic virus disease. But there are two pests of cassava that are particularly significant in Malawi, as they are now widespread, and cause severe crop losses.

The first of these is the cassava green mite, *Mononychellus tanajoa* (*Acarina,* family: *Tetranychidae*), which is known locally as *nsabwe za chinangwa*, the 'louse of the cassava' (Tumbuka: *nyinda*). This exotic pest was first discovered in Brazil in 1921, and given the Portuguese name *tanajoa de mandioca* – 'disease of the cassava'. It was introduced accidentally into Africa, and was first discovered near Kampala, Uganda, in 1971. Since then it has spread throughout the cassava belt of the continent, and reached Malawi in 1981. The mite seems to be restricted to its host, *Manihot* spp. It is a tiny organism, pale brown and barely visible to the naked eye, and usually feeds on the growing parts of the plant, the buds and young leaves. These become deformed and marked with yellow spots, so as to appear mottled, having a mosaic pattern that resembles the cassava mosaic disease. When the plant is severely attacked it becomes stunted, and there is a reduction in the leaf available for relish, as well as a loss of root crop. There appears to be a considerable difference in losses between the different varieties of cassava, but with the more susceptible kinds up to 20 per cent of the crop may be lost. Experiments on the biological control of this mite are presently being conducted in Malawi (Phiri 2000).

The second important pest of cassava is the cassava mealy bug (*Phenacoccus manihotis*). Its local name is *kodikodi* ('what is it') (*syn. milebagi, swanya*). It is a tiny white bug (HB 1–2 mm) that attacks the terminal shoots of the cassava, causing the leaves to become wrinkled and bunched up, and it can reduce yields by up to 70 per cent. More than 60 per cent of farmers in the Mulanje and Kasungu districts reported that mealy bug was a problem throughout the year, and around the same number suggested that mealy bug reduced the root yield by more than half. The bug came into prominence in 1986, when the Nkhata Bay area – where cassava is the staple food – experienced the virtual destruction of the cassava crop by the mealy bug. The government thus had to distribute emergency food aid to the stricken area. Although some farmers attempt to control the cassava mealy bug by removing the affected plants and burning them, by crop rotation, or by the use of clean plant material, it was discovered that in the Mulanje district almost half the farmers did nothing to control cassava pests. As insecticides are expensive and beyond the reach of most Malawians, research in Malawi is concentrating, as with the cassava green mite, on developing some form of biological control, in this case parasitic wasps (Moyo *et al.* 1998).

Sweet Potato, Mbatata *(*Ipomoea batatas*)*

Also a native of the Americas, the sweet potato is widely grown throughout Malawi, and is an important security crop. An area of around 36,846 ha is under sweet potato production (NRI 1996: 40). Rooting freely from cuttings, it is planted in the early rains, to be harvested between February and June. The tubers are eaten boiled or roasted, and the leaves (*kholowa*) are also cooked as a side dish. Like the pigeonpea and cassava, it is often sold as a cash crop.

Although attacked occasionally by termites, wireworms and small beetles, the main pest of this crop is the sweet potato weevil (*Cyclas puncticollis,* Family: *Curculionidae*). Its common name is *nankafumbwe wa mbatata*, the weevil of the sweet potato, given its affinities to the common maize weevil. It is a small, snouted, black weevil (HB 8 mm), with characteristic swollen joints on the legs. The weevil can be a serious pest of sweet potato, although it is not mentioned in early crop protection handbooks (cf. Matthews and Whellan 1974). It can, however, cause losses of up to 50 per cent of the crop. Local farmers have little knowledge of its life-history, and seem unaware of possible control measures, although they tend to harvest early to avoid damage, and unconsciously engage in many cultural practices that tend to inhibit the insect pest. These include crop rotation, banking up the soil, and destroying plant debris by burning or burial. But most farmers practised no explicit method of pest control, and many that I knew personally in the Namadzi area did not recognize the pest or perceive it to be a problem. Thus researchers have concluded that there is plenty of scope for reducing crop losses in the sweet potato through education and by explicitly practising various cultural controls of the weevil. For many smallholder farmers this is the only serious pest of sweet potato they encounter (Munthali *et al.* 1993: 46; Ritchie and Muyaso 2000: 351–66).

In a survey I made in villages adjacent to Kapalasa farm near Namadzi, I asked around 70 people what they considered to be the most troublesome (-*bvuta*) pest of their gardens (*munda*), and the response was as follows:

Chiswe	Termites	20 (28%)
Kapuchi	Maize stalk borer	15 (21%)
M'Nunkhadada	Elegant grasshopper	12 (17%)
Mkupe	Leaf beetle	10 (14%)

The remainder suggested aphids (*nsabwe za masamba*), ants (*nyerere*), grasshoppers (*chitete*) and a hairy caterpillar (*chiyabwe*).

Insect Pests of Cash Crops in the Smallholder Sector

Cotton, Thonje *(*Gossypium hirsutum*)*
The history of Malawi is intricately bound up not only with the hunting of elephant and the 'ivory economy', as I have discussed elsewhere, but with the rise of the cotton industry. Indeed, the cultivation of cotton was a flourishing, commercial venture in Malawi even prior to the colonial period, as Livingstone's Zambezi journals indicate. During colonial times cotton became a major export crop, grown mainly by local people along the Lakeshore and in the Lower Shire Valley, and marketed mainly through the Empire Cotton Growing Corporation (Terry 1962; Mandala 1990). But from the outset cotton growing in Malawi (then Nyasaland) was beset with difficulties, as the cotton plant is the host of numerous insect pests, many of which, like the bollworms, can completely destroy the crop. There is, however, a tendency nowadays among academics –

who themselves know precious little about agriculture – to belittle the authoritarian and paternalistic attitudes, the inconsistency and the blunders of so-called colonial 'experts' as they struggled to come to terms with crop devastations and the other problems of agriculture (McCracken 1982). Personally, I can only express my admiration for the work done by such colonial 'experts' as Edward Lawrence, Colin Smee, Hugh Stannus and William Lamborn, who spent the greater part of their lives in Malawi, often in difficult circumstances, struggling to understand and alleviate the problems experienced by local people, particularly in relation to crop pests and human diseases. Their scholarly output and social commitment is hardly matched by that of the contemporary 'experts', now known as 'consultants', who swan around the country in air-conditioned landrovers, hardly ever go into the rural areas, live in modern houses with electric lights, computers and e-mails, hold conferences in the most expensive hotels, and are paid exorbitant salaries! Nothing is to be gained by a dismissive, disparaging and patronizing attitude towards an earlier generation of colonial 'entomologists', nor by exaggerating the supposed ecological wisdom of local people: neither the colonial experts nor local Malawians fully understood the ecology and habits of the many and varied insect pests that laid siege to cotton during the colonial period, and that are, in fact, still a persisting problem.

Although declining in importance, cotton is still a viable cash crop in Malawi, especially along the Lakeshore and in the Lower Shire Valley, and an area of 53,691 ha continues to be under cotton production, in spite of declining prices. Around sixty thousand smallholders plant cotton as a cash crop, with yields of around 250–450 kg/ha. But 'pest management' by local people is described as 'poor' (Ritchie and Muyaso 2000: 1/48).

Around three hundred insects have been recorded as pests on the cotton plant. In a check list of cotton insect pests of Nyasaland, compiled by Colin Smee at the outbreak of the Second World War (1940), over eighty insects were recorded as attacking cotton – sometimes as seedling plants, as well as affecting the different parts of the plant, roots, shoots, leaves, flowers and bolls (MNA/51/30/40). Some twenty years later Charles Sweeney made a detailed study of the insect pests of cotton and recorded the following number of species attacking cotton.

Beetles (*Coleoptera*)	141
Bugs (*Hemiptera*)	68
Butterflies and Moths (*Lepidoptera*)	50
Grasshoppers and Crickets (*Orthoptera*)	30
Other orders	14
Total	**303**

A pioneer entomologist, Sweeney outlined in some depth the identification, life-history, distribution, ecology, forms of damage inflicted on
cotton, and various modes of control of these many insect pests. Long ago
he was advocating, like Smee, integrated pest management of the insects,
by means of biological control (particularly the encouragement of natural
enemies such as parasites and predators, and the elimination of alternative host plants), chemical control (DDT was then in vogue), and cultural
control (handpicking, clean weeding, appropriate tillage, crop rotation,
the development of resistant cotton varieties, and the burning of plant
debris at the end of the growing season) (Sweeney 1961–3).

It is far beyond the scope of the present study to discuss in detail the
numerous insect pests that damage cotton: I will instead focus on nine
species that are among the major pests, and are generally well known to
local people. But it is worth noting, by way of preface, that as far as
local people are concerned, four insects have particular salience – the
bollworms, the harvester termite, the elegant grasshopper and the
cotton stainers. For instance, when I visited cotton gardens near
Bangula in April and May 2001, local people were adamant that four
pests were particularly troublesome: the larvae of certain moths, the
bollworms, *mbozi/mfunye*, especially those of *Diparopsis castanea*; the
cotton stainers, *kamatowo* (*Dysdercus* spp.); the elegant grasshopper,
m'nunkhadala (*Zonocerus elegans*); and the harvester termite, *nthusi*
(*Hodotermes mossambicus*). At Chauka village near Kasinje on the
Southern Lakeshore, I found a similar situation three weeks later.
Walking through the cotton fields with local growers, the same four
insect pests were constantly described to me as the most troublesome.
Indeed, although one person said he used *lipkodi* (Ripcord) as an insecticide, cotton stainers were extremely abundant in the gardens, and a
large proportion of the cotton bolls were infested with caterpillars
(*mbozi*).

This tends to confirm one particular survey of thirty-four farmers from
the Lower Shire Valley, who were asked to identify what cotton pests were
important to them. The results are shown in Table 4.4.

Elegant Grasshopper, M'Nunkhadala, *(*Zonocerus elegans*) (Family:*
Pyrgomorphidae*).* As we have noted earlier, this is an important insect
pest on a wide variety of crops, including cotton. To some extent cotton
suffers to a greater degree than other crops, as it is widely grown in the
low-altitude areas where the elegant grasshopper is most common. Thus
this grasshopper is an important pest, attacking cotton in all cotton-
growing areas. It is particularly prone to attack young cotton, and is most
numerous during dry periods.

Table 4.4 Numbers of Farmers in the Lower Shire
Valley Identifying Particular Cotton Pests as
Important to them

Pest	Number of Farmers
Red bollworm	21
African bollworm	27
Pink bollworm	19
Aphids	6
Cotton stainers	24
Elegant grasshopper	27
Termites	6
Jassids	25

Source: Munthali *et al*. 1990.

Many other species of grasshoppers and crickets (Order: *Orthoptera*)
occasionally feed on cotton, but do not normally cause extensive damage
to the crop – although in certain years they may occur in such large
numbers that they inflict local damage that can be quite serious, or even
total. These include the following species:

Gryllotalpa africana
Gryllus bimaculatus
Brachytrypes membranaceus
Enyaliopsis petersi
Cymatomera sp
Homorocoryphus vicinus
Pseudorhynchus pungens
Nomadacris septemfasciata
Acanthacris ruficornis
Ornithacris (orientalis) cyanea
Ornithacris magnifica
Cyrtacanthacris aeruginosa
Phymateus viridipes
Acrida sulphuripennis
Acrotylus patruelis

Harvester Termite, Nthusi *(*Hodotermes mossambicus*) (Family:*
Hodotermidae*)*.   Although Sweeney suggests that there is no local name
for this termite, apart from *chiswe*, it is often described as *nthusi* or
*nthedz*a. It is generally absent from the Shire Highlands, but common in
all cotton-growing areas. Other termites might attack cotton, but this

species is certainly the most important, causing serious damage to young cotton plants, especially during a dry spell. Damage may be so severe as to warrant, Julian Mchowa informed me, the complete replanting of the cotton crop.

Cotton Stainer, Cham'Matowo *(*Dysdercus *spp.) (Family:* Pyrrhocoridae*).* There are three forms of cotton stainer that are common in Malawi, which to an ordinary person look very similar. The species involved are *Dysdercus intermedius* (which I found to be common at Kapalasa), *Dysdercus fasciatus* and *Dysdercus nigrofasciatus.* Given their association with the *mtowo* shrub (*Azanza garckeana*), they take the common name *cham'matowo* or *kamatowo.* But the bugs are found on many other plants, including the boabab, *mlambe* (*Adansonia digitata*), the *ngoza* (*Sterculia appendiculata*) and many species of *Hibiscus.* The cotton stainer feeds on the green boll, and thereby introduces a fungus disease (*Nematospora*) that causes serious yellowish discoloration of the cotton – hence its common name. It is found in the cotton fields near the southern Lakeshore in May. Sweeney recommended many different strategies to control the cotton stainer – encouraging insect predators, such as the assassin bug *Phonoctonus nigrofasciatus,* which mimics the stainer; keeping cotton away from alternative host plants and destroying these if necessary; making traps for the bugs using *ngoza* and *njale* seeds; clean weeding of the crop; hand-picking; and the use of insecticides – at the end of the colonial period DDT was the recommended chemical control (Sweeney 1961–3: 3–10). What was more controversial was the suggestion of destroying *mgoza* trees in the attempt to control the cotton stainer – in one experimental area near Sorgin, 4,000 trees were destroyed, but the experiment proved to be inconclusive. At the present time spraying the crop with Carbaryl is recommended by the Ministry of Agriculture. Sweeney used the term *nkhunguni za thonje* (cotton bug) to describe the cotton stainer, but the name seems to have been his own invention – *nkhunguni* is the common name of the green shield bug (*Nezara robusta*).

The cotton stainer can also be a pest on *Macadamia*, especially when these trees are grown at the lower altitudes.

Jassid, Majasidi*, (*Empoasca fascialis*) (Family:* Jassidae*).* The cotton jassid is a 'leaf hopper', a tiny yellowish-green insect that is found on the leaves of the cotton plant, its nymphs often resembling aphids. It feeds on a variety of plants, and like the cotton stainer is particularly associated with the *Malvaceae* family. It is generally found on the underside of the leaves feeding on the plant juices, and causes the yellowing or slight curling of the leaves. The jassid may do a lot of damage to young cotton, and reaches its peak population around April. Cotton varieties vary in their resistance to jassid attack, but none are completely resistant (Sweeney 1961: 10–12).

Four other bugs are often noted as occasional pests on cotton. These are: the green shield bug (*Nezara viridula*), which is a cosmopolitan pest occurring on many crops; the bow-legged bug, *nandoli* (*Anoplocnemis curvipes*); the iridescent cotton bug *Calidea dregii*, which is a bright, shiny blue insect; and the cotton aphid, *nsabwe zo m'thonje*, ('lice of cotton') (*Aphis gossypii*), which feeds on the tips of young shoots and the leaves of the plant. When infestation is severe it turns the leaves yellow.

But, as a general rule, these four bugs occur in small numbers, and are of no serious economic importance.

Black Boll Beetle, Bingiza *(*Diplognatha gagates*) (Family:* Cetoniidae*).* This is a large black beetle (HB 24 mm), given the name *bingiza* by Sweeney, which feeds on the green bolls of the cotton. It often creates a lot of white frash as it feeds its way into the boll. Only a few bolls tend to be damaged in a garden, and it is usually noted only in the months May–June. It feeds on many other kinds of fruit (Sweeney 1964a: 35).

As was noted above, 141 species of beetles have been recorded as causing some damage to cotton, but only two other species have been noted as particularly troublesome, both of them weevils (family: *Curculionidae*). These are:

- *Alcidodes brevirocostris*, a small black snouted beetles (HB 9 mm), which feeds on the bark of the cotton plant, leaving a typical ring of frayed fibres around the stem. The plant may then die, or become susceptible to attacks by termites.
- *Microcerus spiniger* is a dark brown, warty, terrestrial weevil lacking wings (HB 27 mm), the larva of which feeds on the root stems of the cotton just below the soil surface. The adults feed on the leaves of the cotton. Along with termites, this was a major pest of cotton recorded by the soil pests project (1990–2), some 4–9 per cent of plants in the Lower Shire, it was noted, being attacked by this weevil (Munthali *et al*. 1992: 94). As this weevil feigns death, it is often described as *kafadala*.

Red Bollworm, Mbozi Yo Fiira *(*Diparopsis castanea*) (Family:* Noctuidae*).* The red bollworm, the larva of a small moth, is greyish with characteristic rose-red markings and a black head (HB 27 mm). Sweeney (1964a: 38) described it as the 'worst enemy' that the cotton farmer has in Malawi – although the red bollworm feeds only on the cotton plant. Indeed, in the first annual report of the government entomologist (1913) it was suggested that it was 'undoubtedly the most destructive insect' in the country. After hatching, the larva bores into the boll of the cotton, and seems to spend all its life right inside the boll, feeding on the flowers. The larva pupates in the ground. Although the larva damages a minimum number of bolls, it is thus difficult to control with insecticides. Even so, the ministry of agriculture recommends control by spraying with Carbaryl. The most important control measure, however, was that first suggested by Colin Smee, and practised – indeed, attempts were made to enforce the practice – throughout the colonial period, namely to have a closed season of two months, involving the uprooting and burning of all cotton plants by the end of July. In the years prior to the Second World War there was considerable debate and dispute as to whether the enforced close season and the uprooting and burning of the cotton was indeed having any real effect in controlling the red bollworm as a pest (MNA/51/189/38). Smee also noted the potential importance of two parasitic wasps that are associated with the red bollworm as control agents (1940: 13).

What was evident, however, is that, throughout the colonial period, losses of cotton crop due to the red bollworm were extremely high, often around 40 per cent of the potential crop. Smee noted that the 1922–3 season was exceptionally bad for bollworm, and on many estates crops were 'practically ruined by this pest' (MNA/Ann. Rept. Dept. Agr. 1924).

Even today, bollworm attacks continue to be the most important constraints on cotton production, and applications of pyrethroid insecticids to control the bollworms seems to have led to an increase in white fly (Ritchie and Muyaso 2000: 48)

Spiny Bollworm, Mbozi ya Minga-Minga *(*Earias biplaga*) (Family: Noctuidae).* Along with those of the related species *Earias insulana*, the larvae have varying colours, mainly brown or greyish, and are characterized by long spine-like hairs on the body. Although not as troublesome as the red bollworm, they are always present in the cotton crop to some extent. The larvae attack the flower buds and the bolls, but unlike the red bollworm they move about a great deal, and may feed on many buds and bolls. They are also associated with many plants of the *Malvaceae* family, to which of course the cotton plant belongs.

Pink Bollworm, Mbozi ya Pinki *(*Pectinophora gossypiella*) (Family: Noctuidae).* As its common name suggests, the larva of this moth when fully grown (HB 13 mm) is of a pinkish coloration. First recorded in Malawi in 1925, it was not until the outbreak of the Second World War that it was noted as common in the Southern region, but even then it was not considered as serious a pest as the red bollworm. It attacks flower buds and the green bolls of the cotton, and is mostly in evidence in May and June, when most of the damage is done. It has been suggested that the uprooting and burning of the cotton at the end of the season tended to keep this pest in check during the colonial period; but it is still considered a serious pest of cotton. As it tends to keep within the boll, spraying with insecticides such as Carbaryl is said to be only slightly effective against it (Sweeney 1962: 26–7).

In the years immediately after independence, pink bollworm became a serious pest in the Lower Shire Valley, and efforts were made to curb the outbreak. Two strategies were employed: a close season of 2–3 months and a re-emphasis on the uprooting and burning of the previous year's cotton plants; and the fumigation of all cotton seed with methyl bromide (BRS/A17A).

African Bollworm, Mbozi ya Chifilika, *(*Helicoverpa armigera*)* *(Family:* Noctuidae*)*
Originally placed in the genus *Heliothis*, the larva of this moth, the largest of the bollworms, goes under several common names – American bollworm, cobworm (on maize), or budworm (on tobacco). Although it is one of the worst pests of cotton in the United States, it is in fact a cosmopolitan species, and is a serious pest on a variety of different crops – especially maize, groundnuts, tobacco, tomatoes and cotton. Sweeney suggests that it may have been of Asiatic origin (1962: 14–16). The larva is greenish-yellow to pale brown, with characteristic black and white stripes along the sides of the body (HB 35 mm). It feeds on the buds, flowers and bolls of the cotton, and although not generally considered a serious pest, often appears suddenly in great numbers, and can thus, locally, cause extensive damage to the crop. It tends to be less serious on cotton than on maize. Ministry of Agriculture recommendations for the chemical control of this pest in the past have included DDT, and now include Carbaryl or endosulfan.

Vegetables
Vegetable gardens in low-lying areas (*dambo*) or near streams – enabling crops to be irrigated – have always been an important part of people's livelihood in rural areas. Many of my elderly women friends in the Domasi valley had their *dimba* gardens for growing vegetables – groundnuts, cabbage, tomatoes, onions, beans – that they utilized as food, as well as selling in Songani market in order to generate the cash necessary to buy their basic household requirements. Over the past three decades, in

order to provision a growing urban population, the production and marketing of *dimba* vegetables have become important occupations for many Malawians. The Integrated Pest Management project (1996–2000) made a particular study of *dimba* crops, and they estimated that 33 per cent of households in the Blantyre district had access to *dimba* land and grew *dimba* crops, and around 21 per cent used pesticides. The two important *dimba* crops are tomato and cabbage.

Tomato, Matimati, *(Lycopersicon esculentum).* A native of South America, the tomato is an extremely important crop to Malawians, and is grown in semi-wild kitchen gardens within the village environs (along with chillies, *tsobola* (*Capsicum annuum*) and spinach, *bonongwe* (*Amaranthus* sp.)), on termite mounds, and in *dimba* gardens. They are seldom eaten raw, but are used as an essential ingredient in relish (*ndiwo*) dishes. Although tomatoes are occasionally attacked by the African bollworm (*Helicoverpa armigera*), the larvae of the semi-looper caterpillar (*Plusia* sp.) and the green shield bug (*Nezara viridula*), the primary pest on tomato is the red spider mite (*Tetranychus evansi*). This mite has been a serious pest in southern Africa since the early 1980s, and first appeared in Malawi in 1993. Two years later it had spread throughout the country, and is now present and a troublesome pest in all tomato-growing areas. It has been given the name *stoniwashi*, because it appeared, I'm told, around the same time as a particular brand of men's jeans that had a mottled appearance. The red spider mite attacks a wide range of crops besides the tomato – beans, sweet potatoes, peppers, citrus, coffee and tea. It feeds on the sap of the tomato leaf, initially giving rise to a yellow mottling; but the leaves then turn bronze and are shed, and the plant may eventually die. The mites themselves are tiny, of variable colour, but often red. They appear mainly during the dry season, from August to November. Much research has recently been undertaken to develop an integrated strategy of pest control in relation to the red spider mite. These measures include crop rotation, the uprooting and burning of infested plants, the use of botanical insecticides that have long been used in Malawi – for example, infusions of the tobacco plant, or of such shrubs as *mphanjobvu* (*Neoravtanemia mitis*) and *ombwe* (*Tephrosia vugelii*); interplanting with aromatic herbs such as *mpungabwe* (*Ocimum canum*); increasing the humidity near the tomato plants by mulching or close planting; the development of resistant varieties of tomato; and the use of insecticides such as Dimethoate (Chongwe 1999; Mtambo 1999).

Cabbage, Kabichi, *(Brassica oleracea).* Cabbages are grown in *dimba* gardens particularly at the higher altitudes; but, whereas tomatoes tend to be a dry season crop, cabbages are mainly grown during the rainy season. Along with related members of the genus – Chinese cabbage, *tanaposi* (*Brassica chinensis*) and rape, *mpiri wotuwa* (*Brassica napus*) – the cabbage is prone to a wide variety of insect pests. These include the shield bug *Bagrada hilaris*, a small yellow and black insect that may be numerous in hot dry weather; the mealy cabbage aphis *Brevicoryne brassicae*, which is wax-covered and infests the heart of the cabbage; and the larvae of the diamond-back moth, *Plutella xylostella*. It is this latter pest that has been the subject of attention and research in recent years.

The adult diamond-back moth is a small grey moth with a wingspan of about 15 mm, and a characteristic diamond pattern on its back, noticeable when the wings are closed at rest. Hence its common name. The larvae are pale green (HB 12 mm), and active, and when disturbed suspend themselves by means of a silken thread. The larvae feed on the leaves of the cabbage plant from the underside, making hundreds of holes that reduce the leaves to a lace-like condition. The moth has a cosmopolitan distribution, and is a serious and widespread pest of cabbage. Harriet Thindwa suggests that the diamond-back moth has become a 'major setback' to the growing of cabbages in Malawi, as it has now become resistant to many brands of insecticide. Thus experiments are now being conducted to find alternative strategies to control this pest. These include biological control, utilizing two parasitic wasps, or the microbial pesticide *Bacillus thuringiensis*; and using botanical insecticides, such as an infusion of the leaves and seed of the *neem* tree (*Azadirachta indica*) or of the wayside shrubby herb *Tithonia diversifolia*. Without control it is estimated that as much as 50 per cent of the cabbage crop may be lost (Thindwa 1999b; Mtambo *et al.* 2000).

The diamond-back moth is particularly noticeable during the dry season, from July to October. Local people simply refer to the larva of the diamond-back moth as *mbozi* (caterpillar), and one of the main forms of control used by local people is the insecticide Carbaryl. It is simply put into a watering can and poured over the cabbages. Stephen Carr (2001) suggested to me that lemon grass, cut and put over the cabbage, is a useful insect repellent, as the moth dislikes its smell. Research studies have shown that insecticides are commonly used by a few smallholders growing tomato and cabbage, and these include organophosphates such as Temik, Lanate and Actellic; synthetic pyrethroids, such as Ripcord and Sherpa, and the well-known carbamate Sevin. Farmers often mix different insecticides – as herbalists combine different roots, as it is thought that this gives them extra strength, and often use concentrations way above those recommended. Many of the insecticides bought at market stalls are obsolete or out-of-date, and several of the insecticides, e.g.

Temik and Lanate, are in the 'extremely dangerous' category. Interestingly, however, few farmers growing cabbage and tomato considered insect pests to be a problem – of more concern to them were the high costs of fertilizer, high transport costs and low prices for vegetables (Ritchie and Muyaso 2000: 2/174–83).

Insect Pests of Crops in the Estate Sector

Although many crops are grown in the estate sector, including for example maize, sunflower, citrus, soybean, macadamia and groundnuts, I shall here focus on the insect pests that are associated with the four crops that constitute the primary agricultural exports: tea, coffee, tobacco and sugar.

Tea *(*Camellia sinensis*)*

Tea is second only to tobacco as an important source of foreign exchange in Malawi, and the total area under tea now stands at around 39,800 ha. Established at the end of the nineteenth century, tea production is mainly focused in the Thyolo and Mulanje districts, and employs over 42,000 people. During the colonial period tea was entirely produced by private estates, usually owned by small European companies, but in 1967 the Smallholder Tea Authority was established, under Roger Royle, to enable local farmers to grow tea. Royle was an experienced agriculturist who had earlier won renown for his support of soil conservation as against biblical fundamentalism (cf. Chakanza 1998: 77–81). At the present time there are around 5,000 local growers in the Thyolo and Mulanje districts, with an average holding of around 0.5 ha per smallholder, amounting to around 2,500 ha in total (TAM 1991). Although, like any other agricultural crop, tea is exposed to many insect pests, what I always found surprising, having worked for over seven years as a tea planter in Malawi, is that the tea bush is relatively free of pests. Indeed, when I discussed tea pests with Alexander Boatman on the slopes of Thyolo Mountain, where he has worked as an instructor for the Smallholder Tea Authority for some thirty years, he was adamant that local growers are not unduly worried about insect pests. This was confirmed in my discussions with Pritam Rattan, a research scholar who is an acknowledged authority on the pests and diseases of tea in Africa. Rattan suggested to me that only three pests have salience in Malawi – thrips, red spider mite and mosquito bug – and none of them constituted a real problem. As the loss of crop through these pests is negligible, he did not think the loss worth the high costs of spraying with insecticides. Even so, some estate managers for 'cosmetic' reasons do use insecticides: Rattan felt that these were not usually cost-effective. It is significant, then, that in his paper on pest and disease control in Africa with respect to tea Rattan should write: 'Surprisingly though, tea in many countries of Africa is almost free from serious pests and diseases' (1992: 331).

But with new cultural practices and with larger areas being planted with vegetatively propagated material, this situation, he noted, may well change. However, it is worth noting that an advertisement in the *Tea Planter's Handbook* (Grice 1990:68) relating to pest control reads: 'Tea planters can lose up to 40% of potential yields through the ravages of insects and pests such as mosquito bug (*Heliopeltis*), thrips and red spider mite.' This seems to be something of an exaggeration.

I will, then, outline briefly the six main pests of tea, keeping this proviso in mind.

*Mosquito Bug (*Heliopeltis schoutedeni*) (Family:* Miridae*).* The mosquito bug is one of the most important pests of tea, as well as being a pest on many other crops, including cassava, groundnuts, cotton, pigeonpea, beans, coffee and many wild plants. It was first recorded in Malawi in the 1920s, and is a true capsid bug. It is bright red and black (HB 10 mm), with long black antennae, and though active it is rarely seen, as it is crepuscular in habits and keeps hidden.

Both nymphs and adults feed by piercing the plant tissues – tender stems, shoots, young leaves and buds – with their proboscis and sucking the sap. The saliva seems to be toxic, and this causes the blackening and withering of the leaves. In severe cases the bush looks scorched, and there may be severe loss of the crop. Although breeding for most of the year it is scarce during the dry season (September–November) and reaches its peak population at the end of the rains, April–May. It can cause serious damage to young tea in nurseries. The insecticide Endosulfan is considered to be the most effective form of control (Sweeney 1965).

*Red Spider Mite (*Oligonychus coffeae*) (Order:* Acarina*).* The red spider mite is a common pest of tea – this particular mite shares the same name as the tomato pest – and, although present throughout the year, it is mainly found during the dry season from September to December. Its numbers decrease during the rains. A tiny mite, bright crimson, and elliptical in shape, it feeds mainly on the sap of mature leaves, which, if the infestation is severe, can turn a reddish or coppery colour. The leaves then wither and drop off. As with the mosquito bug, the local jat seems more susceptible to the mite than the Indian hybrid tea. There seems evidence that they tend to attack weak and unhealthy tea bushes, and so cultural practices, such as clean weeding, mulching and an adequate level of fertilizer, which increase the vigour of the bush, tend to reduce the severity of attack by the red spider mite. Although this pest may cause loss of crop, Pritam Rattan fervently believes, from experimental evidence, that the use of chemical pesticides to control the red spider mite had not led to any increase in yield, and was hardly cost-effective given the high cost of spraying. As with the mosquito bug, the red spider mite is mostly unrecognized by smallholder tea growers. Judging from early reports, the red spider mite was considered a troublesome pest during the 1920s; and often did 'considerable damage'. Applications of lime sulphur were then used as a control measure (Smee, Ann. Rept. Dept. Agr. 1927: 15; Rattan 1992: 337).

Tea Thrips (Scirtothrips aurantii) *(Order:* Thysanoptera). Thrips are ubiquitous in Southern Africa and a pest on a variety of crops – tobacco, citrus, tomatoes, and macadamia, as well as tea. They are tiny delicate insects, orange-yellow, 1–2 mm long, with membraneous wings, and are good fliers. They occur throughout the year, but are commonest during the dry season, September to December, the nymphs and adults feeding on the tender parts of the tea – young buds, leaves and tender shoots. This causes the margins of the leaves to become brown and brittle, and if infestation is severe defoliation occurs, leaving leafless stems. The time of pruning the tea seems to have a significant effect on the local control of the thrips, and applications of insecticides such as Fenitrothion and Malathion are recommended by the tea research foundation (Grice 1990).

Carpenter Moth (Teregra quadrangular) *(Family:* Arbelidae). On my visits to Zoa and to the tea estates in Mulanje I often encountered the occasional tea bush that had been damaged by the larvae of the carpenter moth. The presence of these brown caterpillars (HB 20 mm) is noticeable by a web that each caterpillar spins, although being nocturnal they are rarely seen. Although not a problem on mature tea, the caterpillars of the moth can ring-bark the stems of young tea, which may result in the death of the plant. Carbaryl is seen as an effective insecticide by the research foundation, to be applied in July and August. Problems with the carpenter moth have only been evident in the last twenty years or so (Grice 1990).

Gelatine Grub (Niphadolepsis alianta) *(Family:* Limacodidae). In May 1938 there was a serious outbreak of what became known as the 'gelatine grub' on two tea estates in the Thyolo district. It suddenly appeared in 'colossal numbers', was extremely destructive of the tea, and caused extreme consternation among European tea planters (Smee 1939). It was not heard of again until the 1960s, when high local populations occurred in both the Thyolo and Mulanje districts. Since then the gelatine grub has been a continuous presence on tea estates, without ever becoming a serious pest. The 'grub' is the caterpillar of a small moth, and is rather slug-like. It is a characteristic bluish-green, with longitudinal wavy white lines (HB 10–15 mm), and rather sticky to the touch. The caterpillars normally feed on the mature leaves of the tea bush, and under favourable conditions can occur in large numbers and do considerable damage. Around 500 caterpillars have been counted on one bush. But normally they are not considered a serious pest (Grice 1990).

The allied nettle grub (*Parasa vivida*), a colourful caterpillar with stinging hairs, is also a pest on tea, and can be troublesome to tea pickers. Its local name is *chiyabwe*.

Bagworm, Mtemankhuni (Eumetia cervina *syn.* Clania moddermanni) *(Family:* Psychidae). Various species of bagworms have been recorded from tea, the most noticeable being *Eumetia cervina*. They are well-known caterpillars of moths, which construct a portable home for themselves from bits of twigs, thorns, sand, and leaves, binding the 'bag' together with silk. The caterpillars can be quite active insects, freely moving about the bushes. Colin Smee (1945) long ago in an article on bagworms in tea recorded four essential kinds in relation to the type of bag constructed – pagoda, straight stick, conical silk bag, and criss-cross grass stalk types. What prompted the article is that there had been reports of serious outbreaks of bagworm in tea, especially in the Thyolo area, which had caused considerable damage locally. At the present time they are not a serious pest of tea, although they may do occasional damage; but according to the research foundation they are easily controlled by insecticides (Grice 1990).

The *Tea Planter's Handbook* records several other insect pests on tea, the leaf weevil (*Systates smeei*), white grubs, the elegant grasshopper, aphids and various mites; but only termites seem to be serious pests, as they are prone to ring-bark young tea (Grice 1990). One tea planter suggested to me that only three pests gave him undue concern – mosquito bug, carpenter moth and termites – but even these were not unduly serious. Many planters have suggested that boron is a simple and effective pesticide against termites.

Coffee (Coffea arabica)
In contrast to tea, which seems to have few serious pests, coffee, like cotton, seems to be besieged with insect pests and diseases. Walking through a tea garden one really has to search hard even to find an insect

pest, apart from the odd termite or mosquito bug. Yet on an instructive tour of Nsuwadzi coffee research station in Mulanje with James Biscoe in May 2001, I was shown around a dozen insect pests – and these were not unkempt coffee gardens. Indeed, tea as a crop in Malawi owes its origins at the end of the nineteenth century to the fact that the coffee estates in Mulanje all failed – largely owing to losses from pests and diseases. Coffee still tends to be a subsidiary crop on estates, and the present area under coffee is around 5,000 ha, only a fraction of the land under tobacco and tea, although there has been some expansion in recent years with improved irrigation and concerns over tobacco prices. But, as Colin Smee suggested long ago, although coffee is a very hardy plant it suffers from a large variety of insect pests, practically all through the year, particularly during the flowering season. Coffee prefers slightly humid conditions, and in Malawi it is grown mainly on estates at a height of between 500 and 1,250 m. Among the more significant pests of coffee are the following four species:

*Coffee Stem Borer (*Anthores leuconotus *syn.* Monochamus ruspator*) (Family:* Ceramycidae*).* The stem borer does a considerable amount of damage to coffee. The adult beetle is large and pale grey, with dark greyish-brown bands (HB 30 mm), with extremely long antennae, 70 mm long. This longicorn beetle is common throughout Malawi, especially in the early rains, and it lays its eggs under the bark of the coffee tree. The larvae, described by local people as *mbozi*, bores into the stem of the Coffee, and makes its way down, and then back up the stem, leaving a lot of wood frass at the base of the tree. The stem of the coffee may become riddled with tunnels. The grub eventually pupates in a large cavity within the stem. The coffee plant begins to show the effects of this damage during the dry season, when the leaves begin to turn yellow, wither and are shed. Smee described this beetle as undoubtedly responsible for more damage to coffee than any other insect, and during the colonial period zinc sulphate and lead arsenate were used as control measures (MNA/Ann. Rept. Dept. Agr. 1927:18). According to James Biscoe it was the coffee stem borer that wiped out the whole coffee industry in Mulanje at the end of the nineteenth century. Control measures now include the use of such insecticides as Regent or Parathion, or having children collect the stem-borers (Clowes *et al.* 1989).

Antestia Bug, Nkhunguni *(*Antestiopsis lineaticollis*) (Family:* Penta-tomidae*).* During the colonial period this shield bug was described as the 'Cameron bug', and was recorded as a common pest on coffee, although the damage done was varied and irregular – as the abundance of the insect fluctuated from year to year. The adult is shield-shaped and dark brown, with orange spots and markings (HB 10 mm). It keeps to dense foliage, out of the sun, and is thus rarely seen. It sucks the fruit of the coffee, and can cause considerable damage to the berries, as well as introducing bacteria into the fruit. Insecticides are the recommended control, such as Fenitrothion and Parathion (Clowes *et al*. 1989).

*Dusky Surface Beetle (*Gonocephalum simplex*) (Family:* Tenebrionidae*).* These are small beetles, the larvae of which are described as 'false wire-worms', which lie hidden in mulch and debris during the day. At night they emerge and feed on the stems of the coffee plant at ground level, often ring-barking the plants. Although not usually a problem, in some areas, such as on estates in the Namweras, they can be an acute problem, killing many young coffee plants. It has been suggested to me that where the herb *Arachnis pintoyi*, which is allied to the groundnut, is grown between the rows of coffee, there is little trouble with the dusky surface beetle (Biscoe 2001).

*Leaf Miner (*Leucoptera meyricki*) (Family:* Lyonetiidae*).* This is the caterpillar of a small white moth that feeds on the underside of the leaves, and can cause considerable damage to coffee, leading to severe defolia-tion. It is described as the most important pest of coffee.

The caterpillar of a similar moth, aptly described as a 'leaf-skele-tonizer' (*Leucoplema dohertyi*) is also a problem on coffee, and in recent years serious outbreaks have occurred. To control these caterpillars, chemical insecticides such as Parathion and Fenitrothion are recom-mended by the research foundation (Clowes *et al*. 1989).

Around thirty other species of insects are described as pests of coffee, but undoubtedly the most problematic pests are two pathogenic fungi – the coffee berry disease (*Colletotrichum coffeanum*) and the bark disease (*Fusarium lateritium*) – the latter having almost wiped out the coffee industry in Malawi in the 1950s (Clowes *et al*. 1989). One of my Malawian friends always referred to these diseases as 'leaf lust'.

Tobacco, Fodya *(*Nicotiana tabacum*)*
An annual crop, and originally a native of tropical America, tobacco is the primary cash crop of Malawi, and is grown both on estates and by small-holder farmers. Tobacco has been grown in Central Africa since time immemorial, but the growing of Virginia tobacco on a commercial scale was pioneered by John Buchanan at the end of the nineteenth century. Since the 1970s production of tobacco in Malawi has more than doubled – an area of 113,000 ha is now under tobacco – and, as noted earlier, it

now accounts for over 70 per cent of the country's foreign exchange earnings. Malawi, in fact, is the world's largest exporter of burley tobacco, and produces more than 120 million kg of tobacco, almost all of which is exported (Matthews and Wilshaw 1992). Most of the tobacco now grown in Malawi is either flue-cured Virginia or burley tobacco – the latter being air-cured by hanging it on racks in grass-thatched sheds. Significantly, tobacco is seen as a 'man's crop', even though women make up nearly 70 per cent of all full-time farmers in Malawi. Malawi's heavy dependence on two crops, maize and tobacco, together with an external debt of around $2 billion, is having high social and environmental costs – accelerating degradation of the land through deforestation, loss of soil fertility, depletion of water resources, and high levels of poverty among the rural population.

It is of interest that the *Malawi Tobacco Handbook* (Matthews and Wilshaw 1992) makes no mention at all of insect pests on tobacco – apart from an advert by the company 'Antipest'. Yet throughout the colonial period insect pests were viewed by planters as a serious problem, particularly the white fly (*Bemisia tabaci*), which transmits a disease locally known as 'leaf cure' or 'cabbaging', and the tobacco beetle. The latter species attacks the stored tobacco (MNA/A3/2/267). Discussions I had with local farmers and farm managers in the Namadzi area, together with my own observations, suggests that five species were particularly troublesome on tobacco. These were the following.

Common Black Ant, Nyerere *(*Pheidole spp*.) (sub-family: Myrmecinae).* These ants are prolific everywhere, even entering houses, and have a particular fondness for the tobacco seed. They can therefore cause problems in tobacco nurseries. The activities of these ants are confined to seed beds; but owing to their ubiquity the ants are capable of removing much seed, so that germination is practically negligible.

*African Bollworm (*Helicoverpa armigera*) (Family:* Noctuidae*).* Known to European tobacco farmers as the 'tobacco budworm' and to local people as *mbozi* or *chipukwa*, this caterpillar is a common pest on tobacco. It is usually pale green, with white and black mid-dorsal stripes, and is around 38 mm long. As was noted earlier, it is a cosmopolitan species, and is also a common pest on maize, cotton and groundnuts. It bores into the stem of the tobacco plant, and on tobacco farms near Namadzi it was noted on young tobacco in December and January. One farm manager told me that he had used Tamaron as an insecticide without success, and had then had to use Karate. Only a few kilometres away another tobacco farmer told me he had not been troubled with tobacco 'budworm' that year (2000–1), so that attacks by this pest may be quite local.

Elegant Grasshopper, M'Nunkhadala *(*Zonocerus elegans*) (Family:* Pyrgomorphidae*).* A common pest on both maize and cotton, as noted earlier, the elegant grasshopper is also a pest on tobacco. As it also feeds on a wide variety of other crops, this insect is probably the most troublesome, as well as the best-known, of all Malawian agricultural pests. The recommended insecticide is Baythroid (a synthetic Pyrethroid) or Malathion.

Tobacco Aphid, Nsabwe *(*Myzus persicae*) (Family:* Aphididae*).* This aphid feeds on a variety of plants, and in some years can be abundant on tobacco. It is less a problem in itself, than as a vector for various virus diseases that affect tobacco.

Green Shield Bug, Nkhunguni *(*Nezara viridula*) (Family:* Pentatomidae*).* This is a small green shield bug, with a strong, somewhat unpleasant smell. It is smaller than *Nezara robusta* (which is eaten) (HB 18 mm), but is much more widely distributed, and is common everywhere, attacking a variety of plants – beans, cotton, and macadamia, as well as tobacco. As with other tobacco pests, the commonest form of control seems to be the application of chemical insecticides, such as Bathyroid or Tamaron. In the Neno district I found this bug to be a very troublesome pest on the fruit of macadamia trees.

These five pests were those discussed by local farmers, and familiar to me on the tobacco farms of the Namadzi area. But many other insect pests have been recorded on tobacco, including cutworms (*Agrotis* sp.), white grub (the larvae of *Scarabeid* beetles), the giant cricket (*Brachytrypes membranaceus*), the red spider mite (*Tetranychus* sp.) and the larvae of several moths. Yet the insect that was most discussed during the colonial period was the tobacco beetle, *Lasioderma serricorne*. This is a tiny reddish-brown beetle (HB 2–4 mm) that feeds on stored tobacco, as well as on other stored products, and can cause serious losses. Sweeney records that it was often found living in pyrethrum powder, an insecticide often used to kill it! (1962: 12). In the past, infestations of these beetles were so alarming, that the agricultural department often decreed the destruction of several tons of tobacco in order to eradicate the beetle or to prevent its spreading. As now, the main form of control was by fumigation. Smee argued that all tobacco should be uprooted and destroyed at the end of the season in order to control insect pests (MNA/A3/2/254).

This practice, however, does not seem to be carried out at the present time – for the dried stems of the tobacco plant are collected by women as fuel.

Sugarcane, Mzimbe *(*Saccharum officinarum*).* Although sugarcane is grown all over the country on a small scale, usually in low-lying and *dambo* areas, and is chewed raw by almost everyone for its juice, as a cash crop it is confined to the larger estates. These are located mainly at Dwangwa on the Lakeshore north of Nkhotakota, and at Nchalo in the Lower Shire Valley. Around 19,000 ha of land are under sugarcane production.

Around a dozen insects have been recorded as pests on sugarcane, but surprisingly, compared with Zimbabwe and Mozambique, Malawi has few serious pests. When I discussed insect pests of sugarcane with one estate manager, he suggested to me that there was no real problem with insect pests in the Lower Shire Valley, and if outbreaks did occur they were usually local, and too late to do anything about. When I explored the cane fields at Nchalo Sugar Estate with Henry Moyo, who was responsible for pests and disease control, apart from slight damage from the pink stalk borer, and the occasional termite and elegant grasshopper, we found little evidence of any insect damage. Indeed, Moyo suggested to me that the main problems of sugarcane focused around rodent damage, especially by the cane rat (*nchenzi*) and rust (fungal) disease, rather than insects. The three insects that have caused acute problems elsewhere in Southern Africa – the black maize beetle (*Heteronychus licas*) – both the adult and larvae ('white grub') damage the cane; the larvae of the moth *Eldana saccharina*; and the sugarcane borer, *Chilo sacchariphagus* – have not been recorded as causing problems on the sugar estates of the Lower Shire Valley.

Besides termites, the elegant grasshopper and the mealy bug (*Saccharicoccus sacchari*), and the occasional outbreak of locusts – there was a serious influx of locusts in February 1993 – only the pink stalk borer *Sesamia calamistis* (family: *Noctuidae*) seems to be a serious pest on sugarcane at Nchalo. The larvae are pink to violet, with a brown head (HB 30 mm) and they burrow into the stem of the sugarcane, and feed on the inner pith. They can thus do considerable damage to the cane.

(On the insect pests of sugarcane see Clowes and Breakwell 1998: 213–28.)

Insects and Pesticides

I have discussed above many of the insect pests that damage the main crops of Malawi, in both the smallholder and estate sectors of the economy. There is no doubt that insects in Malawi take a high toll of agricultural production, and perhaps around 10–20 per cent of the main subsistence crops, such as maize, beans and pigeonpea, may be lost to insects. Yet there is also a growing sense in Malawi, as in other parts of the world, that a 'war against nature', which is reflected in an undue reliance on chemical pesticides, is damaging both to ourselves and to the natural world. Yet little more than a decade ago one Malawian scholar was writing: 'Today, agricultural fields are real battle-fields. Anything wanting to grow, creep or fly on the farmlands is inevitably caught in the firing line of chemicals and perishes in it.' And he notes how excessively chemical pesticides have been used in Malawi given their low cost, effectiveness and availability (Manda 1985: 31).

However, the pious platitudes put out by the World Bank and development agencies, namely that a society is only viable and sustainable if both human well-being and the ecosystem are maintained or improved (has anyone ever argued otherwise?) seem increasingly to be unduly compromised by the widespread use of chemical pesticides. Nowadays, these are not only expensive, but are seen as dangerous to human health, and ecologically suspect. Yet our dependence and commitment to pesticides is quite staggering, even though they have led to serious health problems – besides causing asthma, cancer, infertility and chronic fatigue and mood disorders, there are many thousands of fatalities each year from the use of pesticides – as well as to high ecological costs, such as the loss of wildlife, pollution of groundwater, and the elimination of beneficial insects. Rachel Carson's classic study *Silent Spring* highlighted the problematic nature of synthetic pesticides many years ago, although she was not against chemical insecticides *per se* (1962: 11), but only called for a more balanced ecological approach, so that we could find a way both to manage insect pests, and also to protect ourselves and the environment. But the emphasis on the control of insects through pesticides has created two additional problems. Firstly, the insects themselves have become resistant to the pesticides and so we have created a 'quickening treadmill', with the need for ever-increasing use of ever more powerful pesticides. And secondly, the pursuit of biologically based methods of pest control has tended to be hampered by our commitment to pesticides (Winston 1997: 12–16).

Nonetheless, as we have noted above, the emphasis in Malawi over the last decade has been to encourage integrated pest management – if for no other reason than the fact that ordinary farmers in Malawi can no longer afford the high costs of insecticides. A kilogram of Carbaryl, for example, now costs around 475MK (2000), almost half the monthly income of an agricultural worker. Thus, as both Smee and Sweeney advocated many

Figure 5 Market vendor, Zomba, selling insecticides.

years ago, efforts are currently being made – as reflected in the Integrated Pest Management Project (Orr *et al.* 2000) – to encourage non-chemical pest-management strategies. These include: crop rotation, suitable tillage practices, encouraging natural enemies and developing biological controls of the pest, the removal and burning of infested plants, selecting resistant varieties, interplanting with aromatic herbs to keep pests at bay, and the development and use of organic insecticides, such as *ombwe* (*Tephrosia vugelii*) and *mphanjobvu* (*Neorauthanis mitis*). It is thus highly ironic that tobacco farmers and tea estate managers who have for decades been avid enthusiasts for chemical pesticides (and fertilizers) should now, with the potential development of organic crops for export (such as *Echinacea*) have suddenly become converts to organic farming.

There is, however, still a ready market for insecticides among smallholder farmers, and in most markets in Malawi one usually finds two or three vendors selling small packets of insecticides, such as Sevin, Actellic and Temik (Figure 5). Most of these vendors are young men in their early twenties. In a survey I made of Zomba Market Sevin 85c (*Seveni*) was popularly sold as an insecticide, and seen as effective in protecting pumpkin, cabbage, and tobacco against such insects as grasshoppers (*chitete*), caterpillars (*mbozi*), leaf beetles (*mkupe*), termites (*chiswe*), aphids (*nsabwe za m'masamba*, 'plant lice') and cotton stainers (*chamatowo*). The vendors bought the Sevin at 15MK a packet and sold it at 2MK per spoonful. The insecticide was described as medicine (*mankhwala*), and was clearly aimed at farmers growing cash crops in *dimba* gardens. The pesticide Actellic is sold everywhere, and is particularly used to combat house mites (*nyakanyaka*), bed bugs (*nsikidzi*) and the maize weevil (*kafutwefutwe*). One difficulty, however, is that Malawi does not manufacture any pesticides, and so the continued reliance on chemical insecticides for pest control absorbs a substantial amount of foreign exchange. (For general studies of insect pests and their control, particularly relating to Africa, see Smit 1964; Kumar 1984; Van Emden 1989; Geddes 1990; and NRI 1992).

Household Pests and Locust Swarms

Prologue

'The world is a scene of risk', wrote John Dewey, 'it is uncertain, unstable, uncannily unstable. Its dangers are irregular, inconstant, not to be counted upon as to their times and seasons ... plague, famine, failure of crops, disease ... are always just around the corner' (1929: 41). But Dewey, an empirical rationalist, also emphasized the positive aspects of life – abundance, joy, ideals, ceremonies and song. People in Malawi therefore not only have to contend with the ravages of insect pests in relation to agricultural crops, but also find that insects invade their homes and granaries, and at irregular intervals, swarms of locusts descend upon their fields. In this chapter I want to focus on these two categories of insect pests – those that relate to domestic households; and, from a historical perspective, the impact of the larger grasshoppers on the agricultural economy. These represent the inconstant risks of the subsistence farmers in Malawi. As a kind of interlude, I shall also briefly discuss the forest pests of Malawi.

Household Pests

Discussions I had with local people in the Domasi Valley, north of Zomba, and in the village adjacent to Kapalasa Farm, suggest that many different kinds of insects are seen as troublesome (*bvuta*) in varying degrees. But here we may discuss the five key species that have particular salience for Malawians.

Cockroach, Mpemvu *(*Periplaneta americana*) (Order:* Blattoidea*)*
The term 'cockroach' comes from the Spanish *cucaracha*, and it is estimated that these insects have inhabited the world for more than 250 million years, as the earliest fossil cockroaches look very much like contemporary species. They are indeed tough, resilient creatures that have amazing endurance and are able to live in extreme conditions. They appear to live everywhere that humans live. In one apartment in Austin,

Texas, around one hundred thousand cockroaches were found, for they are adept scavengers, and are highly omnivorous, feeding on almost anything (H. E. Evans 1970: 48–61).

Several species of cockroach are found in Malawi, and the large American cockroach is perhaps the commonest, although as Skaife suggests, its name may be somewhat misleading, for it is probable that most of the domestic cockroaches originally came from Africa (1979: 46). The cockroach is ubiquitous in rural areas, and found in most huts and houses, and it is mainly nocturnal. It tends to like warm, damp conditions. Some huts I have slept in have been literally swarming with cockroaches, and they can disturb one's sleep, although they are quite harmless. Given their oval, flattened shape and greasy appearance they are loathed by Europeans; but Malawians tend to tolerate them, even though they find them troublesome and often attempt to eradicate them. As they are seen as defecating a good deal (*nyatsa kwambiri*) and as moving among the relish stores, cockroaches are thought by some people to cause diarrhoea (*segula m'mimba*, 'open stomach'). Evans indeed confirms that, although cockroaches are basically clean animals, they do in fact carry bacteria that can cause intestinal disorder (H. E. Evans 1970: 49; Service 1996: 219; but cf. Lauck 1998: 83). The suggestion that the cockroach is edible always meets with a negative response, and, like the black rat, which also frequents houses, it is never eaten. People also see the cockroach as destroying (*onongeka*) things, and use the insecticide Doom (*Dumu*), bought at local stores to clear their houses of the pest.

Termites, Chiswe (Order: Isoptera)

Termites are seen principally as agricultural pests, particularly on maize, beans and pigeon pea; but they also cause a great deal of damage to houses, especially the traditional 'wattle and daub' huts. As their diet consists essentially of plant material of a woody nature, the termites are apt to cause much damage to the wooden structures of a house – doors, beams, posts, and often their presence is undetected until the structures collapse. During the colonial period considerable damage was caused to houses even within urban areas, and directives were issued regarding measures to be taken in the building of brick houses. This entailed the construction of a termite-proof thick layer of cement, at least an inch (26 mm) thick, and treating the woodwork with creosol or a solution of mercuric chloride. Alternatively, sheets of metal were recommended as foundations to the house (MNA/51/359/31). Brick houses with a 'tin' (*malata*) roof are now generally favoured in rural areas, not only because they give more protection from termites, but also because timber and thatching grass are becoming increasingly scarce, given the widespread deforestation. Apart from the occasional digging-out and destroying of the queen from a termite colony that may be close to a house, or using Sevin as a pesticide, local people rarely practise control measures against termites. These insects also cause considerable damage to forestry plantations and to exotic trees, especially blue gums (*Eucalyptus* spp.). Often tree seedlings are completely lost to termites, specifically through the ring-barking of the base of the plant (Meke 1995).

Bed Bugs, Nsikidzi *(*Cimex hemipterus*) (Family:* Cimicidae*)*
This 'hideous pest', as the bed bug has been described (Johnston 1897: 239), probably belongs to a group of parasitic insects that primarily evolved in relation to bats, but later switched to humans. It has a distinctive odour, which some people can detect in an infested bedroom. This acts as a deterrent to birds, bats and other potential predators (H. E. Evans 1970: 171–3).

Having been bitten by bed bugs while sleeping in both local huts and in rest houses, I can personally vouch that these are troublesome pests. They are small tick-like insects, dark reddish-brown (HB 6 mm) and are wingless, flattened and oval in shape. They are parasitic and feed on the blood of humans, and live by day in the cracks and crevices and in other sheltered places in houses, coming out at night to feed on humans (Sweeney 1970: 40). They have the ability to live for long periods without food, and become particularly evident when a person goes to sleep in an old disused hut. They are very difficult to eradicate. People vary in their reactions to the bites of the bed bug. Some hardly notice the effects, while others may become quite ill. I developed lumps on my back, and the bitten areas were both achy and itchy. For local people it is considered troublesome in that they are not able to sleep well (*samagona bwino*), and their main protection against the bedbug is to plaster the floor and walls of a house in a careful manner so as to eradicate any cracks where the bedbug may take shelter. Others use Sevin as a pesticide, pouring (*thira*) it around the walls.

Maize Weevil, Nankafumbwe *(*Sitophilus zeamays*) (Family:* Curculionidae*)*
For local people this is the best-known of the weevils that feed on maize in the granaries (*nkhokwe*) or in maize stores. Indeed, with increasing thefts of maize in rural areas, and the difficulty of obtaining bamboo and timber to construct granaries, more and more people are storing maize in bags inside the house, which makes the maize harvest even more susceptible to losses from the maize weevil. This insect is a tiny snouted beetle, dark brown, and 3 mm long, which feeds on the grain of maize and other

cereals. It is a strong flier, has a cosmopolitan distribution, and is believed to have originated in India (Sweeney 1962: 20). It inflicts an enormous amount of damage, and losses are incalculable. I have seen bags of maize that were literally riddled with the maize weevil, and losses are said to be bigger with the increasing use of hybrid maize, which has a softer husk than the local maize (*chimanga chamakolo*). Also, maize stored in granaries tended to have fewer maize weevils, as air circulates continuously between the maize cobs. Everyone suggested to me that in the past the *nankafumbwe* affected the maize far less, though rodents were often a problem. It has been estimated that in the past losses caused by the maize weevil were generally low – less than 5 per cent in traditional storage systems – where farmers cultivated local varieties of maize (Schulten 1969; Robertson 1997).

If people discover that maize is infested with weevil, women will put the maize on a reed mat (*mphasa*), in the sun to dry (*yanika*), and then again winnow (*peta*) the maize. An infusion of tobacco is also said to be a control measure, but most people use Actellic, obtained from a market vendor at around 10MK per packet, as the main pesticide. Other people have suggested to me the use of ashes from groundnut husks (*makako anthedza*) as a deterrent to overcome (*gonjetsa*) this troublesome insect.

Although the maize weevil is the primary pest of maize, very often this weevil breaks into the grain, and is then followed by the flour beetle (*Tribolium* spp.) (Family: *Tenbrionidae*), which often destroys much of what is left. Though not as common as the maize weevil, it is nonetheless common in all stored products, especially maize and groundnut flour.

Two other small beetles are common pests of stored maize. Both are also described as *nankafumbwe*, and belong to the family *Bostrychidae*, which is composed of wood-boring beetles. The first is the lesser grain borer, *Rhizopertha dominica*. This is a tiny, dark brown beetle, 3 mm long, its body covered with small tubercles. It is a common pest of stored products, including maize.

The other is the now well-known larger grain borer (*Prostephanus truncatus*). Originally a pest from tropical America, this is a tiny, cylindrical, dark brown beetle, 3–4 mm long, with rather rectangular elytra. It is a strong flier, and was initially detected in Tanzania in 1981, and has since spread throughout eastern Africa, as well as to Ghana, Nigeria and other parts of West Africa. It was first recorded in Malawi in 1991 in the Karonga and Chitipa districts, and in the past decade it has multiplied, and is now found throughout the country. It is thus now described as a 'permanent resident' of Malawi, and causes severe damage to maize cobs and dried cassava. The loss of grain can be as high as 30 per cent, and in the Lower Shire valley in 1999 farmers reported losses as high as 70 per cent. In spite of widespread damage and losses, farmers in Malawi are still unfamiliar with the larger grain borer – frequently dubbed LGB, and so development agencies, such as the Malawian–German Plant Protection Project, funded by GTZ, have been conducting an 'awareness campaign' to help farmers and extension workers to appreciate the damage that this pest is causing to stored maize. Recommended control measures have included the use of such insecticides as the organophosphates and pyrethroids, usually in combination (Actellic). But given the high cost of such pesticides, research has been conducted involving a predator beetle, *Teretriosoma nigrescens*, as a potential biological control agent to reduce the population of the larger grain borers (IPM Newsletter 6/2002; for a pioneering study of the insect pests of stored products in Malawi see Sweeney 1962).

It is of interest that in his *Reminiscences of Livingstonia* Robert Laws mentions that in the past ship's biscuits were heavily infested with weevils. Before eating a biscuit, a seaman would therefore break it and tap it on the table to dislodge any weevils before putting the biscuit in his mouth (1934: 239).

Itch Mite, Chinyakanyaka *(*Sarcoptes scabiei*, Order:* Acarpina*)*

The mites are not insects, but are arthropods allied to the ticks. They are tiny creatures, greyish-white, 0.4 mm long, and barely visible. They are parasitic on mammals, including humans. The itch mite infests humans, burrowing under the skin, and can cause intense itching or scabies. People describe it as taking hold of you (*gwira*), but say that, at a distance, you do not see it (*samaona*), even though it bites you (*luma*). As a control measure people pound the leaves of the cassava plant in water and then sprinkle (*waza*) the infusion near the floor of the house to get rid of them. Alternatively, people use ashes as a deterrent. People suggest that when the itch mites are around there is never any peace (*mtendere*).

There are many other domestic pests that are troublesome to people in Malawi, and these include the human louse *(nsabwe, Pediculus humanus)*, the common house fly *(ntcheche, Musca domestica)*, the tumbu fly *(mphutsi, Cordylobia anthrophaga)*, fleas *(utitili, Ctenocephalides* sp.), the common cricket *(kalijosolo, Gryllus bimaculatus)* and several species of ants that enter houses, particularly in the search for sugar. Two species are particularly involved: the sugar ant *(chimalasuga, Camponotus maculatus)* and the brown house ant *(Pheodole megacephala)*.

From discussions I had with around seventy people in the villages adjacent to Kapalasa Farm where I enquired as to the *most* troublesome pest of the household *(nyumba)*, data contained in Table 5.1 were obtained.

Table 5.1 Numbers of People Considering Specific Insects their most Troublesome Household Pests (of a Total of 70 Interviewees from Villages around Kapalasa Farm)

Pest	Local Name	Number of Persons
Ants	*Nyerere Chimalasuga*	16
Cockroach	*Mphemvu*	15
Bedbug	*Nsikidzi*	9
Itch mite	*Chinyakanyaka*	8
Mosquito	*Udzudzu*	6
Fleas	*Utitili*	4
Human louse	*Nsabwe*	4

Other pests mentioned were the common house fly, the maize weevil, termites, common crickets and *tumbu* fly. People recognize that certain insects like the house fly (*ntchenche*) are troublesome in that they defecate (*nyera*) in food, and spread diseases such as diarrhoea, although one person thought that the fly was a carrier of malaria (*malungo*).

The mosquito (*udzudzu*) was also frequently discussed as a household pest, and considered troublesome (*bvuta* is the common expression), and is associated with malaria – but this is the subject of the next chapter.

Forest Pests

Although efforts have been made to establish community-based forest areas, the majority of woodlands and forestry plantation in Malawi – mainly of pines and eucalyptus – fall under the auspices of the forestry department or private estates. Around 97 per cent of Malawi's forests consist of indigenous woodlands, mostly dominated by *Julbernardia* and *Brachystegia* spp. (*miombo*) trees, and around 38 per cent of this consists of protected forest reserves (781,360 ha) (NRI 1996: 31). Blue gum (*Eucalyptus*) plantations are widespread, and there are extensive forestry plantations on the mountains of Mlanje, Zomba, Dedza and the Viphya, mostly under various pines. In 1966 a forest entomology section of the Forest Reserve Institute (FRIM) was established in Zomba, and much research has been undertaken on the forest insects of Malawi (R. F. Lee 1971; Esbjerg 1976). Forest insect pests are of little interest or concern to ordinary people in Malawi, but four pests are worth discussing here for their wider interest and public concern.

*Eucalyptus Wood Borer (*Phoracatha semipunctata*) (Family:* Cerambycidae*)*

This longicorn beetle is an exotic species, a native of Australia, and seems to have followed the eucalyptus trees in spreading throughout the world. It is now found in South America, the Middle East, the Mediterranean region and most of Africa, and was first recorded in Malawi at Blantyre Sawmill in 1969. A decade later it had spread to virtually all the blue gum plantations in Malawi. It is a typical longicorn beetle: dark brown, with yellowish bands across the elytra (HB 40 mm) and a very long antenna (50 mm long). The beetle favours dead or dying trees, and in Zambia, in drought-stressed areas, up to 90 per cent of the blue gum trees have been reported killed because of infestation. The damage is inflicted by the pale yellowish larvae, which tunnel under the bark, and when infestation is severe, can form a dense network of overlapping galleries, and even ring-bark the tree. In attempts to control the beetle it was deemed advisable to peel the bark off all felled trees soon after logging, and before transplantation, and to remove all dead or dying blue gum trees. The beetle still has a presence throughout the country (Esbjerg 1976: 45; Majawa 1981).

*Pine grasshopper (*Plagiotriptus pinivorus*) (Family:* Eumasticidae*)*

For many decades the exotic pine plantations of Malawi seemed to be relatively free of insect pests. Then in the late 1960s there was a serious outbreak of this grasshopper on Chambe plateau, Mulanje, for in July 1969 this species caused severe defoliation of the *Pinus patula* trees. This necessitated aerial spraying with the insecticide gamma-BHC. The grasshopper is plump, wingless, green and relatively small, 20–30 mm long. Originally it fed on indigenous trees of the *Euphorbiaceae* family, such as *msopa* (*Bridelia micrantha*) and *mpefu* (*Macaranga capensis*); but it seems to have successfully changed its feeding habits, moving on to the pines. It subsequently became a pest on Zomba plateau, and seems to prefer *Pinus patula,* although it also feeds on *Cupressus lindley* (R. F. Lee, 1972).

The outbreak of this grasshopper on Chambe plateau was recorded as the 'most serious insect infestation' that the Forestry Department had so far experienced, but was nonetheless noted as the 'only real pest of *Pinus patula* in this country' (Esjberg 1976: 18; Powell 1977). Less than a decade later there was a serious infestation of aphids on the pines.

Although of less economic importance, the allied species *Malawia leei* (family: *Lentulidae*) is also a pest on *Pinus patula*. A small, wingless, pale reddish-brown grasshopper (HB 20 mm) it feeds on the needles of the pines, and has been recorded on Chambe plateau.

*Pine Woolly Aphid (*Pineus pini*) (Family:* Adelgidae*)*

In 1976 Esjberg wrote that fortunately 'woolly aphids have not yet been recorded from the Malawian forests' (1976: 24). Only eight years later (1984) this exotic pest was recorded in the Chongoni forest, Dedza, where an estimated 1,500 ha of *Pinus kesiya* were severely infested with the aphid. Since then it has been recorded in all parts of the country, and is a great concern, as some 90 per cent of the country's forestry plantations are under pine (62,454 ha), and the aphid, when infestation is severe, can cause losses of up to 30 per cent of the annual growth of the trees.

The pine woolly aphids are tiny and barely visible to the eye, but are usually detected by the presence of small tufts of whitish 'wool' that they leave at the base of pine needles. They feed on the juices of the needles, and on young bark, and whole twigs may become covered with woolly mats. This can cause die-back of the stems, and yellowing of the pine needles, and, where infestation is high, the slow demise of the trees.

The allied pine needle aphid (*Eulachnus rileyi*) (family *Lachnidae*) is also a common pest on pine trees, on both *Pinus kesiya* and *Pinus patula*. Also an exotic, it was first recorded in 1979, having spread through southern Africa in the preceding decade. These are tiny insects, grey to reddish, 1–2 mm long, with wax-covered bodies. They are extremely mobile, and feed on the pine needles, causing yellowish mottling. When infestation is severe, they can inflict much damage, and up to 30 per cent loss in annual tree growth. In 1990 it was estimated that in Malawi, coupled with the pine woolly aphid, this insect caused damage worth US$5.2 million.

Neither insecticides not biological controls have yet proved to be effective in controlling the pine aphid (Atuahene 1992; Chilima 1997).

*Cypress aphid (*Cinara cuppressivora*) (Family:* Lachnidae*)*

This exotic aphid was first recorded in Malawi in 1986 in a cypress hedge on the Viphya plateau, and has since spread throughout Malawi. It feeds mainly on cypress and cedar trees, and does not appear to attack pines, and is chiefly associated with such trees as the cypress *Cuppressus lusitanica* and the Mulanje cedar, *Widdringtonia whytei*. The aphids feed on the slender stems of the trees, rather than on the foliage, and cause yellowing of the leaves. When infestation is severe, whole branches become yellow and die back. The sudden appearance of these aphids in Malawi has caused devastation to the forests of the country, both to the cypress plantations and to the indigenous cedar forests on Mulanje mountain. A survey in 1992 revealed that about 60 per cent of the Mulanje cedar growing in the Tuchila forest had been seriously attacked by the cypress aphid, and that between 10 and 20 per cent of the trees were either dead of moribund (Atuahene 1992).

For some years the unique cedar forests on Mulanje mountain, though within a protected area, had been neglected or mismanaged, and had suffered continuously from illegal felling and uncontrolled fires. Infestation of the aphid has thus proved to be the last straw, a new and disturbing threat to the cedar, which is, in fact, Malawi's national tree (Chapman 1995: 49). Not only does the aphid seriously hinder the regeneration of the cedar, but it is said to kill a mature cedar in as little as twelve months. It is estimated that the aphid has already killed around ten thousand cedar trees on Mulanje Mountain. Damage caused to the plantation and cedar forests of Malawi by these aphids is estimated at around US$3 million (Atuahene and Chilima 1993; Singh 2001: 3).

As chemical control of the aphid was seen as too costly, or problematic on environmental grounds – although the use of such pesticides as Dimethoate is recommended on a limited scale – research efforts have been made to find a feasible form of biological control. The pioneering studies of Clement Chilima and the late and much lamented Sally Singh have indicated the potential of the parasitic wasp *Pauesia juniperum* (Family: *Braconidae*) as a biological control of the aphid (Chilima 1997; Singh 2001).

Locust Swarms

The Red Locust

The red locust (*Nomadacris septemfasciata*) (Family: *Acrididae*) has been described as a 'forgotten menace' (Whellan 1961), as well as the biggest single threat to agricultural production in Malawi. For along with the migrating locust (*Locusta migratoria*) it periodically swarms, and can cause widespread devastation to crops.

Locust swarms or plagues have been known since time immemorial, at least since the origins of agriculture. In the Bible there is the record of the prophet Moses calling upon the Hebrew god (*circa* 1200 BC) to send locusts upon the land, and thus 'the locust went up all over the land of Egypt and … very grievous they were. For they covered the face of the whole earth, so that the land was darkened, and they did eat every herb of the land, and all the fruit of the trees … and there remained not any green thing, either tree or herb of the field, through all the land of Egypt' (Exodus 10: 14–15).

Locusts, or swarming grasshoppers, are found throughout the world, and, as Howard Evans suggests (H. E. Evans 1970: 211), almost every year is the 'year of the locust' somewhere in the world, for locusts have the capacity of building up their population into immense numbers. Studies by the well-known Russian-born entomologist Boris Uvarov

(1928) detailed how the swarming grasshoppers led, in fact, 'a double life', consisting of a solitary phase, when they are sedentary, harmless, feeding on local vegetation and generally of a cryptic coloration, brown or green; and a gregarious phase, when under specific conditions they become highly gregarious, of brighter coloration and extremely active as swarms migrate – disperse – to other areas. As a swarm they usually fly downwind, and a medium-sized swarm may consist of several million insects, feeding on the vegetation on which they land, and eating daily their own weight in food (Newman 1965: 124–8). The devastation to crops that a swarm of locusts may cause is therefore immense. As it moves freely across national borders, the locust has been described as an 'international enemy', one that requires research and pest management strategies on an international scale, particularly as it is suggested that an average-sized swarm of, for example, the desert locust consists of 30 million insects. Such a swarm can, in 24 hours, destroy crops that could feed many thousands of people. In fact, throughout much of Africa, particularly the Sahel region, locusts are still a major problem, which at intervals reaches plague proportions. Over the last decades, millions of dollars have been spent in attempts to control the swarming grasshoppers – the locusts (Baron 1972; Panos Institute 1993).

Four species of locust are important in Africa; the brown locust (*Locustana paradalina*), which is confined to southern Africa, its natural habitat being the Karroo region of the Cape province; the desert locust (*Schistocerca gregaria*), which is found mainly in Africa north of the equatorial rain forest and in Arabia; the migratory locust (*Locusta migratoria*), which has a very wide range, stretching from Africa through Asia to Australia and New Zealand; and finally, the red locust (*Nomadacris septemfasciata*), which is confined to southern Africa and Madagascar. Only the last two species have been found in Malawi.

The red locust is a large grasshopper (HB 75 mm), yellowish- to greyish-brown, with a pale yellowish-brown dorsal stripe, and semi-transparent reddish-purple wings. The forewing is pale greyish-brown with seven dark brown bars – hence its specific name. It has a characteristic short spine between the forelegs. The red locust breeds from November to March, the female laying her eggs in the soil, usually in sandy areas. The adults are mostly active during the dry season, from August to December. In the Lake Chilwa basin they are associated with the flood plains, and during the dry season feed mainly on bushrush (*Typha augustifolia*). It seems to be a characteristic species of floodplain grasslands, and in Malawi, besides Lake Chilwa, it is found in the Ndindi marsh near Nsanje, and in low-lying areas on some tobacco estates near Mchinji. Elsewhere, the main outbreak areas of the red locust are Lake Rukwa in south-west Tanzania, Mweru Wa Ntipa and the Kafue flats in Zambia, and the Gorongosa plains of Mozambique (Sweeney 1964b: Brown 1979).

As with other locusts, the red locust population in its solitary phase remains at a low level for many years, confined to what is described as an 'outbreak area' – and for Malawi, this is essentially the Lake Chilwa basin. Then, at periodic intervals, the red locust swarms, and 'outbreaks' occur; these are often described as if they form cycles. Over the past hundred years several of these periodic outbreaks have occurred in Malawi.

Locust Swarms in the Colonial Period

At the beginning of the colonial period, there were many report of locust swarms, and Harry Johnston writes of the new protectorate, British Central Africa, as being 'much afflicted' by migratory locusts during the years 1893–5. They appear to have come from the north, and passed through Malawi *en route* to South Africa, causing many serious crop losses. Johnston writes of large numbers of local people beating drums and tin pans, shouting and clapping hands to drive off the locusts from the crops, as well as setting off dynamite. He also writes of the many birds – 'allies in combating the enemy' – that were in evidence, feeding on the locusts – kites, hawks, ravens (Johnston 1897: 370). A local European planter in 1896 also wrote of the 'locust scourge' entering its third season, and noted that it was local people who were the chief sufferers. He also mentions that the coffee plantations were not attacked by the locusts, and gives details of a poisonous concoction to eradicate the locusts – a mixture of arsenic, bran and molasses. Apparently, the locusts were attracted by its smell – with fatal consequences (*Central Africa Planter* 1/7 (1896): 119–20). The locust invasion seems to have sporadically recurred until 1910, to the extent that Colin Smee could write of the 'locust outbreak of 1893–1910'. It seems to have principally involved the migratory locust (*Locusta migratoria*) invading the country from the north. Smee also hints that the migration of the Yao people into the Shire highlands in the nineteenth century may have been related to severe locust outbreaks in their homeland (Smee 1941: 20–2).

Few reports of locust swarms were noted until the 1930s, when in December 1932 swarms of red locust invaded the country, coming from both the west (Zambia) and the Zambezi valley in the south-west. During the next few years the red locust spread over much of central and south-eastern Africa, causing serious damage to crops. Numbers decreased until the early 1940s, when the locust virtually disappeared as a problem.

Throughout the 1930s attempts were made through the Department of Agriculture, via the government entomologist Colin Smee, to monitor and control the red locust outbreaks. In 1932 invasions of both the migratory and red locust occurred. During the November and December of that year, flying swarms of migratory locusts came down from the north (Tanzania), traversed the whole of the protectorate, and then went on to the Zambezi valley beyond Nsanje. According to Smee, no egg-laying by these swarms took place. At the same time – at the end of 1932 – swarms of red locust also invaded the country. Large swarms entered the Lower Shire valley from the west; while separate swarms came from what is now north-east Zambia, and moved into the Kasungu and Lilongwe districts. These swarms then penetrated east and south to the southern lakeshore and the Shire Highlands. In the following year, during the rainy season of 1933–4, a similar pattern occurred, with the locust swarms – mainly of the red locust – occurring throughout the protectorate, with the area from Kasungu to the southern lakeshore and the Lower Shire valley being the areas most affected.

As an intensive campaign against the locusts was impossible for financial reasons, the main efforts of the government entomologist were focused on crop protection, employing European locust officers and local personnel as patrols, often people seconded from the police or tobacco boards. Considerable damage was done to crops by the red locust swarms of 1933. In the Lower Shire valley, around 20 per cent of the cotton gardens were attacked, of which around half were totally destroyed. Smee estimated that this represented 213 tonnes of seed cotton, worth £1,263 to the local cotton growers. In the Chiromo and Chikwawa districts the main grain crops suffered heavily in places; and it was estimated that 75 per cent of the sorghum, 30 per cent of the maize, and 30 per cent of the millet crop were lost. Smee also noted that the locusts tended to feed on cereals and grasses such as *nsenjere, Pennisetum purpureum*, and often maize, sorghum, and sugarcane were completely destroyed – but that tobacco, sweet potatoes, pumpkin and sesame (*chitowe, Sesamum indicum*) were not usually attacked. He noted that the locusts were generally described as *dzombe* (or *nazombe*), while hoppers were referred to as *mamseta* or *mandowa*, and the people insisted that lions often ate the locusts. The local belief that 'locusts and drought years go together' does seem to have been confirmed, Smee suggests, by the fact that 1932–3 was a low-rainfall year. Also of interest was the fact that the fungus disease (*Empusa grylii*) quickly took hold of the red locust population (MNA/Ann. Rept. Dept. Agriculture 1943).

In the 1935–6 season reports of flying swarms came chiefly from the southern region, and considerable crop damage was done in the Mulanje district and the Lower Shire valley, especially to cotton and maize. Often people grouped in their hundreds to protect their gardens, and beating was the usual method employed, although, Smee reports, cattle egrets assisted in consuming large numbers of locusts. The locusts, even the hoppers, were invariably collected as food by local people. Smee also felt that clean-weeded gardens tended to be less liable to attack from locusts than neglected gardens.

It is of interest that Smee in a letter to the chief secretary (October 1934) expressed his concern that, while during locust outbreaks the government allocated funds to the problem, as soon as the swarms had ended 'no money is forthcoming to support the study of the solitary phase of the locust in its permanent breeding grounds' (MNA/512.1.8.1). The entomologist Harriet Thindwa expressed the same concerns to me in February 2001, when locust swarms seemed to have abated.

The outbreaks of the red locust during the colonial period are generally considered to have lasted, for Malawi and the neighbouring countries, from 1929 until 1944. During this period, the locusts invaded about five to six million square kilometres of land and caused serious devastation to crops, leading to local famines and serious problems for local people. Following these outbreaks, the International Red Locust Control Organization was established in 1949, with the aim of preventing red locust plagues in the region. Among its programmes were the study of the biology and ecology of the red locust, identifying and locating the sources of the locust swarms, and developing control strategies. What was clearly established is that there were essentially six major breeding areas of the red locust in south-central Africa, the Lake Chilwa basin being one, and that these areas were characterized by similar vegetative types and periodic flooding. The organization also aimed to monitor the locust populations in these key areas, and to implement preventive measures before the locusts reached plague proportions (Bahana and Byaruhanga 1999).

Prior to the establishment of the Red Locust Control Organization there was much discussion of the issue of outbreak areas, and of the need to prevent the initial swarming of the locust or to destroy incipient swarms, rather than simply engaging in crop protection after the event. In the 1945–6 season, therefore, an intensive campaign against the red locust was conducted at Lake Rukwa and Mweru and Ntipa areas, with the aerial spraying of sodium arsenite. This was deemed to have been a success (MNA.512.1.8.2).

Locust Swarms in the Post-Colonial Period
The locust outbreaks seem to have petered out in Malawi in the early 1940s, and between 1944 and 1962 there were no records of locust problems, although a sparse population of the red locust in its solitary phase continued to exist in the Ndindi Marsh and the Lake Chilwa basin.

However, in 1962 there were reports of locust swarms in the Lake Chilwa basin near Chikala Hill, and subsequent control operations led to the spraying of the area from the air with the insecticide Carbaryl. Subsequent visits by locust researchers from the International Red Locust Control Organization who surveyed the Lake Chilwa area reported a stable but local population of red locust throughout the 1960s and 1970s (H. D. Brown 1979). At this time locusts from the Lake Chilwa basin were regularly on sale as food in the Zomba Market, especially around August. Sweeney estimated that the adult population of red locust in the basin was then in the order of ten to fifteen million locusts (Sweeney 1964b: 14). A helicopter survey of the whole Lake Chilwa area in April 1972 found locusts only along the northern shore, and reported that there was no danger from locust swarms and that insecticide spraying would serve no useful purpose – though it emphasized the need to monitor continuously the area (BRS/ENTA 4).

Again there was a lull in terms of red locust activity in Malawi until the 1990s. But during this last decade there have been several major outbreaks in Malawi in many different areas. The first occurred in February 1993, with a locust outbreak on Sucoma sugar estate and the surrounding farmland, the infestation covering 6,340 ha, half of which was local gardens. As a protective measure the area was sprayed by air with some 3,180 litres of Fenitrothion. In May later that year around 10,000 ha of cropland, also in the Lower Shire valley, was affected by migratory locusts, mostly causing damage to sorghum, maize and millet.

In October and November of that same year (1993) locust swarms were reported in the Lake Chilwa basin, as well as on the Lake Chilwa floodplain. Some 5,000 ha of vegetation was infested with locusts, including both red and migratory locusts.

In April the following year (1994), large quantities of dried grasshoppers were being sold in Limbe market, having originated from the Mangoche district. These appear not to have been locusts, but grasshoppers, *chiwala* (*Cyrtacanthacris* spp.) and crickets, *zeche* (*Acanthoplus speiseri*), which at the end of the rainy season April–May 1994 had devastated farmland north of Mangoche, causing severe losses of the maize crop (BRS/ENT A4 B). A survey of the main locust areas in October 1994 – Ndindi marsh, Lake Chilwa floodplain, Mchinji and Lake Chiuta – indicated, however, that few locust were in evidence – apart from a sparse population on the northern side of Lake Chilwa. The outbreaks of 1993–4 were all controlled by aerial spraying of the insecticide Fenitrothion (Thindwa 1999: 353).

In July 1995, a further locust outbreak occurred in the Mpatsanjoka valley near Salima, which infested over 2,000 ha of land, while the following year, in October and November, another outbreak of the red locusts occurred in the Lake Chilwa and Lake Chiuta floodplains. Over 30,000 ha of vegetation were infested with locusts at quite a high density (30–50 locusts per square metre), and most of this area was sprayed with pesticide. The impact of the locusts on the local communities, however, is not recorded.

The last locust outbreak occurred in April–June 1997, again on the Lake Chilwa floodplain, and was perhaps the most intensive outbreak of the decade. An estimated 30,000 ha of vegetation were covered by locusts, mostly young adults, and control operations involved spraying around 10 per cent of this area by air with Fenitrothion pesticide. Thindwa noted that at the time of the outbreak bushfires had just started on the plains. She also noted that spraying the locust swarms with insecticide was perhaps the most efficient and effective strategy for controlling locust swarms in Malawi (1999: 353–4).

Frequently locust outbreaks are reported in the newspapers, but often turn out to be swarms of the elegant grasshopper.

The reasons for the upsurge in red locust activity during the last decade are still unclear. It seems to have coincided with widespread outbreaks of the migratory locusts, not only in Malawi, but in Zambia, Zimbabwe, and Botswana. It has therefore been concluded that forecasts of locust outbreaks still largely depend on surveys and surveillance in recognized outbreak areas – a mundane and essential task that governments are often reluctant to fund (Bahana and Byaruhanga 1999).

With regard to local people it is important to note that folk memories of the past are often dated or highlighted by reference to locust outbreaks or to serious infestations of other agricultural pests.

–6–

Insects and Disease

Prologue

Disease and parasitism play a pervasive role on organic life. The search for food on the part of one organism, whether a micro-organism, insect or human, becomes for another either death, disability or a nasty disease. 'Meat is murder', some moralists proclaim – so is eating insects and carrots. As Jean-Henri Fabre graphically put it: 'life, when all is said, is a knacker's yard wherein the devourer of today becomes the devoured of tomorrow' (1913: 241). Humans are indeed, like many other organisms, 'robbers of the dead'. But they in turn are preyed upon, not only by predators like lions, but by micro-organisms. These express themselves as human diseases, by finding a source of food in human tissues, thereby sustaining their own vital processes (McNeill 1976: 14).

The concept of disease certainly reflects a very anthropocentric view-point. The complex and fascinating history of human diseases has been told in many different ways, and in fact diseases have had a dramatic impact on human history, whether in relation to the bubonic plague, the 'black death' – transmitted by rats and fleas – that decimated the popula-tions of Europe and Asia in the fourteenth century; or cholera, that has swept across the world in seven pandemics since the beginning of the nineteenth century, and to which Hegel succumbed. Diseases indeed have destroyed armies, brought the downfall of empires, and decimated tribal peoples, and at critical conjunctures have changed the course of human history (Zinsser 1934; McNeill 1976; Cloudsley Thompson 1976; Wills 1996).

With respect to many human diseases – tuberculosis, measles, small-pox, influenza – insects are not directly involved in the transmission of the disease; with other diseases, however, insects play a vital role as vectors. Cockroaches, as was noted earlier, are thought to spread a number of diseases, mainly intestinal; fleas are important vectors of bubonic plague and typhus; black flies (*Simuliidae*) are carriers of *Onchocerciasis*, otherwise known as river blindness; and mosquitoes and tsetse fly are, of course, the well-known vectors of malaria and sleeping sickness (Service 1996). It is beyond the scope of the present study to discuss medical entomology in Malawi, which is a project in itself: I will instead focus in this chapter on two insects that have, historically, made a vital impact on the social life of Malawian people – the mosquito and the tsetse fly.

Mosquitoes and Malaria

Malawi is a poor country, and malnutrition is rife in rural areas. Infant mortality is high, and around 60 per cent of children have stunted growth, caused by inadequate food and the high incidence of disease. Besides malnutrition the major causes of death are anaemia, pneumonia, diarrhoea, measles and malaria. Disease and malnutrition are, of course, closely linked, and malaria is a key factor in the high mortality of children: thus more than one in five children die before the age of five years (NRI 1996: 21). But malaria not only takes a heavy toll of children, it is also a major cause of illness, even death, among adults. Robin Broadhead suggested to me that malaria is so prevalent in Malawi that during the rainy season, from December to March, over 50 per cent of hospital outpatient cases may be due to malaria. How prevalent may be judged from the records from one hospital in Mulanje. Some basic statistics are given in Tables 6.1 and 6.2.

Table 6.1 Morbidity and Mortality from Various Causes, Mulanje Mission Hospital, 1998: Children under Five

Diagnosis	Morbidity		Mortality	
	Number of cases	%	Number of cases	%
Malaria	754	42	105	29
Pneumonia	216	12	41	11
Gastro-enteritis/Cholera	131	7	45	13
Anaemia	129	7	46	13
Malnutrition	120	7	53	15
AIDS-related	60	3	23	6
Meningitis	37	2	21	6
Tuberculosis	35	2	5	1
Other ailments	296	18	21	6
Totals	1778	100	360	100

Source: Mulanje Mission Hospital Annual Report, 1998.

Table 6.2 Morbidity and Mortality from Various Causes, Mulanje Mission Hospital, 1998: Adults

Diagnosis	Morbidity		Mortality	
	Number of cases	%	Number of cases	%
Malaria	278	16	24	10
Obstetric	268	16	—	—
Pneumonia	228	13	46	19
Tuberculosis	172	10	52	21
Aids-related	162	10	61	25
Gynaecological	103	6	—	—
Gastro-enteritis	70	4	8	3
Anaemia	—	—	8	3
Other ailments	420	25	46	19
Totals	1,701	100	245	100

Source: Mulanje Mission Hospital Annual Report, 1998.

It will be noted that malaria is responsible for almost half of children's illnesses, and that 29 per cent of children die from malaria. This is confirmed by the Ministry of Health annual report for the Mulanje district (1994), which recorded that malaria accounted for 33 per cent of all outpatient morbidity. This, of course, related to only one district; but it is a reflection of the ubiquity of malaria in Malawi as a whole, and the disease may be even more prevalent in the Lower Shire Valley and along the Lakeshore. A more recent newspaper report from Mzuzu described malaria as a serious health problem in the city. Around 4,000 malaria cases had been reported in February, and twelve deaths recorded from one hospital alone. An environmental health officer emphasized the need to initiate a malaria control programme, involving the eradication of all stagnant water and the spraying of chemicals in all the potential breeding areas of mosquitoes in the city (*Daily Times*, 27 March 2001).

Evidence suggests that during the colonial period malaria was an absolute scourge. Early records describe malaria as endemic throughout the country, and as particularly prevalent in low-lying areas. A note by the director of medical services (1937) suggested that routine examination of the blood of all patients admitted to government hospitals showed that about 50 per cent had the malaria parasite. Although the European population routinely took *Quinine bi-hydrochloride* tablets as a prophylactic (often with alcohol) the majority of the population had no safeguards against malaria. Some effort was made with regard to anti-malaria measures – but only to the extent of digging drainage ditches in some towns, mosquito-proofing European houses, and employing local sanitary inspectors to encourage the eradication of potential breeding sites for the mosquito. In the 1920s one agricultural officer made the observation that the lethargy of many local people may be due not to inherent indolence, but to the fact that they were suffering from malaria (MNA/M2/5/14). How prevalent malaria was during the colonial period can be judged from the fact that out of the total number of cases of all diseases treated in hospitals in November 1939 (i.e. 83,672), some 20,434 (24 per cent) were due to malaria. It is not surprising, then, that one colonial official could complain that most medical doctors and administrators in the country had failed to realize that malaria was the most serious cause of ill health, and probably the greatest single obstacle to economic development in Africa. Most medical officers in Africa, he wrote, had little interest in malaria control (MNA/M2/5/38). There is little to indicate that Malawians are particularly immune to malaria's ravages. Indeed, after the Second World War, when paludrine was introduced as a prophylactic, it was not used to treat local people in Zomba hospital, as it was believed that this would destroy their inherent immunity to the disease (MNA/M2/5/38) – though this did not prevent Malawians then, as now, dying from the disease.

Because of its medical importance, the mosquito has been the subject of a wealth of research. It belongs to a family of small two-winged insects (*Culcidae*) that are clearly distinguished from other flies by their long proboscis and the presence of scales on the wing veins. Over 2,000 species have been described. The mosquitoes that are important as vectors of malaria belong to the genus *Anopheles*. It differs from the allied genus *Culex* in that, when at rest on the water, its body is in a straight line, almost perpendicular to the surface. Only the female mosquito 'buzzes' and sucks blood, the mouth of the male being vestigial. Hence males are not blood-suckers. When biting, the female injects saliva into the blood, which causes the familiar irritation and swelling. Over 60 species of *Anopheles* are vectors of the malaria parasite – the protozoa *Plasmodium* spp., though they are not confined to humans, but also feed on other animals. In Malawi, and throughout much of Africa, two species are of particular importance as vectors of malaria – *Anopheles gambiae* and *Anopheles funestus*. All mosquitoes breed in water, and *A. gambiae* tends to breed in temporary, open and sunlit waters, such as pools, puddles, or hoofprints, whether or not brackish or muddy. It also tends to rest mainly indoors, and is usually commoner in towns. As it tend to breed only in temporary bodies of water, *A. gambiae* is relatively uncommon during the dry season. *Anopheles funestus*, on the other hand, prefers shaded habitats, and breeds at the edge of sluggish streams, or in ditches, and more rarely in rainwater puddles. It is therefore present in reasonable numbers throughout the year. It is also worth noting that mosquitoes are also vectors of human filariasis, a disease caused by filarial worms, which can lead to what is often described as *Elephantiasis* (Goma 1966; Sweeney 1970: 68–9; Service 1996: 35–53).

In Malawi the mosquito is generally described as *udzudzu*, a term not only covering the mosquitoes (of the genera *Anopheles, Aedes* and *Culex*) but also similar flies, including crane flies (*Tipulidae*). People always recognize it as a troublesome pest (*-bvuta kwambiri*), which gives (*-patsa*) a person the disease (*nthenda*) malaria. The insecticide 'Doom' is used to rid the house of mosquitoes, if people have sufficient cash to buy it – and most rural people do not. It should be recognized, of course, that most of the mosquitoes (*udzudzu*) that people encounter, whether in the woodlands or urban areas, are *not* vectors of malaria, even though they may cause intense discomfort. It is also worth emphasizing that in the Lower Shire Valley during the rainy season – as I have experienced myself on many occasions – mosquitoes can be prodigious in their numbers, and being without a mosquito net can lead to sleepless nights. In the past people in the Lower Shire Valley slept in specially woven bags (*mfumba*) made from palm fronds, as a protection against mosquitoes during the rainy season (Talbot 1956). One early European traveller wrote that the mosquitoes in the Shire Valley were almost unbearable, and that his hands became swollen and 'my features distorted by their venomous bites. All night, sleep was, generally speaking, out of the question' (Faulkner 1868: 25). In fact, the sickness and death rates of the first Europeans coming to Malawi, from malaria and other fevers, were extremely high, even though travellers like Livingstone used quinine as a prophylactic (King and King 1992: 17–18). Used since the seventeenth century as a protection against fevers, quinine, however, is quite toxic, causing nausea and deafness. Even so, though the malaria parasite has developed resistance to many of the standard drugs, quinine is still being used in the treatment of malaria in the Blantyre hospitals.

Early campaigns from the 1950s onwards, aiming to control or eradicate malaria, tended to focus on the mosquito rather than on the malarial parasite. It was considered easier to locate and treat with insecticides all the sites where the mosquitoes were likely to be found, and DDT was then relatively cheap, highly persistent, and apparently unproblematic. The World Health Organization launched a global malaria eradication programme in 1956, combining the spraying of DDT with the treatment of individual cases of malaria with drugs such as chloroquine. Although the campaign may have been successful in some places, it was found that the DDT destroyed a wide spectrum of insect life, as well as indirectly many birds and animals (as Rachel Carson (1962) highlighted). It was also discovered that the mosquitoes by degrees became resistant to the pesticide. Thus the eradication campaigns against malaria that have been conducted in the decades since the Second World War have not proved successful, and as Jerry Patterson (1984) noted many years ago, there is probably as much malaria around in Malawi at the present time as there was half a century ago. And mosquitoes are as plentiful as ever. But the government continues to offer guidelines for controlling malaria through encouraging control of its vector – eliminating mosquito breeding sites, such as stagnant water, practising personal protection through mosquito nets and insecticide repellents, and spraying specific sites in urban areas with approved insecticides. But, as was described earlier, malaria still continues to be a significant and pervasive health problem in Malawi. Indeed, a recent report suggests that malaria is far more problematic than AIDS-related diseases in Malawi, that it still accounts for 40 per cent of all hospital admissions, and that Malawi, one of the poorest countries in sub-Saharan Africa, spends around 198 million MK (US$2.7 million) a year to treat cases of malaria. What hope is there for Malawians to escape from this deadly disease, the report asks (*The Nation*, 4 October, 2000).

Hope is now seen to come either through the development of a vaccine, or through the use of the micro-organism *Bacillus thuringiensis*, which produces a toxin lethal to mosquito larvae, as a biological control.

In challenging the 'war against the mosquito', Joanne Lauck lauds the insect as a 'hero of ecology' and as the 'guardian of the planet's rich resources', and emphasizes its positive aspects, ignoring completely the trials and tribulations suffered by humankind. The 'ecological' approach she seems to advocate was of course long ago suggested by René Dubos (1965), but she goes on to suggest that we should learn to 'communicate' (telepathically) with the insect, or develop 'good feelings' towards it, and then the mosquito won't bother you (1998: 106–19). Malawians don't seem to harbour such New Age illusions, nor such anti-humanist sentiments.

(For an interesting account of a biologist who spent much of his life in Africa studying mayflies and mosquitoes see Gillies 2000.)

Tsetse Fly and Sleeping Sickness

The vital years 1885–1930, with the advent of colonial rule, have been described as a period of 'epidemiological disaster' for Africa, particularly for Malawi (Ransford 1983: 3). For during these years tsetse fly threatened colonial Malawi with an ecological catastrophe as it spread across the central region, leading not only to the death of cattle from the disease *nagana*, but to a serious outbreak of sleeping sickness among humans.

This issue has generated much debate among historians, although sleeping sickness and the tsetse fly are hardly mentioned in early Malawian historiography (e.g. Pachai 1972, 1973; MacDonald 1975; Vaughan 1991).

In his now classic study of the social ecology of East Africa, specifically focused on Tanzania, Helge Kjekshus (1977) sought to demonstrate that prior to the colonial impact at the end of the nineteenth century African people had established a degree of ecological control over the natural environment – in spite of inter-tribal conflict and the Atlantic slave trade. He attempted to counter the widespread depiction of the pre-colonial period as one where people were at the mercy of the vagaries of nature, and their political economy one characterized by disorder, violence and under-development. In challenging this view Kjekshus argued that the presence of long-standing cattle traditions implied that people had indeed achieved a degree of control over the environment, and were fully conversant with the problems of tsetse fly; that people had developed a trading economy and thriving small-scale industries, particularly focused around the production of salt, iron and cloth; and that before the full impact of colonialism, people in Tanzania lived in 'comfort and plenty' (1977: 4).

Acknowledging the vitality and the regenerative powers of nature in tropical Africa – its flora, fauna and microbial life – Kjekshus nevertheless felt that in the pre-colonial period humans had achieved a degree of control – 'ecological domination' is the phrase he uses – over nature, and that the dangers stemming from tsetse fly had been kept at bay. Thus the eruption of sleeping sickness epidemics in East Africa at the beginning of the twentieth century, Kjekshus suggests, resulted from the colonial impact, and the subsequent loss by African people of control over their environment (1977: 81, see Lyons (1992) for a similar analysis of sleeping sickness in Northern Zaire, for Lyons suggests that the outbreaks of this disease were intrinsically related to the social upheavals and ecological disruptions concomitant upon the advent of colonial rule).

A similar thesis to that of Kjekshus was also presented by Leroy Vail with respect to eastern Zambia. Like Kjekshus, Vail suggests that prior to the late nineteenth century people of this region were able to sustain a viable ecological relationship with their environment, a degree of control over nature, such that a 'finely-balanced relationship' between humans and their environment obtained. But after 1895 the dual impact of expanding capitalism and colonial administration shattered this relationship, leading to a 'major ecological catastrophe'. Under the impact of colonialism people lost control over the environment, and impoverishment and the spread of disease, particularly sleeping sickness, were the result (1977: 138).

It is important, I think, not to romanticize the economic conditions of the pre-colonial period, for subsistence agriculture is highly dependent on rainfall, and life is experienced as a constant struggle to survive, particularly against the depredations of wildlife. Moreover, the impact of the Atlantic slave trade from the eighteenth century on, and the invasion of the Ngoni 'warriors' into central Africa during the second half of the nineteenth century, also had an important impact on the people of Zambia (and Malawi) *prior* to colonial rule. But the essential thesis of both Kjekshus and Vail is that the people of Tanzania and eastern Zambia became 'out of harmony with the countryside' and thus experienced increased impoverishment as well as epidemics of diseases, of which sleeping sickness was the most important. As Kjekshus expressed it: 'The eruption of tsetse-borne sleeping sickness in East Africa at the beginning of this century ... resulted from a relatively sudden human and cattle depopulation and the attendant loss of control over the environment' (Kjekshus 1977: 52–6, 181; Vail 1977: 154–5, 1983: 228–9).

Malawi, of course, is situated between Tanzania and eastern Zambia, so it is hardly surprising that the Vail/Kjekshus thesis of a loss of environmental control has been applied to the Malawian context. In this regard the seminal studies of McCracken (1987) and Mandala (1990) are important. The essential theme is that during the latter part of the nineteenth century, prior, that is, to colonial rule, village communities in Malawi, together with their ecological environment, were subject to two complex social forces, the invasion of the Ngoni from Southern Africa into the highland area west of Lake Malawi, and the increasing impact of the Atlantic slave trade. Both made their impact at roughly the same time – the decades after 1850 – and their impact was similar, for throughout Malawi they forced communities to concentrate their settlement in fortified villages – as on the Kasungu plain; or to live in rather remote and inaccessible localities – on the rift valley escarpment near the Lakeshore, or high on the mountains of Zomba or Mulanje, or hidden on Chisi island in the Lake Chilwa basin. Whether escaping from the slave trade, or from the Ngoni raiders, settlements took the form of either fortified villages or refugee camps. A consequence of this change in settlement pattern was that large sections of the Kasungu plain, the Shire Highlands – particularly the Thuchila–Phalombe plain – and the Lower Shire Valley became depopulated. This allowed the regeneration of the savannah woodland, and, within a short period of time, game animals began to flourish in these areas. Thus Henry Drummond could describe the Lake Chilwa basin towards the end of the nineteenth century as 'almost uninhabited', and suggest that 'nowhere else in Africa did I see such splendid herds of larger animals as here' (1889: 30–2). Following the analysis of Kjekshus, and emphasizing the dramatic impact of the slave trade and the great famine of 1862–3 (*chaola*), Elias Mandala (1990) suggests that the Mang'anja of the Lower Shire Valley were unable to control nature through the labour process – and with the loss of control came the bush and the wild animals. It was in such circumstances that the tsetse fly 'belts', which had previously been limited in range, began to spread in Malawi – with the subsequent loss of both cattle and human life. In the first three decades of the last century 'tsetse fly' thus constituted a serious problem and a focus of ongoing concern for the colonial government (McCracken 1987: 67; Mandala 1990: 76–8). But it has to be recognized, of course, that the problem with tsetse fly had its origins in the pre-colonial period.

All tsetse flies belong to the genus *Glossina* (family: *Glossinidae*), and they are found only in Africa south of the Sahara. All species of the genus are potential vectors of *Trypanosomiasis*, the human sleeping sickness. Tsetse flies are unique in that the female does not lay eggs, but rather retains them in her uterus, and then deposits the larvae singly in loose soil, or in woodland debris. The adult tsetse are yellow-brown robust flies, HB 14 mm, which are readily distinguished from other biting flies by the position of the proboscis, which, when not in use, projects forward from the lower part of the head. Tsetse also, unlike most other flies, fold their wings when at rest. They are active mainly during the daylight hours, and vision plays an important part in locating their hosts. They are particularly attracted to dark moving objects, and when travelling through Nkhotakota game reserve on my motor-cycle, I was invariably attacked by tsetse fly. They take blood meals about every 2–3 days. Sometimes the blood is that that of humans, but mainly of bushpig, warthog, and buffalo. According to Selous 'tsetse' is a word derived from the Tswana (Bechuana) language (1908: 170).

In Africa two species of 'tsetse' are particularly important: *Glossina palpalis*, which is a riverine species found mainly in West Africa, Zaire and Uganda, and which is associated with the sleeping sickness parasite *Trypanosoma brucei gambiense* (first identified in 1901 by Everett Dutton); and *Glossina morsitans*, which is associated with the parasite *Trypanosoma brucei rhodesiense*. This is the parasite that was (and is) responsible for sleeping sickness in Zambia and Malawi. It was discovered in 1912 by Warrington Yorke and Allan Kingham, who showed that it was transmitted by the common tsetse fly *Glossina morsitans*. It was subsequently found that other members of the genus were also vectors of the parasite. Tsetse fly is also an important vector of the cattle disease *nagana* – which is a Zulu word, meaning 'to be depressed or low in spirits'. Wild mammals thus form an important reservoir for the sleeping sickness parasite (Pollock 1969; Lambrecht 1970: 92–3; Service 1996: 126–37). By local people in Malawi tsetse fly is described as *kashembe* (syn. *kanzemba*) or *kambalame* ('small bird'), and tsetse fly and horse flies (*Tabanidae*) are usually closely identified.

Tsetse Fly Control During the Colonial Period

It is possible that both *nagana* and sleeping sickness have existed in Africa since the earliest times. The trypanosomes are normal parasites on several species of ungulates, and do not cause illness either to the tsetse fly or to their main hosts – which include, in particular, kudu, bushpig, warthog, elephant and buffalo – an indication of an 'ancient, well adjusted parasitism'. It has even been suggested that the fact that these parasites produced such debilitating illness in humans may have been conducive to the survival of the African ungulates (Nash 1969: 90–5; McNeill 1976: 28; Lyons 1992: 51). But throughout much of east central Africa, the opening up of land for settlement, and the clearing of the woodland through bushfires, allowed some degree of control by humans over the tsetse fly – a balance that, so both Kjekshus and Vail suggest, was disrupted only at the end of the nineteenth century. It was then that epidemics of sleeping sickness began to sweep through Africa, causing serious loss of life (Nash 1969: 177–92; Lambrecht 1970: 93; Ford 1971; McKelvey 1973; Ransford 1983: 109–32).

Compared with the neighbouring countries Tanzania and Zambia, Malawi in pre-colonial times had a fairly high population density – especially around the Lakeshore and in the Lower Shire Valley, and lacked communities with a pastoral economy, apart from the Ngonde in the extreme north, and the Ngoni immigrants. The Ngoni came to Malawi towards the end of the nineteenth century, and settled mainly in the Mzimba, Dowa and Dedza highlands (D. D. Phiri 1982). But, as McCracken has discussed, the colonial administration in Malawi followed the same pattern as that described by Vail and Kjekshus, in attempting to consolidate village settlement in order to have effective control over the local population, in limiting the use of firearms by Africans, and in enacting game laws that were aimed to curtail local subsistence hunting, particularly the communal hunts (*uzimba*). These colonial policies only had a limited success. But there can be no doubt that game animals increased substantially during the early colonial period, and crop depredations became an increasing cause for concern among local communities in certain areas. McCracken suggests that in the Kasungu district and on the South-eastern lakeshore the colonial occupation was marked 'by an increase in the number of wild animals' (1987: 71; see my discussions of wildlife depredations and wildlife conservation in Malawi, Morris 1995, 2001a).

But equally important in disturbing the ecological balance between humans and wildlife at the end of the nineteenth century was the rinderpest epidemic among cattle. This is a virus disease that is spread not by an insect but through the air. Kjekshus suggests that it was the rinderpest epidemic that initiated the 'breakdown' of the long-established ecological balance between humans and nature (wildlife), and placed 'nature again at the advantage' (1977: 126).

Rinderpest is reputed to have first made its appearance in Somaliland in 1889. By 1890 it had reached Uganda, and then spread like wildfire throughout eastern Africa. Its impact was 'catastrophic' on many pastoral people, and it had a far-reaching economic and social consequences (Van Onselen 1972). The rinderpest epidemic reached Malawi in the dry season of 1893, and according to the Rev. James Stewart of the Ekwendeni mission almost all the cattle in Mombera's (M'Mbwela's) kingdom had perished before the rains broke. The epidemic seems to have completely undermined the economic power of the Ngoni – although the cattle soon recovered their numbers. After the epidemic, buffalo and eland almost disappeared in the Henga valley and near Lake Kazuni – the Rev. Stewart records – and so had tsetse fly. Yet by the 1920s, he continued, the wildlife (game) had increased in numbers in its old haunts, together with the tsetse fly. This episode lodged in the minds of many missionaries the idea that game animals and tsetse fly are closely entwined (MNA/51/1721A/123). Indeed, when Frederick Selous was hunting in central Africa some twenty years before, he noted that tsetse fly were particularly abundant in the Zambezi valley, and he put this down to the enormous numbers of buffalo that frequented the river bank. Tsetse, he wrote, seem 'very partial' to these animals (1881: 131).

The exact distribution of tsetse fly in pre-colonial Malawi is difficult to ascertain, but it is probable that it was restricted to uninhabited woodland on the Lakeshore and upper Shire, and on the Thuchila/Phalombe plain. Harry Johnston suggested that it was not found over 3,000 ft (900 m), nor was it found in low-lying areas, like the Lower Shire Valley, where there was extensive human settlement, although it abounded near the Elephant Marsh, near Chiromo. He noted that the wild game of Africa – the buffalo, zebra and antelopes – were quite unaffected by the bite of the tsetse fly, but their nearest congeners among domestic animals – cattle, goat and horse – were killed by the fly. As an observant naturalist Johnston fully understood the close association between tsetse and wild game, and noted that the tsetse 'tends to disappear before the presence of man'. A certain cure, then, for tsetse fly, he suggested, would be human settlement and putting the low-lying parts of the protectorate under cultivation (1897: 377–80). This was the lesson that Lamborn learned later in his attempt to stem the spread of tsetse fly in the 1920s.

In the early years of the last century the spread of tsetse fly threatened Malawi in ways comparable to the effects it had had on Tanzania and eastern Zambia, and heralded what McCracken, following Kjekshus, has described as an 'ecological catastrophe' (1982: 105). Although in the late nineteenth century, the missionary Dr Walter Elmslie and the hunter-naturalist Richard Crawshay had reported both larger game animals and tsetse fly to be common in the Henga valley, from the South Rukuru river in the Mzimba district south to Dedza appeared to have been completely free of tsetse fly (MNA/NNK1/20/9). According to Dr George Prentice, a missionary of Kasungu, no tsetse fly existed in the Kasungu district in 1900 when he established the Livingstone mission there. But the tsetse fly belt soon spread eastwards from the Luangwa Valley, and in 1908 a case of sleeping sickness was reported by Dr J. B. Davey, a medical officer at Dowa, and substantial numbers of cattle became infected with the *Trypanosomiasis* disease. By September 1909 five other cases of sleeping sickness had been discovered. In 1910, Dr Prentice, who did pioneering medical work at Kasungu, diagnosed the first case of sleeping sickness at Kasungu, and between 1909 and 1911 around 66 cases had been recorded, particularly in the Dowa district. In 1909 Dr Hallam Hardy, the medical officer-in-charge of the West Nyasa district, succumbed to the disease. By 1913 there had been 163 confirmed cases of sleeping sickness, and two years later it had risen to 240 cases. In addition, there had been a great loss of cattle through the disease trypanosomiasis (*nagana*), particularly in northern Ngoniland – the Mombera (Mzimba) district. Sleeping sickness was known to local people as *n'tola*, as it implied being carried away from the village, and abandoned in the woodland (-*tola*, to be picked up) [MNA/M2/18/1; Ransford 1983: 109; King 1992: 114–19]. Thereafter the epidemic seems to have died out gradually.

Although in retrospect historians such as McCracken (1982) can disparage and even ridicule the efforts made by Dr William Lamborn and the colonial administration in their attempts to halt the spread of tsetse fly, it has to be recognized that the panic and concerns of the administration were well justified. For between 1898 and 1906 an estimated 200,000 Africans in Uganda had died of sleeping sickness, and colonial officials in Malawi, as well as in Zambia (then Northern Rhodesia) were in a high state of alert when the sleeping sickness epidemic hit Malawi, and so felt that drastic measures might be needed. Several conferences had been held to discuss the issue of sleeping sickness – what research needed to be done, and what strategies would be most effective in halting the spread of the tsetse fly, and thus the ravages of sleeping sickness (Nash 1969: 32; Pollock 1969: 1–5; on tsetse fly and trypanosamiasis in Zambia see Scudder 1962: 165–73).

The causes of the spread of tsetse fly and the outbreak of sleeping sickness are undoubtedly complex. McCracken suggests that the causes include: 'the changing settlement patterns of the late nineteenth century, the impact of the rinderpest epidemic of 1893, the effect of government game policies and the drain of labour from the north' (1982: 105–6).

Following the perspectives of John Iliffe and other scholars, he thus suggests that the effects of these changes were devastating for local people. For they essentially led to an increase in wildlife and tsetse fly – 'nature was reconquering the land'. This included increasing crop depredations, problems with predators, especially lions, and diseases of both cattle and humans (1982: 106; cf. Morris 1995).

The expansion of the tsetse fly belt continued, and in 1922 there was a serious outbreak of sleeping sickness on the Kasungu plain. Some seven cases of sleeping sickness were definitely diagnosed by the local medical officer in August 1922, and the 'endemic centre' and focus of the infection was felt to be among the villagers on the Lingadzi river, now in the heart of the present Kasungu National Park. It was therefore suggested by the provincial commissioner W. Kirby Green, in consultation with the resident at Kasungu and a local – and rather vocal – missionary, Dr George Prentice, that the best means of dealing with the epidemic would be to evacuate the people from the area. This entailed the movement of some fifty-eight villages, comprising 150 huts – a sizeable population of over 2,000 people – and their resettlement in the east, in the Dwangwa valley north of Kasungu Hill, near Kasungu hill itself, and on the Lisisadzi river near Ngara hill. The area from which they were evacuated was to be declared a forest reserve, and no shooting of game animals was to be allowed within its boundaries – it being felt that any hunting within the reserve would scatter the game and 'spread the fly'. But the country south and east of the game reserve was declared a 'free-shooting area', and both Europeans and Africans were to be encouraged to shoot all the wild game they could find.

This idea of containing both the game and the tsetse fly in an ecological enclave came from the activities of an eccentric, Austrian nobleman, Count Marian Steblecki. This ardent hunter owned a large estate of around 16,000 acres, some 40 km north of Salima. This area he considered his own private game sanctuary, and no other person was allowed to hunt there, certainly no Africans. The theory implied that while his estate was 'full of game and swarms with fly', outside the estate the tsetse fly was no longer found and cattle moved freely. Kirby Green seems to have applied this notion to the outbreak of sleeping sickness in the Kasungu area; thus in 1923 this area was declared the Fort Alston forest (game) reserve, to contain the tsetse fly and to protect the wildlife; outside the reserve was declared a 'free-shooting' zone. Although some questioned the logic of this proposal, it was nevertheless enacted, and so Kasungu National Park, as a wildlife sanctuary, owes its existence to the tsetse fly (MNA/S1/1951/22).

However, the establishment of Fort Alston (Kasungu) wildlife sanctuary, and the proclamation of a free-shooting area, did little to halt the spread of the tsetse fly belt, which moved progressively southwards. It eventually reached the outskirts of Mchinji, and stretched between Kasungu and Nkhotakota, thus cutting off the northern cattle from markets in the south. Throughout many parts of the protectorate there was a serious loss of livestock, particularly cattle, and large areas of the territory reverted to 'bush' (woodland) because of the prevalence of tsetse fly. In the Namwera, Chikwawa and Liwonde districts during the 1920s the tsetse fly increased its range, and a loss of cattle from the *nagana* disease was regularly reported (MNA/M2/23/2; McCracken 1982: 106–7).

There ensued a heated debate among colonial administrators, big-game hunters, missionaries and entomologists, regarding the best strategy to halt the spread of the tsetse fly. One strategy was the simple eradication of game animals, given the close association of wild mammals and tsetse fly. The missionary, Dr George Prentice, for example, like Harry Johnston, saw a clear link between tsetse fly (and sleeping sickness) and the prevalence of game animals. In a series of communications with the government he continually urged that the only satisfactory measure to repel the tsetse fly would be the decimation of the large game animals. Since game animals are carriers of the trypanosomes that cause sleeping sickness, wildlife, Prentice contended, should be eradicated. The increase of the tsetse fly, he wrote, 'is due entirely to the European policy of game protection'.

Although he was himself, like many other missionaries, a keen hunter, Prentice was very critical of wildlife preservation, and tersely noted: 'One might say that a huge culture medium is being prepared under the protection of European powers or European sportsmen for the spread of trypanosomiasis ... the protection of game, and the consequent spreading of tsetse with sleeping sickness threatening this country, is about as sane a policy as the protection of rats when bubonic plague is threatening a home community' (King and King 1992: 118). He therefore repeatedly demanded the introduction of free-shooting zones, where African hunters could hunt without hindrance, and thus eliminate the wild game – and the tsetse (MNA/51/700/20; King and King 1992: 18).

In the early decades of the century a great debate sprang up among European hunters as to whether there was indeed any link between wild game and the tsetse fly. This was aired in the famous sporting magazine *The Field* in 1907, and the two figures in the controversy were both famous hunter-naturalists, who had travelled extensively in Central Africa as elephant hunters. Alfred Sharpe, who had spent twenty years in the region, and was later to become governor of Nyasaland, firmly believed that the existence of tsetse fly was not dependent on wild game, and that the presence of tsetse was related to altitude and to the type of local vegetation. Frederick Selous, on the other hand, stressed the close relationship between tsetse and the buffalo, for where buffalo had been exterminated, it was his experience that tsetse too disappeared. This was particularly evident at the time of the rinderpest epidemic, for when buffalo disappeared from any locality the 'fly' soon followed suit; when the buffalo returned to its former abundance, so the tsetse fly again became prevalent (Selous 1908: 149–58). Another big-game hunter, Reginald Maugham, who travelled extensively in Northern Zambezia in the early part of the century, sided with Sharpe, and felt that the tsetse fly also found nourishment from sucking plants. He observed that tsetse fly was found in areas of Malawi where 'game is decidedly scarce'. On the other hand, the research scientist Warrington Yorke, who had conducted researches in Zambia in 1912 and shown that the tsetse fly *Glossina morsitans* was indeed the vector of the sleeping sickness pathogen, agreed with Johnston, Prentice and Selous that there was a close connection between game animals and tsetse fly. Thus Yorke advocated driving back game from the neighbourhood of human habitations (Maugham 1914: 347–55).

But there were many who felt that free shooting was a disastrous policy, as it tended to scatter game animals, and thus spread the tsetse fly. Others suggested that it was quite common to find areas where there were few or no larger mammals, but where the tsetse fly were plentiful. The resident of the Liwonde district, J. O'Brien, for example, wrote (in July 1926) that in the Liwonde area it was apparent that big game and tsetse fly bore little relationship to one another, as tsetse fly was abundant, but that area had been completely depleted of 'game' animals. Another administrator, A. G. O. Hodgson, who was a keen amateur anthropologist, had a more nuanced approach. He wrote: 'I have always belonged to the school which while admitting a connection between tsetse and game, does not believe that the disappearance of tsetse is an inevitable result of the extermination of game. Even if there were no game, there are other hosts for the tsetse besides pigs and baboons.' And like Johnston many years before him, he argued that opening up the land for cultivation was the best way to rid the country of the tsetse fly (MNA/GFT 1/5/11/M2/23/3).

At the end of the First World War a new initiative against the tsetse fly was launched, and the Nyasaland government appointed a medical entomologist, Dr William A. Lamborn, to study the problem, and to offer practical suggestions for dealing with both the cattle disease trypanosomiasis and the human sleeping sickness. Lamborn was short-sighted and a poor shot, as he freely admitted, but he travelled extensively throughout Malawi on *ulendos*, on foot or bicycle, and based himself at Fort Johnston (Mangoche) far 'from the urban delights of the capital Zomba' – as McCracken puts it (1982: 108). McCracken, however, is rather disparaging and dismissive of Lamborn's work as an entomologist – one wonders what the historian would have done in the same circumstances?; but it is clear from Lamborn's reports that he was, like Charles F. M. Swynnerton in Tanganyika (Tanzania), willing to try, with very limited resources, any number of strategies in an attempt to curb the spread of tsetse fly, and the possibility of a serious outbreak of sleeping sickness. Personally, I have nothing but admiration for Lamborn, who constructed his own laboratory in order to undertake entomological research, spent over forty years in tropical Africa attempting to understand and alleviate problems relating to insect pests, and was willing in his retirement, aged 65, to continue work at Mangoche (then, not the healthiest of places) as a humble medical doctor, in the hope that he could also continue his scientific work: to add, in a small way, to our knowledge of nature – as he put it. He was not only engaged in work on the tsetse fly, however, but conducted research and produced scientific papers on cockroaches, mosquitoes and biting flies (*Tabanidae*). He was clearly admired by his contemporaries (MNA/M2/23/3, M4/1/135).

Lamborn was opposed to the policy suggested by Prentice for dealing with tsetse fly, namely the complete eradication of game animals. This, he felt, was entirely impracticable, and the shooting would result in the dispersal of the game animals into other areas, taking the fly with them. On the recommendation of Dr Prentice the government had indeed, in 1915, suspended the Game Ordinance of 1911, and allowed the free shooting of game to the south and east of Kasungu game reserve. But on his return to the country in 1919, after an absence of two and a half years, Lamborn found that the tsetse fly belt had actually advanced southwards. He thus concluded that: 'If free shooting did not actually hasten the spread of fly it had certainly been ineffectual in preventing it.' The free-shooting proclamation was therefore revoked in December 1919.

Lamborn was adamant, and in this he was supported by colonial administrators like W. Kirby-Green and A. G. O. Hodgson, that the 'game extermination' policy was counter-productive in the control of tsetse, for it was felt that the 'disturbance of game' simply helps to 'spread the fly'.

Thus, although the free-shooting policy in the Kasungu district had led to over 1,200 game animals being shot, this had not led to a reduction in the tsetse fly belt, but rather to its expansion southwards (MNA S1/700/20; McCracken 1982: 108).

Having abandoned the eradication of game animals as a policy, Lamborn, following the suggestions made by Charles F. M. Swynnerton in Tanganyika, decided that the best strategy in dealing with the problem of tsetse fly involved combining several methods. These included: firing the woodlands inhabited by tsetse; the judicious settlement of local people so as to form a barrier against the spread of fly; the encouragement of both local and commercial agriculture, with the growing of such crops as tobacco and cotton; the breeding and release of parasites that were destructive of the tsetse fly; and the clearing of bush to create a 'defensive line' to stop the spread of the fly southwards.

When Lamborn made his initial surveys in the early 1920s he found that the tsetse fly belt stretched over much of the Kasungu and Dowa districts, that there had been a substantial loss of cattle, and that the only area free of tsetse fly in the central region was between Ntchisi Mountain and the Dowa *boma*. Although he experimented with various methods of controlling the spread of the fly, none were much of a success, and Lamborn himself was sceptical of firing the bush as a means of control – for the tsetse were strong fliers, and the warthog, which was a favoured host of the fly, actually flourished as a result of the burning of the undergrowth. Between 1925 and 1927 Lamborn supervised the construction of a 'buffer line' of cleared bush between the Bua and Nkamyo hills near Kabadula. But even this was not a great success.

Lamborn seems to have come to the conclusion, along with the chief veterinary officer J. A. Griffiths and the District Resident at Dowa, A. G. O. Hodgson, that the only solution to the 'tsetse fly menace' (as he called it) was not the eradication of game – a policy that did more harm than good, by causing the game to scatter – but human settlement. Opening up the land to human settlement, it was contended, was the only satisfactory method of clearing the area of tsetse fly. In 1927 he concluded that tsetse fly then covered at least two-thirds of the country, and the main infected areas comprised two zones – one covered the Shire Valley from Chikwawa to the Lake, and thence along the lakeshore to the Dwanga river in the Nkotakota district; and the other covered most of the Kasungu and Lilongwe districts, embracing the Bua, the Rusa and the Namitete Rivers (MNA S1/700/20).

Malawi was thus spared such a wholesale destruction of game animals as occurred in Tanzania, Zambia and Natal (McKelvey 1973: 148–54). McCracken points out that the major hosts of tsetse were the bushpig and warthog, and that as late as 1954 one of the heaviest concentrations of tsetse fly in the country was near Mangoche, where, apart from warthogs, all game animals had been eliminated (Mitchell and Steele 1956; McCracken 1987: 72).

Just as the advent of colonialism and the penetration of capitalism at the end of the nineteenth century stimulated the expansion of tsetse, so, some thirty years later, McCracken writes, the expansion of commercial agriculture, in the form of tobacco estates, signalled the eradication of tsetse fly over large areas of the central region. Initiated by A. F. Barron in 1922, tobacco cultivation expanded greatly and rapidly, to the extent that, by 1928, over 25,000 growers had been registered. European settlers purchased leasehold estates in the vicinity of the Mudi, Bua and Ludzi rivers – areas which had earlier been teeming with game, as MacPherson (1973) records, and infested with tsetse fly. Hundreds of African cultivators took up the tenancies, and extensive areas of savannah woodland were cut back to make way for tobacco cultivations. This immediately curtailed the spread of the tsetse fly. In a similar fashion, increasing human population and settlement in the Lower Shire Valley and on the Thucila/Phalombe plain resulted not only in the eradication of most of the larger mammals, but also of the tsetse fly in these regions.

McCracken thus concludes that the colonial administration was much less effective and powerful than it is often assumed to be, and that the impact of capitalism on African communities, those of Malawi in particular, was both complex and contradictory in character (1987: 72).

By 1954 tsetse fly had been eradicated over much of Malawi, the remaining belts roughly corresponding to areas where game animals were still to be found – the Vwaza Marsh, Nkhotakota and Kasungu game sanctuaries, the Phirilongwe region and parts of the Upper Shire, and the Western scarps of the Lower Shire Valley (Mitchell and Steele 1956). It was thus estimated that at the end of the colonial period some 12 per cent of the total land area was still covered by tsetse fly belts. However, with tsetse having been eradicated over much of the central region and the Lower Shire Valley, the number of livestock increased substantially in both these areas (Pike and Rimmington 1965: 193–6).

In the low hills between Chitipa and Karonga, however, there is still a small population of the tsetse fly *Glossina brevipalpis*, and during the 1950s there were various reclamation schemes to extend the areas available for domestic livestock (MNA/PCNI/17/19). Also towards the end of the colonial period there were several reports, focused on the Lower Shire Valley, which then had around 5,000 head of cattle, suggesting ways of controlling the tsetse fly. Yet in 1957 there were still 130 confirmed cases of trypanosomiasis (*nagana*) in cattle (Chorley 1944; Matson 1959).

Epilogue

At the present time pockets of tsetse fly are still to be found in and adjacent to all the wildlife sanctuaries in Malawi – Vwaza Marsh, Kasungu, Nkhotakota, Liwonde and Mwabvi – and it has been suggested that the long-term future of the national parks and game reserves depends on the long-term control of the tsetse fly. Two problems are still evident. Firstly, uncontrolled tsetse fly represents a significant health hazard to people working for the Department of National Parks and Wildlife, as well as for tourists and people living close to the park. Sleeping sickness outbreaks still periodically occur. From about 1980, for reasons unknown, tsetse fly began to increase both in Kasungu and in other protected areas, and there have regularly been reported cases of sleeping sickness. An American friend of mine who worked on an environmental education project in the Nkhotakota game reserve contracted the disease, and was forced to return to the United States. Each year 10–12 cases of sleeping sickness are reported, and in 2001 some 23 cases were recorded in the first five months of the year, and it was suggested by the Ministry of Health that sleeping sickness cases may well be on the increase (*Daily Times* 11 May, 2001).

Secondly, the presence of tsetse fly render impossible the keeping of livestock within about 20 km of wildlife conservation areas, and this has had important consequences for the farmers living adjacent to these areas (WRU/1/54/10/1).

Although certainly not the scourges that they once were, sleeping sickness and the cattle disease *nagana* nevertheless still have a presence in Malawi.

Cultural Entomology

Insects as the Enemy

'What sort of insects do you rejoice in, where you come from?', the Gnat inquired.
'I don't rejoice in insects at all', Alice explained, 'because I'm rather afraid of them.'
Lewis Carroll, Through the Looking Glass (1872)

In recent years two excellent films have been produced on insect life, reflecting very contrasting attitudes towards the natural world. The first is entitled 'Microcosmos', made by Claude Nuridsany and Marie Perennou (1996). Inspired by the writings of Jean-Henri Fabre, it depicts the insect life in the alpine meadows of the French Pyrenees. Without any commentary, the film begins at daybreak and is exquisitely made – simply depicting the sights and sounds of the meadow, time measured in moments – ants drinking from a dewdrop, ladybird beetles feeding on aphids, a swallowtail butterfly emerging from its chrysalis, damsel flies mating, flies held in a sundew trap, rhinoceros beetles fighting on a log, bees feeding on salvia flowers, a small grasshopper caught in a spider's web. As with the deep ecologists, it emphasizes ecological relationships, and expresses a detached, aesthetic attitude towards the natural world, focusing specifically on insect life. No humans are depicted in the film; it simply takes the viewer on a journey into another world, pristine, intricate, fascinating – the miniature world of another life-form.

The film 'Alien Empire', produced in the same year (1996) specifically for the BBC, is very different. Equally well made, and with a haunting sound track by Martin Kiszko, it is based on the premise that since the dawn of time insects and humans have been in conflict with each other, and that humans are slowly losing the 'war' against these ultimate 'aliens'. Significantly, although insects evolved on earth some 350 million years ago, long, long before humans, it is they who are portrayed in the film as the 'aliens', and are depicted as invading our houses, damaging our crops, destroying our buildings, and as engaged in a continual warfare against humans. Insects themselves are described in mechanistic terms as alien 'monsters', as machines with elegant 'hardware' and sophisticated 'software', and insect ecology itself is described in terms of conflict – a 'battle-zone'. Insects, the film suggests, are 'in conflict with everything', and engage in 'secret wars' unseen by humans; they live in a world of 'attack and defence' and every rainforest is thus a 'deadly battleground'. As insects have invaded every corner of the human world, and are beyond the ultimate control of humans, the future for *Homo sapiens* is bleak indeed! In this rather one-sided portrait of insect life, the importance of mutual aid and symbiotic relationships, long ago stressed by Kropotkin (1902), is ignored; the positive aspects of insects in regard to human life are bypassed; and the crucial ecological role that insects play in almost all biotic communities is barely mentioned. Indeed, rather than being 'aliens', engaged in constant conflict with humans, insects, as the dominant terrestrial life-forms, provide crucial ecological support for the very existence of human life.

The film 'Alien Empire' expresses sentiments very similar to those of the colonial administrator Harry Johnston, who wrote of his revulsion from and hatred of the 'insect race', and with the exception of the bee and the cochineal aphid (which produces dyes) suggested that he could not 'call to mind one insect that is of any benefit to man'. He next posed the question whether this hatred of insects was well founded, and then gave a catalogue of insects that created problems for humans. He mentions: the tsetse fly; the jigger flea, which makes people lame; the mosquitoes that spread diseases; the bluebottle fly, which spreads blood poisoning; the lakefly, which gives rise to choking clouds; the ants that get into our sugar; the termites that undermine our houses; the maddening sandflies; locusts that ravage continents and cause widespread famine; bugs that damage valuable crops; hornets – social wasps – that inflict an almost deadly sting with little or no provocation; the beetles that destroy our timber. It is a formidable list. There is one insect, however, that invokes Johnston's extreme ire, and is considered the 'foulest of all insects', namely the cockroach, the very sight of which 'in its mad malicious lustful flight on some hot breathless night ... in one's room fills one with more abject terror and shuddering revulsion than the entry of any wild beast' (1897: 366–7). Having shared accommodation with the cockroach in many a hut and resthouse in both India and Malawi, I can't ever recall feeling terrorized by these harmless creatures – but the sentiments expressed by both Johnston and the film 'Alien Empire' indicate a key relationship or social attitude that humans have towards (some) insects – one of revulsion, hatred, conflict, opposition. It is an attitude expressed by all humans to some degree and in some contexts – and indeed, in a recent anthology of writings on insects, Hoyt and Schultz write (1999: 52) that 'perhaps the most prevalent view of insects in human culture – certainly so in modern times – has been one of revulsion'. People have thus reacted with fear, hatred, aversion, disgust, and with motivations directed towards the extermination of any insect that invades the human sphere.

In the last three chapters I have discussed in some detail those insects in Malawi that are considered by local people to be troublesome (*-bvuta*), or to create difficulties for human life, whether as agricultural or domestic pests, or as vectors of life-threatening diseases. Malawians, as far as I am aware, do not see mosquitoes and cockroaches as 'voices of the infinite', or hold conversations with house flies – as some new age spiritualists seem to affirm (Lauck 1998; Hartmann 1999). But, given the pervasive influence of Cartesian mechanistic philosophy, and the predominance of the ethic of capitalism – with its emphasis on control, domination, utility, detachment and even extermination, many Europeans have become increasingly estranged from nature, and have thus not only exaggerated the dangers emanating from the insect world, but have lost the ability to distinguish one insect from another, and thus, as Hoyt and Schultz suggest 'our negative emotions have become generalized to almost all insects' (1999: 52). Compared with Malawians, many Europeans are indeed entomophobic. But it is simplistic in the extreme to equate European culture with Cartesian philosophy and the anthropocentric outlook as expressed in such films as the 'Alien Empire' or in the writings of a colonial administrator like Johnston. While Johnston can express loathing towards the cockroach – and Malawians may also express similar, though not so exaggerated, sentiments – some writers, such as Howard Evans, have expressed positive attitudes towards the cockroach, though recognizing that this insect can be something of an 'unwanted pet'. *Note*: he wrote 'pet', not 'pest' (1970: 48–61, cf. Schweid 1999). Thus we have to recognize that although there is a pervasive tendency in Western culture to suggest that the insect is an 'alien' and 'does not belong to our world' (as Maurice Maeterlinck put it), and that the eradication of insects has become something of a fetish (Swan 1964: introduction) – this attitude is not the only sentiment that Europeans express towards insects. For, as with those of other 'cultures', Western attitudes towards insects are diverse, complex and multifaceted. Indeed the emphasis on the biological control of insect pests, eloquently expressed by Rachel Carson (1962), has been the expression of an ecological approach to the natural world that repudiates the fetish of insect eradication. Insects themselves are often the primary means of controlling insect pests: hence the title of Lester Swan's study *Beneficial Insects* (1964) (cf. Hoyt and Schultz (1999) for the many and varied attitudes expressed by Western scholars who have been fascinated by the insect world, from Aristotle to such contemporary entomologists as Howard Evans and Edward Wilson).

Nevertheless, the tendency to view all insects as the 'enemy', to be met with hostility and revulsion, is a deeply pervasive cultural bias in Western societies, as Joanne Lauck describes (1998: 1–16), and is reflected both in literature and contemporary film, as well as in pest control strategies. Lauck even considers biological pest control – using insects to kill other insects – as an expression of this cultural bias, and seems to repudiate or be untroubled by the fact that mosquitoes spread malaria, and locusts and armyworms can devastate people's crops and thus cause local famines. She presents, however, an equally monolithic portrait of tribal people – depicting them as new age spiritual mystics.

The film 'Microcosmos', inspired as it was by Fabre's writings on insects, expresses a very different attitude towards nature – a common-sense approach to the world that recognizes the diversity of organic forms, and their relationships and dynamic unity. It is a form of naturalism that is essentially aesthetic (in the original sense of this term). It implies both phenomenal recognition and empathy towards natural beings, specifically insects, and a responsiveness to what Gregory Bateson describes as the 'pattern that connects' (1979: 16–17). It is a way of knowing that may be described as 'natural history', wherein people 'take note' of the variety of living things and their interactions – not for their use and meaning, but simply for the wonder of it. It is a form of knowledge that in Europe in the eighteenth and early nineteenth centuries led to an obsession with classification and collecting (Pickstone 2000: 60), as well as in the development of natural theology. Although language usually reflects a subject–predicate logic (in both English and Chewa) nobody, as far as I am aware, views the world as consisting of self-existent entities – certainly not Aristotle, who, as we have seen, was not only interested in the morphology of insects, but also in understanding how their 'natures' were nourished, moved and reproduced. A 'relational epistemology' is therefore simply a reflection of our common-sense understandings of the world, an aesthetic naturalism that is not dependent upon the divinity, the insights of the Buddha, animism, or what is now described as 'spiritual ecology'. That there are no 'isolated phenomena', that all things are interdependent and interconnected, and that humans are an integral part of nature are basic premises of our common-sense understandings of the world, a 'natural history' or phenomenal approach to nature that was graphically illustrated in the film 'Microcosmos'. In Chapter 1 I have outlined the basic insect life-forms recognized by Malawians, and their folk classifications of insects, that is, their 'natural history'.

Both our phenomenal recognition of insect life, and our aversion and hostility towards insects suggest but two contrasting attitudes towards insects. But, as I have emphasized in my other writings, people's social attitudes and relationship to the natural world – including insects – are always diverse, complex, multifaceted, and often contradictory, and cannot be reduced to a single paradigm, let alone to a single metaphor. The common tendency of anthropologists to describe other people's conceptions of nature in monadic terms – usually with a spiritualist bias – and to contrast this, in Gnostic fashion, with a crude and simplistic account of Western attitudes (usually equated with the mechanistic philosophy of the seventeenth century) seems to me quite unhelpful, if not misleading. In my studies of the role of mammals in the social and cultural life of the matrilineal people of Malawi I thus attempted to show the *multiple* ways in which they relate to animals – pragmatic, intellectual, realist, practical, aesthetic, symbolic and sacramental (1998: 168–70). The same pluralism applies equally to their relationship to the various forms of insect life.

Cultural Entomology: a Comparative Perspective

In recent years, with the emergence of 'cultural entomology' as a sub-discipline, there has been a growing recognition of the diverse ways in which people throughout the world use and relate to insects. For insects are never seen, even in Western cultures, simply as pests to be eradicated. It is beyond the scope of this present study to review this extensive literature here; but we may note briefly some of these varied uses.

Insects as Food
As we have described in Chapter 3, throughout human history insects have been an important source of food for human communities, and it is only in recent times that Western cultures have developed an aversion to insects. Insects have significant nutritional value, and in many communities, as in Malawi, they form an important supplement to the diet.

Insects as Medicine
Throughout the world insects are reputed to possess medicinal properties, and are widely used in the treatment of many ailments. Honey is almost universally recognized as having healing powers, and is used to cure coughs, stomach problems and a variety of diseases throughout Africa, especially in Islamic communities. Beetles, of many different species, have been widely used as medicine. In Europe in the past fireflies 'drunk in wine' were used as an aphrodisiac, and blister beetles (*Meloidae*) are

commonly noted as medicine. *Cantharidin*, a blistering agent, has been extracted from these beetles, and employed in the treatment of urinary ailments. In large doses it can be a corrosive poison and was well known to the Greeks, *Kantharos* being the Greek term for 'beetle' (Frost 1942: 61; G. Evans 1975: 179). Many other beetles have been used in folk medicine – stag beetle, dung beetle, weevil; and, as was noted in Chapter 2, the larvae of beetles play a crucial role in the production of arrow poison for hunting. Throughout many parts of South Central Africa, the small *Pheidole* ants, which commonly invade houses, are consumed, as they are believed to cure stomach problems (Van Huis 1996: 11). Throughout Africa, too, pregnant women eat the clay from termite mounds, which clearly provides them with an essential source of minerals, as we have noted earlier in the study. Fly maggots, particularly of the genus *Wohlfahrtia*, have been used to clean up decaying tissue in wounds, and, as bacteria are now proving resistant to antibiotics, fly maggots are 'returning to service', as Lauck puts it (1998: 51).

Insects in Art
Throughout the world human communities have utilized insects – their forms, shapes and colours – in the decorative and graphic arts. Insects have been depicted on ceramics, in the making of jewellery and bodily ornaments, and as textile designs, as well as in the form of pictographs and paintings. In the sandpaintings of the Navajo, for example, insects such as the blowfly, cicada, cornbug and dragonfly are depicted as symbolic figures, while among the Hopi insect motifs, particularly of the butterfly, which may represent the *kachinas*, are drawn on their pottery, or represented as masked dancers. The *kachinas*, who essentially represent the spirits of the dead, may also include the bee, wasp, cicada, robber fly, cricket and dragonfly (Capinera 1993: 223–5). In fact, insects are depicted in the earliest rock art, especially bees and honey-hunting (Pager 1973). The concentric patterns found in the red schematic paintings that occur throughout Malawi and Zambia could well represent the combs of honey bees (Van Huis 1996: 14; Morris 2002). The shiny green elytra of the buprestid beetles, such as *Sternocera* spp., familiarly known as jewel beetles, are worn as necklaces and earrings in both Africa and South America. Depictions of bees, butterflies, dragonflies, crickets and cicadas are often featured in the art of classical Greece, as well as in China and Japan, and several insects appear in early European Christian art as universal religious symbols (Frost 1942: 65–6; Hogue 1987: 185). Finally, one may mention that insects and their products are frequently used in the art of the Australian Aborigines. Limonite oxide from ants' nests was used for a yellow pigment in paintings; beeswax was shaped

into ritual objects; and insects themselves were depicted in cave paintings (Cherry 1993: 12). Many of these insects, of course, had totemic associations.

Insects in Music

Many insects produce various forms of sound: the buzzing of bees, and the 'songs' of such insects as cicadas, crickets and katydids, produced by stridulating various parts of the body, are well known. Such sounds have always intrigued humans, and in China crickets have long been kept in cages, as their song is thought to bring enjoyment and tranquillity to the household (Laufer 1927). The songs of insects have inspired many European composers, such as Grieg and Rimsky-Korsakov, and insects have often been incorporated into popular songs – such as the well-known 'blue-tailed fly' (Frost 1942: 64).

Insects in Folklore, Mythology and Literature

Insects play an important part in the folklore and mythology of indigenous people throughout the world. Among native Americans, for example, insects such as beetles, ants, bees, fireflies and wasps frequently appear in their mythology, especially in relation to the creation of the world and its various inhabitants (Clausen 1954; Cherry 1993b). Many of the myths and legends of classical antiquity relate to insects, and there are, of course, numerous references to insects in the Bible (Cansdale 1970). Keith McE. Kevan (1974) compiled an intriguing and interesting collection of the many sayings, hymns, verses and poems relating to the grasshoppers, crickets and katydids, drawn from across the world, and throughout history. Many of the earliest verses, in fact, relate to locust swarms laying 'waste' to the land. Insects also play a role in some African folktales, which often explain why specific insects, such as the dung beetle or termite, look and behave the way they do. Insects are equally important in many African proverbs (Van Huis 1996: 15–16). Insects continue to play an important part in contemporary literature, and many short stories and novels have insects engaging in prominent roles – for they are useful in conveying various moods and images, both positive and negative (Hogue 1987: 182–3).

Insects and Recreation

Insects have long been used for recreational purposes, especially as pets. In China, as was noted earlier, singing crickets have been popular pets for many centuries, and the cricket *Gampsocleis gratiosa* (family: *Tettigoniidae*) is still sold as a pet in many markets in China. Crickets are also used in China as a popular form of entertainment, for gambling-based cricket fights are staged in similar fashion to cockfights. Crickets were often selected for their fighting abilities (Laufer 1927). 'Flea circuses' were, of course, once common in Europe. Throughout the world, cocoons of the larger moths are utilized in the making of dance rattles – as both hand and ankle rattles (Peigler 1994).

Children, of course, often play with insects, capturing antlions, grasshoppers, beetles and dragonflies, and utilizing them in various games. The goliath beetle, for example, may be captured, and tied to a stick, and the insect then allowed to whirl around (Clausen 1954; Van Huis 1996: 14).

Insects as Oracles

Throughout the world insects, as with other life-forms, have been utilized in divination rites. The best-known of these is the termite oracle among the Azande of the Sudan, as recorded by Evans-Pritchard. The *dakpa* or termite oracle is considered to be the poor man's oracle, because little expense is involved: a person simply finds a termite mound and inserts two branches of different trees into one of the chambers of the mound. The person will return the next day to see which of the two branches the termites have eaten. The problem with this form of divination is that it takes an entire night to answer a question, and very few questions can be asked at any one time (1937: 352). But Evans-Pritchard emphasizes that the termites are not perceived by the Azande as persons. 'They are simply termites and nothing more, but if they are approached in a correct manner they are endowed with mystical powers' (1937: 321). Termites are also used as oracles among the Lugbara of Uganda, and the Ndembu of Zambia utilize small black ants (probably *Pheidole* sp.) in all modes of divination as they are said to be 'always looking for things' (Middleton 1960: 261; Turner 1975: 338).

Insects as Religious Symbols

The most famous insect that has religious significance is the scarab beetle of Egypt (*Scarabaeus sacer*), which has had an important influence upon the cultural life of Egypt for several millennia, and is still important as an icon for visiting tourists. The dung beetle was seen as the symbol or manifestation of the sun-god Khepri, and the beetle pushing a ball of dung was deemed to symbolize the movement of the sun across the heavens. The beetle was therefore a symbol of rebirth and regeneration (Armour 1986: 26). In early European culture the stag beetle (*Lucanus cervus*) was associated in mythology with the thunder god Thor (G. Evans 1975: 177). Equally well-known is the importance of the 'praying' mantis in the mythology and religion of the San. *Kaggen*, the mantis, represents the deity, and is variously responsible both for the creation of the moon and the animals, and for the maintenance of human sociality. He is not prayed to, but is rather a trickster figure, and has the power to bring the dead back to life, and to transform himself into different forms (Barnard 1992: 84). Laurens van der Post refers to the mantis as the 'voice of the infinite', and Joanne Lauck (1998) vicariously and misleadingly not only generalizes this perspective to all insects, but assumes in monadic fashion that it is the world-view of all tribal people. This is not to deny that insects – of specific species – do not in many cultures have a religious significance, and are seen as the embodiment or manifestations of various spiritual beings – deities, spirits and souls of the dead: but to equate the religious beliefs of tribal people with the neo-Platonic Christian mysticism of Meister Eckhart or new age spiritualism is unhelpful. Insects, however, have a religious significance in many societies throughout the world. Among the Hopi, as was earlier noted, the *kachina* spirits often took the form of insects, represented as figurines, as masked dancers, or as naturalistic designs on pottery. Several insects, such as the 'cornbug' or 'big fly', were also important in the religious life of the Navajo, mediating between people and the deities (Capinera 1993; Morris 1979). Throughout West Africa butterflies may be associated with the divinity. Insects are, of course, also associated in a negative sense with witchcraft, and either viewed as manifestations of witches or instruments of their malevolence (Van Huis 1996: 12–13).

Such are the diverse ways that people throughout the world relate to insect life, reflected in the various influences that insects have had on human social existence – in medicine, art, aesthetics, poetry, music, mythology, recreation, divination and religion. I turn now to exploring the important ways that Malawian people relate to insect life – not simply as a food resource (*chakudya*) or as a pest (*chirombo*), but rather the important role that they play in their broader cultural life. I thus examine their use as medicine, and the role that they play in oral literature, folklore and religion.

Insects as Medicine

As I have described in detail in my earlier studies (Morris 1996, 1998: 215–22), medicines play a crucial and significant role in the social and cultural life of Malawian people, although they tend to be ignored by visiting scholars, who are generally more interested in the more esoteric or political aspects of Malawi culture. The term for medicine is *mankhwala*, which is a cognate of the widespread term *bwanga*, and is used to cover a variety of substances believed to possess inherent potency and efficacy. In fact, the term essentially refers to this vital power. It thus covers various charms, amulets, and protective medicines, as well as medicines in the normal sense. Western pharmaceuticals, agricultural fertilizers and pesticides are also called by the same term. The general term for the traditional healer in Malawi, *sing'anga* is derived from the term for medicine, and essentially means 'medicine person'. The proto-typical *sing'anga* is the herbalist, but the term is extended to cover other healers, such as diviners and spirit mediums.

The majority of substances used for *mankhwala* are plant materials: the roots, leaves, bark, fruit and seeds of various plant species. In my earlier studies I recorded over 500 species of plants used as medicine in some way, and it was estimated that around 120 herbs were widely used by herbalists in the treatment of various ailments (1996: 61). But importantly such medicines may be used for a variety of purposes, extending far beyond the therapeutic context: as good luck charms; for assistance in a variety of activities and concerns (hunting, friendship, employment, marriage, agriculture, court cases); as protective medicine against witches; for potency and reproductive purposes; and for life-cycle rituals, as well as being herbal remedies for a wide variety of ailments (*math-enda*). Equally importantly, animal substances are utilized – especially in countering sorcery or witchcraft, or the influence of malevolent spirits – as 'activating' medicines (*chizimba*) that give additional power to the plant substances (Morris 1998: 217–20).

In the past I studied as an 'apprentice' to two local *asing'anga*, herbal-ist-diviners (Useni Lifa and Samson Waiti), although I have never felt the need to describe my personal encounters with them, or pretend to my friends that I myself believed in the reality of the ancestral spirits or witches. But as far as I can recall insects were never employed, or even mentioned, as a medicine, or utilized in their divinatory rites. More recent studies seem to confirm this, for insects are not widely used as medicine. But from my observations and my discussions with several herbalists, there are a number of insects that seem to be widely recognized as *mankhwala*, and these include the following.

Snouted Beetle, Kafadala, Brachycerus nr labrusca

This is a distinctive dark grey beetle, covered in warty tubercles, which has the habit when touched of feigning death. Hence its common names *kafadala* or *mndaferamwendo* (*-fa*, to die). It is thus used as an amulet, worn (*-zobvala*) on a string around the neck, to stop fainting or fits (*-komoka*), especially with regard to someone suffering from epilepsy (*khunyu*). Other herbalists suggest reducing the beetle to ashes (*-wocha*), and then rubbing the ashes into incisions made on the sides of the head

(-*temera mutu*) as a cure for the same ailment, or for someone losing consciousness. Among the Yao, in the past, the beetle was used as 'gun medicine' to help in the killing of game, and as an item in a divining gourd (*ndumba*). Its Yao name is *chiwamsagaja* (Stannus 1922: 302; Sanderson 1954: 66).

Bagworm, Mtemankhuni, Eumeta cervina

The bagworm is universally recognized as a 'poison' or as 'bad medicine' (*mankhwala woipa*), and it is believed that any person or livestock animal eating the insect will die. Its Chewa name *lipepedwa* (-*pha*, to kill) suggests this. There is, however, little empirical evidence to support this assertion, and Sweeney notes (1970: 29) that the Medje of the Ituri forest regard the bagworm larvae as a delicacy. However, the bagworm is widely used as medicine. The insect, including the silken 'bag' of twigs, is mixed (-*sanganiza*) with various plant medicines, usually roots, and then reduced to ashes. These are then rubbed into incisions made on the temple as a cure for various head ailments associated with sorcery (*matsenga*). It thus may be described as *mankhwala amutu*, 'head medicine'. More often the insects and twigs are reduced to ashes and rubbed into incisions made on the legs of a young child who is slow or unable to walk (*saenda*). This is also used as a cure for swollen legs. The ashes of this insect, together with those of various herbs, are usually kept in a small calabash (*nsupa*). Many suggest that people are afraid (-*opa*) of the bagworm, and that unlike other caterpillars it is always found alone. Interestingly, this is the only insect noted as medicine in Ken Kalonde's little booklet on medicinal plants *Mankhwala a Zitsamba* (2000). It suggests charring (-*psya*) the insect (*kachirombo*) and turning it into ashes (charcoal) (*kusanduka makala*), with the ashes then rubbed into incisions – *mphini* (tattoo marks) – made on the legs and around the knees. This is the cure for a child or elderly person (*kholo*) who has difficulties in walking. The booklet suggests, in a concluding note, that if the medicine does not work after several attempts, then a person should run to the hospital immediately (*thamangirani ku chipatala msanga*)! (2000: 103–4). Also of interest is that the bagworm (*Psychidae*) is the only insect used as medicine by the Kalahari San (Nonaka 1996: 37). But besides being widely recognized as a medicine to assist children to walk, or for rheumatism (*nyamakazi*), the ashes of the bagworm have also been noted as a cure for headaches, as a strengthening medicine, and for stomach ailments. It is thus usually the only insect to be found on the stalls of market herbalists.

Lake-fly, Nkhungu, Chaobora edulis

Although, as we have discussed earlier, the lake-fly is an important source of relish, it is also used in the northern region as a medicine. The well-known 'African doctor' of Mzuzu market, J. Chiwanda Uka Lyoka, informed me that the lake-fly has many medicinal uses (*nchito kwambiri*), and is utilized as a cure for heart problems, pneumonia (*chibayo*), and drowsiness, as well as to assist in difficult court cases (*mlandu*). The lake-fly cake is usually ground up, made into an infusion and drunk; or it may be rubbed into incisions. He also suggested that if the infusion is poured (*-thira*) on a termite mound, it will encourage the flying termites to emerge in abundance.

Blister Beetle, Dzodzwe, Mylabris dicincta

This beetle is often associated by local people with the red-banded longi-corn beetle (*Ceroplesis orientalis*), as both are conspicuous red and black beetles, although the longicorn beetle belongs to a different family and has very long antennae. The local name *ligombera* is also used for both insects. The blister beetle is used as a medicine to treat venereal diseases such as gonorrhoea (*chisonono*) and syphilis (*chindoko*) – known by men as 'diseases of women' (*mathenda yaakazi*). The beetle is pounded in a mortar with various plant medicines, such as *mdima* (*Diospyros* spp.), and an infusion made of the pounded material is drunk as a remedy. It is also used as a medicine for swollen necks (*khosi wotupa*), the insect being charred, ground (*-pera*) into powder, which is then rubbed into incisions made in the neck. This complaint is known as *chotupa* ('swelling'). Hugh Stannus noted that this beetle, which contains Cantharidin, is a recog-nized poison among the Yao, and may be used with intent to murder, as well as for suicidal purposes. The symptoms, as described by local people, include constipation, followed by high fever and death around eight hours later (1922: 292).

Water Beetle, Chinsambisambi, Cibister vulneratus

This shiny black beetle is recorded as an ingredient in the preparation of a medicine to protect (*-tsirika*) a house against the malevolent influences of witches (*afiti*), spirits (*ziwanda*) and human thieves (Van Breugel 2001: 248).

Ground Beetle, Chikodzera, Tefflus cypholoba

This common, black, solitary beetle has a characteristic habit of squirting fluid if provoked, which can be painful if it comes into contact with tender skin or the eyes. It is recognized as a 'poison'. Its common name refers to this mode of defence (*-kodza*, 'to urinate'). The insect is charred on the fire, together with (*-phatikiza*) several plant medicines, and rubbed into incisions as a cure for headaches and urinary problems.

Toad Grasshopper, Tsokonombwe, Lobosceliana haploscelis

This conspicuous, fat, wingless grasshopper is widely used as a medicine to encourage plant growth, particularly of pumpkins. The insect, whose call is a harbinger of the rainy season, is roasted and then mixed with pumpkin seeds on planting. It is said to make the pumpkins very sweet. The ashes of the insect were also noted as a cure for asthma and chest complaints (*chifuwa*).

Mutillid Wasp, Nthumbathumba, Mutilla dasya

Often described as the 'velvet ant', this insect is widely associated throughout Malawi with luck, and is often described as *mankhwala wamwayi* – good luck medicine. Its ashes are either used to anoint the body (*-dzola*) or rubbed into incisions (*-temera*) to bring good fortune – in marriage, friendship, work, and other undertakings.

I have brief notes on the occasional use of other insects as medicine for various ailments – the king cricket, *chiboli* (*Henicus* sp.) as a cure for swollen lymph glands (*mabomu*) and headaches; the dragonfly *tombolombo* (*Philonomon luminans*) mixed with other plant medicines, is used as a wash to bring good luck (*mankhwala amwayi*); the tree locust, *chiwala/mphangali* (*Acanthacris ruficornis*) is noted as a medicine for urinary problems and bilharzias (*likodzo*); and finally, the irritating fluid of the armoured ground cricket, *Mvimvi* (*Enyaliopsis petersii*) is used as a cure for sores and abscesses (*kanjinji*).

It is of interest that many of the herbalists I met in urban areas had little knowledge of insects generally, and apart from the use of bagworm as a cure for rheumatism knew little about the medicinal uses of insects. It seems that much indigenous knowledge of insects is being lost with urbanization.

Insects in Oral Literature

The matrilineal people of Malawi have a rich oral tradition, expressed in historical narratives, folk tales, songs, proverbs and riddles. Early missionaries often published important collections of this oral literature, and more recently Steve Chimombo (1988) has written a pioneering study of what he describes as the 'aesthetics' of the indigenous arts of Malawi. Although animals, particularly mammals, play an integral role in the folk tales and proverbs of Malawi – as I have discussed elsewhere

(1998: 173–85) – indeed the local literature journal was called *kalulu* ('hare') – insects seem to have a more marginal role. Two important collections of the folk tales of Malawi, for example, make no mention at all of insects (Singano and Roscoe 1980; Schoffeleers and Roscoe 1985), although one Lomwe story relates to a young man called *Kansabwe* (small louse) – a name given to him an account of his dishevelled and dirty appearance. But one (Tumbuka) folk tale relating to insects has been recorded by Boston Soko. It runs as follows:

Njuchi the bee and some other insects were bored. As they didn't have a profession, they spent their time buzzing. They really envied the spider who weaves a web, the ant who builds anthills, Mbewa the mouse and others too who dig tunnels. But one day, god let them know that he was going to teach them a job, which is to make sweet products. All the insects who make honey met on that day, including Zoli, the carpenter bee. God started to explain their job. At first, he taught them how to make a hive with lots of cells. These will be used as honey stores. Then, he said, one has to find some grains of pollen, which the insects will work with their saliva to make honey. Zoli, the carpenter bee, who was always impatient and in a hurry, got up and said 'I'm going to put this into practice right now.' Then he left. But it was not over, because god still had a lot of things to teach them. Njuchi the bee and his companions who had stayed learnt how to conserve the honey, how to feed from it, and how to feed the larvae. Happy, the insects went back home. Today when you compare the honey made by Zoli the carpenter bee and that made by Njuchi the honey bee you can see a big difference

(Soko 1994: 1, translated from the French)

The story indicates of course a good understanding of the habits of honey bees (*njuchi*), which contrast with those of carpenter bees (*bemberezi*).

I have noted earlier a song relating to the *mphalabungu* caterpillar sung by children; but several other songs (*nyimbo*) focused on insects and other small invertebrates have been recorded. Some examples may be noted.

Analimvimvi teyeni
Ulendo wanga uno
Wokamelo mapiko
Anabwera nalira
Ana m'mana mapiko

Armoured ground cricket, let's go
My journey is now

To grow wings.
He returned weeping
As he was denied wings.

The song alludes to one of the creation stories in which all winged creatures went to the creator (*namalenga*) to be given wings. Friends called on the armoured ground cricket to join them, but this fat cricket (actually a long-horned grasshopper) did not go immediately, as he was more concerned with eating. As a result he arrived too late, and never acquired wings.

There is also a children's song about the jewel beetle *nkhumbutera*, which runs:

Nkhumbutera, tera! tera!
Kwanu kulibe mtengo, eh!

Jewel beetle, land! land!
At your home there is no tree.

The song is supposed to entice the insect, who flies to a tree close to the singer, where it can be easily captured. The beetle, as we have noted, is commonly eaten. The millipede *bongololo* (it is not a centipede, as *chimombo* calls it) is also the subject of many songs. These include:

Bongololo wafera panjira
Miyendo khumi-khumi
Mafuta kusana ng'ani ng'ani

The millipede died on the path
With lots of legs.
Its back was oily and shiny.

Bongololo tiye! tiye!
Bongololo tiye! tiye!
Chisese, se! se!

Millipede, come along, come along,
Millipede, come along, come along,
Lets sweep, sweep, sweep.

In the latter song the children imitate the actions of the millipede. They hold hands in a long line, which then curls up like a disturbed millipede, later to re-open and move again across the playground (Chimombo 1988: 159–62).

> Nyerere, nyerere, eh, nyerere,
> Nyerere, nyerere, eh, nyerere
> Ndikanakhala nyerere, eh!
> Nyerere ndikanakumba ndilowe eh!

> Ant, ant, eh ant
> Ant, ant, eh ant
> I am living with an ant
> Ant, I dig and enter, eh!

The woman who sang this song explained to me that good husbands should be like ants – always industrious.

Another song recorded by Chimombo relates to the *mopane* or stingless bee (*nsikisa*).

> Fikisa anamwali, eh
> Fikisa anamwali ndi uchi, eh
> Fikisa za pa chulu

> Stingless bee maidens, eh
> Stingless bee maidens are honey, eh
> Stingless bees are from the termite mound
> (Chimomombo 1988: 154)

This song is sung during a *Nyau* ritual and makes an analogy between the young girls and the sweetness of honey. The stingless bees often nest in termite mounds, which in turn is associated with fertility.

There is also a children's counting song that alludes to the thief ant, *mafulufute*.

> Modzi, wiri, ndiwerenga
> Ndawerenganji?
> Mapira, mapira si anga
> Nga fulufute
> Fulufute si wanga, nga, nga, nga

> One, two, I've counted
> What have I counted?
> Millet, millet, that's not mine.

It's the thief ants.
The thief ant is not mine, mine, mine.
                    (Chimombo 1989: 17)

Both male and female thief ants, as we have noted, are important as relish, but they are often elusive to capture as they emerge singly from the hole on their nuptial flight.

At Migowi, as part of the *Chiputu* ritual for young girls, I heard one typical song relating to the *Pheidole* ants. It went:

Kuli nyerere
Ine osagona

There are black ants,
I do not sleep.

It was sung to the accompaniment of handclapping, and with the women forming a circle, several of the younger girls lying on the ground, gesticulating and moving as if being attacked by ants. The movement of their hips made it evident that the play act was a euphemism for sex.

A final song, recorded among the Yao, is the following:

Litono, tuti! tuti!
[O little] dung beetle, push, push

with the refrain:

Likutata manyi
It's rolling its dung.

It is sung as part of the *Likwata* dance during the initiation of girls, the women imitating the actions of the dung beetles, pushing and pulling each other (Stannus 1922: 366).

Proverbs

Proverbs (*chisimo*) and riddles (*ndawi*) play an important part in the cultural life of Malawian people, both in an everyday context and during the rituals associated with puberty. Some of these proverbs and riddles relate to insects, but they often include archaic words or expressions, and frequent ideophones, and thus their meaning is often esoteric and difficult to understand. Several important collections of proverbs have been made

(Gray 1944; Salaun 1978: 100–10; Van Kessel 1989; Chakanza 2000), and those relating to insects are listed below.

General

Tiri tiwiri ndianthu, kali kamodzi n'kanyama
Those that are two are humans;
That which is alone is a small animal [insect].

Nthawi yamvula kuchuluka zoliralira
At the time of the rains there is a lot of 'crying'.

Kachirombo kofula m'njira katama mano
The insect that digs the path trusts its teeth.
Zonse ndi moyo
Everything is life.

Cockroaches

Mphemvu yodyera ku mthiko
The cockroach eats the porridge stick.

Termites

Chulu cha ndiwo
The termite mound is relish.

Chiswe chikoboola chikwa, chayambira patali
[When] the termites bore into the basket [for grain storage], they
    have started from afar.

Chiswe chimalowa m'mphasa yongoimika
The termites enter the mat just as it stands.

Chiswe chimodzi sichiumba chulu
One termite does not make a termite mound.

Chulu sichiyendera chiswe; chiswe chimayendera chulu
The termite mound does not go to the termite; the termite goes
    to the termite mound.

Kalindelinde adalinda chiswe
"Wait, wait', waited for the termites.

Moyo saika pa chiswe
Don't put [your] life on the termite.

Zidzalezidzale zidalinda chiswe
To be filled, wait for the termite.

Achoke malizangundu, tiyanike inswa
[Zachoka ndundu, tiyanike inswa]
The black army ants have left, let's put the termites out to dry.

Inswa ikaola imodzi, zaola zonse
If one flying termite is rotten, all are rotten.

Pakamwa padzaulukira mbereswa
The small flying termite will fly from the mouth.

Grasshoppers and Crickets

Tsokonombwe adatha dziko n'kulumpha
The toad grasshopper reached the end of the world by jumping.

Mpemphetsa sakulitsa chitete
The beggar does not enlarge the grasshopper.

Kaphovu walowa m'dzombe
The disease (*kaphovu*) has struck [entered] the locust.

Nkhululu yatcheru ndiyo imaimba zokoma pachilimwe
The giant cricket is the one with the fine song in the dry season.

Dyera kudamanitsa bvimbvi mapiko
Gluttony prevented the armoured ground cricket from getting wings.

Bololo sakonda madzi
The mole cricket does not like water.

Lice

Chala chimodzi sichiswa nsabwe
One finger cannot crush a louse.

Nsabwe yoyendayenda idakomana ndi chikhadabo
The louse that is always on the move meets up with the finger nail
[that crushes it].

Chizolowezi chinalowetsa nsabsw ku munthu
'Getting used to' made the louse come to the person [head].

Bedbugs

Nsikidzi (nkhufi) zinachilira kwa alendo
The bed bug (tick) got a good return [feed] from the visitors.

Nsikidzi (nkhufi) zikalumaluma zilowa m'tsekera
After the bedbug (tick) bites, it enters the thatching grass.

Flies

Chakometsa ntchenche, ina chilimika ku uluka
What makes the fly likeable (fortunate) is that it depends upon flying.

Kalionera adaphika ntchenche nayesa ana anjuchi
The watcher [imitator] cooked flies, mistaking them for bee larvae.

Dyera linapititsa ntchenche ku manda
Gluttony brought the fly to the graveyard.

Choka mmbuyo khwangwala atole mphutsi
Leave from behind, so that the crow can pick up the fly maggot.

Kuwerengera (wakhalira) madzi a mphutsi
Rely on the water for the fly maggot.

Butterflies/Moths

Nda onera momwemo: mwambo wa gulugufe
That is how it's seen: is the tradition [way] of the butterfly.

Wasps

Ukapanda mng'oma umadya mabvu
If you do not have a beehive, you will eat wasps.

Chimvano cha mabvu n'choning'a pamimba
It is by mutual agreement that the wasp has a thin waist.

Bees

Bemberezi adziwa nyumba yake
The carpenter bee knows its own home.

Kusafunsa asadya njuchi izi
Not asking one eats the bees.

Njuchi yako ndi iyo yaluma
Your bee is the one that has stung [you].

Njuchi zikachuluka siziika
If the bees are too numerous they do not put [make honey].

Njuchi zikachuluka ziliba usinda
If the bees are too numerous there is no wax.

Chuluke-chuluke ngwa njuchi, tsatsa yakuluma
There are many bees, just follow the one that stung [you].

Zingalume phula nditenga
Let the bees sting, I will collect the wax.

Ants

Pachedwa msulu (khakhakha) pali nyerere
When the banded [water] mongoose is late, there are ants.

Makomakoma a nkhuyu m'kati muli nyerere
The figs are tasty, but inside there are ants.

Zikubwerera anafa ndi linthumbu
'If you return' was killed by the red driver ants.

Kutsinira mafulufute ku una
Don't squeeze the thief ant at the hole.

Mafulufute akamatuluka usamatsinira kudzenje (una)
When the thief ant is coming out, do not squeeze them at the hole.

Mafulufute umalinda atuluke
Wait for the thief ant to leave [the hole] by itself

Ukapeza nyamu ziku uluka, ima pambali uzitula imodzi imodzi, upeza zadzala nsengwa
If you find the thief ant flying [emerging], stand aside and pick them up one by one, and you will fill the basket.

Millipedes

Bongololo anali ndiwo; timadyi ndi auje
The millipede was relish: we ate it with 'you know who'.

Bongololo ndi ndiwo, uli ndi mnzako amene umadya naye
The millipede is relish, when you have a friend to eat with.

Bongololo sadzolera mafuta pagulu
The millipede does not anoint itself with oil in public [in a group].

Bongololo sadzolera mafuta pali anthu
The millipede does not anoint itself in the presence of people.

Riddles

Many well-known riddles also refer to insects; the following have been recorded (see Rattray 1907; Gray 1939; Mvula 1976; Singano and Roscoe 1980: 84–106).

Termites

Q. Munthu wangu wawuluka kumwamba, koma pabwera wabera opanda
My person flies high, it returns without wings.
A. *Inswa/mbereswa*

Q. Adamunyengera kutsetse
She eloped with someone at the valley.
A. *Inswa*

Q. Munthu akaponya mubwi wache kumwamba, ndipo pobwera ubwera wopanda bango
A person shoots his arrow high, when it returns it is without its shaft.
A. *Inswa*

Q. Ombani m'manja akulu-akulu adutse
Clap hands as the elders pass by.
A. *Chiswe*

Q. Ndinapita kudondo ana amandiombera m'manja
I went to the forest, children clapped hands for me.
A. *Chiswe*

Q. Make mariya madzi ndikatunga kuti
Mother Mary, where can I draw water?
A. *Chiswe*

Q. Amfumu momwe analowera nkhoti sanatuluke
The chief has not left [the courthouse] since it entered it.
A. *Manthu wa chulu* (termite queen)

Q. Chakhala pa chulu chidazi lamba
Living at the termite mound is a bald one.
A. *Chiswe*

Q. Ndidapita kwa bwenji langa adandiphikira ntchima ndiwo kangali matumbo
I went to my friend's [house] and she cooked *nsima* porridge and relish [has no intestine].
A. *Mbulika*

Crickets

Q. Kamnyamata kanga kamayimba ng'oma nkumbuyo
My boy plays on a drum behind [on his back].
A. *Nkhululu*

Q. Ng'oma ya atate/bamboo anga yo imbira ndi kumbuyo
My father's drum is beaten at the rear [behind].
A. Nkhululu

Q. Mfuti yanga yowomba ndi kumsana
My gun is fired at the back.
A. *Nkhululu*

Q. Nkhalamba za kwathu zimaimba ng'oma ndi kumbuyo
The old folks at home beat the drum at the back [behind].
A. *Nkhululu*

Q. Jekete abvalira ku likulu
He wears a jacket in old age.
A. *Nkhululu*

Q. Kankalamba aka kupambukapambuka
The old person breaks out often.
A. *Chiboli*

Q. Ndapeza mfumu ya dazi mutu onse
I found a completely bald chief.
A. *Chiboli*

Lice

Q. Kuli konse kumene upite kamba ndiwe
Wherever you go you will be my relish [meal].
A. *Nsabwe*

Q. Kali m'chiputu kandgodya nyama
In the short grass it eats meat.
A. *Nsabwe*

Q. Ndapha nyama ndi ndodo ziwiri
I can kill an animal with two sticks.
A. *Nsabwe*

Jigger Fleas

Q. Galu wanga kusagonetsa tulo
My dog makes me have sleepless nights.
A. *Thekenya*

Flies

Q. Kagalu kanga kamanunkhiza kwambiri ungabisitse kako kakalon-dola
My small dog has a strong smell, and if you hide something it finds it.
A. *Ntchenche*

Q. Ndanka kwa bwenzi langa wayamba kunditpatsa moni ndi mwana
I went to [visit] my friend, and the first to greet me was a child.
A. *Ntchenche*

Q. Ndikayalira alendo mphasa iye ndiye ayamba kukhalapo
Each time I spread the mat for the visitor, he begins to sit [on them].
A. *Ntchenche*

Q. Kanthu konunkiza, ungabisitse kako kakalondola
Something sweet swelling; if you hide it, I will seek it out.
A. *Ntchenche*

Q. Ndidachoka pano kupita ku chipyera ndalendo wanga m'mbuyo, kufika ku chipyera ndati ndkhale pantchi nawo akhala
I left here to go to Chipyera with my visitor behind; I arrived at Chipyera and sat down, and he also sat down.
A. *Ntchenche*

Q. Mfumu ya kumpoto poenda imati kudzera ine nkwabwino kupita ine nkwabwino
The chief from the north when walking says: 'Where I come from is good, [where] I go is good.'
A. *Ntchenche*

Q. Mkhuku zanga zimayikira podekha pokha pokha
My chicken lays its eggs only in calm places.
A. *Udzudzu*

Q. Zoluma zedi koma kukagwira sikakhalira kuswanyika
It bites, but if you get hold of it, it will not break easily.
A. *Chimbu*

Butterflies/Moths

Q. Namwali, taona! Taona! Taona!
Girl, look, look, look!
A. *Gulugufe*

Q. Kankhalamba ka imvi kupambuka pambuka
Grey-haired old person breaks out often.
A. *Makula aimvi*

Wasps

Q. Mfuti yanga yolasa nkumbuyo
My gun cuts [shoots] from behind [the tail].
A. *Mabvu*

Honey Bees

Q. Kuluka achita kuziluka sindingakuthe
Weaving they do, but I can't.
A. *Njuchi*

Q. Bambo amandimenya chifukwa cha chuma chawo, koma amalume
sindidziwa chifukwa chomwe amandimenyera
My father beats me because of his wealth, but as for my uncle I
don't know the reason why he beats me.
A. *Njuchi and Mabvu*

Q. Amayi anga amaphika zakudya zokoma kwabasi, koma chimoji
chokha, ufiti
My mother cooks delicious food, but one thing only, witchcraft.
A. *Njuchi*

Q. Kanthu kang'onong'ono kapanga tokoma
A very tiny thing makes [something] tasty.
A. *Njuchi*

Q. Mubvi wanga ulasa ndi kuthera
My arrow wounds with its end.
A. *Njuchi*

Ants

Q. Ndiri ndi nkhumba zanga zakuda kwambiri ngati dothi la
ngonondiyani
My pigs are as black as dirt.
A. *Mafulufute*

Q. Ndanka kwa bwenzi langa andiphikira ndiwo makala
I went to [visit] my friend, and he cooked me relish like char-
coal.
A. *Mafulufute*

Q. Zungulira chulu ndikupatse mchere unyambite
Circle around the termite mound, and I will give you salt to taste.
A. *Mafulufute*

Q. Anandiphikira nsima ndiwo makala
They cook me porridge with charcoal as relish.
A. *Mafulufute*

Q. Ng'ombe zanga zukuda
My cattle are black.
A. *Mdzodzo*

Q. Chipaza ndi gombe nkumati chigwa
It skirts around the banks of the valley [but never falls in].
A. *Linthumbu*

Millipedes

Q. Pafera amayi makoza ndvu!
Wherever mother dies, there are [many] ivory rings.
A. *Bongololo*

Q. Sitima ipaza ndi dondo
The train skirts around the woodland.
A. *Bongololo*

Proverbs and Riddles: Discussion

Both the proverbs and the riddles indicate a wealth of empirical knowledge about the morphology, habits and ecology of insects. With regard to termites, for example, there is the recognition that the reproductive termites lose their wings during the nuptial flight, that the queen has a smooth, hairless body and never leaves the nest, that they may do much damage to baskets and other household utensils, and that the black army ants frequently feed on the termites. Similarly, with the giant cricket there is the recognition that this insect sings at the end of the dry season, and does so by means of stridulation. The proverb *Wakhalira madzi aphutsi,* 'rely on water for the fly maggot', relates to the fact that in the past boiling water was poured on the floor of the hut to destroy the blood-sucking congo-floor maggots (*Auchmeromyia luteola*). This no longer seems to be the pest that it once was.

But what the proverbs essentially affirm metaphorically is what are considered to be important social and moral values: to share and not to be greedy or selfish; to respect elders; to persevere in a task in spite of difficulties; to listen to others and to be attentive to their well-being; to be patient and show discretion, and, above all, to use one's common sense. Thus the proverb *Kutsinira mafulufute kuuna* ('don't squeeze the thief ant at the hole') – which has many variants – essentially signifies the importance of patience, for a person only captures these insects as they emerge singly from their nest, if he or she is not *too* eager, as I learned from my own experience collecting this relish. The well-known proverb: *Tsokonombwe adatha dziko n'kulumpha*, ('the toad grasshopper travelled the whole world by jumping') also expresses the need for patience and perseverance in spite of limitations. Unlike other grasshoppers, the toad grasshopper is plump, slow-moving and wingless. The proverb *Bololo sakonda madzi* ('the mole cricket does not like water') also expresses the need for perseverance, determination and courage, for although this cricket lives in marshy areas, it is oily to the touch and never becomes wet. The importance of honesty and being sincere is also emphasized in such proverbs as *Bongololo anali ndiwo: timadyi ndi auje* ('the millipede was relish: we ate it with "you know who" '). In fact the millipede is not relish and is never eaten – and the proverb alludes to be importance of not being boastful, or too proud, or dishonest. In Malawi, there is a pervasive emphasis on sociality, and on being open, friendly, hospitable, and civil to other people. Hence the proverb: *tiri tiwiri ndi anthu, kali kamodzi n'kanyama* ('those that are two are human: that which is alone is a small animal [insect]'). Greed and gluttony are therefore always reproached:

Dyera linapititsa ntchenche ku manda
Gluttony brought the fly to the graveyard.

Dyera kudamanitsa bvimbvi mapiko
Gluttony prevented the armoured ground cricket from getting wings.

The proverbs and riddles tend to focus around a number of insects that have cultural salience for Malawians, and these include those detailed in Table 7.1.

Although some of the proverbs and riddles relate to 'insects' that have only an aesthetic interest to local people, such as the toad grasshopper (*tsokonombwe*) and millipede (*bongololo*), the majority of insects are either household pests or edible species. Among the former are the bedbug (*nsikidzi*), louse (*nsabwe*) and fly (*ntchenche*); with regard to the insects utilized as food the termites (*chiswe/inswa*), crickets (*nkhululu, bololo*), honeybee (*njuchi*) and thief ant (*mafulufute*) are of particular salience.

Table 7.1 Types of Insect Mentioned in Malawian Proverbs and Riddles

Insect	Number of Proverbs	Number of Riddles
Cockroaches	1	—
Termites	10	9
Grasshoppers and crickets	6	7
Lice	3	3
Fleas	—	1
Bedbugs	2	—
Flies	6	8
Butterflies/moths	1	2
Wasps	2	1
Bees	7	5
Ants	7	6
Millipedes	4	2
Totals	**49**	**44**

Proverbs and riddles are said to express the 'cultural memory' of Malawian people, and thus to encapsulate the *mwambi* (the folk traditions) or the *nzeru za kale* (wisdom of olden times) (Kumakanga 1975; Chakanza 2000). Insects, in a small way, are still utilized as a means of expressing these folk traditions.

Insects in Folklore and Religion

As in other societies throughout the world, insects in Malawi are not simply seen either as pests – although the term *kachirombo* itself implies something that is useless and harmful to humans – or as a food resource, but rather they reflect the many different ways in which humans relate to the natural world. There are many ways of being, and thus our social attitudes to insects – as well as to other animals, mushrooms, plants and inanimate things – are always complex and diverse. Thus Malawians do not conceive of insects as a homogeneous category, nor do they approach them only in a utilitarian fashion – for insects also have significance in their wider culture. I have noted earlier in the study many of the insects that have particular cultural salience in conveying specific meanings or attitudes; some of these may be recalled. Thus, throughout Malawi the mantis *chiswambiya* (Yao, *chikasachigwa*), a term that covers not only several mantis species but also the stick insects (*Phasmatodea*), is held in a particular kind of reverence. It is not conceived as a person or as having subjective agency; but the harming or killing of a mantis is believed to result in dire consequences, so that thereafter – as its name suggests – a person will be continually breaking pots (*mbiya*). Similarly, the mutillid wasp, *nthumbathumba* (Yao, *ndupatumba*), is commonly associated with good luck – as a sign. If a person sees the wasp he (or she) may pat its belly, and then rub his own, and this will bring him luck for that day. If a person is embarking on a journey he or she may wrap a mutillid wasp in a piece of cloth and carry this with them – again to bring good luck. And as we noted earlier, the wasp is often utilized as medicine. The caterpillars of the large hawk moths *chilumphabere* (Yao, *chisumbila mawele*) (*Acherontia atropos, Hippotion osiris*) are believed by many people to 'jump at the breast' – hence their common name. The caterpillars bear a characteristic 'horn' (*nyanga*) at their rear end, and look rather formidable. The black army ant, *mdzodzo*, though associated with witchcraft, is also used as a protective medicine against sorcery and witchcraft, the live ants being placed in the shell of a large snail (*nkhono*), and kept in order to protect (*-tsirika*) the house from adverse influences. Equally important: if this ant is seen carrying eggs – it often moves over the ground in long lines – this is said to indicate that a person will find luck (*-peza mwayi*). Malawians often speak of black army ants' ability to subdue and carry off as food the much more abundant termite – especially *nthusi*, the harvester termites.

Even the cockroach, which is essentially viewed as a pest to get rid of (*-chotsa*), is meaningful in other contexts. There is thus the Yao saying:

Kuluma upeu
To bite the cockroach.

For local people the cockroach has a peculiar way of eating, remaining still and quiet, and then suddenly taking a bite of food. This may be said of a person who is 'two-faced' – coming up to you smiling, and then hitting you (Stannus 1922: 327).

Some insects are neither viewed as food nor pests, or even used as medicine, but are approached from an essentially aesthetic perspective. This applies particularly to butterflies/moths (*gulugufe*) and dragonflies (*tombolombo*). One person suggested to me that butterflies were created by god (*mulungu*) in their many forms, to make people happy (*-sangalasa*), and that their varied colours and markings gave people ideas in the designing of clothes. And she affirmed that these insects are important because of their beauty (*-kongola*). Indeed, some people suggest that if you kill a butterfly you will become deaf. Dragonflies are also approached in a similar manner. Although recognized as carnivorous insects, and believed to drink water by means of the tail, they are seen as happy creatures that are pleasing for humans to behold. I recorded one song relating to the dragonfly:

Tombolombo sangalasa ukuone ambuye ako
The dragonfly is happy to see his grandparent (god) (× 2)

People say that what makes a dragonfly truly happy is that, like humans, it enjoys capturing and eating winged termites.

Another insect that is invariably associated with feelings of happiness and joy is the jewel beetle, *nkhumbutera*. Not only the subject of a song, it is also kept by children as a pet, and in the past its wing cases were used in the making of a musical instrument. Children still keep this iridescent beetle as a pet, along with its 'egg'; both are esteemed as food.

In the past, it seems, several other beetles were kept as pets by children and used as toys – being whirled around on a string – or utilized in the making of musical instruments. The pretty green and white flower beetle, *nangalire* (Yao, *chiwauwau*) (*Taurhina splendens*) was impaled on a split stick, which, held in the teeth, was then used as a musical instrument. The positioning of the buzzing insect on the stick gave rise to different sounds. Stannus offers notes on another insect *matecheteche*, a lamellicorn beetle whose wing cases were used by women in the making of a musical instrument. He writes: 'The wing covers of some twenty of these insects are threaded on a string arranged around the shoulders and the feet of the player as she sits on the ground ... the wing covers give the buzzing quality to the notes which all natives like' (1922: 365).

In recent years there has been a lamentable tendency to posit a kind of Gnostic dualism between so-called 'Western' thought –largely equated with the Cartesian metaphysics of the seventeenth century – and the 'relational' epistemology of hunter–gatherers, and tribal peoples more generally. Thus whereas 'Western' people (supposedly) see nature as lifeless, homogeneous, inert, passive, and mechanistic, and all living things (including humans) as unitary, isolated and self-existent, tribal people see the world as animate, and as a web of interconnected things, and view all things – animals, plants, stones, sky, wind as 'persons', with consciousness and subjective agency (Bird-David 1999; Hartmann 1999; Peterson 2001: 222). This gnostic vision misrepresents both 'Western' thought and the conceptions of the natural world held by non-Western peoples. With regard to Malawian people, they do not, as I have discussed elsewhere, see, the whole world as 'animate' (1998: 141). There is in fact a riddle that runs:

Chamoyo chabereka chakufa,
Chakufa chabereka chamoyo

The living brings forth the dead, the dead brings forth the living.

The answer, of course, is chicken and egg.

Nor do Malawians go around 'personalizing nature' and seeing everything as 'persons' (Milton 2002: 40–54). It is well to note, however, that the concept of 'person' has several distinct meanings which are invariably conflated in discussions of 'relational' epistemology – which, as I noted earlier, largely reflects the common-sense understandings of people everywhere.

The first meaning of personhood alludes to an anthropomorphic perspective – people behaving towards other animals or natural phenomena as if they were 'humans'. Thus in Malawi folk tales animals – hare, bushpig, kudu, lion – have human characteristics and desires and live like humans – they live in villages and have chiefs, they hunt, set traps and cultivate gardens, eat meat and maize porridge, and use medicines; and they are depicted as human personalities with human foibles, idiosyncrasies and behaviour. But importantly, such descriptions always refer to a past time (-*kale*), and as far as I am aware nobody in Malawi thinks that real, contemporary hares or tortoises have gardens, make traps or eat maize porridge, and I doubt very much if such 'anthropomorphism' had any 'practical value' for hunter–gatherers in the upper Palaeolithic (Mithen 1996; Morris 2000: 39). Insects play a minor role in Malawian folk tales, and are not conceived as 'human'-like, although, as in other cultures, they may be described as being 'angry' (-*kwiya*), as 'hating' (-*dana*) humans, as 'happy' (-*sangalala*), 'liking' (-*konda*) certain things, and in need of respect (*ulemu*).

A second meaning of personhood relates to the fact that non-human animals, particularly the larger mammals, are viewed – as Ernest Thompson Seton (1898) described them at the end of the nineteenth century – as having complex and intricate forms of communication and sign language, so that much of their behaviour is social, learned rather than instinctive, and that they express emotions and have consciousness, subjective agency and unique personalities (Morris 2000: 38–40). Malawians, like many biologists (e.g. Griffin 1992) and people throughout the world, often views animals as 'persons' in this sense, and each species-being is viewed as having its own unique dispositions, habits and perspective on the world. Insects, however, tend to be seen by Malawians as having a more limited form of subjectivity and consciousness: they are, unlike mammals, never spoken of as possessing moral sentiments or knowledge (*nzeru*). And certainly they are not seen as the embodiment or manifestation of some kind of 'universal mind' of which Lauck writes (1998: 73), even though insects are held by Malawians to be created beings (-*lengedwa*).

The third meaning of 'person' in relation to animals refers to those contexts when animals (or other phenomena) are conceptualized as legal subjects or moral agents. (In this sense, in some cultures, many humans are *not* considered persons (Morris 1994: 11–12)). An example are the well-known 'animal trials' in medieval Europe, when animals were put on trial for damaging human interests. Thus weevils and beetle larvae were accused by villagers of damaging crops, and put on trial as legal persons – represented, of course, by a human lawyer. Interestingly, a judge may decide in the insects' favour, granting that they were creatures of god and that it would thus be unjust to deprive them of their natural subsistence – human crops. Equally, the insects' damage to crops may have been interpreted as a scourge sent by god to punish humans for their sins, or as their acting as instruments of the devil (Ferry 1995: ix-xiii). Malawians do not conceive of insects as moral agents, as persons in this sense.

The final way in which animals may be conceived as 'persons' is when they, or other natural phenomena (such as wind, trees, stones, and sun, as well as human artefacts), are conceived as embodiments or symbols of spiritual beings – the divinity, deities, ancestral spirits – that are then addressed as if they were persons. The term 'enspirited' is now a fashionable term, but as I explored in my earlier studies the relationship between the spirits (*mizimu*) and the animals that embody them is best seen as one of transformation, metamorphosis (*-sanduka*), rather than as possession or incarnation (2000: 221–6). Thus a spirit (*mzimu*) of the ancestors, or a malevolent spirit (*chiwanda*), or even a witch (*mfiti*) may transform itself into an animal, and thus be addressed as a quasi-human (person), although (importantly) people address the spirit, not the animal-form in which is it embodied. Significantly, of course, a witch or malevolent spirit – or even a person with knowledge of powerful medicines – that transforms itself into a leopard, behaves as a leopard, and thus may wreak havoc amongst a person's livestock.

Insects in Malawi are not usually seen as manifestations of ancestral spirits or of the divinity (*mulungu*) – and I found no evidence to suggest that Malawians think that insects have 'souls' or are 'voices of the infinite' (Lauck 1998). But there are some insects that do have religious significance, and in a sense become manifestations of the ancestral spirits during the *Nyau* rituals. For example, the louse (*nsabwe*) and the toad grasshopper (*tsokonombwe*) are represented by masked dancers, who in a sense unite, during the *Nyau* ritual, the human, the animal (insect) and the spiritual dimensions.

Pali Nsabwe is a black clay mask from Mua, and is a type of *kapori* that represents an old man, full of wrinkles, missing his teeth, dirty and unshaven, a person covered in lice and miserable. Usually appearing at funerals, his dancing movements are uncontrolled, and in response to his singing 'I dress like this because I am poor: I am covered in lice'; the gathering responds 'he is full of lice'. Father Boucher suggested that this *Nyau* figure indicated an important message: that people should respond to and feed a person even though he has an unkempt and repulsive appearance.

Tsokonombwe is a brown mask from the Pemba district. The mask has a broad mouth, large eyes, and two small horns that represent the antennae of the toad grasshopper. The dancer wears a headgear made of rags, and clothing with patches to represent the insect's body, and enters the ritual arena carrying maize or some other crop stalk. Also appearing at funerals, this *Nyau* figure enters to the accompaniment of the song: '*Tsokonombwe* makes noise the whole night, all night long; how can I sleep, *Tsokonombwe*?', and performs a dance with much jumping and chasing of the women.

The jewel beetle (*Nkhumbutera*), butterfly (*Gulugufe*) and millipede (*Bongololo*) have also been recorded as masked dancers during the *Nyau* rituals, representing the ancestral spirits (Boucher 2001; on *Nyau* rituals see Morris 2000: 131–50).

Insects, however, are not always seen in a positive light, as they may also be interpreted as instruments or manifestations of malevolent spirits or witches. Witchcraft beliefs in Malawi are intrinsically linked both to the use of medicine and to the conception of the person as a moral being. A witch (*mfiti*) can indeed be defined as a generic human being who is not a real person (a social and moral being), but who, motivated by envy, greed, malice and anti-social tendencies, and using medicines, wreaks harm on, and even kills, his or her kin and neighbours. Witches are associated with animals in several ways. Firstly, an animal may be a sign (*chizindikiro*) of the presence of a witch, and seen as a creature of ill-omen. A bat (*mleme*) or barn owl (*kadzidzi*) seen near the vicinity of the house may thus be interpreted as the presence of a witch. In some contexts ants may thus be associated with witchcraft. Secondly, witches may use an animal as an instrument or familiar, or may transform (*-sanduka*) themselves into animals – and thus steal or destroy crops, or take domestic livestock, or even kill a human. Thus a swarm of locusts or armyworms that devastates a crop may be interpreted as due to the machinations of some local witch. In the Mangochi district a specific ceremony, the *kapuche* ritual, is enacted, in which the help of the rain-maker *Bimbi*, and his associated spirit, is sought to protect crops from the depredations of armyworms or the maize stalkborer – which may have been sent by a witch (Amanze 1986: 236). People may also use special medicines to protect (*-tsirika*) their crops and houses from damage wrought by termites, which have been sent by some malevolent person using sorcery (*matsenga*) or by a witch (*mfiti*). But although both a pest and an important source of relish, termites (*chiswe*) are also significant in many rituals as a religious symbol. The termite mound (*chulu*) and the termite colony itself, particularly the queen termite (*manthu*), are seen as a cosmological icon and a source of vitality, health, fertility and well-being. The colony is seen as analogous to the matrilineal kin group, and the queen as the 'mother' of the colony (kin group), an endless, inexhaustible source of fertility. The queen has high medicinal value, and is eaten to give strength and procreative power. Whereas an early European traveller like Henry Drummond can describe the termite as a 'repulsive' insect and suggest that this creature is 'hated and despised by all civilized peoples' (1889: 123–31), Malawian people, while recognizing the destructive potential of the termite, tend to have very positive attitudes towards the insect. Thus the wife of Chief Tengani in the Lower Shire Valley was called 'manthu' ('the queen termite'), and she was seen as the 'mother of all people' and the ritual source of fertility (Schoffeleers 1997: 43). Importantly, however, Drummond recognized the vital role that termites played in the ecology of the African savannah, and noted the importance of termite mounds in the making of bricks. Indeed, throughout Malawi the clay from termite mounds is widely used in the making of bricks, and, in the past, was used in the construction of iron-smelting kilns (*ng'anjo*) (Msamba and Killick 1992: 17). Equally importantly, there seems to be a close ritual association between rain and termites, which usually emerge at the beginning of the rains, thus making the symbolic equation:

$$\text{RAIN} = \text{TERMITES} = \text{FERTILITY}$$

Conclusions

In this study I have attempted to explore the many and varied ways in which Malawian people relate to the world of insects, and have thus focused specifically on human–insect interactions. I have stressed that Malawians do not see insects – *kachirombo* – as a homogeneous category, nor is their relationship to the natural world, and specifically towards insects, to be interpreted in monadic fashion, in terms of a single paradigm. For their interactions with insects, and the various conceptions they have of insect life, are diverse and complex – empirical, pragmatic, practical (social), aesthetic, symbolic and sacramental. Thus an insect, such as a termite (*chiswe*) may be recognized (*-zindikira*) as a specific life-form or folk generic, and its morphology, habits and ecology known, particularly what it eats and what its principal predators are. This is a mode of understanding that may be described as empirical naturalism – a relational epistemology that is prior to and distinct from symbolic thought or religious conceptions (spiritualism). Such common-sense understandings of insects Malawians share with myself. But in some contexts the termite may be viewed as a harmful pest (*chirombo*) that damages crops and destroys the timber of houses. Indeed, as we have noted in Chapter 4, termites are one of the principal pests of maize, and in the early part of the season may damage around 20 per cent of the crop. In the Lower Shire Valley the harvester termite may completely ruin the cotton crop in its early stages. But in other contexts, particularly if a household is experiencing many acute problems, termite damage to a house or garden may be interpreted as the machinations of a local witch (*mfiti*). The termites may then be seen as the instrument or even the embodiment of some witch. Yet people generally have very positive feelings towards termites, for they are well-liked and important as a source of relish, particularly during the rains, and in their life-cycle and rain rituals, the termite, especially the termite mound and queen, have an important symbolic significance, being expressions of fertility and social well-being. Thus Malawians relate to termites, and to all insects, in diverse ways that express divergent interests, and several distinctive perspectives on the natural world. But importantly, for Malawians, insects are life-forms with which they share the earth; they are not conceived of as an 'alien empire' in need of eradication, nor as the voice of the infinite, the manifestation of some mystical 'world spirit'.

Appendix
Insect Life of Malawi

In the appendix I give a descriptive outline of the common insects of Malawi, focusing on those species that have salience for local people. This salience relates either to those insects that impinge on peoples lives in some way – damaging crops, inflicting stings, pests within the household – or that are utilized as food or medicine, or are items of cultural significance. Long ago Charles Sweeney indicated that around 4,000 species of insects had been collected from Malawi (1970: 32). This is a highly conservative estimate of actual numbers, and Cornell Dudley (1996) has recently calculated that there are probably well over 200,000 species of insects to be found in the country, many of which are still undescribed. Those insects that have cultural significance for local people are therefore only a tiny fraction of the insects that one is likely to encounter in Malawi. The local names denoted are essentially of Nyanja derivation (Mang'anja), but I have noted all the names suggested to me by local people during my researches in Malawi. The linguistic origins of these are indicated as follows:

C   Chewa
S   Sena
Y   Yao
L   Lomwe
T   Tumbuka

Under each species I have given a short description of the insect, and notes on its distribution and ecology.

With regard to taxonomic matters I have drawn freely on the pioneering studies of African insect life by Skaife (1979) and Sweeney (1970).

ORDER: ODONATA   Dragonflies

FAMILY: AESHNIDAE

1.   IMPERIAL DRAGONFLY
Anax imperator
Tombolombo
syn. *dombolombo, mweteteri* (L), *tombolinyo* (Y), *kumachenjezi* (T).
The well-known entomologist Eliot Pinhey (1966, 1979) recorded 154
species of dragonfly from Malawi, belonging to ten families. They are
predacious insects with biting mouthparts, and are ubiquitous, hunting
over water, or around the tops of *Brachystegia* trees, particularly at dusk
during the early rains. In Japan and South-east Asia dragonflies have an
important place in literature and the arts, and have long been esteemed as
food (H. E. Evans 1970: 63). But in Malawi, though they attract attention,
they are never eaten and have little cultural significance.

It is of interest that the predacious robber fly *Alcimus rubiginosus* is
also described occasionally by the term *tombolombo*. Many species of
dragonfly were recorded as common in the Shire Highlands, and all were
described by the taxon *tombolombo*. These include the following.

FAMILY: GOMPHIDAE

Ictinogomphus ferox

FAMILY: LIBELLULIDAE

Rhyothemis semihyalina
Brachythemis leucosticta
Philonomon luminans
Palpopleura lucia

FAMILY: PROTONEURIDAE

Elattoneura glauca

ORDER: BLATTODEA   Cockroaches

2.   COMMON COCKROACH
Periplaneta americana
Mphemvu
syn. *mbendule, mathuru* (L), *berethe* (S), *mbewu* (Y), *suche,*
maphere (T).

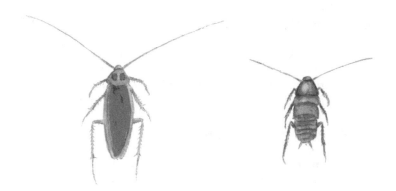

Figure 6 Number 2. *Blatoidea, Periplaneta americana*, Cockroach, Mphemvu, Makwawa, 3 July 2001.

Cockroaches, which are among the most primitive of insects, the earliest cockroaches appearing on earth some 350 million years ago, are allied to the grasshoppers, mantids and crickets – although rural Malawians see them as quite distinct. They are ubiquitous, and there is hardly a house in the rural areas of Malawi without its company of cockroaches. Numerous species have been recorded from Malawi, and cockroaches are plentiful among debris in *Brachystegia* woodland, but it is as household pests that they are well known, and three cosmopolitan species are fairly common: *Blatella germanica, Blatta orientalis* and *Periplaneta americana*.

ORDER: ISOPTERA   Termites

Both economically and culturally termites play an important part in the social life of the Malawian people. They are erroneously called 'white ants'. In reality they are quite distinct from the ants – and Malawians themselves see them as quite different, for termites have been described as highly evolved social cockroaches. As social insects they live in large and complex communities, which are essentially divided into three castes – the wingless, sterile workers and soldiers, and the winged reproductives. The latter swarm at certain times of the year – and having shed their wings they mate, and a pair forms a new colony. The termite queen is the most prolific of all insects, and during a lifetime may produce millions of eggs. The termites are soft-bodied insects; but soldiers, who form about 5 per cent of the colony, are often equipped with huge mandibles, and can easily draw human blood.

The generic term for termite is *chiswe*, and all language communities in Malawi have equivalent terms:

syn. *oweshe* (L), *ucheche* (S), *lucheche* (Y), *chimehe* (T).

Flying termites, mainly the winged reproductives of the sub-family *Macrotermitinae*, are specifically recognized as *ngumbi* (N/Y)

syn. inswa (c/s), shede (L), mpharata, mbulika (T).

as are the soldier termites (*agang'a*, *mgagadula*).
Termites belonging to two families have significance for local people.

FAMILY: TERMITIDAE

This large and complex family contains the vast majority of termites, and there are probably around a hundred species to be found in Malawi (Sands and Wilkinson 1954). It is very difficult to distinguish these various species in the field, but Malawians essentially recognize three kinds of termite within this family, in relation to their general ecology and habits.

3.   SUBTERRANEAN TERMITE
Chiswe Cha Micholo

This is a group of termites, of diverse species, which live in subterranean nests with little or no mound (*chulu*) and have fungus combs within the nest. They embrace the following species:

> *Pseudacanthotermes militaris*
> *Pseudacanthotermes spiniger*
> *Odontotermes nr mediocris*
> *Odontotermes nr badius*
> *Microtermes spp*
> *Ancistrotermes latinotus*

The alates of these various subterranean termites normally take to the wing towards the end of the rains, and usually around midday – hence they may be described as *chiswe chamasana* (*msana*, back, noon). Those of *Pseudacanthotermes militaris* are dark, reddish-brown, almost black, HB 12 mm, with pale brown wings 20 mm long, while alates of *Odontotermes nr. Badius* are larger, reddish-brown, HB 15 mm and with the wings a dark, smokey brown 28 mm long.

4. LARGE MOUND TERMITE
Macrotermes falciger
Chiswe Chapachulu

Termites of the genus *Macrotermes* are common throughout Malawi, and are particularly characteristic of *Brachystegia* woodland, although they are also common along the Lakeshore and in the Lower Shire Valley. Their large mounds form a significant part of the landscape, and many reach a height of several metres. The mounds of *Macrotermes falciger* near Namadzi may be 20 m in diameter and covered in large trees. Other common members of the genus include *Macrotermes goliath, Macrotermes bellicosus* and *Macrotermes natalensis*. The alates of all these termites form an important source of food for people throughout Malawi, and are commonly sold on the roadside or in markets during the rainy season. The alates of *Macrotermes falciger* are much larger than the worker termites, which measure less than HB 10 mm. The alates, in contrast, are dark reddish-brown, almost black, HB 21 mm, with pale brown wings having a chestnut edge, 35 mm long. Local people recognize two kinds of *ngumbi*, which vary in the timing of the nuptial flight. These are termed *chiswe chausiku* (*Macrotermes subhyalinus*), which is said to be paler and smaller and to emerge at night during the early part of the rains, and *chiswe chamadzulo* (*Macrotermes falciger*) which is larger, darker and emerges in the late afternoon in December and January.

5. SMALL MOUND TERMITE
Cubitermes spp.
Chiswe Cha Chikula

The genus *Cubitermes* is widespread and common throughout Malawi, and around 20 species have been collected. They are particularly common at the edge of *dambos* and in montane grasslands, where their small, very hard, brown, hillock-like mounds, 35–40 cm high, form a characteristic feature of the landscape. Donovan (1999) found a very high density of these mounds on Nyika plateau. Many other species of termites live in association with these termites – e.g. *Ancistrotermes* spp., *Microtermes* spp. These mounds are described as *chikula*. These termites are not eaten.

FAMILY: HODOTERMITIDAE

6. HARVESTER TERMITE
Hodotermes mossambicus
Nthusi
syn. *mnanthusi, mtusi, kanthusi, nthedza* (S).

This is a common and widespread termite, and is chiefly found in the Lower Shire Valley and along the Lakeshore – though I have found it common by the roadside in Rumphi. Unlike other termites, it forages on the surface during the day, particularly on cloudy days, without making any protective tunnels. It has a subterranean nest, and workers on the surface cut and collect grass, which forms their staple food – though they often cause great damage to seedling crops such as maize and cotton. The large black army ant, *mdzodzo*, is an important predator. It is not eaten.

ORDER: MANTODEA   Mantids

7.   BARRED MANTIS
Polyspilota aeruginosa
Chiswambiya
syn. *chiswamphika*, *mphwesakadi* (L), *nyaswankhali* (S), *chisoka-soka* (Y), *gogomthiko* (T), *chikasachiwiga* (Y).

There are many different kinds of mantids to be found in Malawi, all easily recognized by their elongate bodies, their small, mobile triangular

Figure 7 Number 7. *Mantidae, Polyspilota aeruginosa*, Barred Mantis, Chiswambiya, Kapalasa, 14 March 2001.

heads with large eyes, and their spiny forelegs, which are adapted for seizing prey. They hunt by lying in wait, usually well-camouflaged at the top of some shrub or grass stem. All mantids are carnivorous, mainly eating other insects, although they have been known to capture frogs and lizards, and John Wilson records observing a large mantis near Lake Chilwa holding a fire finch, a bird which is many times larger than the mantis. Their mode of capturing prey is reflected in their other names: *chilandamphuno* or *mdulamphuno* (*ku-landa*, to seize, *ku-dula*, to cut, *mphuno*, nose).

Many of the larger mantids in Malawi are extremely colourful: *Tenodera* sp. HB 10 mm is an attractive leaf green; the barred mantis, *Polyspilota aeruginosa*, is of similar size with brown and maroon barring on the wings; and *Pseudocreobota wahlbergi*, the flower mantis, has a spectacular a beautiful eye-like pattern on the forewings – undoubtedly to ward off enemies. Mantids are adept fliers, and the larger species are capable of drawing blood from a finger if handled carelessly. Other mantids I recorded during my research include:

Rhomboderella scututa
Popa spurca
Damuria thunbergi
Epitenodera capitata

All these share the term *chiswambiya*.

ORDER: PHASMATODEA   Stick Insects

8.   STICK INSECT
Chiswambiya
syn. *chikasachiwiga* (Y).

Though rarely noticed, stick insects are abundant in Malawi, and many species have been described. As their common name suggests, they are slender insects, often resembling twigs or grass, and are usually dull-coloured, greyish-brown, and sometimes green, with long legs and antennae. The insect shares the same name as the mantis, *chiswambiya*, which in many ways it resembles; but the stick insects are vegetarian, and most cannot fly, simply 'freezing' when approached. One species of stick insect, recorded from Zomba Mountain, *Bactrodema sp.* is around ten inches long (250 mm), and is illustrated in early texts (Johnston 1897: 372; Sweeney 1970: 151).

ORDER: DERMAPTERA   Earwigs

9.   COMMON EARWIG
Forficula senegalensis
Katambala
These small insects are largely scavengers, feeding on organic debris, and they are easily recognized by the pair of pincer-like cerci at the end of the body. Several genera are recorded from Malawi. The common earwig is widespread, and dark brown, almost black in colour, HB 14 mm. No uses are recorded.

ORDER: ORTHOPTERA   Grasshoppers and Crickets

Grasshoppers and crickets are some of the most common and striking insects of Malawi, and their 'songs' are familiar to all. They are stout and rather well-built insects, with the hindlegs adapted for jumping. *Orthoptera* means 'straight-winged', the forewing being straight and leathery; the hindwing is broader, membranous and often with brightly coloured – though some species are wingless. The 'song' is characteristically achieved by the male, who rubs one part of the body against another, this 'stridulation' attracting the female. The females of many species have a conspicuous ovipositor that is used for laying eggs in the ground.

FAMILY: PAMPHAGIDAE   Toad Grasshoppers

10.   TOAD GRASSHOPPER
Lobosceliana haploscelis
Tsokonombwe
syn. *khoyowoyo* (L), *chisokosoko* (Y), *jaghayagha* (T).
There are three closely allied species, all of which seem to be widespread and are described as *tsokonombwe*. *Lobosceliana haploscelis* seems to be

Figure 8 Number 10. *Pamphagidae, Lobosceliana brevicomis*, Toad Grasshopper, Tsokonombwe, Kapalasa, 20 January 2001.

the commonest, and is active by night as well as by day. Its loud stridulation may frequently heard at night. Widely distributed, ranging from Nsanje (200 m) to Chambe plateau and Mulanje mountain (2000 m), it is a fat, humped, wingless grasshopper, HB 70 mm, pale greyish-brown with dark chocolate patches on the thorax shield. Its femur is winged, with spines. It is said to cry (*ku-lira*) at night at the end of the dry season (October), and this is thought to herald the coming of the rains, when people hurry to the gardens to commence hoeing. It is not eaten by many people, though the *Nyasaland Survey* (1938) records that they were eaten by children in the Dowa district.

The two other species noted were:

Lobosceliana brevicomis
Lobosceliana loboscelis.

FAMILY: PYRGOMORPHIDAE

11. ELEGANT GRASSHOPPER
Zonocerus elegans
M'Nunkhadala
syn. *chitsidze* (C), *shankha* (L), *mbobo* (S), *balamanunkha* (T).
This attractive grasshopper is one of the best-known insects in Malawi, and a serious agricultural pest in many places, especially in the Lower Shire Valley, where it is abundant. The hoppers are striped yellow and black, and the adults most colourful: it has short black and orange antennae 15 mm long; a greyish-blue thorax shield, edged yellow; short non-functional wings that are reddish and mottled; and a yellow abdomen banded dark blue, HB 48 mm.

It is invariably described by Malawians as a kind of *chitete* (a generic term for small grasshoppers); but, unlike other grasshoppers, it does not stridulate. But what is most characteristic of the elegant grasshopper is that, despite its rather elegant appearance, it has a most disgusting smell (*fungo loipa*) produced by a yellow fluid that it exudes when threatened – hence its common name (*ku-nunkha*, to smell).

Several other similar *Pyrgomorphid* grasshoppers may be described as *nunkhadala*, such as *Taphronata cincta*, an orange-winged grasshopper that may be a serious agricultural pest, and *Dictyophorus griseus*. The latter species, HB 40 mm, has a pink and black hindwing. Both species seem to be widespread, especially at the higher altitudes above 850 m.

12. COFFEE LOCUST
Phymateus viridipes
Nunkhadala wamkulu

Allied to the elegant grasshopper but much larger, the coffee locust is equally evil-smelling and distasteful, as it exudes a poisonous, frothy secretion. Charles Sweeney describes it well: 'It is a massively-built, clumsy grasshopper, the adult all green above when the leaf-like wings are closed, except for the reddish spines and tubercles on the thoracic shield and the coloured parts of the legs, but in flight the magnificent bright red hind wings spotted black and blue may be seen, and then it is like some small but exotic bird' (1970: 34). The abdomen is olive green, HB 80 mm. It can be a serious agricultural pest, but it prefers shrubs and trees such as coffee and cassia, and it has been recorded as severely defoliating *Gmelina arborea* trees.

At the end of the rains it seems to be plentiful in the montane grasslands and around the pine plantations of Zomba, Mulanje and Dedza mountains, though widely distributed elsewhere. I noted it as common on Chambe Plateau at 1,900 m in May.

13. GREY GRASSHOPPER
Maura bolivari

This is a plump, wingless grasshopper, HB 34 mm, dark grey with a white or yellowish 'chin', and two yellow spots on the thorax shield. Slow-moving, found in gardens during the early rains, it has a wide distribution. Although sometimes described as *chitete*, it is essentially unnamed, and is not eaten.

FAMILY: ACRIDIDAE   Short-horned Grasshoppers

The short-horned grasshoppers are abundant throughout Malawi, and in a preliminary annotated checklist Whellan (1975) described over a hundred species as occurring in the country. Three general terms are utilized by local people in describing grasshoppers:

Chitete is a generic term used to describe all grasshoppers, but it excludes the crickets, and tends to focus particularly on the smaller species of *Acrididae*.

syn. *nswala* (C), *chamukoto* (L), *nthete* (S), *litete, zolo* (Y), *mphazi* (T).

Chiwala is used to describe the medium to large species that display colourful hindwings when in flight (*ku-wala*, to shine, to be bright).

Dzombe refers to the larger grasshoppers, not only those, like the red locust, that have a tendency to swarm, but to all the larger species.

syn. *musererbo* (L), *nyadzombe* (S), *chinthuli*, *dziwala*, *lusombe*, *liwalangulo* (Y), *phanana* (T), *nazombe*, *namseta* (hoppers), *nkhwiya* (L).

A. **Chitete** Small grasshoppers

14. CHILWA GRASSHOPPER
Leptacris monteiroi
Magazini (Y)
syn. *etokoro* (L).

This is a small grasshopper, HB 60 mm, with pale maroon hindwings and a rather pointed fish-like head: hence its name *magazini* – after the small fish (*matemba*), *Barbus aluminous*. It is found in grassland during the dry season, especially around Lake Chilwa.

15. GREEN-STRIPED GRASSHOPPER
Heteracris attentuatus
Chadambo

This is a small colourful grasshopper, HB 37 mm, with conspicuous yellow and black banded hindlegs and a red tibia, and with two green stripes on the thorax shield. The hindwing is yellow.

The allied *Heteracris pulchripes* is similar but slightly smaller. Both are common and widespread, found in low-lying grassland: hence their common name (*dambo*, marsh, valley, grassland), although the term may also be applied to the bush grasshoppers *Afroxyrrhepes spp.* Commonly hunted by small boys and eaten.

16. CRESTED GRASSHOPPER
Abisares viridipennis
Chansasi
syn. *kam'satsi*, *nakasasi*, *makita* (L), *nakambalika* (Y).

This grasshopper is rather dull-coloured, and is always described as being 'khaki', its wings at rest being a mottled greyish-brown; the hindwings when opened are greyish, HB 60 mm. The thorax is reddish-brown with a characteristic ridge in the form of a crest. It is associated with the castor oil plant, hence the name (*nsatsi*, *Ricinus communis*) and is reputed to have a bad smell, like the crushed seeds of the shrub. The castor oil plant is of course poisonous, and most people do not consider the grasshopper edible. One person described it to me as *gontham'kutu*, a name usually associated with inedible termites. It is a fairly common species, found throughout the country, usually singly on shrubs.

17. YELLOW-WINGED GRASSHOPPER
Gastrimargus africanus
Chidyamamina
syn. *gulumamina, chikwakwa* (Y).
A small dark chocolate brown grasshopper, HB 50 mm, with conspicuous bright yellow hindwings with a black banded border. It is a common
species, found in grassland and in abandoned cultivations throughout the

Figure 9 Number 17. *Acrididae, Gastrimargus africanus*, Yellow-Winged
Grasshopper, Chidyamamina, Makoka, 23 May 2001.

country, and may be encountered at all times of the year. Its name is
derived from the fact that it is reputed to eat mucus (*ku-dya*, to eat,
mamina, mucus of the nose), and is therefore not considered edible.

A smaller grasshopper *Pycnodactyla flavipes*, with a dark pink or
orange hindwing banded brown, HB 26 mm, is also described as *chidyamamina* and thus not eaten.

18. SULPHUR ACRIDA
Acrida sulphuripennis
Chigomphanthiko
syn. *nyadedengwa* (S), *chigombanthiko* (Y) (*ku-gompha*, to peck,
nthiko, porridge stick).

This grasshopper is easily recognized by its pointed head, and its flat, blade-like antennae, 22 mm long. The thorax and wings are green, the long slender legs also green, tinged red, HB 75 mm. The hindwings when open are golden yellow. Common and widespread throughout Malawi, it feeds on grass, and is especially noted at the end of the rains (April–May).

Three other species of the genus are commonly noted, all very similar and sharing the name *chigomphanthiko*:

Acrida acuminata
Acrida bicolor
Acrida turrita

Figure 10 Number 18. *Acrididae, Acrida sulphuripennis*, Sulphur Acrida, Chigomphanthiko, Kapalasa, 30 May 2001.

Several other small grasshoppers were recorded, mostly at the end of the rainy season, and identified as *chitete*.

19. BLUE-WINGED GRASSHOPPER
Catantops spissus
Nakagunda
A small grasshopper, HB 42 mm, with pale chestnut thorax and blue hindwings. Widespread and common in open grassland.

Figure 11 Number 19. *Acrididae, Catantops spissus*, Blue-Winged Grass-hopper, Nakagunda, Kapalasa, 12 May 2001.

20. CRYPTIC GRASSHOPPER
Morphacris fasciata
Chifiira
A very common species in dry grassland. Not usually eaten.

21. SCARLET-WINGED GRASSHOPPER
Acrotylus nr patruelis
Kamwendo
A small grasshopper, HB 30 mm, with blue tibia and red hindwing. It is a ground species, feeding on grasses and is widely distributed.

22. YELLOW SPOTTED GRASSHOPPER
Euproacris cylindicollis
A small grasshopper with yellow spots on the thorax, a blue tibia and pale scarlet hindwings, HB 40 mm. It is widespread, mainly found on shrubs, and is evident throughout the rainy season.

B. Chiwala/Dzombe Locusts and larger grasshoppers

These are medium to large grasshoppers, usually of cryptic coloration – brown or green – but with colourful hindwings, which are displayed in flight.

23. SNOUTED GRASSHOPPER
Acanthoxia gladiator
Nakawago (Y)
A large grasshopper with an elongated snout 30 mm long. It is pale brown with pale yellow hindwings, HB 96 mm. Evidently common in grasslands around Lake Chilwa.

24. BUSH GRASSHOPPERS
Afroxyrrhepes acuticerus
A medium-sized grasshopper, wholly pale brown with a chocolate patch on the thorax, a pinkish-brown forewing and a pale yellow hindwing, HB 60 mm.
Afroxyrrhepes procera is similar but smaller, HB 45mm.
The allied species *Homoxyrrhepes punctipennis* is a brown grasshopper with a yellow band on the side of the head, and almost transparent hindwings, tinged yellow, HB 66mm.
All three species are common in grassland and waste cultivations at the end of the rains, and seem to be widespread. All are similar in having unbarred forewings, and are considered edible.

25. YELLOW LOCUST
Cyrtacanthacris tatarica
A medium-sized yellow locust with a pale brown forewing that has two distinct bars; the hindwing is pale yellow or greyish-green; the hindleg, reddish-brown, HB 58 mm. Found mainly on grasses and shrubs, including the castor oil plant (hence described as *kams'atsi*).
The allied species *Cyrtacanthacris aeruginosa* is also common.

26. COMMON LOCUST
Ornithacris magnifica
Mphangala

This is a large species, HB 82 mm, with a prominent pale ridge or crest to the thorax. The antennae are yellowish-brown and 27 mm long, the tibia purple, the forewings brown with three distinctive bands, and the hindwings vermilion. It is a large and attractive grasshopper with a wide distribution, and is generally found in grasslands and open country.

An allied species *Ornithacris (orientalis) cyanea* is particularly common around Lake Chilwa and in the Lower Shire Valley, but is smaller, HB 55 mm.

Figure 12 Number 26. *Acrididae, Ornithacris magnifica*, Common Locust, Mphangala, Makwawa, 14 March 2001.

Figure 13 Number 26. *Acrididae, Ornithacris (orientalis) cyanea,* Oriental Locust, Chiwala, Kapalasa, 12 February 2001.

27. TREE LOCUST
Acanthacris ruficornis
A common, medium-sized locust, HB 52 mm. The forewing is mottled and barred; the hindwing pale yellow. The thorax is chocolate-brown with a pale ridge; the femur sometimes bluish. It has a wide distribution, and has been recorded attacking cotton. Found mainly in grasslands.

28. RED LOCUST
Nomadacris septemfasciata
A large yellowish-brown grasshopper with a pale dorsal stripe, HB 65 mm. The forewing has around seven distinct dark bands – hence its specific name. Localized populations are found around Lake Chilwa and Nsanje, and on Zomba and Mulanje plateau, and at intervals these have migrated to other parts of the country, sometimes reaching 'plague' proportions.

Figure 14 Number 27. *Acrididae, Acanthacris ruficornis*, Tree Locust, Chiwala/Dzombe, Kapalasa, 14 March 2001.

29. MIGRATORY LOCUST
Locusta migratoria
Chilimamine

This locust is focused on tropical West Africa, but at intervals swarms and becomes widespread throughout Southern Africa. The last invasion of to Malawi by this species occurred in 1932.

Almost all the larger grasshoppers and locusts of the family *Acrididae* (*dzombe*) are considered to be an important source of relish.

FAMILY: TETTIGONIIDAE   Long-Horned Grasshoppers

30. COMMON KATYDID
Homorocoryphus vicinus
Bwanoni
syn. *noni, mphombo* (C/S), *mpopo, mbubunika, lakabalu* (Y), *epwano* (L), *ndafu* (T).

Figure 15 Number 30. *Tettigoniidae, Homorocoryphus vicinus,* Common (Green) Katydid, Bwanoni, Kapalasa, 24 May 2001.

This is a small, slender, green grasshopper, with a pointed head and long, slender antennae 48 mm long. It has a characteristic yellow patch around the mouthparts and dark brown eyes. The legs are slender and green; the hindwing pale green, and almost translucent. The length HB is 33 mm. It is reputed to contain a lot of fat (*mafuta*), and to call (*ku-lira*) when hiding in the maize gardens, and it regularly comes to the light at night, when it is gathered as food. It is a very common species, and in the past large swarms were recorded, often attacking crops (*Report of the Department of Agriculture* 1945).

Two similar species that are often described as *bwanoni* are:

Tylopsis rubrescens, with extremely long antennae 70 mm long. HB length 24 mm.

Pseudorhynchus pungens, which has a very long pointed head, and pale brown, almost translucent wings, HB length 40 mm.

31. ARMOURED GROUND CRICKET
Enyaliopsis petersi
Bvimbvi

syn. *mbvivi, nalivivi, mvivi, chikodzera, elupharakito* (L), *naghateriteri* (S), *nantundira* (Y/T).

These are rather bizarre creatures: sluggish, wingless, rather plump, and with a thorax armed with horns and sharp spines, they have strong legs and are able to exude a white, rubbery fluid in self-defence – which is said to blister sensitive skins. Hence their common name, *chikodzera* (*kukodza*, to urinate). They are pale brown, HB 47 mm, with long, slender antennae, 40mm long. Locally, they are often described as *chirombo choipa* – harmful organism. They are common insects, especially along the Lakeshore and the Lower Shire Valley, and feed on trees and shrubs. I found them frequently at Zoa and in the Domasi Valley in the early part of the rains.

32. MOTTLED GRASSHOPPER
Cymatomera denticollis
Nazombe

A pale greyish-brown grasshopper with long slender antennae 100 mm long. Forewing broad, mottled grey; hindwing almost translucent; length HB 40 mm. Often noted in the Shire Highlands, but not recognized locally.

33. GREEN LONG-HORNED GRASSHOPPER
Clonia wahlbergi
Gomphanthiko
syn. *nyadedengwa*.

A large green grasshopper with long spiny legs, long, slender antennae 110 mm long, and with strong mandibles that can inflict a bite. The abdomen is yellowish-green; length HB 55 mm; the wings when present are almost transparent, mottled brown. Found mainly during the rains, they are, unlike many other grasshoppers, exclusively carnivorous. As they prey on other insects, they are often described as *chiswambiya* (the mantis) or *fisi* (hyena). But they are more often associated with the slender green *Acrida* spp. (which are vegetarians) and share the same common name.

34. SPOTTED GRASSHOPPER
Microcentrum rhombifolium

A medium-sized grasshopper, HB 56 mm, with slender antennae, up to 50 mm long. The forewings are smoky green with characteristic dark spots, while the brown hindwings are almost transparent. Not recognized locally.

FAMILY: GRYLLIDAE   Crickets

35. GIANT CRICKET
Brachytrypes membranaceus
Nkhululu
syn. *kwiritoto, sondoro* (L), *njelemba, njerere* (Y), *nkhuluzi* (T).
The giant cricket is one of the best-known insects, for it makes its holes
in garden lawns – it seems to prefer open spaces under trees – and its song
may be commonly heard just after sunset during the rains – when it is
most commonly found. Its holes are about 20 mm in diameter, and it
burrows to a depth of 15–20 cm. It is rather squat, dark chestnut in colour,
with white on the sides of the abdomen, and has long antennae, to 30 mm.
It is much larger than the common cricket, HB 47 mm. It is a common
and well-liked relish, as it contains a large amount of fat, as well as being
a serious agricultural pest.

36. COMMON CRICKET
Gryllus bimaculatus
Kalijosolo
syn. *kajosolo, njenjete* (C), *chikululu, makantusi, khwiritoto* (L),
njolokoto (S), *chijosolo* (Y), *kabanthira* (T).
This is a very common cricket in houses and cultivations, and stridulates
loudly during the night in the rainy season. It is dark brown in colour, HB
25 mm, with long antennae, 29 mm. But several species of cricket –
Gryllus argentea, Gryllus campestris, Gryllacris lyrata – have been
noted, and all are recognized as *kalijosolo* (*njenjete*), and seen as clearly
distinct from the giant cricket, which has lots of fat and is edible.
Although some people eat the common cricket, it is usually associated
with destroying the seeds of cultivated plants (like beans and tomato) and
with entering houses at certain times of the year and damaging clothing.
The common cricket has a cosmopolitan distribution.

FAMILY: GRYLLOTALPIDAE

37. MOLE CRICKET
Gryllotalpa africanus
Bololo
syn. *lololo, libololo* (L), *chisugugu* (Y), *chitutira.*
This is an unusual insect having its front legs like those of a mole, highly
adapted to digging, being enlarged and armed with strong teeth. It is
found throughout Africa and is very common in Malawi, but it is confined
to low-lying marshy, *dambo* areas. Hence it has been described to me as
chamathope ('of the mud'). But it is a strong flier, and comes to the light

at night. Its song is a quiet churring. The body of the mole cricket is much more slender than that of the common cricket, a rich reddish brown in colour, HB 30 mm in length, and furry; and, as local people say, it never gets 'wet'. On the Shire river it is commonly used as fish bait.

FAMILY: STENOPELMATIDAE

38. KING CRICKET
Henicus sp.
Chiboli

This is a well-known, nocturnal wingless cricket with a very stout body, HB 33 mm, and a large head and long antennae 22 mm long. It is dark, shiny, almost black in colour, and burrows, although unlike the giant cricket it is said to have no 'nest'. It is eaten and has lots of fat, and is normally encountered in the early rains.

FAMILY: LENTULIDAE

39. LEE'S GRASSHOPPER
Malawia leei

A small wingless grasshopper, light reddish-brown with darker stripes. HB 20 mm. It is a pest on *Pinus patula* on Chambe plateau and on Mulanje mountain.

FAMILY: EUMASTACIDAE

40. PINE GRASSHOPPER
Plagiotriptus pinivorus

A small green wingless grasshopper, HB 30 mm, that has become a serious pest on pine trees on Zomba and Mulanje mountains. It is a grasshopper that originally fed on indigenous shrubs (mainly *Euphorbiaceae*), but has in recent years moved into pine plantations. It has no local name (Esbjerg 1976: 18–19).

ORDER: PHTHIRAPTERA   Lice

41. HUMAN LOUSE
Pediculus humanus
Nsabwe

syn. *ethupo* (L), *nsawawa* (S), *luchipi* (Y), *nyinda* (T).

Lice are wingless parasites of mammals and birds, very small, with a pear-shaped body, and are exclusively blood-sucking. They have two forms, head and body lice, the latter being slightly larger (HB 4 mm).

Well-known to Malawians, they are capable of transmitting diseases, including typhus fever. In rural areas it seems very troublesome (*opsya*) and its bites are said to bring sores (*zilonda*). Clothes are boiled, and then pressed with a hot iron to kill the lice. The eggs of the lice are described as *nyena* or *mina*.

ORDER: HEMIPTERA   Bugs

Although the term 'bug' has a wide reference, to an entomologist it is reserved for the members of the order *Hemiptera*. Although variable in form, bugs usually have two pairs of wings, the front pair normally hardened, at least in part, and the mouthparts are adapted to sucking juices from plants or other animals. Many bugs, such as aphids, mealy bugs and scale insects, are serious crop pests.

FAMILY: PENTATOMIDAE   Shield Bugs

42. GREEN SHIELD BUG
Nezara robusta
Nkhunguni
syn. *ntalamira* (Y), *owinkha* (L).

This is a common bug, particularly in the Neno and Thyolo districts, where it feeds on *Brachystegia* and *Julbernardia* trees, as well as on blue gums (*Eucalyptus* sp.). It is a robust bug in the shape of a shield, and is bright leaf green, HB 30 mm, and gives off a powerful smell that can carry great distances. Hence it is often described as *chinunkha*, that which smells – 'stink bug'. It is found from May to September, and is collected as a relish food.

The small green bug *Nezara viridula*, HB 18 mm, a cosmopolitan species, is common in Malawi, and in places a serious pest of *Macadamia* trees, while the 'Cameron bug', *Antestiopsis lineaticollis*, a small black shield bug with orange and white spots, HB 11 mm, is a serious pest on coffee, sucking the fruit.

FAMILY: COREIDAE

43. BOW-LEGGED BUG
Anoplocnemis curvipes
Nandoli
syn. *nkhamila* (L), *gongoni* (C).

This is also a stinkbug, and is one of the commonest wayside insects in Malawi, feeding on numerous plants. It is found throughout Africa. It is dark greyish-brown or black, with long antennae, 20 mm, that have an orange tip; there are spines on each side of the thorax and prominent curved hindlegs – hence its specific name. Total length HB 28 mm. It secretes a foul-smelling liquid, and is therefore associated with the Armoured ground cricket (*bvimbvi*) and several blister beetles as *chikodzela*.

A similar, smaller, dark grey species *Anoplocnemis montandoni*, HB 22 mm, is also widespread, and is described as *nandoli*. There are many other Coreid bugs in Malawi, but these are rarely given cultural recognition.

FAMILY: PYRRHOCORIDAE

44. COMMON STAINER BUG
Dysdercus intermedius
Cham'matowo

This is a well-known species, not only as a pest on cotton, but as common wherever there are plants of the *Malvaceae* family, such as *Hibiscus*. They are brightly coloured bugs, usually pale reddish-brown or brick red, with a black tip to the wings and long antennae, HB 16 mm. A pair is often seen together mating, and thus their Yao name is *chilombere* (*kulomba*, to marry). Sweeney gives them the common name *nkhunguni za thonje* (cotton bug), but I never heard this term used, and they are widely described as *cham'matowo* (of the *mtowo* shrub – *Azanza garkeana*, also of the *Malvaceae* family). Two other similar species are also common: *Dysdercus fasciatus*, and *Dysdercus nigrofasciatus*. They are called stainer bugs because they pierce the bolls of cotton, and so introduce a fungus that stains the cotton fibre.

FAMILY: MIRIDAE   Leaf Bugs

45. MOSQUITO BUG
Helopeltis schoutedeni

These are small, soft-bodied insects with long black antennae, HB 10 mm. Generally bright crimson and black in colour, they are seen mainly in the rainy season, and as sap-sucking bugs are a serious pest at times, of many crops, especially pigeonpea, cotton, mango, pepper and tea. The bug has long been known as a pest on tea, and in recent years has become widespread, causing heavy losses, especially among smallholders. It reaches its peak population at the end of the rains (March–May). It is widely distributed in Malawi.

(On the biology of the mosquito bug see Sweeney 1965.)

FAMILY: REDUVIIDAE Assassin bugs

46. ASSASSIN BUG
Platymeris rhadamanthus
Molosi
This carnivorous insect is easily recognized by its short, curved proboscis or beak, which is normally three-segmented, and which is used to stab other insects, especially honey bees, and to suck out their juices. *Platymeris rhadamanthus* is one of the larger members of the family, shiny black in colour, with two orange-yellow patches on the body, and black and yellow legs, HB 41 mm. It can inflict a painful bite on people.

A smaller species *Rhincoris segmentarius*, with a black and white barred abdomen and dark brown wings, HB 23 mm, is also common. Some members of the family mimic and prey upon cotton stainer bugs (*Dysdercus* sp.).

FAMILY: BELOSTOMATIDAE Water Bugs

47. GIANT WATER BUG
Lethocerus niloticum
Nyamalaza
This is probably the largest bug in Malawi, HB measuring 72 mm. It is dark greyish-brown, rather flat, with sharp edges to the wings: hence its common name, *malaza* (razor).

It has long legs: the front pair are raptorial, the hindlegs used for swimming. It has large, bulging eyes at the front of the head. It is thus a rather formidable insect that attacks small fish and tadpoles, and is confined to water. But it is a strong flier, and often comes to light at night. It was very common at Nchalo sugar estate in the rainy season. Many people describe this bug as *nkhumbutera*, which it superficially resembles; but this name is usually reserved for the jewel beetle, *Sternocera orissa*.

FAMILY: NEPIDAE Water Scorpions

48. WATER SCORPION
Laccotrephes ater
Mwinimadzi
This is a very common insect in Malawi, especially in the Shire Highlands. As with the giant water bug, its front legs are powerful, and adapted to seizing prey – mainly tadpoles, aquatic larvae and crustaceans. It is dark greyish-brown in colour with a rather flat body, HB 37 mm, and

it has a long hollow 'tail' used for obtaining air from the water surface. Hence the common name 'scorpion', although the insect is perfectly harmless. The Nyanja name means 'chief or guardian of the water'.

FAMILY: CIMICIDAE   Bed Bugs

49. COMMON BED BUG
Cimex hemipterus
Nsikidzi

This is a wingless parasitic bug that seems to be common throughout Malawi, especially in huts and old buildings. I was badly bitten by these bugs in Bangula resthouse. It is a flat, dark reddish-brown, tick-like insect, HB 6 mm, which lives in cracks and crevices during the day, emerging at night to suck the blood of sleeping people. It is an extremely resilient insect, and may live in unoccupied houses for many months – re-emerging when humans return. Other members of the family are parasitic on mammals, particularly bats.

FAMILY: CICADIDAE   Cicadas

50. CICADA
Ioba leopardina
Nyenje
syn. *enyende* (L), *nyesele* (Y), *chenje* (T).

At the end of the dry season, in October, the shrill call of the cicadas in *Brachystegia* woodland is one of the most memorable sounds in Malawi. The whole woodland it seems, resonates with their sound – although it is only the males that call, and it is extremely difficult to detect the exact whereabouts of the individual insects making the sound. The cicadas have large eyes on the side of the head, a squat, tapering body, HB 30 mm, which is yellowish-brown with black blotches, and transparent wings with black barring.

A smaller species, *Platypleura brevis*, has an olive green-body, with a chestnut band and white patches on the thorax, and transparent wings, HB 25 mm. In Yao this is described as *lilangwe*, in contrast with the longer *Ioba* sp., which has the generic term *nyesele* (*nyenje*).

Cicadas are common throughout Malawi, and are particularly associated with *Brachystegia* trees. They are an important source of relish, being caught by means of a long tapering bamboo or reed stem tipped with *ulimbo*, the sticky latex of *Ficus natalensis*, which adheres to their wings. Several genera of cicadas have been recorded from Malawi.

FAMILY: CERCOPIDAE   Spittle Bugs

51. FROGHOPPER
Ptyelus flavescens
Throughout Malawi certain trees are known as 'rain trees', as when one is under a tree, even on a cloudless day, drops of rain appear to fall to the ground, often forming puddles. Such trees are often called *mulilira* (*kulira*, to cry), and have important medicinal uses, and the most well known of these is *mpakasa* (*Lonchocarpus capassa*) (see Hargreaves 1978). As is well known, the 'rain' is caused by spittle bugs or froghoppers, whose larvae suck the sap of the tree. These are small soft-bodied bugs, green or brown in colour, HB 10 mm, which are usually enveloped in a mass of protective frothy secretion. There are a number of species in Malawi, although no local names have been recorded.

FAMILY: CICADELLIDAE   Leafhoppers

52. COTTON JASSID
Empoasca facialis
Majasidi
These are rather small (HB less than 10 mm), green, agile insects, which as their name suggests are active 'hoppers' or jumpers. Members of the family are ubiquitous, and are usually found on the undersides of leaves. The cotton jassid is an important pest of cotton, although it has been found on a variety of other plants – sweet potato, groundnuts, castor oil – and is often a vector in spreading plant diseases. It has no local name, but extension workers describe it as *majasidi*.

ORDER: NEUROPTERA   Antlions

53. ANTLION
Palpares cataractae
Tombolombo
Adult antlions are rather like dragonflies, and like them are carnivorous, plucking small insects from plants – hence they share the same name, *tombolombo*. But unlike that of dragonflies, their flight is slow and weak, and they fold their wings roof-like over the back when resting. They also tend to be nocturnal. The body of *Palpares cataractae* is long, slender and soft, HB 45 mm, the wings greyish and membranous, with a dense network of cross veins. The larvae, as is well known, construct a pitfall trap in sandy soil, making a sort of crater that serves to trap other insects, especially ants, which slip to the bottom of the pit – to be seized upon by

the antlion larva, which then proceeds to suck its body dry of juices. The larvae are brown and plump, with sickle-like jaws, HB 17 mm. They are described as *kamfulifuli* (*ku-fula*, to dig out) or *chauli* (syn. *nalikhungulu* (Y)).

ORDER: COLEOPTERA   Beetles

Beetles are quite ubiquitous in Malawi, and found in almost every type of habitat. Beetles are easily recognized by their thick leathery forewings (elytra), under which they keep folded their membranous hindwings, which are used in flight – although there are some beetles that are unable to fly. Having strong mandibles used for chewing and biting, beetles are essentially insects of the ground and vegetation, and many are serious pests of agriculture.

FAMILY: CARABIDAE   Ground Beetles

54. GROUND BEETLE
Tefflus cypholoba
Chikodzera
syn. *chinkhanira, namankha* (L), *namtundira* (Y).
These are solitary beetles that hunt their prey chiefly at night, and feed on a variety of invertebrates. They thus have powerful mandibles and can move quite quickly. A characteristic of the ground beetles, particularly the larger species, is that as a mode of defence they are able to squirt formic acid in any direction and over surprisingly long distances – up to 30 cm (cf. Esbjerg 1976: 45). The fluid can be painful if it comes into contact with human skin or the eyes – hence the common name *chikodzera*, a name they share with the armoured ground cricket, which has a similar protective mechanism. *Namtundira* carries the same meaning (*ku-tunda* (Y), to urinate).

Tefflus cypholoba is a large, black beetle with long legs, HB 48 mm, its elytra grooved, with chocolate-brown mottling. The antennae are black, 22 mm long. It is very common during the rainy season. *Tefflus carinatus* is smaller, HB 35 mm, with beautiful iridescent blue or violet elytra – mentioned by Johnstone a century ago, with the note that 'it can take a piece out of the finger if incautiously handled' (1897: 368).

This family of predacious ground beetles contains many other genera in Malawi, but they have no cultural significance.

FAMILY: DYTISCIDAE   Water Beetles

55. WATER BEETLES
Cibister vulneratus
Chinsambisambi
syn. *checheche, nkulunga, chinjelanjela* (Y).

There are many families of water beetles in Malawi, and several species are attracted to the light during the rainy season. This common species is rather oval-shaped, smooth, shiny, and black in colour, with pale chestnut brown along the edge of thorax and elytra; front legs short, hindlegs protruding beyond the elytra, HB 27 mm. They are carnivorous, feeding on tadpoles and other aquatic creatures, and are said by Lake Chilwa fishermen to eat the flesh of dead fish. The local names relate to *swimming* (*ku-sambira*) and to floating on the surface of the water (*ku-jelajela* (Y)).

FAMILY: DYNASTIDAE

56. RHINOCEROS BEETLE
Oryctes boas
Chipembere
syn. *hunyamari* (L).

Figure 16 Number 56. *Dynastidae, Oryctes boas*, Rhinoceros Beetle, Chipembere, Blantyre, 3 October 2000.

This is a large glossy black beetle, HB 45 mm, the males of which have a characteristic large horn on the head, 17 mm long, which is apparently used as a weapon in fights between males. Their larvae are huge white grubs that are common in horse manure. It is not generally recognized by local people. Equally common is *Oryctes monoceros*, HB 35 mm, which is a serious pest on palm trees.

A small black beetle, *Cyphomstes vallatus* (Gongoni) with a small horn 4 mm long, often comes to light in the Shire Valley, and its grub is said to feed on sugarcane roots.

57. BLACK MAIZE BEETLE
Heteronychus licas
Matono

This is a rather shiny, thick-set, black beetle, HB 20 mm that is evident in the early rains. It is nocturnal, but often comes to light. Its larva is a dirty-white, C-shaped grub (*mbozi zoyera*, white grub) that is a serious pest on maize and sugarcane, feeding on the roots. and thus causing the wilting and yellowing of the leaves.

FAMILY: SCARABAEIDAE   Dung Beetles

58 • DUNG BEETLE
Garreta azeurus
Chitutamanyi
syn. *chifulamanyi, mfulatubzi, mtengamatuvi.*

Dung beetles are of crucial importance in ecosystems owing to their activity in recycling animal dung – and Fabre indeed described them as 'the dealers in ordure' and the scavengers of the meadows (1911: 3). All their local names refer to this activity – of digging (*ku-fula*), or carrying (*ku-tuta, ku-tenga*), dung (*thubzi*, excrement). There are over 150 species of dung beetles in Malawi, and one of the most common is *Garreta azeurus*. This is a small dung beetle that collects the droppings of the baboon (*nyani*), and has been noted in *Brachystegia* woodland. It is almost round, HB 21 mm, and a shiny metallic dark green in colour. The beetle rolls and then buries the dung, which provides the food for its larvae (grubs).

Three other species have been noted; all are larger, HB 30–45 mm, and glossy black in colour:

Catharsius satyrus (*bingiza* (T));
Anachalos procerus; and
Heliocopris hamadryas.

(On the ecology of dung beetles see Dudley 1977.)

FAMILY: CETONIIDAE   Flower Beetles

59. GOLIATH BEETLE
Goliath albosignatus
Nkangala
syn. *khawa* (L).

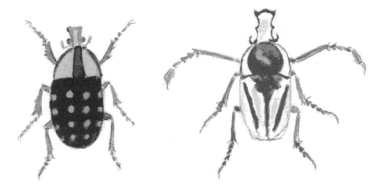

Figure 17 Number 59, left. *Cetoniidae, Amaurodes passerinii* (*Mecynorrhina passerinii*), Nsopa Beetle, Kapalasa, 30 November 2000.

Figure 18 Number 59, right.. *Cetoniidae, Ranzania petersiana* (*Taurhina splendens*), Green Flower Beetle, Kapalasa, 3 February 2001.

Flower beetles includes some of the most attractive beetles to be found in Malawi. They feed principally on pollen or on the sap of trees, and though they are very conspicuous and colourful they are not usually recognized by local people and have no common name. The largest of the flower beetles is *Goliath albosignatus*. This is a robust beetles HB 50 mm, greyish-white with characteristic black stripes on the thorax and black markings on the elytra. The legs are long, and fringed with reddish hairs.

Several other species were noted as frequent in the Shire Highlands:

Mecynorrhina passerinii (*Amaurodes passerinii*) has a greenish-yellow thorax with a broad black central stripe, and black elytra, spotted with old gold, HB 30 mm. It feeds on the sap of the *Bridelia micrantha* tree (*nsopa*).

Taurhina splendens (*Ranzania petersiana*) is a colourful beetle with dark green legs, fringed with red hairs, and with iridescent green and black markings on the white thorax and elytra; the underside an iridescent purplish-brown; full length HB 30 mm. Found during the rains in *Brachystegia* woodland.

Stephanorrhina princeps has a chestnut/green thorax, and iridescent olive green elytra covered in white spots, HB 25 mm. Feeds on *Compositae* flowers.

None of these three attractive species have names or cultural significance.

60. SPOTTED FLOWER BEETLE
Psadacoptera simonsi
Litamila (Y)
syn. *chilota mvula*.
This is a small, pale chocolate flower beetle, HB 15 mm, with four black spots, which is said to call (*ku-lira*) when the rains are close.

FAMILY: RUTELIDAE   Chafers

61. CHOCOLATE FLOWER BEETLE
Anomala cingulata
This is a very common small beetle, HB 14 mm, pale chocolate brown with two black spots on the thorax. It eats foliage and fruits, and its larvae feed on the roots of plants. It often comes to light at night.

The allied family of cockchafers, *Melolonthidae*, have similar habits, and the larvae 'white grubs' of the chafer *Schizonycha* sp., inflict damage on the roots of many crops, such as maize or groundnuts.

FAMILY: BUPRESTIDAE   Jewel Beetles

62. JEWEL BEETLE
Sternocera orissa
Nkhumbutera
syn. *mpumbutera, ekhumbunya* (L), *lichetechete* (Y), *gongoni* (C).
This is a family of 'wood-borers' for the larvae, which have a flattened pro-thorax, excavate long galleries under the bark of trees (cf. Esbjerg 1976: 44). The adults are usually brilliantly coloured and metallic, hence their common name. Over 50 species of this family have been recorded from Malawi, many collected by Rodney Wood, but the only jewel beetle familiar to local people is *nkhumbutera*, *Sternocera (variabilis) orissa*. This is an attractive beetle with a rather streamlined body: the thorax is black covered with white hairs; the elytra a metallic black or deep blue; and the underside has silvery-white hairs. Full length: HB 37 mm.

Figure 19 Number 62. *Buprestidae, Sternocera (variabilis) orissa,* Jewel Beetle, Nkumbutera, Makwawa, 26 January 2001.

FAMILY: ELATERIDAE   Click Beetles

63. BLACK CLICK BEETLE
Tetralopus terotundifrons
Chindenga

If a member of this family is placed on its back it will sham death for a while, and then, with an audible click, leap into the air. The larvae, which live in the soil or in decaying wood, are smooth, tough-skinned yellow

Figure 20 Number 63. *Elateridae, Tetralopus terotundifrons,* Black Click Beetle, Chindenga, Zoa, 11 February 2001.

grubs, generally known as 'wire-worms'. Only one species of this family was noted during my research.

The black click beetle is rather elongate, shiny black, HB 48 mm, with conspicuous 'frilly' – many-leaved – antennae. This species has been described to me as *chikumbu*. I recorded it as common at Zoa from February to May.

FAMILY: LYCIDAE   Net-winged Beetles

64. ORANGE NET-WINGED BEETLE
Lycus constrictus
Nakurutu (L)

Netwinged beetles are fairly common, and often congregate on shrubs or wayside vegetation, or are seen flying around trees on mating flights. They feed on decaying organic matter.

Lycus constrictus is a colourful beetle, pale orange with strangely expanded elytra that are round and have black tips. The body is completely hidden by the wings. Antennae black, 10 mm long. The total length is around 27 mm. No cultural uses recorded.

FAMILY: LAMPYRIDAE   Fireflies

65. FIREFLY
Luciola caffra
Chiphaniphani

syn. *mawaliwali, ng'ambang'ambi* (C), *nyetanyeta* (Y).

'Fire-flies' are in fact beetles, and they are very common during the rainy season, flying at night, especially just after dusk. They are small, winged, and brown, with large eyes, HB 6 mm, with the 'light' at the end of the abdomen. All local names allude to their ability to produce light: (*ku-nyetula* (Y) to shine like stars, *ku-wala*, to shine, *ng'amba*, to shine, like the stars, or the sky).

FAMILY: TENEBRIONIDAE   Darkling Beetles

66. MOSS BEETLE
Catamerus rugosus

This is one of the most commonly seen insects in Malawi, especially during the rainy season, when it feeds on the moss and lichens of rocks, and is often gregarious. It is extremely common in *Brachystegia* woodlands, particularly on the foothills of the Zomba and Mulanje mountains.

The adult beetle is slow, wingless, and a dark metallic blue-black, the thorax being round and especially shiny, with a total length HB of 20 mm. The beetle has no common name, although it will occasionally be related to the ground beetle and be described as *namtundira*; but its larvae are even more conspicuous: they are a glistening bluish-black in colour and look rather like woodlice, and they form large masses on rocks around February. They are described as *unyala* (wrinkles) or *unyawi*.

67. GREY BEETLE
Anomalus heraldicus
This is a slow-moving, greyish-brown beetle, with the thorax and elytra both broad and angular, HB 28 mm. It is very common in *Brachystegia* woodland and gardens, and terrestrial, feeding on the leaves of *Costus* and other plants. It has no cultural significance, even though it is very common.

68. BLACK HUMPED BEETLE
Dichtha inflata
Kafadala
syn. *gonondo* (C).
An oval-shaped, thick-set black beetle, with 'humped' thorax, and the elytra striped dark maroon, and long brown legs, HB 25 mm. It feigns death: hence its common name.

69. FLOUR BEETLE
Tribolium confusum
Nankafumbwe
Many members of the family *Tenebrionidae* are adapted to dry conditions, and some are serious pests of grain. The flour beetle is a small insect, HB 4 mm, and is a serious though secondary pest of maize – the maize weevil breaking into the grain initially, and the flour beetle following up and destroying much of what is left (Sweeney 1962: 27). It also feeds on groundnut flour.

70. DUSTY SURFACE BEETLE
Gonocephalum simplex
Both the larvae – 'wireworms' – and the adult beetle are well-known agricultural pests, attacking coffee, maize, cowpea, groundnuts, beans and cotton.

FAMILY: MELOIDAE   Blister Beetles

71. BLISTER BEETLE
Mylabris dicincta
Dzodzwe

syn. *kazodzwe, sitinyope* (L), *ligombera* (Y), *kafikifiki, mang'ombe* (T).

The blister beetles are well-known and colourful insects that feed on flowers, especially *Hibiscus* and legumes – *Tephrosia*, pigeon pea, *Vigna* and *Dolichos*. The larvae are often parasites on the eggs of bees or grasshoppers, and have a complex life history. What characterizes the blister beetles – and why they have such warning colours – is that they contain the chemical cantharidin, which is a poison and a blistering agent – hence their common name.

Several species of this genus have been recorded. *Mylabris dicincta* is one of the commonest. It is a black beetle with orange antennae 8mm long, a narrow thorax, and a black elytra with two broad red bands. HB 36 mm. It is plentiful towards the end of the rainy season.

Three other species of *Mylabris* are also common:

Mylabris amplectens: probably the commonest of the blister beetles; with orange antennae, it is black with three lateral yellow stripes, HB 18 mm. It is common on pumpkin flowers, though it has no recognized common name.

Mylabris tricolor. This is a black beetle, HB 35 mm, with a broad belt of yellow across the elytra, a front pair of yellow spots, and a hind pair of red spots – giving it three colours, as in the specific name. It has bright yellow antennae, 7 mm long. It is particularly associated with *Xerophyta* shrubs.

Mylabris tripartita is a black beetle with three broad bands of pale yellow on the elytra, and orange antennae 6 mm long. Full length: HB 32 mm.

All the *Mylabris* species are strong fliers.

FAMILY: CERAMBYCIDAE   Longhorn Beetles

72. REDBANDED LONGHORN BEETLE
Ceroplesis orientalis
Ligombera

syn. *chigombera*.

This family is highly important as a forest pest all over the world, as the larvae are wood-boring and very destructive, although they mostly only attack trees that are dead or dying. Many longhorn beetles make a feeble

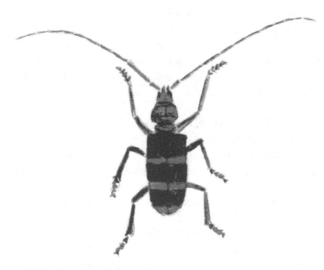

Figure 21 Number 72. *Cerambycidae, Ceroplesis orientalis*, Redbanded Longhorn Beetle, Ligombera, Kapalasa, 6 January 2001.

squeaking noise when picked up. There are many species to be found in Malawi, and R. F. Lee's (1971) listing of forest insects records 162 species belonging to this family. Most are colourful beetles, feeding on flowers, and have very long antennae. Usually nocturnal, they often come to light. The species mostly recorded was *Ceroplesis orientalis* which is a large black beetle with three red bands across the elytra, and with long black tapering antennae 44 mm long. The full HB length is only 28 mm. It is invariably given the name *dzodwe* or *ligombera* (Y), as it is closely identified with the blister beetle *Mylabris dicincta*, which it resembles, apart from its long antennae.

73. GREY LONGHORN BEETLE
Monochamus (anthores) leuconotus
Chipokodzi
syn. *mununu, chipukusu*.

This is the well-known 'coffee stem borer', for its white larva bores into the stem of the coffee plant and causes considerable damage, its presence being indicated by loose droppings – frass – at the base of the coffee stem. It is most troublesome when the coffee is near natural woodland. The adult beetle is pale grey with dark brown patches on the elytra, and a dark grey head and thorax, HB 30 mm. Antennae dark grey, very long, to 70 mm. It is widely found in *Brachystegia* woodland.

74. BLACK LONGHORN BEETLE
Acanthophorus (tithoes) confinus
This is an extremely large and formidable-looking beetle, with massive mandibles and long antennae. It is dark grey, almost black, mottled with pale brown, HB 82 mm. It is nocturnal, though often comes to light. It seems to be widely distributed.

75. EUCALYPTUS BEETLE
Phoracantha semipunctata
This is an exotic beetle, of Australian origin, first noted at Blantyre sawmill in 1969, and now widely distributed. It can be a problem on *Eucalyptus* trees, its larvae burying under the bark. But it is not common. The adult beetle is brownish black, with yellowish patches on the elytra.

76. BLUE LONGHORN BEETLE
Mecosaspis plutina
Mwase
syn. *nalungo.*
A widely distributed beetle with a tapering body; elytra iridescent blue, with long black legs. Antennae 28 mm long. Full length: HB 35 mm. No cultural recognition.

Figure 22 Number 76. *Cerambycidae, Mecosaspis plutina*, Blue Longhorn Beetle, Mwase, Kapalasa, 9 November 2000.

FAMILY: BOSTRYCHIDAE

This is a family of wood-boring beetles that includes the famous bamboo-borer (*Dinoderus minutus*), which is common along the Lakeshore. But it also includes several species that are important grain pests.

77. LESSER GRAIN BORER
Rhizopertha dominica
Nankafumbwe

This is a small, brownish-black beetle, its thorax covered in brown tubercles, HB 3 mm. It is widely distributed, and a common pest of stored products.

78. LARGER GRAIN BORER
Prostephanus truncatus
Nankafumbwe
syn. *njowu* (S).

Originally a pest of South America, this was found attacking stored maize and cassava in Tanzania in 1980, and has since then spread to many countries of Africa, including Malawi. In 1991 it was found in Chitipa and Karonga, and is now a serious pest of maize and dried cassava, causing severe damage, with losses as high as 34 per cent (GTZ – German Techniczl Development Agency). It is a small beetle, cylindrical, and dark brown in colour, with rows of teeth at the front edge of the thorax and a flat end to the elytra, HB 4 mm.

FAMILY: GALERUCIDAE   Leaf Beetles

79. PUMPKIN BEETLE
Ootheca mutabilis
Mkupe
syn. *nkupe*, *nkhupe* (T), *ununda* (L), *chechereche*.

A small beetle with orange head and thorax, and iridescent blue-black elytra, HB 6 mm. It is commonly found on pumpkin and beans, and is well known to local people, as it feeds on the leaves.

FAMILY: PASSALIDAE   Wood Beetles

80. PINCER BEETLE
Didymus sansibaricus
Nyangi

A gregarious insect that forms colonies in decaying logs, and often comes to light at night during the rains. It is widely distributed, but noted by myself only from Nchalo. A medium-sized beetle, black, with narrow 'waist' between thorax and abdomen, and pincer-like mandibles, HB 31 mm. The local name is from nyanga, 'horn'.

FAMILY: CURCULIONIDAE   Weevils

81. SNOUTED BEETLE
Brachycerus nr labrusca
Kafadala

> syn. *gonondo, kafalubvu, mndafera mwendo, mnangalire, chiswansagaja* (Y).

This is a large family, and R. F. Lee's (1971) checklist of Malawi forest insects records 59 species. It is characterized by its snouted head and elbowed and clubbed antennae.

Brachycerus nr labrusca is one of the largest of the family in Malawi, and is common in *Brachystegia* woodland. Its body has three distinctive parts: and it has a 'humped' appearance. Dark grey in colour, it is covered in rows of warty tubercles: its long legs are often barred yellow. Full length: HB 28 mm. Its common name relates to its habit of feigning death when disturbed (*ku-fa*, to be dead, *dala*, intentionally).

A much smaller snouted beetle *Lixus praegrandis*, is very common in scrub woodland, although not recognized by local people. It has a relatively long snout (6 mm), and is dark mottled grey in colour, HB 25 mm.

82. MAIZE WEEVIL
Sitophilus zeamays
Nankafumbwe

> syn. *fuse, futwefutwe, kafumbwefumbwe, chipukusu* (Y), *kapeche-peche, tuphwitha* (L).

This is a common pest of stored maize, whose original home is believed to be India. It is ubiquitous, and does an immense amount of damage. It has a long, slender snout, and is dark reddish-brown in colour, HB 3 mm, and is a strong flier.

The similar but much larger sweet potato weevil *Cylas puncticollis*, is described as *nankafumbwe*. It is brown, with a long snout and swollen leg joints, HB 7 mm. It is a serious pest on sweet potato.

The common name is derived from their feeding habits (*ku-fumbwa*, to be eaten into holes).

ORDER: SIPHONAPTERA   Fleas

83. CAT FLEA
Ctenocephalides felis
Utitili
syn. *ukuku, utata, azukuku* (T).

Fleas are small, well-known insects, winged, with laterally compressed bodies, HB 2 mm. Their hindlegs are long and strong, enabling them to jump astounding distances. They are parasites on birds and mammals, adapted to living within fur or feathers, and suck the blood of their hosts. They can survive long periods without feeding. The human flea, *Pulex irritans*, is essentially a temperate species, and its status in Malawi is problematic. The cat flea, however, is common, and along with the fleas that infest the black rat (*Rattus rattus*) and gerbils (*Tatera* spp.), can transmit the bubonic plague bacillus.

The dog flea, *Ctenocephalides canis*, is also recognized, but is less common and it shares the same local name, as do the fleas that infest domestic fowls.

84. JIGGER FLEA
Tunga penetrans
Thekenya
syn. *litekenya* (Y).

This flea, introduced into Africa from South America in the seventeenth century, arrived in Malawi in 1891, and, according to Harry Johnston, became a great pest in the Shire Highlands three years later (1897: 369). It is similar in habits to other fleas, and will feed on a wide range of hosts, but is particularly fond of humans. The fertilized female, however, burrows under the skin, especially between the toes, and this can cause serious inflammation and infection. It seems to be widely distributed in Malawi, mainly in sandy areas. I never encountered the flea myself during my research, but it is still prevalent, and Robin Broadhead informs me that this troublesome pest is mainly dealt with by local herbalists using heat and a sharp instrument to extract the flea. This flea, reddish-brown in colour, seems to have been very troublesome in the past, and Robert Laws records that at Livingstone the pupils were so infected with the jigger, that they were examined every morning, and had the flea painfully extracted (1934: 245).

ORDER: DIPTERA   Flies

This family consists of the true flies, which possess only one pair of wings: hence the name of the order. The hindwings are modified to form club-like halteres that vibrate in flight and function as balancing or controlling organs. Flies have large compound eyes, and their mouthparts are adapted to piercing or sucking, and they feed on a variety of items – nectar, the sap of plants, decaying organic matter or blood. There are numerous species of flies to be found in Malawi, belonging to around twenty-six families. Only the more prominent or salient species are recognized by local people.

FAMILY: CHAOBORIDAE

85. LAKE-FLY
Chaobora (eucorethra) edulis
Nkhungu
Allied to the mosquito, lake-fly are a common sight on Lake Malawi, forming dense clouds during the mating flight. They are, tiny black flies, very greasy to the touch, the wings shorter than the body, HB 3 mm. They are an important source of relish, and were described in detail by many early travellers to Malawi.

FAMILY: TABANIDAE   Horseflies

86. HORSE FLY
Tabanus nyasae
Chimphanga
syn. *chimbu, nyumbu, mphanga, mzazu, mukhanga* (L), *ngulembe, liguwoguwo* (Y), *balang'ombe.*
These are large, biting flies, active on humid and sunny days, and which are well known as they are irritating blood-suckers, causing inflammations around the bite. Over 60 species of the family have been recorded from Malawi (Sweeney 1970: 70). They have conspicuous heads with large compound eyes, and powerful wings. *Tabanus nyasae* has a yellowish abdomen with dark patterns, HB 19 mm. They feed on a variety of mammals, including humans, but especially cattle, horses and antelopes, worrying the animals. But it is only the female horsefly that sucks blood, the males feeding on nectar. The common name refers to the taking of blood (*ku-phanga*, to steal) and the harming of livestock (*bala*, a wound, *ng'ombe*, cattle).

A large horsefly, with a reddish body that is associated with lions, is described by Scott as *nkango* (1929: 392).

87. BITING FLY
Haematopota insatiabilis
Kamphwayi
syn. *liguwoguwo* (Y).
A very common biting fly, wings greyish, mottled, HB 12 mm, found in open country. Sweeney describes this species as abundant in the Shire Highlands, and as 'voracious blood suckers' (1970: 71).

FAMILY: CALLIPHORIDAE Blowflies

88. BLUE FLY
Chrysomyia putoria
Membi
syn. *membi, nchenchemsipu, lumembe* (Y), *nalupisu* (Y), *ekulihi* (L).
There are a number of species of this genus, otherwise known as 'blue-bottle' or 'greenbottle' flies, which feed on dead flesh or the blood from wounds, especially of the larger mammals.
Chrysomyia putoria has a brownish head, with chestnut eyes, and a bluish-black body with a brilliant sheen, HB 9 mm. Seen feeding on dead frog. The local name *nchenchemsipu* refers to its colour (*nchenche*, generic term for fly, *msipu*, fresh green grass).

89. TUMBU FLY
Cordylobia anthropophaga
Mphutsi
syn. *nyamphutsi.*
This is a most troublesome fly, the tiny larva of which burrows under the skin of humans and other animals, and causes severe inflammation – which eventually becomes a painful boil until the full grown larva – a white maggot 13 mm long – is fully grown and wriggles out. A common remedy is to smear the inflammation with Vaseline, when, as the larva needs to breathe, it will come to the surface, and can then be squeezed out. The fly itself is a large, robust yellowish-brown insect with dark lines on the thorax, HB 14 mm. *Tumbu* is the Zulu name for the fly.
   In the past an allied species, known as the Congo floor maggot, *Auchmeromyia luteola*, was a prevalent and well-known pest. Its blood-sucking larvae lived in the crevices and cracks in the floors of huts, and like the bed bug, came out at night to suck the blood of the sleeping occupants. The adult flies are dark orange-brown with smoky wings. In Yao it is called *mbisu* or *liche'chenengo*. At the present time it is rarely encountered, but the *mphutsi* fly is common.

FAMILY: ASILIDAE   Robber Flies

90. ROBBER FLY
Alcimus rubiginosus
Kango
syn. *nsosa* (Y), *kharamo* (T).

These are active flies that are not really robbers, but, as Skaife suggests, assassins – for they attack a variety of other insects, including wasps, dragonflies, bugs, grasshoppers and other flies. Their prey is often much larger than themselves, They often perch on a bush waiting for potential prey, and then take off suddenly in pursuit. When the prey is captured they suck its blood. Because of their predatory habits, people often describe them as *tombolombo*, a name usually reserved for the dragon-flies.

Robber flies are elongate, bristly flies with large eyes and mobile heads, strong probosces and long powerful legs. *Alcimus rubiginosus* has a characteristic chestnut patch on the thorax, edged with two black lines, HB 34 mm.

Two smaller robber flies were also recorded during the research: *Bactria adamsii* and *Microstylum nr helenae*. The latter has smoky brown wings, HB 30 mm. Both were described as *nsosa* (Y).

FAMILY: CULCIDAE   Mosquitoes

91. COMMON MOSQUITO
Anopheles gambiae/funestus
Udzudzu
syn. *mbudu, imbu* (S), *njenjema* (Y), *nyimbo* (T).

Mosquitoes are well-known insects that not only transmit the serious disease malaria, but in the rainy season can be extremely troublesome, particularly in the Lower Shire Valley, and along the Lakeshore. Mosquitoes are small, fragile insects, but they can be divided into two groups: *Anopheles*, which are associated with malaria (two species are common in Malawi), and *Culex* spp., which are common around houses. The former group can be distinguished by the fact that when at rest their bodies stand upright in an almost perpendicular position, while with the *Culex* the wings lie flat, parallel to the surface. All mosquitoes breed in water.

The larger crane-flies (Family: *Tipulidae*), which are common around houses, are also described as *udzudzu*.

FAMILY: MUSCIDAE   Houseflies

92. HOUSE FLY
Musca domestica
Ntchenche
syn. *membe* (Y/T), *gwili* (L).

The term *ntchenche* is used to cover all the common flies, particularly those associated with houses, and of the genus *Musca*, the cosmopolitan housefly *Musca domestica* is widespread and common. As it is associated with human food, excrement and refuse, it is considered a major health hazard. Houseflies are generally much smaller than blowflies, with bristles on the thorax and transparent wings, HB 7–8 mm.

Hover-flies (Family: *Syrphidae*), which are ubiquitous in Malawi are normally described as *ntchenche*. One species, *Protylocera haemorrhoea*, with black markings to the wings and a chestnut tip to the abdomen, HB 15 mm, was noted from Kapalasa.

FAMILY: GLOSSINIDAE   Tsetse Flies

93. TSETSE FLY
Glossina morsitans
Kashembe
syn. *kambalame, kazembe, kaodzera, kamphwayi, kamdoni* (T).

In the naming of flies there is a good deal of overlap between the names given to the tsetse and the horseflies, and the former may also be described as *chimphanga* (*liguwoguwo* (Y)).

The tsetse fly are related to the *Muscidae*, and are yellowish or dark brown, with dark bands on the abdomen, HB 10 mm. A characteristic feature of the tsetse fly is that its proboscis projects forward. Active during the day, both sexes are blood-suckers, and they feed on a variety of mammals, besides humans, the warthog and buffalo being favourites. The tsetse fly is locally recorded: mainly at Nkhotakota, Liwonde and the Lower Shire Valley.

The related species *Glossina brevipalis* has been recorded from the Karonga district.

FAMILY: DIOPSIDAE   Stalk-eyed Flies

94. STALK-EYED FLY
Diopsis macrophthalma

These unusual small flies are easily recognized, as they bear eyes and antennae at the end of stalk-like projections on either side of the head.

They are slow fliers, and often swarm in shady places. They have proved to be a major pest of rice on the Lake Chilwa plains, the larvae attacking young rice seedlings. Up to 10 per cent of the seedlings may be destroyed. No local names are recorded (Kalk *et al.* 1979: 279).

FAMILY: SIMULIIDAE   Black Flies

95. BLACK FLY
Simulium damnosum
These are tiny midges, robust, dark, and almost black in colour – hence their common name – with a rather lumped thorax, HB 4 mm. As with mosquitoes, only the females suck the blood of mammals, the males feeding on plant juices. Although black flies can inflict painful bites, they are also vectors of the disease river blindness (*onchocerciasis*), which Robin Broadhead described to me as a 'nasty itching' of the eye, not blindness. The black fly breeds in clear running streams, and is locally common in the Thyolo and Mulanje districts. No local names recorded.

ORDER: LEPIDOPTERA   Butterflies and Moths

The total number of butterflies and moths in Malawi probably runs into the thousands, and Gifford's checklist of the butterflies (1965) records 528 species, belonging to ten families. In Malawi the butterflies and moths are all recognized by the generic term *gulugufe*, and there are many synonyms: *pherupheru* (C), *chiphepheru*, *balaula*, *nikuruthu* (L), *chipuluputhwa* (Y), *burawuru* (T).

Those with nocturnal habits (moths) are described as *chifukufuku*. I made a record of the common butterflies in open woodland near Namadzi, and noted the following species, all of which were described under the taxon *gulugufe*.

FAMILY: ACRAEIDAE

The Wanderer *Bematistes aganice*
Dancing Acraea *Acraea eponina*
White-barred Acraea *Acraea encedon*

FAMILY: SATYRIDAE

Evening Brown *Melanitis leda*
Grizzled Bush-brown *Mycalesis ena*

FAMILY: NYMPHALIDAE

Common Barred Sailor *Neptis alta*
Golden Piper *Eurytela dryope*
Diadem *Hypolimnas misippus*
Gaudy Commodore *Precis octava*

FAMILY: PAPILIONIDAE

Emperor Swallowtail *Papilio ophidicephalus*
Green Banded Swallowtail *Papilio nireus*
Mocker Swallowtail *Papilio dardanus*

FAMILY: PIERIDAE

Common Grass Yellow *Eurema hecabe*
Dotted Bonder *Mylothris chloris*

Although Malawians recognize the colourful aspects of butterflies, and suggest that they make people happy because of their beauty (*-kongola*), they have little interest in distinguishing the many kinds of butterflies and moths that adorn the local landscape. What is important for local people are the larvae, and *mbozi* is a general term for caterpillars (its synonyms are *chimbozi, chiungu* (Y), *mbungu* (T)). Caterpillars with irritant hairs are *chiyabwe* (*-yabwa*, to itch).

Caterpillars have salience for Malawians in two contrasting ways: either they inflict damage on agricultural crops (this particularly relates to the larvae of the moths of the family *Noctuidae*), or they are edible, and in this regard the caterpillars of the large nocturnal moths, the *Saturniidae*, the Emperor moths, are important. We shall consider those moths that have particular relevance under their various families.

FAMILY: NOCTUIDAE   Owlet Moths

This is a very large family of moths, mostly small to medium-sized, with wingspan around 30 mm. Most of the important species are rather nondescript, with the forewings buff to dark brown, the hindwings usually paler or white. The larvae are usually smooth, with four pairs of prolegs, or are semi-loopers. One of the largest of the family Walker's owl, *Erebus macrops*, was commonly noted at Kapalasa.

96. AFRICAN BOLLWORM
Helicoverpa (heliothis) armigera
Mbozi ya Chifilika
syn. *chipukwa.*

In the past this was described as 'American Bollworm', but this is a misnomer, as it has a cosmopolitan distribution. It derives its name 'boll-worm' from being a common pest of cotton, but the larva attacks many other crops – maize, tomato, tobacco, groundnuts and sweet potato among them. It thus has many common names: for example, maize earworm, tobacco budworm. It is not however a serious pest of cotton, except when, in the past, cotton was planted close to maize.

The adult moth is yellowish to dark brown, with the forewing mottled dark brown; wingspan is 35 mm. The larva is variable in colour, green to reddish-brown, with a white mid-dorsal line edged black, 35 mm long.

97. ARMYWORM
Spodoptera exempta
Ntchembere Zandondo

This is the well-known pest that at intervals has a swarming phase, when there is an outbreak of caterpillars that move through the garden like an 'army', causing widespread damage to maize. Hence its common name. The Nyanja name refers to its habit of moving in a line (*ntchembere*, a mature woman, *ndondo*, to follow in line). The adult moths have dark brown forewings and white hindwings; the wingspan is 40 mm. The caterpillars are variable in colour, but usually yellowish-green, darker above, with white lines along the sides, 30 mm long, with the head shiny black. It feeds chiefly on grasses, but also on maize and sugarcane, though it is not a common pest of cotton.

The lesser armyworm (*Spodoptera exigua*) has been recorded from Malawi. It is closely related to the armyworm, and is similar in appearance; but it does not form such dense swarms, and is not confined to maize, but may be a pest on a variety of crops – tobacco, cotton, potatoes, rice, beans, cowpeas and groundnuts.

98. GRASS MOTH/CATERPILLAR
Spodoptera sp.
Mphalabungu
syn. *mbalaungu, imphe, nthupa, mpusi* (S), *mpherebungu* (T).

This is a common and well-known edible caterpillar whose identification is as yet uncertain. During a serious outbreak in the early months of 1930 of armyworm that damaged young maize and that were eaten by an enormous number of pied crows, Colin Smee wrote that the armyworm 'is not the same as the caterpillar that can be found in swarms annually about May, on the higher slopes of Zomba mountain. The latter has the native name *mbalaungu* and is utilized as food by the natives, whereas the true swarming caterpillars are not so eaten' (MNA. Ann. Rept. Dept. Agr. 1930). Some years later Jessie Williamson recorded that a 'very popular kind of edible caterpillar *mphalabungu*' feeds on the leaves of the shrubby herb *nthupa* (*Dolichos kilimanscharicus*) (1975: 100).

This caterpillar is widely distributed, and I have recorded it throughout Malawi from Thyolo to Mzuzu. People suggest that eggs are laid by the moth on the *Dolichos* (*nthupa*) or *Mucuna* (*dema*) shrub, and that the caterpillars then move into the surrounding grassland. It is usually found on the slopes of mountains, but I found it common in grassland *dambos* near Namadzi. It seems to be particularly associated with *tsekera* grass (*Pennisetum purpureum*). It is likened to the maize stem borer (*kapuchi*).

The caterpillar is pale yellowish-green, with a faint black line along the side, head orange-yellow, underside of belly black, 33 mm long. They are usually to be found in the late rains (February –March).

99. SPINY BOLLWORM
Earias biplaga/insulana
Mbozi ya Minga-Minga

This moth is particularly associated with the *Malvaceae* family, and the caterpillar may be a serious pest of cotton, not only attacking the flowers and bolls, but also boring into the stem of the cotton plant. The forewing of the adult moth is golden-brown, marked with darker brown; the hind-wing silvery white; wingspan 22 mm. The larva is usually grey or brown, spindle-shaped with darker markings, and with spine-like hairs on the body, whence its common name (*minga*, thorn). Up to 18 mm long.

100. RED BOLLWORM
Diparopsis castanea
Mbozi Yofiira
syn. *mfunye yofiira* (S).

Sweeney described the red bollworm as the worst enemy of the cotton farmer in Malawi, and the visits I made to the cotton fields at Bangula and Kasinja certainly confirmed this. For the caterpillars were ubiquitous in the cotton bolls, inflicting a great deal of damage on the crop. The adult moth has straw-coloured or reddish forewings, the hindwings being white edged with straw brown, with a wingspan of 35 mm. It is strictly nocturnal. The larva is yellowish green, becoming reddish when mature, each segment with three dark red marks – hence its common name. It seems to live practically all its life inside the cotton boll, and to be restricted to the cotton plant.

101. MAIZE STALK BORER
Busseola fusca
Kapuchi
syn. *mphuchi.*

This is probably one of the most destructive pests of maize, and Stephen Carr suggested to me that in many areas of Malawi between 5 and 10 per cent of the maize crop may be lost each year through the maize stalk borer – although the burning of the stalks annually no doubt keeps the population of the caterpillar in check. In Malawi it is commoner above 1,200 m, being replaced by the spotted stalk borer (*Chilo partellus*) at the lower altitudes. The adult moth has dull coppery-brown forewings, with a row of spots near the margin; the hindwings are paler, with a wingspan of 40 mm. The moth lays its eggs on the inside of the leaf sheath, and the emerging caterpillar bores into the stem of the maize, causing the plant to become stunted and the leaves to wilt. The larva is dirty white in colour, with a dark stripe along the side and a dark reddish-brown head, 30 mm long.

102. COMMON CUTWORM
Euxoa (agrostis) segetis/ypsilon
Mbozi Zamdothe

This is an important pest of young maize, but will attack many other crops – cabbage, tomatoes, beans, tobacco. The adult moths have buff or dark brown forewings: the hindwings are much paler, with a wingspan of 32 mm. The caterpillars are smooth, waxy, dull grey or brown in colour, and 30 mm long. They spend the day curled up in the soil and come above ground at night to feed, often cutting through the stems of the plants. A single caterpillar may cause considerable damage to the crop in a single night.

103. PINK STALK BORER
Sesamia calamistis
Kapuchi
syn. *mbozi.*

The caterpillar of this moth has been recorded as a stalk borer on maize, sorghum and sugarcane, but it is especially common on the latter crop at Nchalo. The adult moths are nocturnal, with light yellowish-brown forewings, with the hindwings white, and a wingspan of 35 mm. The larvae are pink to violet, with brown heads, 30 mm long. They bore into the inside of the maize or sugarcane, where they pupate.

Another well-known stalk borer, sharing the same common name, is the spotted stalk borer *Chilo partellus* (Family: *Pyralidae*), which is common in the Lower Shire Valley.

FAMILY: PLUTELLIDAE   Cabbage Moths

104. DIAMOND BACK MOTH
Plutella xylostella
Mbozi

The diamond back moth is a cosmopolitan species that occurs everywhere in the world where cabbages are grown. In Malawi it is a serious and widespread pest of cabbage, which tend to be grown in *dimba* gardens. It occurs all the year round, but is particularly serious during the dry season (July–October). The adult moth is ash-grey with a characteristic diamond pattern on its back: hence its common name. The wingspan is 15 mm. The larvae are a translucent or yellowish green, 12 mm long, with a yellow head; when disturbed they drop to the ground by a silken thread. They feed on the undersurface of the leaves of the cabbage – as well as on cauliflower, broccoli, rape and other crucifers.

FAMILY: GELECHIIDAE

105. PINK BOLLWORM
Pectinophora (platyedra) gossypiella
Mbozi ya Pinki

This was a serious pest of cotton in Egypt in the early part of the century, and during the 1920s it began to spread southwards, being first recorded in Malawi in 1925. By 1940 it had established itself in all the Shire Valley cotton-growing areas. The adult moth is small, and grey in colour. The larvae are yellowish, becoming dark pink 15 mm long. The moths are nocturnal and feed on *Hibiscus* sp., and it is not considered a serious pest of cotton in Malawi, and tends to inflict damage only towards the end of the dry season.

FAMILY: THAUMETOPOEIDAE

106. PROCESSIONARY MOTH
Anaphe panda
Nchiu
syn. *masopa, kadzola, maleweza* (T), *awauleni* (L), *chikalakala* (Y).

Figure 23 Number 106. *Thaumetopoeidae*, *Anaphe panda*, Processionary Moth, *Ntchiu*, Collective Cocoon on *Bridelia micrantha*, Kapalasa, 2 February 2001.

This is a common and widely distributed moth that is specifically asso-ciated with the *nsopa* tree (*Bridelia micrantha*). The moths, which are common in the early part of the rains, are attractive: the body is yellow-ish-buff, HB 25 mm; the forewing white with black patterning; the hind-wing white but buff towards the base; the wingspan is 65 mm. The larvae have a dark grey body covered with long dirty-white hairs; the head is reddish brown or shiny black, and the prolegs reddish brown; they are 35 mm long. It is gregarious and is commonly seen moving in lines: hence the common name processionary moth/caterpillar. I have counted 180 caterpillars moving in a single line. When fully grown the caterpillars form a collective cocoon that may contain several hundred caterpillars. The large oval cocoons are pale yellowish brown and consist of three layers of silk, with a smooth, tough outer layer. The collective cocoons (*chikwa*) vary in size, but measure around 120 × 95 mm, although many are much larger, depending on the number of occupants.

The term *nchiu* is the name of the *Dombeya rotundifolia* tree, with which the caterpillar is also associated. *Malewezi* is the Tumbuka name of *Bridelia micrantha*.

A similar species, *Anaphe reticulata*, is also a processionary caterpillar. The moth is slightly smaller, and is associated with the *tenza* tree (*Grewia pachycalyx*), and the caterpillars spin separate cocoons contained within the large communal cocoon. The edible caterpillar *kamonde* (*nyamkamondo*) described from Chimaliro Forest probably relates to this species, which is associated with the *msolo* tree, *Pseudolachnostylis maprouneifolia*.

FAMILY: PSYCHIDAE   Bagworms

107. COMMON BAGWORM
Eumeta cervina
syn. *Clania moddermanni*.
Mtemankhuni
syn. *chitebere* (L), *mteba*, *chitemangu* (Y), *mtemang'ombe*, *chisalanda* (T).

Bagworms are common and widespread, and are so called because the caterpillars of the *Psychid* moth weave around themselves a silken bag

Figure 24 Number 107. *Psychidae*, *Eumetia cervina* (*Clania moddermanni*), Bagworm Moth, Ntemankhuni, Kapalasa, 12 May 2001.

covered in twigs, thorns or pieces of grass. Fabre described them as 'twig faggots' who build for themselves a portable shelter (1912: 185), and the Nyanja name means 'to cut firewood' (*ku-teba, -tema*, to cut, *nkhuni* firewood). The females are wingless and grub-like and never leave the bag of twigs they have made for themselves. The male moths are winged and diurnal, but rarely seen and have a transient life, as they die soon after mating with the female. The bundle of twigs that constitute the bag of *Eumetia cervina* are about 45 mm long and 16 mm round, and the inside is filled with grey, silky material. The caterpillars that dwell inside the bag are whitish, barred with black, and their heads and upper parts protrude some 15 mm beyond the bag when they move about – and they can be quite active.

Throughout Malawi people consider the bagworm to be extremely poisonous – and it is widely used as medicine – although there is no real evidence that they are indeed toxic, and experiments in South Africa proved that no harm was caused when sheep were fed on bagworms mixed with their feed (Smit 1964: 189; Pinhey 1975: 39).

FAMILY: LIMACODIDAE

108. STINGING CATERPILLAR
Latoia (parasa) vivida
Chiyabwe

These are small attractive moths: forewings a vivid green edged with pale brown; the hindwings white with yellow border; wingspan 32 mm. The larvae, which are often described as 'nettle grubs', can be a pest on tea and coffee. They are rather slug-like, 30 mm long, translucent green or yellow, with a pale blue stripe running along the back and with dark markings; and they are further covered with tufts of hair that are poisonous and can cause intense irritation to the skin. They can therefore be troublesome to tea-pickers.

Chiyabwe is a generic term for all stinging caterpillars (*ku-yabwa*, to itch), and thus includes members of many different families (e.g. *Lymantriidae, Lasiocampidae* and *Artiidae*).

109. GELATINE GRUB
Niphadolepsis alianta

This is another slug-like caterpillar that is a pest on tea and coffee. The adult moth is small, and brown, HB 10 mm, and has a jerky flight. The larva, often called 'jelly grub', is soft, gelatine-like, sticky, and whitish, becoming bluish-green, 15 mm long.

FAMILY: GEOMETRIDAE

110. PINE LOOPER MOTH
Buzura abruptaria

The family *Geometridae* are mostly moths with small and slender bodies and relatively large wings, triangular-shaped and marked with wavy lines. The larvae, which are known as 'loopers', – have only two pairs of prolegs, including the claspers, and so move in a characteristic looping fashion. *Buzura abruptaria* is a well-known pest on *Pinus patula*, often causing severe defoliation of the trees. The adult moth is creamy-white, with dark brown bars on the wings; a wingspan of 45 mm, and feathery antennae. The larvae are elongate and slender, and resemble small twigs.

FAMILY: SPHINGIDAE   Hawkmoths

111. DEATH'S HEAD HAWKMOTH
Acherontia atropos
Chilumphabere
syn. *chisumbila mawele* (Y).

The hawkmoths are well represented and well known in Malawi, as they often come to light at night. They are strong fliers, and have the ability to hover in front of flowers while collecting nectar. They have strong, streamlined bodies, rather narrow wings, and a long coiled proboscis. *Acherontia atropos* is a cosmopolitan species, so named because it has a yellow skull-like pattern on its thorax. The forewings are deep brown, mottled with yellowish brown, while the hindwings are yellow with two dark brown bands; the wingspan is 100 mm. It squeaks when handled, and often raids beehives in search of honey. The caterpillars are large, and green or yellow, with seven blue or purplish slanting stripes, and as with other members of the family, they have a short horn (*nyanga*) at the end of the body. The caterpillar is said to make an audible clicking sound. It feeds on the potato family, particularly sweet potato and cape gooseberry. Ray Murphy suggested to me that it also feeds on *nthula* (*Solanum incanum*) and *mpindimbi* (*Vitex doniana*). Because of its green colour the caterpillar may be described as Matondo, although it does not feed on *Julbernardia* trees.

FAMILY: SATURNIIDAE   Emperor Moths

The emperor moths are amongst the largest and most attractive moths in the world, and certain species have a wingspan of over 20 cm. In Malawi they are particularly associated with *Brachystegia* woodland, and their larvae form an important source of relish, even though many species are armed with conspicuous tubercles or spines.

The adult moths are heavily scaled, the wings often glistening, and each wing has a conspicuous eye-spot. They are nocturnal and thus rarely seen. Most species have a single generation a year, with a pupal diapause in the dry season, though John Wilson informs me that some species may breed twice during the rainy season. As the identification of the caterpillars was based only on field observations and local descriptions, the scientific names can only be considered tentative. For such identifications I have relied heavily on Pinhey's pioneering study of emperor moths (1972) and discussions with Ray Murphy and John Wilson.

112. PINE EMPEROR MOTH
Nudaurelia (imbrasia) cytherea
This is a well-known forest pest in Southern Africa, widely distributed and causing considerable damage to pine plantations, often defoliating trees. The moths are brownish-yellow, with dark, wavy markings, and typical eye-spots; the wingspan is of up to 15 cm. The caterpillars are described as having a 'remarkable' colour – a red body with bright blue, green and yellow spangles, up to 130 mm long. In Malawi, only a few records exist of its infesting pines (Esbjerg). Its status is doubtful in Malawi, although because of its association with *Rhus spp*, the edible caterpillar *matatu* may refer to this species (*mtatu, Rhus longipides*) – the name refers to the trifoliate leaves (Berry and Petty 1992: 271).

113. COMMON EMPEROR
Bunaea alcinoe
Mabwabwa
syn. *chandimbo, malasalasa, maphombo* (T), *nkalati* (S).
This is the commonest emperor moth, and its caterpillar is found on a variety of trees, but it is particularly associated with the tree *mbwabwa*, (*Cussonia (kirkii) arboria*) and typically feeds on its leaves. Hassam Patel showed me one tree in Mzuzu botanical gardens that had been completely defoliated by this caterpillar, which is well-liked as a relish. It is often described as *mphalabungu*, although this term is more usually associated with the grass moth/caterpillar (*Spodoptera* sp.). The moth has reddish-brown wings, the forewing with a clear spot, the hindwing having an orange eyespot ringed black and white. The caterpillar is black, with black spines on the first two segments, and six rows of wavy white spines along the rest of the body; the head is black; and there are orange spiracles along the side of the body, which is 65 mm long. On account of its spines it may be described as *malasalasa* (*ku-lasa*, to

wound), although this term may be applied to any caterpillar with spines. The *mabwabwa* caterpillars are usually found during the rains, from January to April.

114. WAHLBERG'S EMPEROR
Nudaurelia (imbrasia) wahlbergi
Maphombo
syn. *mapondo*, *viphombo* (T).

This is a similar species to the common emperor. Local people invariably associate it with the *msuku* tree (*Uapaca kirkiana*), although Ray Murphy informs me that it particularly feeds on *Allophylus* and *Croton* trees, as well as on guava, castor oil and mango. The caterpillar has a black body and three rows of red spines along the body, with white hairs at their base; the spiracles are white, along the side of the body; and the head is black; it is 65 mm long. It is to be noted that *chipombora* (T) is the tree *Cussonia arborea*. The caterpillars are edible and collected at the end of the rains (March–June).

115. ZAMBESI EMPEROR
Gonimbrasia zambesina
Chilungulungu
syn. *malasalasa*, *vilungulungu* (T).

In the idenitification of the caterpillars there is a good deal of overlap between specific species and various vernacular names, as these vary between localities. *Chilungulungu* thus covers essentially three species of *Gonimbrasia*, while this particular species, *G. Zambesina* may also be described as *mabwabwa* and *nyamanyama*. It is particularly found at low to medium altitudes, and has been noted from Blantyre, Zomba and the lakeshore, and is associated with mango and *msumwa* (*Diospyros mespiliformis*) trees. The caterpillar of *Gonimbrasia zambesina* has a black head and body, with the body densely mottled with white, yellow and red spots, except between segments; and with rows of red or black short spines; the spiracles are along the body, and black; and in all it is 70 mm long.

Gonimbrasia belina is the familiar 'mopane worm' – although the term 'worm' is something of a misnomer, nevertheless the *mopane* moth is particularly associated with the *mopane* or *tsanya* tree, *Colophospermum mopane*. The adult moth has pale orange-brown wings, with a small orange eye-spot, ringed black and white, on the forewing, and a larger orange eye-spot on the hindwing. The caterpillar of the *mopane* moth has a black head, legs and body, with the body covered with numerous yellow and white spots except between the segments; the fine rows of short spines are black, with short white hairs at the base, and its length runs to 100 mm. I recorded this caterpillar at Liwonde on mango trees. *Gonimbrasia belina* has been recorded from Kasungu National Park (Munthali and Mughogho 1992: 145), but this may be a misidentification, as this species is mainly found in Tsanya woodland at the lower altitudes – Liwonde, Mpatamanga and the Lower Shire – and there are no *Colospermum* trees to be found in Kasungu National Park. The chilunglungu of Kasungu and Chimaliro forest is probably *Gonimbrasia rectilineata*. The caterpillar of this species is similar to the so-called '*mopane* worm', but it has a reddish-brown head and short red spines. The *Gonimbrasia* caterpillars (*chilungulungu*) are mostly collected for relish at the end of the rains (February–March).

116. DIVERSE EMPEROR
Imbrasia ertli
Mapala
syn. *makalampapa, makulaimvi, makuluaimvi.*
A large moth, ochraceous-brown, forewing with a very small eye-spot; hindwing with large orange eye-spot, with black, pink and white rings. The caterpillars have a characteristic reddish-brown head, and a black body, sparsely covered with long, white downy hairs, mainly between segments, and with no spines; they are 90 mm long. This is widely distributed and one of the commonest emperor moths, found at all altitudes from the Lower Shire to the Nyika plateau. The caterpillar is edible, collected mainly at the beginning of the dry season, May–July, and it feeds on a variety of plants. One of its common names describes it as the 'grey hair of the ancestors' (*makolo*, matrilineal ancestors, imvi, grey hair).

117. IRIAN EMPEROR
Pseudobunaea (irius) pallens
Matondo
The term *matondo* seems to cover a variety of emperor moths whose caterpillars are large, green and without conspicuous spines, and that are specifically associated with the *mthondo* tree (*Julbernardia paniculata*). The caterpillar of *Pseudobunaea pallens*, which has been described to me as *matondo*, is large, and green with swollen ridged segments, silvery speckling, and minute black dorsal spots, with the head green, while the spiracles along the side of the body are reddish; it is 80 mm long. It seems to be widespread in Malawi, and has been recorded as feeding on *mseza* (*Brachystegia bussei*), *mpandula* (*Bauhinia petersiana*) and *kasakolowe* (*Uapaca nitida*). The edible caterpillars are collected in the early rains, from October to December.

Two species of the genus *Athletes* also appear to be described as *matondo*, and both are associated with *Julbernardia* trees. *Athletes gigas* is found at medium to high altitudes, and appears to be widespread. The caterpillar is glaucous green, with a violet suffusion, but the head and spiracles brown; and it has a series of golden-yellow thorns.

Athletes semialba is similar, the caterpillar green with a bluish tinge, and with rows of golden spines.

The caterpillar of the giant emperor, *Pseudimbrasia deyrollei*, a species that appears to be common and widespread, may also be described as *matondo*, for it is a large, bright green caterpillar with swollen segments, small reddish brown spines and orange spiracles, to up to 110 mm long. John Wilson informs me that it is particularly associated with the *mwabvi* tree (*Erythrophleum suaveolens*).

Gynanisa maia, the speckled emperor, has been noted as the *matondo* collected in Kasungu National Park (Munthali and Mughogho 1992: 145). But Ray Murphy informs me that this moth tends to be restricted to the low veld of Southern Africa, and that it has not been recorded from Malawi. It is possible that the caterpillars in Kasungu belong to the related species *Gynanisa carcassoni*, which has been noted in *Brachystegia* woodland in Mzuzu.

118. PALLID EMPEROR
Cirina forda
Kawidzi
syn. *kawichi, maiye* (Y).

The adult moths have pale pinkish brown or russet wings; forewings without an eye-spot; hindwings with an eye-spot. The caterpillars are yellowish with long white hairs and black transverse segmental bands. The head and 'tail' are black, and it is 60 mm long. The edible caterpillars are collected mainly in January and February and are associated with the *mkalati* (*Burkea africana*) (*kawidzi* (T)), *mwabvi* (*Erythrophleum suaveolens*) and *mpambulu* (*Carissa edulis*) trees. It is widespread, but not common. It is widely eaten in Zambia (Silow 1976: 88).

The tailed emperor, *Urota sinope*, may also be described as *kawidzi* (Berry and Petty 1992: 271).

119. AFRICAN LUNAR MOTH
Argema mittrei
This is a large and attractive moth; the wings are yellowish-green with conspicuous wingspots; the hindwings with long tails (100 mm). Wingspan 140 mm. Mainly found on the Lakeshore and in the Shire Highlands below 920 metres. The caterpillars are green, feeding on *mfula*

(*Sclerocarya caffra*) trees; they are probably eaten, but there is no definite information.

ORDER: HYMENOPTERA   Wasps, Bees and Ants

After the beetles, this is probably the largest order of insects, which includes not only bees, wasps and ants, but also sawflies. They are characterized by the narrow 'waist' (actually the first segment of the abdomen) between the thorax and the abdomen, and the fact that the smaller hindwings are interlocked with the forewings by a row of minute hooks. Many species possess a long ovipositor that they utilize for egg laying, as well as for sawing and stinging – especially the wasps. The larvae are usually legless, but with a well-developed head, and either live as parasites, or in the case of bees, in the food-laden cells prepared by the adults.

FAMILY: ICHNEUMONIDAE   Ichneumon Wasps

120. ICHNEUMON WASP
Osprynchotus gigas
Nalugumbu (Y)
syn. *namlondola* (C), *lilumasya* (Y), *likwi, namukoro* (L), *botomani.* This is one of the most commonly seen insects in Malawi, for it frequently enters houses during the day – particularly the females. It is especially noted suring the dry season, from August to November. It is a parasitic wasp, though it does not sting and is quite harmless. It seems to be a parasite on mud wasps, and its ovipositor is able to 'drill' through the nud nest, enabling the ichneumon wasp to lay its eggs on the developing mud wasp larvae (Skaife 1979: 211). It is a slender black wasp, HB 25 mm, with long black and yellow legs, and a long petiole: the ovipositor is needle-like, up to 10 mm long. The wings are bluish-black.

The local names allude to the fact that the ichneumon wasp is closely identified with the mud wasp (-*gumba* (Y), to mould pots, plaster with mud). Other members of this family are parasitic on other insects, especially the larvae of moths and butterflies.

There are numerous species of wasps to be found in Malawi, belonging to several families, but few are recognized by local people. Those which have salience are noted below.

FAMILY: SPHECIDAE   Digger and Mud Wasps

121. MUD WASP
Sceliphron spirifex
Nalugumbu (Y)
syn. *namukoro* (L), *chiumbambiya* (C).

This is the family of solitary wasps that so fascinated Fabre in Southern France, who closely observed how the female wasp (of the genera *Sphex*, *Bembix*, and *Ammophilia*), after capturing the prey that was to form the food of her larvae – grasshopper, fly and caterpillars respectively – would not kill the victim, but would inject a toxin that would only paralyse it, preventing it from rotting for several weeks (Fabre 1916).

This species is the true *nalugumbu*, which is a common wasp that builds its small mud nest in buildings and outhouses, and provisions its larvae with spiders that are stuffed into the nest and on which the eggs are laid. The female will often make a series of mud cells side by side, each containing spiders, and will cover them with a thick layer of mud. It seems to be widespread in Malawi, and I have recorded it from both the Shire Highlands and the Lower Shire Valley, and its presence is often indicated by a high-pitched buzzing. It is a black wasp with a slender yellow petiole, and yellow and black legs. It has transparent wings, 15 mm long, with a total length HB 27 mm. It is common throughout the rains until May. Its common name *chiumbambiya* refers to its habits (*ku-umba*, to make, mould bricks, *mbiya*, clay pot).

FAMILY: EUMENIDAE   Mason Wasps

122. ORANGE-TAILED WASP
Paragris analis
Nalugumbu (Y)

These are solitary wasps that build small nests of mud. *Pagaris analis* is the commonest species. It is a black wasp with the lower half of the abdomen – the 'tail' – bright orange, and the wings iridescent bluish-black, HB 25 mm. It is frequent in the early part of the rains (October–January).

FAMILY: POMPILIDAE   Spider-hunting Wasps

123. SPIDER WASP
Pseudagenia brunniceps
Nalugumbu

Also known as the digger wasps, this is a family of slender, long-legged wasps, with smoky wings and curled antennae. This species, noted only infrequently, is black with orange curled antennae, metallic bluish-black wings and long orange legs, HB 19 mm. It is a very active species, and like other members of the family is probably a digger wasp, hunting spiders to provision larvae.

FAMILY: SCOLIIDAE

124. BLACK WASP
Scolia ruficornis
This family, which includes some very large solitary wasps, are parasitic on the larvae of beetles, particularly dung beetles, and the habits of the European species were graphically described by Fabre (1919: 30–54). The only species I recorded was *Scolia ruficornis*, which was a large, thickset black wasp, with black wings and antennae, and long hairy legs, HB 25 mm. This species occasionally enters houses, but was not recognized by local people.

FAMILY: VESPIDAE   Social Wasps

125. SOCIAL WASP
Belonogaster junceus
Mabvu
syn. *li/matendeu* (Y), *davu, bavu* (sing.), *nalume* (Y), *muhonyope* (L), *sanganavu* (T).
These are truly social wasps that build their papery 'honey comb' nests hanging down on verandahs, or under the eaves of houses. There are usually about 8–12 wasps to a nest, although Sweeney records as many as 32 individuals in one nest (1970: 85). The larvae are reared in the cells of the nest, being fed by the females on chewed caterpillars, and when they hatch the young females stay with the mother and assist in the food gathering. The adults themselves seem to feed on nectar. *Belonogaster junceus* has a grey thorax, a reddish-brown pointed abdomen and a slender long petiole. The wings are dark reddish-brown, and the full length is around HB 35 mm though, they are variable in size. It can inflict a painful sting, but if unmolested it is not particularly aggressive. It is a very common wasp, present mostly during the rains, and is widely distributed, usually described by using the plural term *mabvu* (*matendeu* (Y)). Two other common species of *Vespidae* share this name.

  Belonogaster griseus is a slightly smaller species, reddish-brown with two pale yellow spots on the abdomen; the wings are pale brown; full HB length 27 mm. It is mainly seen during the rains.

Icaria distigma is a small reddish-brown social wasp, which builds papery nests under the eaves or on the verandas of houses. It is pale reddish-brown, with the wings transparent with a black spot, HB length15 mm. The wasp can inflict a painful sting.

FAMILY: MUTILLIDAE

126. MUTILLID WASP
Mutilla dasya
Nthumbathumba

syn. *chisulu* (C), *upile, ndupatumba* (Y), *mwayi, chisoni, ekhari* (L). Although often described as the 'velvet ant', this is not in fact an ant but a wasp, the females of which are wingless and have a velvety appearance. They are often seen wandering about on the ground, especially on hot days, and can inflict a painful sting. Seeing one is thought to bring good fortune – hence the term *mwayi* (good luck) – although you are unfortunate if you happen to tread on a mutillid wasp with bare feet. There are many species to be found in Malawi, and they appear to be parasitic on other members of the order. *Mutilla dasya* is fairly common. It is a black hairy wasp with several white spots on the abdomen, which are characteristic, HB 16 mm, and often larger.

FAMILY: HALICTIDAE   Mining Bees

127. MINING BEE
Crocisa picta
Mpasi

syn. *pasi, chitani* (Y), *tefunte* (T). There are many members of the family *Halictidae* whose habits are not well known. Some are solitary bees, and others form small colonies, usually in the ground, often in banks, and their honey is well-liked and collected by people. The only species I personally recorded was *Crocisa picta*, which is a beautiful small bee, sky blue with black patterning on the abdomen; the forewings are dark brown; the hindwings transparent; the full length HB 17 mm.

FAMILY: APIDAE   Social Bees

128. HONEY-BEE
Apis mellifera
Njuchi

syn. *nyuchi* (Y), *oravo* (L).

Common and widely recognized throughout Malawi, both as a wild species and as domesticated for beekeeping. Several sub-species are recognized, those in Malawi being of the race *Apis mellifera scutellata*, which is the typical honey-bee of east and southern Africa. They are well known for the readiness to defend their colonies. Malawians describe them as dreadful (*opsya kwambiri*), and recognize that if one bee bites you then others will quickly follow, and they suggest that bees may kill animals. The bees differ from ants and wasps in that their food is composed of pollen mixed with honey derived from the nectar of flowers, and thus bees have a complex and intricate relationship with flowering plants. Bees usually establish their colonies in houses or in hollow trees.

129. MOPANE BEE
Trigona bottegoi
Nsikisa
syn. *mfikisa, chipita, gulumba* (C), *chisugugu* (Y), *munya* (T).
Often called '*mopane* flies' these are small dark-coloured social bees, with yellowish antennae, HB 3–4 mm, that were originally placed in the family *Meliponidae*. They are not specifically associated with *tsanya* (*Colosphospermum mopane*) woodland, but are widespread in savannah woodland. They may also be called 'sweat flies', as they can become very annoying when walking through the woodland, as they attack the ears and eyes, seeking wax. But they cannot sting and are often called 'stingless bees'. They nest in hollow trees, in holes in walls or rocks, or in termite mounds, and at the entrance to the hive there is a long wax tube 20–30 mm long. Malawians are very fond of the honey, which is usually described as *tongole*, and consider it very sweet (*otsekemera*).

FAMILY: XYLOCOPIDAE   Carpenter bees

130. CARPENTER BEE
Xylocopa mossambica (caffra)
Bemberezi
syn. *ling'ong'olo* (L), *kamchenjezi* (T), *zoli* (T).
There are no bumble bees in Malawi, but there are large bees that make their nests in wood, excavating long galleries, and are thus known as carpenter bees. And they can often do much damage to the beams of houses. Having cut a long tunnel in the wood, the female partitions it into a series of cells, each of which is provisioned with a pasty mixture of pollen and nectar, on top of which an egg is laid, the larvae subsequently feeding on the mixture. *Xylocopa caffra* is a large black bee with two

Figure 25 Number 130. *Xylocopidae, Xylocopa mossambica (caffra)*, Pied Carpenter Bee, Bemberezi, Kapalasa, 11 November 2000.

Figure 26 Number 130. *Xylocopidae, Xylocopa flavorufa*, Rufous Carpenter Bee, Bemberezi, Kapalasa, 2 October 2000.

Figure 27 Number 130. *Xylocopidae, Xylocopa nigrita*, Large Carpenter Bee, Bemberezi, Kapalasa, 6 May 2001.

broad white bands across the body, the wings dark brown, HB 22 mm. The legs are short and hairy.

Two other species are common and share the name *bemberezi*. These are *Xylocopa flavorufa*, which has a deep chestnut thorax, HB 25 mm, and *Xylocopa nigrita*, which is the largest of the genus. The female is glossy black, with white hairs on the side of the abdomen; wings dark brown; length HB 30 mm; the male is rusty brown and larger, HB 34 mm.

Many Chewa dictionaries suggest that the *bemberezi* is the 'ichneumon fly' (e.g. Massana 2000: 2), but my own researches suggests that *bemberezi* is specifically related to the carpenter bees.

FAMILY: FORMICIDAE   Ants

This is an extremely large family of insects, which is ubiquitous in Malawi, and found everywhere. All species are social, living in colonies of various sizes, and in diverse habitats, the colonies consisting of individuals of various castes. The workers are always without wings – only the reproductives have wings, and the queens lose these soon after mating. Numerous species are to be found in Malawi, but, though they are not eaten (apart from *mafulufute*), many forms are recognized by local people.

SUB-FAMILY: PONERINAE

131. BLACK ARMY ANT
Paltothyreus tarsatus/Pachycondyla tarsata
Mdzodzo

syn. *nyanyao* (C), *nsoso* (Y), *mwisoso* (L), *phomboni* (T), *sisinya* (T). These ants are regarded as the most primitive ants of Africa, and they tend to live in small colonies, and to forage singly. But sometimes they forage in long lines, and hence their common name 'army' ants. One early writer described them as going around in bands to 'wage war' on termites (Scott 1929: 291). They are large black ants, some 19 mm long, with strong mandibles, and have a very strong smell; hence they are also described as 'stink ants'. They are armed with a powerful sting, and can inflict pain. They are described by local people as 'fierce' (*-kalipa*). When approached they often make a 'buzzing' sound. All are carnivorous, hunting insects and other arthropods, and seem to prey especially on termites. In Lengwe National Park in October I watched a column of black army ants, about 4 metres long, attacking a colony of harvester termites (*Hodotermes mossambicus*), carrying away the helpless termites, even though the soldier termites put up a gallant defensive fight. Nesting in the ground, with holes around 50 mm apart, with loose soil at their entrance, the army ants have their nuptial flight at the end of October.

The allied species *Megaponera foetens* is similar in habits and also common, and is also described as *mdodzo*. Many other species of the sub-family are found in Malawi.

SUB-FAMILY: DORYLINAE

132. RED DRIVER ANT
Anomma (dorylus) nigricans/molestus
Linthumbu
syn. *nthumbu, liragudu* (C), *salau* (Y), *mtalakwi* (L), *nkhulande* (T), *onthumbwi* (S).

This is one of the most familiar insects of Africa, and all the early Europeans who came to Malawi wrote about its marching columns and its predatory habits. Hans Coudenhove wrote of them, as 'warrior ants', and described them by the Swahili term *siafu* – for Swahili seems to have been widely spoken during the colonial period; and he writes of the ants swarming through the camp, or entering the huts of local people, forcing them to leave the house temporarily (1925: 210–15). This still often happens. (See Faulkner 1869:273; Foran 1958: 137–46; and Sweeney 1966: 83–4 for similar accounts of these 'pugnacious insects', which are often described as 'safari ants' in east Africa.)

Such experiences are common to anyone who spends time in the 'bush' in Malawi, and when red driver ants are on the move and in the vicinity people often protect their houses by encircling them with ashes.

The red driver ants are entirely carnivorous, and have such large colonies that they are largely nomadic, and continually on the move, although they may spend some days resting in same damp spot at the base of a tree. When foraging they spread over an area, and will attack and devour not only other insects, but any animal they are able to overcome. At Zoa I lost two pet rabbits one night to a swarm of red driver ants. They thus may devour snakes, lizards, young birds and small mammals – although some of the stories regarding their predatory nature may be a little exaggerated. But according to local people, the *linthumbu* may provide a useful service, for they often rid a house of rats and other unwanted invertebrates. Some people say that if a driver ant enters your ear you will die. They are particularly noticeable at the beginning of the rains (October–January) and on humid, overcast days.

The red driver ants have a single pedicel and no eyes, and are reddish-brown in colour; the workers vary in size, ranging from 5 to 9 mm long. The soldiers are larger – 14 mm long – with large heads and strong mandibles, and are able to inflict a painful bite – they do not sting. Only the males are winged, and these are the familiar insects known as the 'sausage fly' (not usually recognized by local people, but sometimes called *nsatafisi*), which often come to the light at night. They have a hairy thorax, a long reddish-brown abdomen, and pale smoky brown wings with strong black veins. Around 30 mm long and with large eyes, they thus bear little resemblance to other members of the colony. It is of interest that while on the march the red driver ants – fierce as they are – are attacked themselves by a parasitic fly *Bengalia depressa*, which robs the ants of their larvae (Sweeney 1970: 75).

SUB-FAMILY: MYRMICINAE

133. BROWN HOUSE ANT
Pheidole megacephala
Nyerere
syn. *nyele* (Y), *enenere* (L), *nyerera* (T).
The sub-family *Myrmicinae* contains numerous genera and species in Malawi, and they are characterized by a 2–segmented petiole. The brown house ant is perhaps the most widespread, and is ubiquitous, and can be a serious pest both in houses and in tobacco nurseries. It is a tiny dark brown or black ant, only 2–4 mm long, withlong antennae. It nests in the ground, bringing up small heaps of loose soil, and during the dry season seems to disappear entirely. The concept *nyerere* is a generic term for all small ants. Sweeney notes that there are around 15 species of the genus *Pheidole* to be found in Malawi, and these, together with the small species of the sub-family *Formicinae* (e.g. the introduced ant *Paratrechina longicornis*, which is found in the Lower Shire and along the Lakeshore) may all be described as *nyerere* (Sweeney 1970: 95). People often complain about *nyerere*, entering the house, keeping you awake and not giving you peace (*ntendere*), as well as carrying away food.

134. SHINY BLACK ANT
Myrmicaria eumenoides/natalensis
Mapipi
syn. *ndundu* (C), *mayiphini* (L), *vindundu* (T).
This is a small shiny black ant, 7 mm long, that is particularly common in woodland habitats and in gardens, where it forms populous colonies in underground burrows with large openings. It throws up lots of soil, and unlike most ants it has the unusual habit of coming to the surface in large numbers when the ground is stamped near its burrow. It eats seeds, and like other ants often attends aphids; but it also feeds on other insects. If

winged termites or dried crickets are placed near its nest, these are quickly discovered by foragers, and consumed. The whole gathering of ants become oily as they engage in food-sharing.

135. THIEF ANT
Carebara vidua
Mafulufute
syn. *nyamu* (N/Y), *manyenye* (T), *nyamunyamu* (S).

This is a very unusual ant that lives in termite mounds. It seems to be common throughout the country, especially along the Lakeshore and in the Lower Shire Valley – but I also found it plentiful in the Shire Highlands. It is usually described as *chiswe*, as the worker ants are minute, reddish-yellow, with dark heads, some 1–2 mm in length. If they come into contact with the skin they can cause an irritable itching (-*yabwe*). In contrast with the workers the reproductives are enormous; the females are large, shiny black with a globose abdomen, and dark brown wings and some 25 mm long; the males are slightly smaller, also winged, with a black head and thorax, and a bright ochre-yellow abdomen, HB 17 mm. The winged ants are widely described as *nyamu* (*nyama* = meat), and they emerge from the termite mounds, or holes in the ground (from underground termite nests) in the early rains (November–December). They come forth singly, usually around midday, or the early afternoon. Both reproductives are considered an important food source, and well liked, as they contain a large amount of fat. They seem to be the only species of ant eaten in Malawi.

136. EUPHORBIA ANT
Cataulacus nr intrudens
Nkhungunkuma
syn. *ipalankongo* (Y), *nsungununu* (C), *amaluma*.

This is a small ant, usually nesting in holes in *Euphorbia* shrubs, or in trees. It is about 5 mm in length, with spines on the lower part of the thorax. It is fairly common, but of little cultural significance, apart from the fact that it inflicts a sharp bite, which is said to cause blisters (-*luma*, to bite).

SUB-FAMILY: FORMICINAE

137. TAILOR ANT
Oecophylla longinoda
Mzukira
syn. *msuchila* (Y/N).

Members of this sub-family have a single pedicel and no sting, but are able to squirt formic acid from a gland into the wounds made by their mandibles, thus inflicting a fierce and painful bite. Several common species have been recorded from Malawi, belonging to many genera. The tailor ant is widespread in Malawi, but seems to have a local distribution. I found it common in mango trees at Zoa. It makes a remarkable nest by weaving leaves together using silk produced by the larvae, and several nests may be found in the same tree. Livingstone noted that these ants 'give battle readily and sting keenly' (Wallis 1956: 1/74), for they are very aggressive in protecting their nests. They are medium-sized reddish-yellow ants, about 10 mm long. They are omnivorous in habit, foraging through the branches of the trees.

138. GREY ANT
Camponotus rufoglaucus
Mphembedzu
syn. *lupambesu* (Y), *empepesu* (L), *belethe* (S).
This is a small ant, 6–10 mm in length, with a reddish head and a grey abdomen. It lives underground in small colonies, and is mainly active at the onset of the rains. Largely vegetarian in habit, it also feeds on the secretion of aphids. People always describe this ant as 'urinating' (-*kodza*) on a person's leg, the urine causing severe pain if it enters a wound (*bala*). It is thus described as fierce (-*ukali*). As with the black army ant, people describe this ant as storing food, and thus not being in evidence for a greater part of the year – through the dry season.

Sweeney suggests that the cocktail ant (*Crematogaster tricolor*) (sub-family: *Myrmecinae*), which is a common and widespread species, making its nest in the branches of trees or the walls of houses, is also described as *mphembedzu* (1970: 93).

139. SUGAR ANT
Camponotus maculates/etiolipes
Chimalasuga
syn. *nakasuga* (C).
This is a rather large ant, about 16 mm in length, black with slender antennae and long reddish legs. It normally has four pale brown spots on the abdomen. As its local name suggests, it commonly enters houses in search of sugar and sweet substances. It is not usually aggressive, and it seems to live in small colonies under stores, in dead wood, or among debris, and to be mainly nocturnal.

140. MAKWAWA ANT
Polyrhachis gagates
Gugudira
syn. *liragudu, nyalagudu.*

These are large black ants (HB 10 mm), with a globose abdomen and a spiny pedicel. They are family common in *Brachystegia* woodland, living in large mound-like colonies. A similar species was noted in sugarcane at Nchalo in February. They do not appear to be aggressive, and feed mainly on honeydew and nectar.

OTHER ARTHROPODS

CLASS: DIPLOPODA

141. COMMON MILLIPEDE
Spirostreptus sp.
Bongololo
syn. *dzongololo* (C), *lijongolo* (Y), *njelenyenye* (Y), *mongoro* (L), *nyabanda* (T).

Often misidentified as a centipede, and described by one early writer as a 'very ugly burrowing caterpillar' (W. P. Johnson 1922: 16) – it is neither ugly nor a caterpillar – the *bongololo* is one of the most familiar creatures of Malawi. It is a long, cylindrical, many-jointed arthropod, dark chestnut in colour, with around 60 segments, each segment bearing two pairs of legs. The larger species are about 150 mm in length. They are mainly scavengers and diurnal in habit, feeding mainly on decaying plant matter, dead animals or dung. Hence they tend to be slow-moving. They are quite harmless, but are able to discharge an unpleasant protective fluid, and so have few predators – apart from hedgehogs and scorpions. When touched, they roll themselves up into tight spirals for protection. For Malawians they have few uses, but are of great cultural significance, being the subject of many proverbs.

CLASS: CHILOPODA

142. CENTIPEDE
Scolopendra morsitans
Kalizi
syn. *karisi* (Y), *nankalizi, linyetsa* (small red centipede).

There are many species of centipede in Malawi, and local people tend to be familiar only with the larger kinds – although all are described by the term *kalizi*, a complex that also embraces scorpions. Centipedes have long, flattened bodies, consisting of around 20 segments, each segment bearing one pair of legs. They are reddish-brown to black, with bluish legs, the front legs being pincer-like and used as venomous jaws. They can inflict a severe bite on humans, which can cause intense local pain. They are nocturnal in habit, and are quick-moving, and found primarily in damp places, under logs or stones, or in debris. They are essentially predators, feeding on insects, slugs and other small creatures. As centipedes have the habit sometimes of raising up their last segments when disturbed, and inflict a painful bite, it is not surprising that local people identify them with scorpions, which belong to a very different group of arthropods (Class: *Arachnida*).

CLASS: ARACHNIDA

ORDER: ARANEAE

143. SPIDER
Kangaude
syn. *nthandaude, lutathavu* (T).
There are several hundred different spiders in Malawi, and though familiar and common everywhere, there has been no serious research undertaken in Malawi on this fascinating group of organisms. Apart from the occasional mention in folk traditions, they have little salience for Malawians, and all the spiders I encountered – but was unable to identify – were described by local people under the single taxon, *kangaude*.

ORDER: SOLIFUGAE

144. HUNTING SPIDER
Solpuda sericea
Chindalandala
syn. *buwe, duwiduwi, psyapsyapsyao.*
These are large spider-like creatures with long legs, brown, hairy, with a pair of front appendages equipped with claws, so that the 'hunting' spider appears to have five pairs of legs. They move very quickly on the ground, or on rocks, hunting their prey, which consists mainly of insects; hence their name 'hunting' or 'wind' spider. They have a reputation for being poisonous, and although they may bite if handled roughly, they have no venomous glands.

ORDER: ACARINA

FAMILY: IXODIDAE

145. TICK
Nkhufi
syn. *kamanya, nkhupakupa, likupe* (Y).

Africa has been described as the 'home of ticks' (Smit 1964: 19), as there are so many species to be found on the continent, and in Malawi they are ubiquitous – and common parasites on cattle, dogs and humans. A walk through the long grass in woodlands or *dambos* at the end of the rains will invariably lead to ticks attaching themselves to the legs, or clothing, and people spend time removing bloated ticks from their pet dogs. And, of course, ticks have great economic and medical importance in being vectors of diseases of both livestock and humans.

Ticks are small, blood-sucking external parasites that have a hard dorsal shield that covers the whole upper surface in the male. The adults have four pairs of legs, and live on their hosts for varying periods of time. They have a complex life-cycle, and can live for long periods without food. Malawians recognize the differences between the ticks that are to be found on different hosts.

Nkhufi is the common term for the tick (*Ornithodorus moubata*) that is parasitic on humans and a vector of relapsing fever. It is a soft tick, lacking a horny shield, greyish, and about 12 mm long. Like the bed beg, it lives in cracks and crevices of houses. The term may, however, be extended to other ticks.

Nsakapuka (syn. *nkumbakumba*) is used to refer to the ticks of live-stock, particularly cattle and dogs, and embraces the common blue tick (*Boophilus decoloratus*) and the brown ticks (*Rhipicephalus* spp.), the species *Rhipicephalus sanguineus* and *Haemaphysalis leachii* being found mainly on dogs (*mbapani* (Y), *kabali* (T)).

Mites, which are allied to ticks, are serious pests in Malawi, both on such crops as cassava and tomato, and in the house. The latter, the itch-mites (*Sarcoptes scabiei*) are minute, greyish, cause intense irritation or scabies, and are generally described as *chinyakanyaka*.

Bibliography

Archival Material
National Archives of Malawi (MNA), Zomba.
Library, Bvumbwe Agricultural Research Station (BRS).
Wildlife Research Unit, Kasungu National Park, Department of National
    Parks and Wildlife (WRU).

References

Abbot, P. G. (1998) 'The Supply and Demand Dynamics of Miombo Woodland'. Aberdeen University: Ph.D. thesis.

Abram, D. (1996) *The Spell of the Sensuous*. New York: Random House.

Amanze, J. (1986) 'The Bimbi: Cult of Malawi'. Oxford University: Ph.D. thesis.

Aristotle (1937) *Parts of Animals*. trans. A. L. Peck. Cambridge, MA: Harvard University Press

—— (1965–1970) *History of Animals*, trans. A. L. Peck, 3 vols. Cambridge, MA: Harvard University Press.

Armour, R. A. (1986) *Gods and Myths of Ancient Egypt.* Cairo: American University Press.

Atran, S. (1990) *Cognitive Foundations of Natural History.* Cambridge: Cambridge University Press.

—— (1999) *Itzaj Maya Folkbiological Taxonomy,* in D. L. Medin and S. Atran (eds), *Folk Biology,* pp. 119–203. Cambridge, MA: MIT Press.

Atuahene, S. K. (1992) *Exotic Insect Pests of Forestry in Malawi.* Zomba: FRIM Dept 92007.

Atuahene, S. K. and Chilima, C. Z. (1993) *Aspects of the Biology and Ecology of* Cinara Cuppessi. Zomba: FRIM Dept 93001.

Bahana, J. W. and Byaruhanga, E. K. (1999) 'Advances and Review of Strategies for Red Locust Plague Preservation', *Insect Sci. Applic.* 19(4): 265–72.

Bahuchet, S. (1999) 'Aka Pygmies', in R. B. Lee and R. Daly (eds), *The Cambridge Encyclopaedia of Hunters and Gatherers*, pp. 190–4. Cambridge: Cambridge University Press.

Baker, C. A. (1962) 'Nyasaland, the History of its Export Trade', *Nyasaland Journal* 15(1): 7–35.

Banda, A. S. *et al.* (1991) *Beekeeping Handbook.* Mzuzu Malawi–German Beekeeping Development Project.

—— (1997) *Consolidation of Beekeeping Clubs.* Mzuzu: Dept National Parks and Wildlife Dept Border Zone Development Project.

—— (2001) Personal communication.

Banda, E. A and Morris, B. (1986) *Common Weeds of Malawi.* Zomba:

University of Malawi.

Banda, S. W. (1967) 'The Khungu of Lake Malawi', *Malawi Sci. Teacher* 3 (1): 68–70.

Barnard, A. (1992) *Hunters and Herders of Southern Africa.* Cambridge: Cambridge University Press.

Baron, S. (1972) *The Desert Locust.* London: Methuen.

Bateson, G. (1979) *Mind and Nature.* London: Fontana.

Bequaert, J. (1921) 'Insects as Food', *Journal American Museum Natural History* 21(2): 191–200.

Berg, S. and Critchlow, D. P. (2001) 'Honey Production Losses Due to Vandalism in Nykia National Park', *Nyala* 21: 41–7.

Berkes, F. (1999) *Sacred Ecology.* Philadelphia, PA: Taylor & Francis.

Berlin, B. (1972) 'Speculations on the Growth of Ethnobiological Nomenclature', *Language & Society* 1: 51–86.

—— (1992) *Ethnobiological Classification* Princeton, NJ: Princeton University Press.

Berlin, B, Breedlove, D. E. and Raven, P. H. (1974) *Principles of Tzeltal Plant Classification.* New York: Academic Press.

Berry, V. and Petty, C. (1992) *The Nyasaland Survey Papers 1958–1943.* London: Academy Books.

Berry, W. T. C. (1984) *Before the Wind of Change.* Suffolk: Halesworth Press.

Bird-David, N. (1999) ' "Animism" Revisited: Personhood, Environment and Relational Epistemology', *Current Anthropology* 40: 67–91.

Biscoe, J. (2001) Personal communication.

Bodenheimer, F. S. (1951) *Insects as Human Food.* The Hague: Junk.

Bookchin, M. (1990) *The Philosophy of Social Ecology.* Montreal: Black Rose Books.

Boucher, C. (2001) Personal communication.

Bowie, F. (2000) *The Anthropology of Religion.* Oxford: Blackwell.

Bowker, G. C. and Star, S. L. (1999) *Sorting Things Out.* Cambridge, MA: MIT Press.

Bricmont, J. (2001) *Sociology and Epistemology,* in J. Lopez and G. Potter (eds), *After Postmodernism.* London: Athlone Press.

Brown, C. H. (1979) 'Folk Zoological Life Forms: Their Universality and Growth', *American Anthropologist* 81: 791–817.

—— (1984) *Language and Living Things.* New Brunswick, NJ: Rutgers University Press.

—— (1985) 'Mode of Subsistence and Folkbiological Taxonomy', *Current Anthropology* 26: 43–64.

—— (1995) 'Lexical Acculturation and Ethnobiology: Utilitarianism versus Intellectualism', *Journal Linguistic Anthropology* 50(1): 51–64.

Brown, E. S. (1970) 'Control of the African Armyworm, Spodoptera exempta — an Appreciation of the Problem', *E. A. Agriculture & Forestry Journal* 35(3): 237–45.

Brown, H. D. (1979) 'Lake Chilwa and the Red Locust', in M. Kalk *et al.* (eds), *Lake Chilwa: Studies of Change in a Tropical Ecosystem*, pp. 282–5. The Hague: Junk.

Bunge, M. (1996) *Finding Philosophy in Social Science.* New Haven: Yale University Press.

—— (1999) *Dictionary of Philosophy.* New York: Prometheus Books.

Cansdale, G. S. (1970) *Animals of Bible Lands.* Exeter: Paternoster Press.

Capinera, J. L. (1993) 'Insects in Art and Religion: The American Southwest', *American Entomologist* 39: 221–9.

Carr, A. (1965) *Ulendo.* London: Heinemann.

Carr, S. (2001) Personal communication.

Carson, R. (1962) *Silent Spring.* London: Hamish Hamilton.

CCAM (1992) *Malawi's Traditional and Modern Cooking.* Blantyre: Blantyre Print.

Centre for Language Studies (2000) *Chinyanja Dictionary.* Blantyre: Dzuka Publications.

Chakanza, J. C. (1998) *Voices of Preachers in Protest.* Blantyre: Claim.

—— (2000) *Wisdom of the People.* Blantyre: Claim.

Chapman, J. D. (1995) *The Mulanje Cedar.* Blantyre: Society of Malawi.

Cherry, R. (1993) 'Australian Aborigines', *American Entomologist* 32: 8–13.

—— (1993) 'Insects in the Mythology of Native Americans', *American Entomologist* 39: 16–21.

Chilima, C. Z. (1997) *Biological Control of Conifer Aphids.* Zomba: FRIM Project Report.

Chimombo, S. (1988) *Malawian Oral Literature.* Zomba: University of Malawi.

—— (1989) 'Flora and Fauna in the Folksongs of the Chewa', Nyanja-Manganja Speaking Peoples *Nyala* 13: 3–20.

Chimwaza, B. M. (1982) 'Food and Nutrition in Malawi'. University of London: Ph.D. thesis.

Chongwe, E. H. (1999) 'Out of Season Tomato Production Tips', *Horticulture in Malawi* 4: 19–22.

Chorley, J. K. (1944) *A Report of a Visit to Southern Province of Malawi: Anti-Testse Fly Measures* Zomba: Government Print.

Clark, L. R. (1970) 'Analysis of Pest Situations through the Life System Approach', in R. Rabb and E. F. Guthrie (eds), *Concepts of Pest Management*. Raleigh, NC: North Carolina State University Press.

Clausen, L. N. (1954) *Insect Facts and Folklore.* New York: Macmillian.

Clauss, B. (1982) *Beekeeping Handbook*. Gaborone: Ministry of Agriculture

Cloudsley Thompson, J. L. (1976) *Insects and History*. New York: St Martins.

Clowes, M. St J. and Breakwell, W. L. (1998) *Zimbabwe Sugarcane Production Manual*. Chinedzi: Sugar Experimental Station.

Clowes, M. St J. *et al.* (1989) *Coffee Manual for Malawi*. Mulanje: Tea Research Foundation.

Coudenhove, H. (1925) *My African Neighbours*. London: Cape.

Crane, E. (1999) *The World History of Beekeeping and Honey Hunting*. London: Duckworth.

D'Andrade, R. (1995) *The Development of Cognitive Anthropology*. Cambridge: Cambridge University Press.

DeFoliart, G. R. (1975) 'Insects as A Source of Protein', *Bulletin Entomological Society of America* 21(3): 161–3.

—— (1989) 'The Human Use of Insects and Food and as Animal Feed', *Bulletin Entomological Society of America* 35: 22–35.

—— (1995) 'The Human Use of Insects and Food in Uganda', *Food Insects Newsletter* 8(1): 1–10.

—— (1999) 'Insects and Food: Why the Western Attitude is Important', *Annual Review Entomology* 44: 21–50.

De Meza, J. (1918) *The Common Ticks of Nyasaland*. Zomba: Dept. of Agriculture Bulletin No. 1.

Dempster, J. P. (1975) *Animal Population Ecology*. London: Academic Press.

Denis, L. (n.d.) *French Chichewa Dictionary*, 2 Vols. Mua: White Fathers.

Devitt, M. (1984) *Realism and Truth*. Oxford: Blackwell.

Dewey, J. (1929) *The Quest for Certainty*. Carbondale, IL: Illinois University Press.

—— (1929) *Experience and Nature*. New York: Dover.

Diamond, J. (1991) *The Rise and Fall of the Third Chimpanzee*. London: Random House.

Donovan, S. (1999) 'Termites', in M. Overton (ed.), *Bioresearch Nyika*. Lincolnshire: Wellborn.

Douglas, M. (1966) *Purity and Danger*. Harmondsworth: Penguin.

—— (1975) *Implicit Meanings*. London: Routledge and Kegan Paul.

—— (1990) 'The Pangolin Revisited: A New Approach to Animal Symbolism', in R. Willis (ed.), *Signifying Animals*. London: Unwin Hyman.

—— (1999) *Leviticus as Literature*. Oxford: Oxford University Press.

Dreyer, J. J. and Wehmeyer, A. S. (1982) 'On the Nutritive Value of Mopane Worms', *South African Journal Science* 8: 33–5

Drummond, H. (1889) *Tropical Africa*. London: Hodder & Stoughton.

Dubos, R. (1965) *Man Adapting*. New Haven, CT: Yale University Press.

Dudley, C. (1977) 'The Natural History of Dung Beetles', *Nyala* 3(1): 38–47.

—— (1979) 'The Dung Beetles of the Western Grasslands of the Chilwa Area', in M Kalk *et al.* (ed.) *Lake Chilwa: Studies of Change in a Tropical Ecosystem* pp. 286–7. The Hague: Junk.

—— (1996) 'How Many Species of Insects Does Malawi Have? *Nyala* 19: 13–16.

Dupré, J. (1981) 'Natural Kinds and Biological Taxa', *Philosophical Review* 90: 66–90.

Eccles, D. H. (1985) 'Lake Flies and Sardines: A Cautionary Note', *Biological Conservation* 33: 309–33.

Elais, N. (1994) *The Civilizing Process*. Oxford: Blackwell.

Ellen, R. (1978) *Nuaulu Settlement and Ecology*. The Hague: Martinus Nijhoff.

—— (1993) *Cultural Relations of Classification*. Cambridge: Cambridge University Press.

Ellert, H. (1984) *Material Culture of Zimbabwe*. Harare: Longman.

Epulani, F. (1996) *Kuweta Njuchi*. Limbe: Wildlife Society of Malawi.

Esbjerg, P. (1976) *Field Handbook of Malawian Forest Insects*. Copenhagen.

Evans, G. (1975) *The Life of Beetles*. London: Allen & Unwin.

Evans, H. E. (1970) *Life on a Little Known Planet*. London: Deutsch.

Evans-Pritchard, E. E. (1937) *Witchcraft, Oracles and Magic Among the Azande*. Oxford: Clarendon Press.

Fabre, J. H. (1911) *The Life and Loves of the Insect*. London: Black.

—— (1912) *The Life of the Caterpillar*. London: Hodder & Stoughton.

—— (1913) *The Life of the Fly*. London: Hodder & Stoughton.

—— (1916) *Hunting Wasps*. London: Hodder & Stoughton.

—— (1917) *The Life of the Grasshopper*. London: Hodder & Stoughton.

—— (1919) *The Mason Wasps*. London: Hodder & Stoughton.

Faulkner, H. (1868) *Elephant Haunts*. London, Hurst & Blackett.

Feijen, H. R. (1979) 'Pests of Rice in the Chilawa Plain', in M. Kalk *et al.* (eds) *Lake Chilwa: Studies of Change in a Tropical Ecosystem*, pp. 275–91. The Hague: Junk.

Ferry, L. (1995) *The New Ecological Order*. Chicago: Chicago University Press.

Foley, R. (1987) *Another Unique Species*. London: Longman.

Foran, W. R. (1958) *A Breath of the Wilds*. London: Hale.

Ford, J. (1971) *The Role of Trypanosomiasis in African Ecology*. Oxford: Clarendon Press.

Foster, J. B. (2000) *Marx's Ecology*. New York: Monthly Review Press.

French, R. (1994) *Ancient Natural History*. London: Routledge.

Frost, S. W. (1942) *Insect Life and Insect Natural History*. New York: Dover.

Geddes, A. M. (1990) *The Relative Importance of Crops Pests in Sub-Saharan Africa*. Chatham: Natural Resources Institute.

Gelfand, M. (1971) *Diet and Tradition in an African Culture*. London: Livingstone.

Gellner, E. (1973) *Cause and Meaning in the Social Sciences*. London: Routledge & Kegan Paul.

Gifford, D. (1965) *Butterflies of Malawi*. Blantyre: Society of Malawi.

Gillies, M. (2000) *Mayfly on the Stream of Time*. Hamsey: Messuage Books.

Goma, L. K. (1966) *The Mosquito*. London: Hutchinson.

Gomez, P. A., Hault, R. and Cullin, A. (1961) *Production de proteines animals, au Congo, Bulletin Agriculture Congo* 52(4): 689–815.

Goodwin, B. (1994) *How the Leopard Changed its Spots*. London: Orion Books.

Gotthelf, A. and Lennox, J. G. (eds) (1987) *Philosophical Issues in Aristotle's Biology*. Cambridge: Cambridge University Press.

Gould, S. J. (1980) *The Panda's Thumb*. London: Penguin Books.

Gray, E. (1939) 'Some Riddles of the Nyanja People', *Bantu Studies* 13: 251–91.

—— (1944) 'Some Proverbs of the Nyanja People', *African Studies* 3(3): 101–28.

Green, S. (2001) 'The Caterpillar Coin and a Cautionary Tale', *Antenna* 25(3): 157–9.

Grice, W. J. (1990) *Tea Planter's Handbook*. Mulanje: Tea Research Foundation.

Griffin, D. R. (1992) *Animal Minds*. Chicago: University Chicago Press.

Hamilton, III, W. J. (1987) 'Omnivorous Primate Diets and Human Overconsumption of Meat', in M. Harris and E. B. Ross (eds) *Food and Evolution*, pp. 117–32. Philadelphia: Temple University Press.

Hammond, P. (1992) 'Species Inventory', in B. Goombridge (ed.) *Global Biodiversity*. London: Chapman & Hall.

Hargreaves, B. (1978) 'The Raintree of Misuku Society', *Malawi Journal* 31(1): 36–9.

Harris, M. (1999) *Theories of Culture in Postmodern Times*. London: Sage.

Hartmann, T. (1999) *The Lost Hours of Ancient Sunlight*. London: Hodder & Stoughton.

Hattingh, C. C. (1941) *The Biology and Ecology of the Army Worm in South Africa*. Pretoria: Dept Agriculture Bulletin No 217.

Hays, T. E. (1983) 'Ndumba Folkbiology and General Principles of Ethnobiological Classification and Namenclature', *American Anthropology* 85: 592–611.

Henderson, J. and Harrington, J. P. (1914) *Ethnozoology of the Tewa Indians*. Washington, DC: Smithsonian Institute Bulletin No. 56.

Hetherwick, A. (1902) *A Handbook of Yao Language*. London: SPCK.

Hogue, C. L. (1987) 'Cultural Entomology', *Annual Review Entomology* 32: 181–99.

Holden, S. (1991) 'Edible Caterpillars – A Potential Agroforestry Resource?', *Food Insect's Newsletter* 4(2): 3–4.

Holt, V. M. (1885) *Why Not Eat Insects?* Farringdon: Classey.

Holy, L. (1986) *Strategies and Norms in a Changing Matrilineal Society*. Cambridge: Cambridge University Press.

Honderich, T. (ed.) (1995) *The Oxford Companion to Philosophy*. Oxford: Oxford University Press.

Hooper, A. (1989) 'Mutualism Between Man and Honey Guide', in J. Clutton-Brock (ed.) *The Walking Larder*. London: Unwin Hyman.

Hovington, A. [*Bibi Minus-Habens*] (1971) *On the African Way of Life Around the Southwest Shores of Lake Malawi*. Mua: White Fathers.

Howard, L. O. (1915) 'The Edibility of Insects', *Journal Econ. Entomology* 8(6): 549.

Howell, S. and Willis. R. (eds) (1989) *Societies at Peace*. London: Routledge.

Hoyt, E. and Schultz, &. (1999) *Insect Lives*. Edinburgh: Mainstream Publications.

Hunn, E. (1975) 'A Measure of Degree of Correspondence of Folk to ScientificBiological Classification', *American Ethnologist* 2: 309–27.

—— (1977) *Tzeltal Folk Zoology*. New York: Academic Press.

—— (1982) 'The Utilitarian Factor in Folk Biology Classification', *American Anthropology* 84: 830–47.

—— (1993) 'The Ethnobiological Foundation for Traditional Ecological Knowledge', in N. M. Williams and G. Baines (eds) *Traditional Ecological Knowledge*, pp. 16–20. Canberra: Australian National University.

—— (1999) 'Size as Indicating the Recognition of Biodiversity in Folkbiological Classification', in D. L. Medin and S. Atran (eds) *Folkbiology*, pp. 47–69. Cambridge, MA: MIT Press.

Ichikawa, M. (1981) 'Ecological and Sociological Importance of Honey to the Mbuti Net Hunters, Eastern Zaire', *African Studies Monographs* 1: 55–68.

—— (1987) 'Food Restrictions of the Mbuti Pygmies, Eastern Zaire', *African Studies Monographs* 6: 97–121.

Illgner, P. and Nel, E. (2000) 'The Geography of Edible Insects in Sub-Sahara Africa: A Study of the Mopane Caterpillar', *Geographic Journal* 166(4): 336–51.

Imms, A. D. (1947) *Insect Natural History*. London: Collins.

Ingold, T. (ed.) (1994) *Compendium Encyclopaedia of Anthropology*. London: Routledge.

—— (2000) *The Perception of the Environment*. London: Routledge.

Ironside, D. A. and Fero, W. K. (1993) *Macadamia Pests and Disease Management in Malawi*. Bvumbwe Dept of Agriculture.

Irvine, K. (1995) 'Ecology of the Lakefly, Chaoborus Edulis', in A. Menz (ed.) *The History Potential and Productivity of the Pelogic Zone of Lake Malawi*, pp. 109–44. Chatham: Natural Resources Institute.

Johnson, S. A. (1995) *A Visitor's Guide to Nyika National Park, Malawi*. Blantyre: Mbabzi Book Trust.

Johnson, W. P. (1922) *Chinyanja Proverbs*. Cardiff: Smith Bros.

Johnston, H. H. (1897) *British Central Africa*. New York: Negro University Press.

Jones, S. *et al.* (ed.) (1992) *The Cambridge Encyclopaedia of Human Evolution*. Cambridge: Cambridge University Press.

Kalk, M. *et al.* (ed.) (1979) *Lake Chilwa: Studies of Change in a Tropical Ecosystem*. The Hague: Junk.

Kalonde, K. (2000) *Mankhwala a Zitsamba*. Lilongwe: Sunshine Publications.

Kesby, J. (1979) 'Rangi Classification of Animals and Plants', in R. F. Ellen and D. Reason (eds) *Classifications in Their Social Context*. New York: Academic Press.

Kevan D. K. McE. (1974) *The Land of the Grasshoppers: Being Some Verses on Grigs*. Toronto: Memoir of the Hynan Entomological Museum, McGill University.

Khonga, E. B. (1997) *Integrated Pest Management of Soil Pests in Malawi*. Zomba: Chancellor College.

Killick, J. (2001) Personal communications.

King, M. and King, E. (1992) *The Story of Medicine and Disease in Malawi*. Limbe: Mountfond Press.

Kjekshus, H. (1977) *Ecology Control and Economic Development in East African History*. London: Heinemann.

Kropotkin, P. (1902) *Mutual Aid: A Factor in Evolution*. Harmondsworth: Penguin Books.

Kumakanga, S. L. (1975) *Nzeru za Kale*. Blantyre: Dzuka.

Kumar, R. (1984) *Insect Pest Control with Special Reference to African Agriculture*. London: Arnold.

Kuper, A. (1994) 'Culture, Identity and the Project of Cosmopolitan

Anthropology', *Man* 29: 537–54.

Lamborn, W. A. (1926) *Memorandum on Game Destruction in Relation to* Glossina Morsitans. Zomba: MNA 51/665/26.

Lambrecht, F. L. (1970) 'Aspects of Evolution and Ecology of Tsetse Flies and Trypanosomiasis on Prehistoric African Environments', in J. D Fage and R. A Oliver (eds) *Papers on African Prehistory*, pp. 87–96. Cambridge: Cambridge University Press.

Latham, P. (1999) 'Edible Caterpillars of the Bas Congo Region of the Democratic Republic of the Congo', *Antenna* 23(3): 134–39.

Lauck, J. E. (1998) *The Voice of the Infinite in the Small*. Mill Spring: Swan Raven.

Laufer, B. (1927) 'Insect Musicians and Cricket Champions in China', *Natural History* 22: 1–27.

Laws, R. (1934) *Reminiscences of Livingstonia*. Edinburgh: Oliver & Boyd.

Lea, A. (1938) *Investigations on the Red Locusts in PEA and Nyasaland in 1935*. Pretoria: Dept. Agriculture Bulletin No. 176.

Leach, E. R. (1964) 'Anthropological Aspects of Language: Animal Categories and Verbal Abuse', in E. Lennenberg (ed.), *New Directions in the Study of Language*. Cambridge, MA: MIT Press.

Lee, R. B. (1979) *The !Kung San*. Cambridge: Cambridge University Press.

Lee, R. F. (1971) *Preliminary Annotated History of Malawian Forest Insects*. Zomba: FRIM Record No. 40.

—— (1972) *A Preliminary Account of the Biology and Ecology of Plagiotriptus sp.* Zomba: FRIM Record No. 48.

Lennox, J. G. (2001) *Aristotle's Philosophy of Biology*. Cambridge: Cambridge University Press.

Livingstone, D. and Livingstone, C. (1865) *Narrative of an Expedition to the Zambezi and its tributaries 1858–64*. London: J Murray.

Loveridge, A. (1954) *I Drank the Zambezi*. London: Lutterworth Press.

Luhanga, W. W. (1988) 'Armyworm Outbreaks and Control in Malawi', Bvumbwe: *Agricultural Research Studies Newsletter* 3: 69–72.

Lyons, M. (1992) *The Colonial Disease*. Cambridge: Cambridge University Press.

McCracken, J. (1982) 'Experts and Expertise in Colonial Malawi', *African Affairs* 81: 101–16.

—— (1987) 'Colonialism, Capitalism and The Ecological Crisis in Malawi — a Reassessment', in D. Anderson and R. Grove (eds), *Conservation in Africa*. Cambridge: Cambridge University Press.

MacDonald, R. J. (ed.) (1975) *From Nyasaland to Malawi*. Nairobi: East African Publishing House.

McGregor, J. (1995) 'Gathered Produce in Zimbabwe's Communal Areas: Changing Resource Availability and Use', *Ecology Food Nutrition* 33: 163–93.

McKelvey, J. L. Jr (1973) *Man Against Tsetse! Struggle for Africa*. Ithaca, NY: Cornell University Press.

Mackenzie, J. M. (1930) 'Means of Defence in Insects', *Journal Bombay Natural History Society* 33: 100.

McNeill, W. H. (1976) *Plagues and People*. Garden City, NY: Anchor Press.

MacPherson, D. W. K. (1973) 'Wild Life of the Central Region', *Society of Malawi Journal* 20(2):48–66.

Majawa A. O. (1981) *Phoracantha Beetle in Malawi*. Zomba: FRIM Leaflet No. 4.

Malaisse, F. (1978) 'The Miombo Ecosystem', Paris: UNESCO/FAO *Natural Research* 14: 589–606.

Malaisse, F. and Lognay, G. (2000) 'Le Chenilles Combustibles d'Afrique Tropical', *Colloque: Insectes et tradition orale*. Paris.

Malinowski, B. (1974) *Magic, Science and Religion and Other Essays*. London: Souvenir Press.

Manda, D. R. (1985) 'Pesticide Use by Cash Crops Farmers in Malawi', in Nairobi: USAID, *Workshop Proceedings on Pest Management*, pp. 31–3.

Mandala, E. C. (1990) *Work and Control in a Peasant Economy*. Madison, WI: University of Wisconsin Press.

Marcus, G. E. (1995) 'The Redesign of Ethnography After the Critique of its Rhetoric', in R Goodman and W. R Fisher (eds) *Rethinking Knowledge*. Albany, NY: State University New York Press.

Margulis, L. and Sagan, D. (1986) *Microcosmos*. Berkeley, CA: University of California Press.

Marshall, L. (1976) *The !Kung of Nyae Nyae*. Cambridge, MA: Harvard University Press.

Massana, J. M. (2000) *Chichewa-English Dictionary*. Dowa: Franciscans.

Matson, B. A. (1959) *An Investigation into the Livestock Problems of the Lower Shire Valley of Nyasaland with Particular Reference to the Disease Trypanosomiasis*. Zomba: Dept. Veterinary Science.

Matthews, A. and Wilshaw, C. (1992) *Fodya: The Malawi Tobacco Handbook*. Blantyre: Central Africana Ltd.

Matthews, G. A. and Whellan, J. A. (1974) *Malawi Crop Protection Handbook*. Lilongwe: Ministry of Agriculture.

Maugham, R. C. F. (1914) *Wild Game in Zambezia*. London: Murray.

Mayr, E. (1982) *The Growth of Biological Thought*. Cambridge, MA: Harvard University Press.

—— (1988) *Towards a New Philosophy of Biology*. Cambridge, MA: Harvard University Press.

Medin, D. L and Atran, S. (eds) 1999 *Folkbiology*. Cambridge, MA: MIT Press.

Meke, G. S. (1995a) *Termite Control Options for Trees on Farms in Malawi: A Review*. Zomba: FRIM Report No 95003.

—— (1995b) *A Preliminary Study to Appraise the Importance of Edible Caterpillars and Potential for Expanding this Resource in Some Ngoni Villages around Chimaliro Forest Reserve*. Zomba: FRIM Report.

Meke, G. S. *et al.* (2000) *Edible Insects in Tsamba Forest Reserve and Surrounding Areas*. Zomba: FRIM Report.

Menzel, P. and D'Alvisio, F. (1998) *Man Eating Bugs*. Berkeley: Ten Speed Press.

Middleton, J. (1960) *Lugbara Religion*. Oxford: Oxford University Press.

Mills, D. Y. (1911) *What We Do in Nyasaland*. London: UMCA.

Milton, K. (2002) *Loving Nature*. London: Routledge.

Mitchell, B. L. and Steele, B. (1956) *A Report on the Distribution of Tsetse Flies in Nyasaland*. Zomba: Government Press.

Mithen, S. (1996) *The Prehistory of the Mind*. London: Thames & Hudson.

Mkanda, F. X and Munthali, S. M. (1994) 'Public Attitudes and Needs Around Kasungu National Park', *Malawi Biodiversity and Conservation* 3: 29–44.

Morris, B. (1970) 'Nature and Origin of Brachystegia Woodland', *Commonwealth Forestry Review* 49: 155–8.

—— (1976) 'Whither the Savage Mind? Notes on the Natural Taxonomies of a Hunting and Gathering People', *Man* 11: 542–59.

—— (1979) 'Symbolism and Ideology: Thoughts Around Navaho Taxonomy and Symbolism', in R. F. Ellen and D. Reason (eds), *Classifications in Their Social Context*, pp. 117–38. New York: Academic Press.

—— (1980) 'Folk Classification', *Nyala* 6: 83–93.

—— (1982) *Forest Traders*. London: Athlone Press.

—— (1984) 'The Pragmatics of Folk Classification', *Journal of Ethnobiology* 41(1): 45–60.

—— (1987a) *Anthropological Studies of Religion*. Cambridge: Cambridge University Press.

—— (1987b) *Common Mushrooms of Malawi*. Oslo: Fungi Flora.

—— (1989) 'Notes of the Dualistic Worldview of Tim Ingold', *Critique of Anthropology* 9/(3) 71–9.

—— (1994) *Anthropology of the Self*. London: Pluto Press.

—— (1995) 'Wildlife Depredations in Malawi: The Historical Dimension', *Nyala* 18: 17–24.

—— (1996) *Chewa Medical Botany*. Hamburg: Lit I. A. I.

—— (1997) 'In Defence of Realism and Truth', *Critique of Anthropology* 17(3): 313–40.

—— (1998) *The Power of Animals*. Oxford: Berg.

—— (2000) *Animals and Ancestors*. Oxford: Berg.

—— (2001a) 'Wildlife Conservation in Malawi', *Environment and History* 7(3): 357–72.

—— (2001b) 'Kropotkin's Metaphysics of Nature', *Anarchist Studies* 9: 165–80.

—— (2002) 'Nyau and Rock Art in Malawi', *Society of Malawi Journal*.

Morris, B. and Patel, I. H. (1994) 'Ulimbo: Morphological and Pragmatic Aspects of Plants Classification in Malawi', in Proc. XII Meeting Aetfat, *Malawi* 1: 103–111.

Moyo, C. C. *et al.* (1998) *Current Status of Cassava and Sweet Potato Production and Utilisation in Malawi*. Bvumbwe: Dept Agriculture.

Msamba, F. and Killick, D. (eds) (1992) *Kasunga and Kaluluma Oral Traditions*. Phoenix, AZ: Dept Agriculture.

Mtambo, C. (1999) 'The Fight Against The Red Spider Mite (*Tetranychus*) in Malawi', *Horticulture in Malawi* 4: 23–4.

Mtambo, C. *et al.* (2000) *Control of the Diamond-back Moth (*Plutella Xylostella*) Using Botanical Pesticides in Malawi*. Lilongwe: Malawi-German Plant Protection Project.

Munthali, D. C. *et al.* (eds) (1990) *Farmer's Perceptions of Insect Disease and Weed Problems in Small-scale farms*. Zomba: Chancellor College, Soil Pests Project Report No. 1.

—— (1992) *The Major Insect Pests, Plant Diseases and Weeds Affecting Subsistence Farmers' Crops in Southern region of Malawi*. Zomba: Chancellor College Soil Pests Project Report No. 2.

—— (1993) *Relative Importance of Different Insect Pests, Plant Diseases and Weed Species Affecting Farmers' Crops in Southern Malawi*. Zomba: Chancellor College Soil Pests Project Report No. 3.

Munthali, S. M, and Mughogho, D. C. (1992) 'Economic Incentives for Conservation: Beekeeping and Saturniidae Caterpillar Utilisation by Rural Communities', *Biodiversity & Conservation* 1: 143–54.

Mvula, E. T. (1976) 'An Appendix of Malawi Riddles', *Kalulu* 1(1) 1–16.

Mvula, L. V. and Nyirenda, G. K. (1995) *Preliminary Investigation into the Incidence of Bean Flies (*Ophiomyia spp.*) and Their Parasitism in Select Grain Granaries in Malawi*. Lilongwe: SADC Workshop Proceedings.

Nash, T. A. M. (1969) *Africa's Bane: The Tsetse Fly*. London: Collins.

Newman, L. H. (1965) *Man and Insects*. London: Aldus Books.

Nkouka, O. (1987) 'Les Insectes Comestibles dans les Sociétés d'Afrique

Centrale', *Muntu* 6: 171–8.

Nonaka, K. (1996) 'Ethnoentomology of the Central Kalahari San', *African Studies Monograph* 22: 29–46.

NRI (Natural Resource Institute) (1992) *A Synopsis of Integrated Pest Management on Developing Countries in the Tropics.* Chatham: NRI.

—— (1996) *Renewable Natural Resources Profile: Malawi.* Chatham: NRI.

Orr, A. *et al.* (2000) *Learning and Livelihoods: The Experience of the FSIPM Project in Southern Malawi.* Greenwich: University of Greenwich IPM Project.

Pachai, B. (ed.) (1972) *The Early History of Malawi.* London: Longman.

—— (1973) *Malawi: The History of a Nation.* London: Longman.

Pager, H. (1973) 'Rock Paintings in Southern Africa Showing Bees and Honey Hunting', *Bee World* 54: 61–8.

Panos Institute (1993) *Grasshoppers and Locusts: The Plague of the Sahel.* London: Panos Institute.

Patterson, J. (1984) *Malaria.* Zomba: Chancellor College Seminar Paper No. 42.

Peham, A. P. K. (1996) *Non-Timber Products as Miombo Resources: A Malawian Case Study.* Vienna: University für Bodenkultur.

Peigler, R. S. (1994) *Non-Sericultural Uses of Moth Cocoons in Diverse Cultures.* Denver, CO: *Proc. Mus. Nat. Hist* 3(5): 1–20.

Perchonock, N. and Werner, O. (1969) 'Navaho Systems of Classification', *Ethnology* 8: 229–42.

Peterson, A. L. (2001) *Being Human.* Berkeley, CA: University of California Press.

Phiri, D. D. (1982) *From Nguni to Ngoni.* Limbe: Popular Publications.

Phiri, G. S. N. (1995) 'Interaction of the Spotted Stem Borer with Some Alternative Hosts and a Larval Parasitoid in Malawi'. University of Reading: Ph.D. thesis.

—— (2000) *Malawi Cassana Green Mite Project.* Lilongwe: Malawi-Germany Plant Protection Project Report.

Pickstone, J. V. (2000) *Ways of Knowing.* Manchester: Manchester University Press.

Pike, J. G. and Rimmington, G. T. (1965) *Malawi: A Geographical Study.* Oxford: Oxford University Press.

Pinhey, E. (1962) *Hawk Moths of Central and Southern Africa.* Cape Town: Longmans.

—— (1966) 'Checklist of Dragonflies From Malawi', *Arnouldia* 2(33): 1–24.

—— (1972) *Emperor Moths of South and South Central Africa.* Cape Town: Struik.

—— (1975) *Moths of Southern Africa*. Cape Town: Tafelberg.

—— (1979) 'Additions and Corrections to 1966 Checklist of Dragonflies from Malawi', *Arnoldia* 8(38): 1–14.

Pollock, N. H. (1969) *The Struggle Against Sleeping Sickness in Nyasaland and Northern Rhodesia 1900–1922*. Athens, OH: Ohio University Paper on International Studies No. 5.

Posey, D. A. (1983) 'Ethnobiology as an Emic Guide to Cultural Systems: The Case of the Insect and the Kayapo Indians', *Rev. Brazil Zool.* 1: 135–44.

Powell, W. (1977) *Plagiotriotus Species*. Zomba: FRIM leaflet No. 2.

Preuss, A. (1975) *Science and Philosophy in Aristotle's Biological Works*. New York: Hildesheim.

Quin, P. J. (1959) *Foods and Feeding Habits of the Pedi*. Johannesburg: Witwatersrand University Press.

Randall, R. A. and Hunn, E. S. (1984) 'Do Life Forms Evolve or do Uses For Life? Some Doubts About Brown's Universal Hypothesis', *American Ethnology* 11: 329–47.

Rangeley, W. H. J. (1948) 'Notes on Chewa Tribal Law', *Nyasaland Journal* 1(3): 5–68.

Ransford, O. (1983) *Bid the Sickness Cease*. London: Murray.

Rattan, P. S. (1992) 'Pest and Disease Control in Africa', in K. C. Wilson and M. N Clifford (eds), *Tea: Cultivation to Consumption*, pp. 331–52. London: Chapman & Hall.

Rattray, R. S. (1907) *Some Folklore Stories and Songs in Chinyanja*. London: SPCK.

Riley, C. V. (1876) *Eighth Annual Report on the Noxious, Beneficial and Other Insects of the State of Missouri*. Jefferson City: Regan & Carter.

Ritchie, J. M. and Muyaso F. (eds) (2000) *Integrated Pest Management Project: Selected Reports 1996–2000*, 3 Vols. Bvumbwe: Agricultural Research Station.

Robertson, H. G. (1997) *Insects in African Economy and Environment*. Pretoria: Entomological Society of Southern Africa.

Roy, M. N. (1940) *Materialism*. Delhi: Ajanta.

Salaun, N. (1978) *Chichewa: An Intensive Course*. Likuni: White Fathers.

Sanderson, G. M. (1954) *A Dictionary of the Yao Language*. Zomba: Government Print.

Sands, W. A. and Wilkinson, W. (1954) *A Report on a Survey of the Termites of Nyasaland*. Muguga: Termite Research Unit.

Schneider, D. (1976) *Notes Towards a Theory of Culture*, in K. Basso and H. Selbey (eds), *Meaning in Anthropology*. Albuquerque: University of New Mexico Press.

Schoffeleers, J. M. (1997) *Religion and the Dramatisation of Life*.

Blantyre: Claim.

Schoffeleers, J. M. and Roscoe, A. A. (1985) *Land of Fire*. Limbe: Popular Publications.

Schulten, G. G. M. (1969) *Maize Storage Problems in Malawi*. Zomba: Science Conference Report.

Schweid, R. (1999) *The Cockroach Papers*. New York: Four Walls.

Scott, D. C. (1929) *Dictionary of the Nyanja Language*. London: USCL.

Scudder, T. (1962) *The Ecology of a Gwembe Tonga*. Manchester: Manchester University Press.

Searle, J. (1999) *Mind, Language and Society*. London: Weidenfeld & Nicolson.

Selous, F. C. (1881) *A Hunter's Wanderings in Africa*. London: Bently 1908 *African Nature Notes and Reminiscences* London: Macmillan.

Service, M. W. (1996) *Medical Entomology for Students*. London: Chapman & Hall.

Seton, E. T. (1898) *Wild Animals I Have Known*. New York: Scribners.

Shaxson, A., Dixon, P. and Walker, J. (1974) *The Cook Book*. Zomba: Government Printer.

Sherry, B. and Ridgeway, A. J. (1984) *A Field Guide to Lengwe National Park*. Limbe: Mountfield Press.

Silberbauer, G. B. (1981) *Hunter and Habitat in the Central Kalahari Desert*. Cambridge: Cambridge University Press.

Silow, C. A. (1976) *Edible and Other Insects of Mid-Western Zambia*. Almquist & Wiksell, Uppsala: Studies in Ethnoentomology.

Singano, E. and Roscoe, A. A. (eds) (1980) *Tales of Old Malawi*. Limbe: Popular Publications.

Singh, S. R. (2001) *Mulanje Cedar and Cypress Aphid Project*. Newcastle: University of Newcastle Report of Expedition to Mulanje.

Skaife, S. H. (1955) *Dwellers in Darkness*. London: Longman.

—— (1979) *African Insect Life*. Cape Town: Struik.

Skinner, J. D. and Smithers, R. H. N. S. (1990) *The Mammals of the Southern African Subregion*. Pretoria: University of Pretoria.

Smee, C. (1923–38) *Reports of the Entomologist*. Zomba: Annual Reports of the Dept. Agriculture (MNA).

—— (1936) 'Nyasaland Tea and its Pests and Diseases', *Nyasaland Tea Association Quarterly Journal* 1(2) 1–5.

—— (1939) 'Gelatine Grubs in Tea in Nyasaland', *Nyasaland Tea Association Quarterly Journal* 4(1): 13–15, 2: 14–18.

—— (1940) *Pests and Diseases of Cotton in Nyasaland*. Zomba: Dept. Agriculture (MNA).

—— (1941) 'Notes of the Locust Outbreak of 1893–1910', *Nyasaland Tea Association Quarterly Journal* 1(1): 15–22.

99 (1943) 'Army Worms or Swarming Caterpillars (*Laphygama Exempta*)', *Nyasaland Tea Association Quarterly Journal* 3(4) 1–14.

—— (1945) 'Bagworms on Tea', *Nyasaland Tea Association Quarterly Journal* 5(1): 1–5.

Smit, B. (1964) *Insects in Southern Africa: How to Control Them*. Cape Town: Oxford University Press.

Sokal, A. and Bricmont, J. (1999) *Intellectual Impostures*. New York: Picador.

Soko, B. J. (1994) *Contes et Legendes du Malawi*. Zomba: Chancellor College Dept French Studies.

Stannus, H. (1922) 'The Wayao of Nyasaland Harvard', *African Studies*, III: 229–372.

Swan, L. A. (1964) *Beneficial Insects*. New York: Harper & Row.

Sweeney, R. C. H. (1961–1963) 'Insects Pests of Cotton in Nyasaland', 4 Vols. Zomba: *Dept Agriculture Bulletins* 18–21.

—— (1962) 'Insect Pests of Stored Products in Nyasaland', Zomba: Dept of Agriculture.

—— (1964) *Insect Pests of Cotton*. Limbe: Farmer's Marketing Board.

—— (1964) *Red Locusts in Nyasaland.* Zomba: Government Press.

—— (1965) 'The Mosquito Bugs of Malawi (*Helopeltis spp*)', *Farm & Forester* 6(4): 11–19.

—— (1966) *The Scurrying Bush*. London: Chatto and Windus.

—— (1970) *Animal Life of Malawi, Vol. 1, Invertebrates*. Beograd: Institute for Publication. Belgrade.

Talbot, I. (1956) 'Mfumba Sleeping Bugs', *Nyasaland Journal* 9(1): 72–3.

TAM (Tea Association of Malawi) (1991) *A Handbook of the Tea Industry of Malawi*. Blantyre: Central Africana.

Terry, P. T. (1962) 'The Rise of the African Cotton Industry in Nyasaland 1902–1918', *Nyasaland Journal* 15(1): 59–71.

Thindwa, H. P. (1999a) 'Red Locust Population in Malawi 1988–1998', *Insect Science Applic.* 19/4: 351–4.

—— (1999) 'Diamond-back Moth (*Plutella Xylostella*) Identification and Control', *Horticulture in Malawi* 4: 25–6.

Turnbull, C. M. (1965) *Wayward Servants*. New York: Natural History Press.

Turner, V. W. (1975) *Revelation and Divination in Ndemba Ritual*. Ithaca: Cornell University Press.

Uvarov, B. P. (1928) *Locusts and Grasshoppers: A Handbook for Their Study and Control*. London: Imperial Bureau of Entomology.

Vail, L. (1977) 'Ecology and History: The Example of Eastern Zambia', *Journal Southern African Studies* 3(2): 129–56.

—— (1983) 'The Political Economy of East-Central Africa', in D. Birmigham and P. M. Martin (eds), *History of Central Africa, Vol. 2.* London: Longman.

Van Alebeek, F. A. (1989) *Integrated Pest Management.* Wageningen: Dept of Entomology.

Van Breugel, J. W. (2001) *Chewa Traditional Religion.* Blantyre: Claim.

Van Emden, H. F. (1989) *Pest Control and its Ecology.* London: Arnold.

Vane-Wright, R. I. (1991) 'Why Not Eat Insects?', *Bulletin Entomological Research* 81: 1–4.

Van Huis, A. (1996) 'The Traditional Use of Arthropods in Sub-Saharan Africa', Amsterdam: *Proc. Exp. & Appl. Entomolgy* 7: 3–20.

Van Kessel, A. C. (1989) *Dzedzere: Dzedzere Salingana N'Kugweratu.* Chipate: White Fathers.

Van Onselen, C. (1972) 'Reaction to Rinderpest in Southern Africa', *Journal African History* 13: 473–88.

Vaughan, M. (1991) *Curing Their Ills.* Cambridge: Policy Press.

Wallis, J. P. R. (1956) *The Zambezi Expedition of David Livingstone 1858–1863.* London: Chatto & Windus.

Waldbauer, G. (1996) *Insects Through the Seasons.* Cambridge, MA: Harvard University Press.

Whellan, J. A (1956) 'The Armyworm and its Control', *Nyasaland Farmer & Forester* 3(2): 48–49.

—— (1961) 'The Red Locust: A Forgotten Menace', *Rhodesia Agricultural Journal* 6(1)4: 67–9.

—— (1971) 'Agricultural Ethnology', Zomba: *Annual Report Department Agriculture.*

—— (1975) 'The Acridoidea of Malawi: An Annotated Checklist', *Acrida* 4: 105–22.

Whitehead, A. N. (1929) *Process and Reality.* New York: Free Press.

Williamson, J. (1941) 'Nyasaland Native Foods', *Nyasaland Times*, pp. 1–25.

—— (1975) *Useful Plants of Malawi.* Zomba: University of Malawi.

—— (1992) *Insects* in V. Berry and C. Petty (eds), The Nyasaland Survey Papers 1858–1943, pp. 270–3.

Wills, C. (1996) *Plagues.* London: Harper Collins.

Winston, M. L. (1997) *Nature Wars: People vs Pests.* Cambridge, MA: Harvard University Press.

Woodburn, J. C. (1968) 'An Introduction to Hadza Ecology', in R. B Lee and I. Devore (eds), *Man The Hunter*, pp. 49–55r. Chicago: Aldine.

Wyman, L. C and Bailey, F. L. (1964) *Navaho Indian Ethnoentomology.* Albuquerque: University of New Mexico, Publ. Anthropology No. 12.

Yellen, J. E and Lee, R. B. (1976) 'The Dobe-Du/Da Environment in', R.

B. Lee and I. DeVore (eds), *Kalahari Hunter-Gatherers*, pp. 27–46. Cambridge, MA: Harvard University Press.

Zinsser, H. (1934) *Rats, Lice and History*. London: MacMillian.

Index

Abram, D. 16
African lunar moth, 275
African people, 57
agriculture, 109–11
alien empire, 181–2
ant, 2, 39, 45, 106, 196
    as pest, 139
    proverbs, 201–2
    riddles, 206–7
antesia bug, 137
antlion, 243
aphid, 152–3
Aristotle, 15–17, 53–4
armoured ground cricket, 33,
    235–6
armyworm, 77, 111–13, 264
arrow poison, 51
arthropod, 3, 13
Atran, S., 5, 14, 19
Australian Aborigines, 50, 52, 186

bagworm, 4, 136, 191, 269–70
Banda, A., 96
Banda, W., 75
Bateson, G., 184
beanfly, 120
beans, 10, 72, 118–21
bedbugs, 10, 32, 147, 200, 242
bee, 10, 38–9, 42, 54, 93–106,
    279–82
    in folktale, 194
    proverbs, 201
    riddles, 206

Beekeeper's Association of
    Malawi, 104
bee-keeping, 10, 96–8, 100–3,
    106–8
bee-keeping clubs, 103–5
beeswax, 97, 100
beetle, 2, 21, 33–4, 41, 45, 50,
    72–3, 85, 244–56
    as pests, 116–17, 128
Bell, R., 101
bemberezi, see carpenter bee
Berkes, F., 19
Berlin, B., 13, 17
Berry, W., 56
Bible, 96
Bird-David, N., 14
Biscoe, J., 137
Blantyre, 83, 119, 151
black army ant, 282–3
black fly, 262
blister beetle, 192, 252
blue monkey, 49
Boatman, A., 133
Bodenheimer, F.S., 50, 53–5
bollworm, 128–30, 139, 264–7
bololo, see cricket
bongololo, see millipede
botanical insecticides, 131, 144
Botswana, 83
Boucher, C., 214
bow-legged bug, 72, 121, 239–40
Brachystegia woodland, 58, 70,
    82–3, 88, 95–7, 107

Broadhead, R., 162
Brown, C. 23–5
Buchanan, J., 138
bug, 10, 31–2, 39, 69–70, 239–43
Bunge, M., 4
butterfly, 35–6, 41, 200, 205, 214,
   262–3
bvimbvi, see armoured ground
   cricket
bwanoni, see common katydid

cabbage, 131–3
carpenter bee, 280–2
carpenter moth, 135
Carr, A., 74, 76, 114
Carson, R., 142, 183
Cartesian philosophy, 8
cassava, 10, 121–2
cassava green mite, 121–2
cassava mealy bug, 122
castor oil, 41
caterpillar, 10, 36–7, 57, 76–7,
   81–90, 112, 264–7
   as pests, 112–15
   collecting, 86–7
   cooking, 82
   ecology, 85–6
   nutritional value, 88
cedar forest, 10
centipede, 287
chacma baboon, 49
Chambe plateau, 151
chansasi, see crested grasshopper
chiboli, see cricket
chidyamamina, see yellow-winged
   grasshopper
chikodzera, see ground beetle
chilumphabere, see death's head
   hawk moth
Chilima, C., 153
chimalasuga, see sugar ant
Chimaliro forest, 6, 76, 82

Chimombo, S., 193
chimphanga, see horse fly
Chinyangala, S., 43
chirombo (wild animal), 25
chiswambiya, see mantid
chiswe, see termite
chitete, see grasshopper
chiyabwe, see stinging
   grasshopper
cicada, 25, 44, 53, 70, 242
   collection 70–1
cockroach, 10, 27, 41, 44, 198,
   210, 218–19
   as pest, 145–6, 161
coffee, 136–7
coffee locust, 226
coffee pests, 137–8
coffee stem borer, 137
colonial experts, 124
common katydid, 67, 234–5
concept of anomaly, 46
cotton, 10, 123–30
cotton jassid, 127–8, 243
cotton pests, 123–30
cotton stainer bug, 127, 240
crested grasshopper, 227
cricket, 10, 31, 39, 41–4, 55–6,
   69, 237–8
   collecting, 69
   riddles, 203–4
cultural entomology, 1, 50
cutworm, 115

Darwin, C., 54
death's head hawk moth, 37, 80,
   271
deductive logic, 15
DeFoliart, G., 50, 54–5
Denis, L., 7, 76, 80
Dewey, J., 15, 145
Diamond, J., 51
diamond back moth, 132, 267

dimba gardens, 130–1
Diodorus of Sicily, 64
Divinity, 213
Domasi Valley, 130, 145
Douglas, M., 4, 46
dragonfly, 20, 26–7, 44, 218
Drummond, H., 168
Dudley, C. 2, 217
dung beetle, 246
dusky surface beetle, 138
dzodzwe, see blister beetle
dzombe, see locust

earwig, 29, 224
Edwards, P., 8
Egypt, 96
Eidos, 15–6
elegant grasshopper, 44, 67–8,
    115–16, 225
  as pest, 118, 121, 125, 140
Elias, N., 54
Ellen, R., 18, 20
emperor moth, 81–3, 271–5
Epulani, F., 102
ethnic groups, 3, 43
ethnobiological classification, 13
ethnobiology, 1, 19
eucalyptus beetle, 151, 254
Evans, H.E., 153, 183–4

Fabre, J.H., 1, 54, 70, 161, 181,
    246
fieldwork, 5–6
firefly, 250
flea, 257
flour beetle, 251
flower beetle, 247–8
fly, 33, 42, 200
  riddles, 204–5
folk classifications, 18–19, 41,
    46
folktales, 194

froghopper, 243
functional classifications, 18,
    42

gelatine grub, 135–6, 270
giant water bug, 241
global capitalism, 55
grasshopper, 10, 20, 29–31, 39,
    42, 44, 47, 55–6, 64, 66–7,
    226–31
  as pests, 126
  collecting, 64–5, 66
  cooking, 65
  proverbs, 199
grass moth, 264
Greeks, 70
green shield bug, 71–2, 121, 128,
    239
  as pest, 140
grey ant, 286
ground beetle, 33–4, 192–3,
    244
ground bug, 120
groundnut, 119
Gruner, S., 77, 112
gulugufe, see butterfly or moth
Gulumba, B. 99, 105–7

Hebrew, 46
Heidegger, M., 5, 8
herbalist, 43
Hodgson, A.G., 175–7
Holt,V., 49, 53
honey, 107
honey hunting, 10, 93–6, 99
horse fly, 258
house fly, 261
household pests, 145–50
humanism, 5
Hunn, E. 18, 20
hunter–gatherers, 8, 18–19, 50,
    54, 57, 93–6, 212

Ichikawa, M., 52, 95
ichneumon wasp, 276
infant mortality, 162
Ingold, T., 14
insecticides, 114, 141–4, 165
insects
    as food, 49–91, 185
    as medicine, 53, 185–6, 189–93
    as recreation, 187–8
    cooking, 10,
    disease vectors, 161–2
    evolution, 3
    folk classifications, 19–24
    in art, 186
    in folklore and religion, 187–9,
        209–15
    in music, 187
    in oral literature, 187, 193–209
    pests, 111–41, 181–2
integrated pest management, 109,
    142, 144
interpretative anthropologists, 4
itch mite, 149
Itzaj Maya, 19
ivory economy, 123

jewel beetle, 195, 211, 214, 248–9
Johnston, H.H. 100, 147, 155,
    174–5, 182–3

kafadala, see snouted beetle
Kalonde, K., 191
Kamalo village, 6, 7, 8
kango, see robber fly
Kapalasa, 2, 6, 7, 65, 77, 114,
    123, 127, 145, 150
kapuchi, see maize stalk borer
Kasungu National Park, 6, 83,
    89–90, 101, 105, 173–4, 176
katambala, see earwig
Kayapo, 26
Kjekshus, H., 167–8, 170–2

Kumar, R.,109
Kuper, A., 5
lacewing, 27

lakefly, 10, 33, 35, 73–6, 192, 258
Lake Chilwa, 154, 157–9, 168
Lamborn, W., 7, 172, 176–7
Langstroth, L.L., 103
Lauck, J., 166, 189, 213
Laws, R., 7
leaf beetle, 120
Lee, R.B., 51, 94
lice, 31, 199, 204, 214, 238–9
life form category, 15, 17, 25
linthumbu, see red driver ant
Livingstone, D., 65, 73, 123
locust, 25, 41, 55–6, 63–5, 153–4,
    231–4
    swarms, 153–9
longhorn beetle, 252–4
Lower Shire Valley, 115, 124–6,
    130, 141, 156, 158, 163, 165,
    169, 171, 178, 215, 221

mabvu, see wasp
mabwabwa, see caterpillar/
    emperor moth
MacPherson, D.W., 178
McCracken, J., 124, 168–70,
    172–3, 176–8
Maeterlinck, M., 183
mafulufute, see thief ant
maize, 111–18, 148
maize stalk borer, 113–14, 266
maize weevil, 147–9, 256
malaria, 150, 162–6
Malata, M., 8, 79
Malawian people, 3, 6, 7, 9–10,
    41–2, 46, 85, 110–11, 146, 189,
    209, 212, 219
Malawi Cookbook, 56, 63, 69, 73,
    76

Malinowski, B., 39
Mandala, E., 169
Mangoche, 71, 75, 158
mankhwala, see medicine
mantid, 28–9, 46, 222–3
mapala, see caterpillar
mapipi, see shiny black ant
market vendors, 144
Marx, K., 4
Maugham, R., 175
Mayr, E., 14–16
mbozi, see caterpillar or white
    grub
Mbunda, 36–7, 76–7, 82–4
Mbuti, 52, 93–4
Mchowa, J., 127
mdzodzo, see black army ant
medicine, 189–90
Meke, G., 71, 76–7, 82, 87
Mgomo, H., 43
microcosmos, 181, 184
Middle East, 55, 63
millipede, 195, 202, 207–8, 214,
    287
mining bee, 98, 279
mkupe, see flower or leaf beetle
m'nunkhadala, see elegant
    grasshopper
mopane worm, 83
mosquito, 10, 164–6, 260
mosquito bug, 134, 240
moss beetle, 250
moth, 263
Moyo, H., 141
mpasi, see mining bee
mphalabungu, see grass moth or
    caterpillar
mphembedzu, see grey ant
mphemvu, see cockroach
mphutsi, see tumbu fly
mtemankhuni, see bagworm
mud wasp, 277

Mulanje, 88, 122, 133, 135–6,
    150, 152, 156, 162–3
Mulanje cedar, 152–3
mutillid wasp, 193, 210, 279
mzimu, see spirit of the dead
Mzuzu, 163

Namwera, 138
nandoli, see bow-legged bug
nankafumbwe, see maize weevil
naturalism, 4, 5
natural kinds, 13–4, 18, 24,
    42
Navajo, 19, 21–3, 186, 189
Nayaka, 18
Nchalo, 6
Ndumba, 17
Neno, 71–2, 86, 140
Ngoni, 68, 170
ngumbi, see termite
njuchi, see bee
nkhufi, see tick
nkhululu, see cricket
nkhumbutera, see jewel beetle
nkhungu, see lakefly
nkhunguni, see green shield bug
Nonaka, K., 51
nsabwe, see lice
nsikidzi, see bedbug
nsikisa, see stingless bee
ntchenche, see house fly
ntemankhuni, see bagworm
ntchiu, see processionary
    caterpillar
Nuaulu, 19–20
nyama (wild animal/meat), 25
nyenje, see cicada
nyerere, see ant
Nyika, 84, 101, 103, 106

Ojibway, 14
oral literature, 193–4

Patel, H., 82
Patterson, J., 166
Pedi, 83
personhood, 212–13
Phiri, G., 114
physis, 15–17
pigeon pea, 115, 119
pine grasshopper, 151, 238
pine plantation, 10, 151
Posey, D., 47
postmodernism, 4–5, 18
Prentice, G., 173–4, 176
processionary caterpillar/moth,
    78–80, 267–9
proverbs, 197–202, 207–9
pumpkin beetle, 255

Rangi, 26
Rattan, P., 133–4
realism, 4–5
red driver ant, 45, 283–4
red locust, 153–5, 233
red spider mite, 131, 134–5
relational epistemology, 15, 184
relativism, 4
rhinoceros beetle, 245
rinderpest, 171
robber fly, 27, 260

San, 19–20, 24, 39, 51, 94
Schneider, D., 4
Selous, F.C., 169, 171
Seton, E.T., 212
shiny black ant, 284
Shire Highlands, 41, 68, 115
Silow, C., 36, 76, 86
Singh, S., 153
Skaife, S.H., 5, 10
sleeping sickness, 166–7, 170–9
smallholder sector, 89, 110–11,
    135, 144
Smee, C., 7, 109, 124–5, 129,

135–7, 140, 142, 155–7
snouted beetle, 190–1, 256
Soil Pests Project, 116
Soko, B., 194
songs, 194–7
spider, 288
spirit of the dead, 213–15
Stebkecki, M., 173
Stewart, J., 171
stick insect, 223
stinging caterpillar, 270
stingless bee, 93, 196, 280
subject-predicate logic, 15
sugar ant, 286
sugar cane, 141
Sweeney, C.H., 7, 10, 75, 124–5,
    127, 140, 142, 191, 217, 226
sweet potato, 10, 122–3
Swynnerton, C.F.M., 176–7

tailor ant, 285–6
Tanzania, 167, 172
tea, 10, 133–4
tea pests, 133–6,
termite, 2, 10, 25, 27–8, 39,
    56–63, 87, 116, 219–22
    as fertility symbol, 215–16
    as pest, 117–18, 126–7, 146–7
    collecting, 58–61
    nutritional value, 62
    proverbs and riddles, 198–9,
        202–3
Tewa, 19
textualism, 7
Thailand, 54
thrips, 135
tick, 289
thief ant, 28, 41, 45, 62–3, 197,
    208, 285
Thyolo, 133, 136
toad grasshopper, 68, 193, 214,
    224–5

tobacco, 138–9
tobacco pests, 139–40
tomato, 131
tombolombo, see dragonfly
top-bar hive, 102–3
tribal people, 8–9
truth, 4–5
tsetse fly, 10, 166, 169–70, 261
tsetse fly control, 170–9
tsokonombwe, see toad
  grasshopper
tumbu fly, 259
Turnbull, C., 52
Tzeltal, 17–20, 26, 39

udzudzu, see mosquito
Uvarov, B., 153

Vail, L., 167–8, 170
Vane-Wright, R., 54
vegetables, 130–3
vervet monkey, 49
Viphya, 52

Waldbauer, G., 3
wasp, 38–9, 45, 200, 206, 276–9

water beetle, 245
weevil, 10, 33, 256
  as person, 213
  as pest, 119–20, 122–3, 128
Western culture/thought, 8–9, 185,
  211
Wheeler, M., 3
White, M., 78
white grubs, 115–16, 118
Whitehead, A.N., 9, 15
wildlife conservation, 101–2
Williamson, J., 56, 62, 68, 71–2,
  82, 100
Wilson, E.O., 3, 184
Wilson, J., 60
witch, 116, 216

yellow-winged grasshopper, 228
Yorke, W., 175

Zambia, 80–4, 86, 167, 169, 172,
  186
Zimbabwe, 64, 116
Zoa, 6, 58, 106
Zomba, 60, 100, 150, 158, 164,
  223